CAMBRIDGE STUDIES IN INTERNATIONAL RELATIONS

Series list continues after Index

D0709083

State Identities and the Homogenisation of Peoples

Heather Rae

Department of International Relations
Research School of Pacific and Asian Studies
Australian National University

CAMBRIDGE
UNIVERSITY PRESS

PUBLISHED BY THE PRESS SYNDICATE OF THE UNIVERSITY OF CAMBRIDGE
The Pitt Building, Trumpington Street, Cambridge, United Kingdom

CAMBRIDGE UNIVERSITY PRESS
The Edinburgh Building, Cambridge CB2 2RU, UK
40 West 20th Street, New York, NY 10011-4211, USA
477 Williamstown Road, Port Melbourne, VIC 3207, Australia
Ruiz de Alarcón 13, 28014 Madrid, Spain
Dock House, The Waterfront, Cape Town 8001, South Africa

http://www.cambridge.org

First published 2002

Printed in the United Kingdom at the University Press, Cambridge

Typeface Plantin 10/12 pt   *System* LaTeX 2_ε [TB]

A catalogue record for this book is available from the British Library

Library of Congress cataloguing in publication data

Rae, Heather.
State identities and the homogenisation of peoples / Heather Rae.
    p.   cm. – (Cambridge studies in international relations ; 84)
Includes bibliographical references and index.
ISBN 0 521 79284 3 (hc.) – ISBN 0 521 79708 X (pbk.)
1. Forced migration – History.   2. Population transfers – History.
3. Genocide – History.   4. Political atrocities – History.   I. Title.   II. Series.
HV640 .R24   2002
303.48′2 – dc21   2002016588

ISBN 0 521 79284 3 hardback
ISBN 0 521 79708 X paperback

For my sister Lesley Cleary

and in memory of my father
John Douglas Rae
1914–1999

Contents

Preface

This book is the result of an abiding interest – perhaps puzzlement would be more apt – in how human beings can come to accept that systematic mistreatment of other human beings is somehow morally justifiable. That the project has taken the particular form it has, as an inquiry into what I call pathological homogenisation – forced assimilation, expulsion, genocide – practised by state-builders, is due to my good fortune in being taught as an undergraduate by Andrew Linklater, now Woodrow Wilson Professor of International Relations at the University of Wales at Aberystwyth.

As well as being an inspirational teacher of international relations, Andrew drew my attention to the problem of inclusion and exclusion in the modern system of states and how the boundary of the state has been drawn not only in territorial form but also as a moral boundary. My sense was that while it is important to search for more inclusive forms of political community, work remained to be done on how exclusion – the sort of moral exclusion that justifies mass slaughter of civilians, for example – can come about. Although this interest has taken me off in a different direction I hope that my intellectual debt to Andrew is obvious, though any shortcomings are of course my own responsibility.

Another important influence that animates this project, though one that I was not perhaps aware of for quite some time, was my father's history as a soldier in the British army between 1933 and the mid-1950s. Starting with a tour of duty in India he then went on to 'scoop the pool' (or the bottom of the barrel) of mid-twentieth-century conflict, serving in Europe during World War II, then Palestine, Korea, Malaya. Like many men of his generation, so much was left unsaid about his experiences – words literally failed him. Despite all that was left unsaid, or perhaps because of it, I have inherited a deep interest (and puzzlement) with the nature and consequences of systematic violence. I hope that words have not failed me in the account that follows.

Of course there is a significant difference between my father's experiences, horrifying as they no doubt were, and those of the people whose stories I tell in this book. My father was a trained soldier, he was armed, and he stood a fighting chance. This has not been the case for the great majority of those who over the last 500 years have been displaced or murdered *by their own rulers* in the name of a unified sovereign identity within the state.

I have benefited greatly from the assistance and encouragement of a number of teachers, colleagues and friends over the years during which this book took shape, first as a Ph.D. thesis submitted to Monash University. From my time at Monash I wish to thank Michael Janover, for his patience and feedback as the project evolved, Roger Spegele, Hugh Emy, Paul Muldoon, Margaret Nash, Robyn Eckersley, Richard Shapcott, Catherine Welch and Christian Reus-Smit. For their support while working on the Ph.D., I would like to thank Lesley and Michael Cleary, Sandra Hacker, Margaret Leunig, Janet Reus-Smit, Tor Roxburgh and Pamela Storm. At Deakin University, Melbourne, I thank Joan Beaumont for her support and also gratefully acknowledge the study leave granted to me by Deakin University from January to June 2000. This time was spent as a Visiting Fellow in the Department of International Relations, Research School of Pacific and Asian Studies, Australian National University, where much of the work on chapter 7 was undertaken.

Since then I have had the good fortune to return to this department as a staff member and it is a great privilege to work in such a vibrant and collegial environment. In the Department of International Relations many thanks are due to Thuy Do for her enthusiastic research assistance and also to Mary-Louise Hickey for her painstaking work in preparing the manuscript for publication. Thanks too to Robin Ward for preparation of the index. I would also like to thank my colleagues in the Graduate Studies in International Affairs programme, the Director Greg Fry, Farnaz Salehzadeh and Suzanne Harding, for their patience and support during the final stages of the book.

Parts of this project have been presented in seminars at the Australian National University, Deakin University, Monash University, The University of Queensland, the Melbourne International Relations Discussion Group, the 'Ethics of Armed Intervention' Workshop held at the University of Melbourne in 1998 and at the APSA Annual Conference, 2000 in Washington, DC. I have benefited greatly from the comments of participants at these seminars. For their comments on various incarnations of the project, or the ideas therein, I thank Peter Katzenstein, Richard Little, Adrian Hastings and once again, Andrew Linklater. Thanks also to Henry Shue, Peter Christoff, Jacqui True, Lynn Savery, Stefan Auer, Jeffrey Checkel, David Wippman, V. P. Gagnon Jnr, Valerie Bunce and Matthew Evangelista. While I have gained immeasurably from the comments of, and conversations with, those mentioned above, any failures of omission or interpretation remain my own.

Finally, thanks are due to my partner Chris Reus-Smit for his unfailing love and support, for his inexhaustible commitment to intellectual engagement, and for his close reading of the manuscript as it evolved. I write this in Canberra, which means we no longer live in our 'House in the Woods'. Instead, these acknowledgements come from our new home, which has been dubbed fondly 'Parrot Point'.

Introduction

The history of the international system of states is replete with examples of states turning on their own citizens and the twentieth century was certainly no exception. Indeed, it was in the twentieth century, as states developed greater bureaucratic and military capacities, that the toll on their citizens rose to unprecedented numbers. This was despite the received wisdom in international relations scholarship that the state performs the cardinal function of providing security for its citizens in an anarchical international environment. Since the end of World War II the international community has developed clear norms of legitimate state behaviour towards citizens, yet in the last decade of the twentieth century the world witnessed brutality on an astounding scale, from Rwanda to the former Yugoslavia, in which segments of populations were targeted for expulsion or extermination.

The recurrence of such practices raises a number of key questions which animate this study: why have such practices been an enduring feature of international history? Why have elites used the resources of the state to persecute large sectors of their populations in ways, and to extents, that have ultimately proven detrimental to those states? Why has the international community failed to eradicate such practices, despite the development of norms which clearly prohibit them and despite the destabilising impact of such practices in terms of both refugee flows and regional conflicts?

Recent waves of 'ethnic cleansing' and genocide have led to a renewed wave of scholarly interest in such practices, yet the favoured explanations tend to focus on the role of virulent nationalism in bringing about and rationalising the mass destruction of one group by another. Such arguments are problematic, though, because forced assimilation, expulsion and genocide have occurred throughout the history of the modern international system, starting well before the age of nationalism. Waves of refugees swept across Western Europe from the late fifteenth to the seventeenth centuries, a result of the burst of state-building that occurred in this period and the repressive policies this entailed.[1] These waves only abated when this first great phase of state-building had passed and those deemed undesirable by state-makers had been either assimilated into dominant identities or excluded from the state. Massive displacements have accompanied all subsequent phases of state formation, culminating in the continuing plight of increasingly numerous refugees at the turn of the twenty-first century, many of whom have either been expelled or have fled in fear of their lives.

Existing theories of state formation struggle to explain such practices, as they overlook the crucial role that the construction of collective interests and identities plays in state formation. Materialist accounts explain the development of states and the states system as a function of the world economy, and regard the 'homogenisation' of peoples as a necessary function of this process which is driven by economic interests. Institutionalist accounts also take the economic motivation of actors as a given, though from a position of methodological individualism. In both accounts the construction of interests and identities within the state is left unexplored. Power-based explanations take for granted the interest of state-builders in the accumulation of the means of violence within the sovereign state. Although such explanations pay attention to the processes of internal pacification that were an important part of early modern state-building, they see this as a function of the administrative centralisation of states, rather than a phenomenon that needs further explanation.

The central argument of this study is that state formation has a crucial cultural dimension, a dimension overlooked by other theories of state formation, which regard culture, if they mention it at all, as merely an instrument of either economic or procrustean interests. State-builders must establish their right to rule, as well as the legitimacy of the political order they seek to establish or consolidate. This involves two tasks: the construction of a unified political community within the bounds of their territorial rule – a community with a single, cohesive identity – and the identification of the monarch or the national government as the political embodiment or representative of that unified community. As Michael

---

[1] Aristide Zolberg, 'The Formation of New States as a Refugee Generating Process', in Elizabeth Ferris (ed.), *Refugees and World Politics* (New York: Praeger, 1985), pp. 33–8. Refugee movements also result from political repression by authoritarian regimes, and civil or international wars that may have little to do with state-building. However by far the greatest number have been generated as states have formed in the wake of imperial breakdown, whether in Europe or in post-colonial states. See Aristide Zolberg, 'Contemporary Transnational Migrations in Historical Perspective: Patterns and Dilemmas', in Mary M. Kritz (ed.), *US Immigration and Refugee Policy: Global and Domestic Issues* (Lexington Books, 1982).

Walzer argues, the political unity of the state 'has no palpable shape or substance. The state is invisible; it must be personified before it can be seen, symbolized before it can be loved, imagined before it can be conceived.'[2]

State-builders cannot do otherwise than draw upon the prevailing cultural resources available to them as they seek to build a unified collective identity, and in doing so mark out the boundaries of the sovereign state as the boundary of a moral community. As Walzer goes on to argue, '[i]f symbolization does not by itself create unity (that is the function of political practice as well as of symbolic activity), it does create units – units of discourse which are fundamental to all thinking and doing, units of feeling around which emotions of loyalty and assurance can cluster'.[3] In drawing on the available cultural resources, state-builders contribute towards changing the very framework on which they draw. For example, early modern state-builders drew on the prevailing religious world view when defining insiders and outsiders, but in so doing they contributed towards the development of the secular world view as they rearticulated religious beliefs which no longer had universal normative purchase across Western Europe.

In the following chapters I trace the relationship between state-building and the strategies of 'pathological homogenisation' used by elites to construct the bounded political community of the modern state as an exclusive moral community from which outsiders must be expelled, and show how this process is intimately bound up with the development of the international system of states. The creation of outsiders as a distinctive social category is an important part of this process, and the investigation of how this has occurred in different times and places is a core concern of this study. The creation of outsiders is a political process in which 'difference' becomes translated into 'otherness' and therefore a threat to be disposed of in one way or another. For many state-builders, it is through this targeting of 'otherness' that a sense of unity in a shared collective identity is pursued. Such unity can only ever be symbolic, though, even if it is symbolised through the mass expulsion or destruction of a targeted group, as diversity in political life as elsewhere can never be fully eradicated. However, the attempt to create unity through the targeting of out-groups has concrete, and often bloody, political effects, as various regimes have attempted to construct homogeneous political communities in the most literal way.

[2] Michael Walzer, 'On the Role of Symbolism in Political Thought', *Political Science Quarterly* 82:2 (1967), 194.
[3] Ibid., 194.

There are many aspects to the modern sovereign state. The term is used here in two ways: the first to denote the state as government, 'the collective set of personnel who occupy positions of decisional authority in the polity'. The second is to denote a 'normative order',[4] which, in turn, elites play an important, though by no means exclusive, part in constructing. The term state-building refers to those practices which elites have more or less consciously employed to consolidate and centralise power within clearly demarcated territorial boundaries. As we shall see, these practices draw on symbolic as well as material resources. For example, early modern state-builders, such as Ferdinand and Isabella, who in the fifteenth century laid the foundations for the Spanish state, were much less consciously engaged in 'state-building' than contemporary leaders such as Slobodan Milosevic, who was intent on building a strong (and expanded, to take in *all* Serbs) Serbian state in the wake of the breakdown of Yugoslavia. Yet the Spanish monarchs and modern nationalists have been involved in similar projects of political consolidation, and the strategies of symbolic manipulation they employ as they attempt to legitimate their authority have much in common.

Despite their many differences, these two cases share the use of what I term 'pathological homogenisation' as a means of state-building. This refers to the methods state-builders have used to define the state as a normative order and to cultivate identification through targeting those designated as outsiders for discriminatory and often violent treatment. According to current international standards of human rights and legitimate state behaviour these means are unacceptable. No such standards existed in the earliest phases of state-building, as Christian universalism lost its normative purchase and state-builders abrogated the authority of the Church, but to describe such methods as 'pathological' is not anachronistic. Such practices have without exception damaged the body politic, despite the benefits that state-builders may perceive, and they have invariably caused human suffering on a vast scale. From very early on in the development of the international system, voices have been raised to question policies so destructive in human and other terms. For example, in the early seventeenth century, Cardinal Richelieu described the expulsion of the Moriscos (Christianised Moors) from Spain as 'barbaric', giving voice to misgivings felt by many at the time about the methods used in this action by the Spanish monarchy, including taking small children from their families.

[4] Stephen D. Krasner, 'Approaches to the State: Alternative Conceptions and Historical Dynamics', *Comparative Politics* 16:2 (1984), 224.

I use the term 'pathological homogenisation' to designate a number of different strategies that state-builders have employed to signify the unity of their state and the legitimacy of their authority through the creation of an ostensibly unified population. These strategies range from attempts to legally exclude minority groups from citizenship rights, to strategies of forced conversion or assimilation, expulsion and extermination.[5] Although these strategies have had very different impacts on those unfortunate enough to be subjected to them, they are all a means to the end of creating a 'homogeneous' population within the boundaries of the sovereign state. For those who pursue such policies, they serve to symbolise and create a 'purer' and thus more unitary sovereign identity within the state, a more unified 'imagined community' to use Benedict Anderson's phrase.[6]

In the pursuit of a homogeneous collective identity within the state various assimilatory policies have been practised. Forced religious conversion is one means of forcibly assimilating a minority within a dominant identity. Such policies often result in the mass movement of people attempting to avoid forced conversion, as occurred in late seventeenth-century France, when French Protestants fled their homeland when their religion was outlawed. In some cases, forced conversion may be posed as a choice: convert or leave. This was the 'choice' presented to Spanish Jews in the fifteenth century. Many did convert to Christianity while others who wished to maintain their Jewish identity were expelled from the state, resulting in the end of the official existence of the Jewish community in Spain. Expulsion may also be ordered with no 'choice' of any other alternative, except perhaps death or imprisonment. In 1609 the Moriscos were not presented with any other alternative but to leave Spain and numerous examples of expulsions can be found in the history of the international system. These include 'population exchanges' such as those between Greece and Turkey early in the twentieth century; the massive displacement of ethnic Germans in Europe following World War II; and the exchange of populations between India and Pakistan at partition, to name just a few.

In the twentieth century, as the bureaucratic and technological capacity of the state has increased, mass murder and genocide have increasingly

---

[5] Paul Brass notes how 'both processes of nationality-formation and state-building may be pushed beyond pluralist accommodations to extreme, even pathological limits, to expulsions, counter-expulsions, the exchange of population groups and even to genocide'. Paul R. Brass, *Ethnicity and Nationalism: Theory and Comparison* (New Delhi: Sage, 1991), p. 21.

[6] Benedict Anderson, *Imagined Communities: Reflections on the Origin and Spread of Nationalism* (Oxford: Blackwell, 1983).

been used as pathological means of homogenisation by state-builders. The intent here goes beyond expulsion to the wholesale removal of the targeted group through obliteration. Forced conversion (though by no means an attractive option) has become less thinkable in the age of national criteria of identification, linked, as these often are, to notions of racial or ethnic identity as inherent in the individual and therefore unchanging.[7] In the case of the genocide of the Armenian people of 1915–16, there were cases of Christian Armenians converting to Islam in order to avoid death (particularly children who were taken into Muslim families), but few were given this option in a genocide in which religious criteria had become inextricably bound up with national criteria of identification. A conception of racial identity as inherent in the person was also behind the Holocaust. A similar view of 'ethno-national' identity as inherent in the person and unchanging, ironically marked out through religious affiliation, informs the virulent ethno-nationalism seen in action during the attempts at state-building which followed the fragmentation of Yugoslavia. From such a viewpoint, expulsion or extermination become much more likely policy 'options' than conversion.

The book is divided into seven chapters. In chapter 1, I argue that mainstream theories of international relations are ill-equipped to explain pathological homogenisation as they explicitly bracket off processes of state formation and the construction of interests and identities. However, as noted above, theories of state formation also fail to investigate the cultural dimension of state formation and the construction of identities and interests, leaving them unable to explain practices of pathological homogenisation. Drawing on critical approaches to international relations, I argue that cultural structures and strategies play crucial roles in the construction of collective state identities and hence in the consolidation of the boundaries between states. It follows, therefore, that these structures and strategies also play an important and often overlooked role in the constitution of the international system of states.

Chapters 2 to 5 illustrate this relationship between state formation, cultural practices and practices of pathological homogenisation. Four case studies range across five centuries and over the geographical spread of much of Europe, broadly defined to include the Ottoman Empire.[8] This broad historical and geographic sweep allows comparison of different regimes, the different criteria of inclusion and exclusion that they have employed as state-builders, and the continuities and discontinuities to be

---

[7] See Craig Calhoun, 'Nationalism and Ethnicity', *Annual Review of Sociology* 19 (1993).

[8] The period covered – the late nineteenth to early twentieth centuries – was when the Ottoman Empire was being 'brought in' to the European society of states.

found in practices of pathological homogenisation across space and time. A central argument of the study is that such processes are not the result of nationalism *per se*. Rather, they are the result of modern state-builders' efforts at building unified states according to different criteria of identification which, since the late eighteenth century, have been primarily national. This argument has informed the selection of case studies which aim to demonstrate that homogenisation played an important role in state formation *before* the age of nationalism.

In Western Europe from the end of the fifteenth century until the end of the seventeenth century, religion was the dominant criterion of inclusion and exclusion. Thus the first two case studies come from the first phase of state-building in Western Europe as the moral authority of the Respublica Christiana and the Holy Roman Empire disintegrated. In this phase the criterion of homogeneous identity could not be anything other than religious, as rulers wrested religious authority from its previously universal sources.

Chapter 2 investigates the expulsion of the Jews from Spain in 1492 and, briefly, the expulsion of the Moriscos in 1609. The expulsion of the Jews of Spain was ordered in an edict issued at the end of March 1492 by Ferdinand and Isabella, the 'Catholic Monarchs'. The Jewish community was given four months to either convert to Christianity, or leave Spain. This expulsion, along with the reconquest of Islamic Spain completed in the same year, represented a final break with the medieval tradition of coexistence between the three great monotheistic religious and cultural groups. As Aristide Zolberg notes, the expulsion was a 'startlingly modern measure'.[9] In its systematic nature, it was unlike previous measures taken against Jews in what was to become Spain. It was also unlike previous expulsions of Jews from England and France, in that the population that was expelled from Spain was a well-integrated, socially diverse population whose forebears had lived in the kingdoms of Castile and Aragon for 1,000 years. The Jews of Spain were as 'Spanish' as anyone else in Spain at that time. Yet the expulsion, along with the forced conversion of Muslims in Spain which followed soon after, allowed the monarchs to emphasise religious unity as the basis of the new state.

Chapter 3 investigates the Revocation of the Edict of Nantes by Louis XIV in late seventeenth-century France. By this act, Louis outlawed Protestantism in France and caused an estimated 200,000 French Protestants to flee the country. This attempt to enforce Catholicism was a systematically implemented programme with a clearly defined goal of a religiously homogeneous population within the state. When, in the

---

[9] Zolberg, 'The Formation of New States', p. 34.

sixteenth century, the Huguenots *did* pose a threat to the stability of a factionalised state, the weak monarchy was unable to take effective action against them. But by the time of Louis XIV, the Huguenots no longer posed any military or political threat to the French state. Yet the very existence of a group with a distinct corporate identity was perceived as a threat to the integrity of the absolutist state and a challenge to the legitimacy of absolutist rule, and they were targeted for repression and the extinguishing of their collective identity. This was an extremely popular policy within France at the time, and it served to buttress Louis' legitimacy, at least in the short term. However, it was widely criticised across Europe and soon came to be seen as a costly mistake within France.

The next two cases in chapters 4 and 5, highlight the importance of the national principle in the nineteenth and twentieth centuries, as providing both the basis of political legitimacy and of collective state identity. At its most extreme, the national principle can be interpreted to justify an absolute conception of sovereign identity which claims that the sovereign state must be exclusively of and for a particular nation. It can thus provide a potent motive for policies of pathological homogenisation. In order to investigate this, chapter 4 focuses on the genocide of the Armenian people in 1915–16, and the role this played in building a unitary sovereign state amidst the breakdown of the Ottoman Empire. The Young Turks and their Party of Union and Progress (CUP), which came to power in 1908, were initially concerned with reforming the empire in order to save it, but ultimately they sought to remake the remains of the crumbling Empire into a centralised, modern and national state, which could stand as an equal among the European powers. Influenced by a virulent strand of Turkish nationalism, the Young Turk regime systematically implemented a policy that sought the extermination of the Armenian people in Anatolia, which Turkish nationalists now considered the national heartland of Turkey. In a time of war and revolution, the Young Turks used the targeting of this minority population to buttress their own fragile legitimacy, at the same time that they sought to mark out the boundaries of the Turkish state. It was no accident that those Armenians who were 'deported' to die in the desert, died within the bounds of the Ottoman Empire, but outside the boundaries of the state of Turkey, recognised as independent and sovereign by the international community in 1923.

Chapter 5 highlights the continued use of methods of pathological homogenisation in the late twentieth century. The emergence of the successor states to the former Yugoslavia was accompanied by 'ethnic cleansing' – the euphemistic phrase that has now entered our lexicon in place of genocide and deportation. Though all parties to the conflict in Bosnia-Herzegovina committed atrocities and forcibly removed people from their homes, the focus of this chapter is on the 'logic' of ethnic homogenisation that drove the ethnic cleansing practised by Serb and Bosnian Serb forces in Bosnia-Herzegovina and subsequently in Kosovo, which led to the North Atlantic Treaty Organization (NATO) intervention in 1999. Behind the rhetoric of this virulent form of nationalism has been the process of state disintegration and reformation, with elites using nationalist ideology to construct a conception of the sovereign identity of the state which buttresses their, otherwise doubtful, legitimacy. However, these strategies do not exist in a cultural vacuum and in the former Yugoslavia elites drew on and exacerbated currents of resentment and cultural stereotypes that exist within a society rendered vulnerable by the historical experience of the last century.

This study draws on a distinction made by Alexander Wendt, between the internal, or corporate, and the international, or social, aspects of state identity construction, though unlike Wendt I do not bracket off the domestic aspects of state identity.[10] Indeed, I argue that we cannot understand relations between states if we do this. Where chapters 2 to 5 focus primarily on pathological means of corporate identity construction, in chapter 6 I turn my focus to the social identity of the state as an actor in the international system and I contend that the relation between the corporate and social aspects of state formation is mutually constitutive. The practices which some political elites have used to construct corporate state identity have pushed states at the international social level to develop norms that proscribe such behaviour. In turn, these norms of legitimate state behaviour play a role, though sometimes an oppositional one, in corporate identity construction. Despite the discourse of sovereignty and the claims by state elites that they possess the right to define the corporate identity of the state, there has long been a dialectical relationship between such claims and the social identity of states which depend for legitimation on adherence to basic norms of acceptable behaviour – within the state as well as in relations between states. However, there are strong tensions between developing norms of what are acceptable means of corporate identity construction and the other important principle of coexistence between states, non-intervention. It is this principle which gives moral and legal form to the inviolability of the boundary of the sovereign state – the very boundary that has so often been constructed by practices which the international community now regards as illegitimate.

As Marc Weller points out, the debates over how to deal with the Kosovo conflict, culminating in the 1999 NATO bombing campaign

---

[10] Alexander Wendt, 'Collective Identity Formation and the International State', *American Political Science Review* 88:2 (1994), 385.

against the Federal Republic of Yugoslavia, was a contest over 'core values' in the international system. The principles of territorial unity, non-intervention and the non-use of force were all subject to intense debate.[11] While the manner of this intervention is open to criticism, the intervention reflects growing acknowledgement that what happens inside the borders of a sovereign state cannot be disconnected from international politics. This is so in two senses. First, with the development since World War II of clear norms that prohibit practices of pathological homogenisation, there is recognition (albeit contested at times) that the human rights of citizens of all states are matters of international concern. Second, such practices still remain attractive means of state-building to some regimes.

This raises the question of under what conditions such strategies will *not* be attractive to state-builders in the first place. In order to investigate this question in chapter 7 I examine two 'threshold cases', the Czech Republic and the Former Yugoslav Republic of Macedonia, both of which have many of the 'preconditions' for pathological homogenisation, most importantly the existence of a clearly defined minority which is regarded with distrust or entrenched prejudice by significant sections of the majority population. During the 1990s, elites in these two states either backed away from, or did not pursue pathological strategies of corporate identity construction. These two cases show how emphasis on the social identity of the state – which in both the cases studied here means gaining recognition as a pluralistic democratic state within Europe – can provide alternatives to state-builders. However, these cases also demonstrate that reliance on the social identity of the state is not enough when there is a significant clash between international norms and strongly entrenched domestic norms. The extent to which recasting the social identity of the state may help reconstitute domestic norms towards less exclusivist notions of citizenship rather than merely acting as an external restraint on the potential for pathological policies of corporate identity construction, is explored in this chapter. In the first case, that of the Czech Republic, I examine the 1992 Citizenship law that came into operation when the Czech Republic and Slovakia separated peacefully at the beginning of 1993. This law had the effect of rendering a large number of Roma, who were permanent residents in the Czech Republic and who had been citizens of Czechoslovakia, stateless. I trace the domestic and international pressure on successive governments to change this law, which some critics claimed was expressly designed to rid the state of members of this underprivileged, yet widely disparaged, minority. Over

---

[11] Marc Weller, 'The Rambouillet Conference on Kosovo', *International Affairs* 75:2 (1999), 213–18.

six years the law was gradually amended to fit the social identity of the state more closely.

As the only state to leave the former Yugoslavia peacefully, the Former Yugoslav Republic of Macedonia found itself in a vulnerable position as war flared around it. With tensions running high between the majority ethnic Macedonians and the minority ethnic Albanians, who constitute at least one quarter of the population, many commentators predicted that ethno-nationalist violence was bound to flare up. Certainly, such violence broke out in 2001 and without the support of the international community Macedonia would most likely have been engulfed by civil war. But how did Macedonia confute these predictions for the best part of the decade and why, when ethnic cleansing was being pursued by state-builders all around it, did Macedonia pursue another path? Again, the social identity of the state as a pluralistic democracy wishing to be integrated into Europe played a central role. However, as I explain, this has not yet had a reconstitutive effect on the dominant forms of corporate identity within the state and thus the preconditions for pathological homogenisation continue to exist in this society which is polarised along ethnic lines.

The method employed in this book is interpretive and comparative. Through the interpretation of a range of historical sources, I have sought to plot the construction of categories of insider and outsider through the interaction of agents and the cultural structures within which they act, which in turn their actions reshape. In so doing, I have endeavoured to trace the processes by which 'difference' is translated into 'otherness', and how once a group is put into the social category of 'outsiders' or 'political misfits' this legitimates political behaviour which ensures their removal from the political community by strategies such as forced conversion, expulsion or genocide. I have sought to trace the role this process plays in the construction of the boundaries of states as moral boundaries. Where a number of scholars investigate how the sovereign state is 'written', through the practices of theorists and diplomats,[12] I have instead traced, through historical records, how the sovereign identity of the state has been constructed through exclusionary practices, directed at the goal of a supposedly homogeneous population.

Thus, this study takes the form of a macrohistorical comparison of an important and often overlooked aspect of state formation.[13] I look at the

---

[12] For example in the work of Cynthia Weber, *Simulating Sovereignty: Intervention, the State and Symbolic Exchange* (Cambridge University Press, 1995).

[13] Aristide Zolberg's work is the exception to this, but he does not explicitly inquire into the cultural dimension of these processes. On macro-history see Charles Tilly, *Big Structures, Large Processes, Huge Comparisons* (New York: Russell Sage Foundation, 1984).

Table 1 *Axes of comparison*

1. Early modern, pre-nationalist (Chapters 2 & 3)	—	**Nationalist** (Chapters 4 & 5)
2. Non-systematic persecution (i.e., not state planned)	—	**Systematic, state sponsored** (Pathological homogenisation)
3. Pathological homogenisation (Chapters 2–5)	—	**Threshold cases** (Chapter 7)

continuity of strategies of pathological homogenisation in state-building across the pre-national and national epochs, hence the selection of two cases from each period. As Table 1 illustrates, within each case study I also draw comparisons between practices towards minorities before and during periods of state-building. It is the *systematic* nature of the policies of state-builders, and their goal of constructing a unitary corporate identity which is to be understood as the only acceptable political identity within the state, that distinguishes acts of pathological homogenisation from earlier acts of discrimination and violence such as various popular uprisings, pogroms and massacres. The final axis of comparison is between those cases where elites have clearly pursued policies of pathological homogenisation and the two threshold cases explored in chapter 7. What, if anything, makes a difference to the range of policies that state-builders consider as 'available options'?

Work on the construction of identities and interests does not have a long history in international relations scholarship. As Paul Kowert and Jeffery Legro point out, most studies which emphasise the social construction of identities and interests do not actually investigate *how* this occurs, focusing instead on the impact of these identities and interests. The result of this is that, 'this research struggles to contribute more to an understanding of political behavior than the work it criticizes. The next task for scholars such as these is to take their own criticisms seriously and to develop more explicitly theoretical propositions about the construction of socio-political facts – the process of building collective norms and political identities.'[14] It is with this task that this study is concerned, by investigating the construction of two kinds of norms: those that make possible and legitimate acts of discrimination and extreme violence in

---

[14] Paul Kowert and Jeffery Legro, 'Norms, Identity, and Their Limits: A Theoretical Reprise', in Peter J. Katzenstein (ed.), *The Culture of National Security: Norms and Identity in World Politics* (New York: Columbia University Press, 1996), p. 469.

the name of a unitary and sovereign identity within the state, and those that reject the normative justification and the political practices of what I call 'pathological homogenisation' and instead assert that state-builders are morally accountable to both their citizens and the wider international community for the policies they employ.

1   State formation and pathological homogenisation

Within the study of international relations surprisingly little attention has been paid to the relationship between strategies of pathological homogenisation and state formation. As a result key questions about the relationship between state formation, sovereignty, changing forms of political legitimacy and the building of collective identities – all areas that have recently received greater attention in international relations – have not been brought to bear on the treatment of those deemed 'political misfits'.[1] Indeed, the targeting of minority groups for expulsion, or other even harsher measures, has until recently been seen as representing crises *within* states, and therefore beyond the provenance of international relations theory. Or, once refugees spill over state borders in large enough numbers, or atrocities reach a level which 'shock the conscience of humankind' and become potentially destabilising, they are regarded as examples of systemic breakdown, as anomalies which must be attended to at a practical level, but which require little further explanation.[2]

These processes, I contend in the following chapters, are an integral part of the state system, and practices of pathological homogenisation have, in part, *constituted* the states system, for it has been constructed in large measure on the exclusionary categories of insider and outsider. This is not to assert that the most extreme forms of mistreatment are in some way inevitable, only that they remain a possibility in a system which is based on a sharp distinction between insiders and outsiders. The assertion that the boundary of the state constitutes the only legitimate moral boundary (and hence it is logical that those who are outside the moral community, however defined, are owed no moral duties and may be removed from the state) only makes sense, and is only morally acceptable, if the 'state monopoly over the right to define identity' is accepted.[3]

---

[1] Aristide Zolberg, 'The Formation of New States as a Refugee Generating Process', in Elizabeth Ferris (ed.), *Refugees and World Politics* (New York: Praeger, 1985), p. 31.

[2] A recent exception to this is Jennifer Jackson Preece, *National Minorities and the European Nation-States System* (Oxford: Clarendon Press, 1998).

[3] Andrew Linklater, 'The Problem of Community in International Relations', *Alternatives* 15:2 (1990), 149.

While the assertion by elites that they have the right to define state identity has been characteristic of the system of states from its inception, there have always been limits to such claims. At the beginning of the twenty-first century it is clear that the state monopoly on the right to define legitimate identity is no longer unequivocally accepted. It is challenged by the international norms of legitimate state behaviour that have developed over the centuries in response to the most outrageous treatment of subjects and citizens. Such international standards have gained moral and legal force, particularly since the end of World War II. Yet despite the articulation of such norms, virulent exclusionary practices remain an attractive option to many regimes in the world today, as recent events in the former Yugoslavia and elsewhere illustrate. Such practices provide a baseline of the most extreme claims that can still be made in the name of a unitary sovereign identity and highlight the problems faced by the international community in dealing with such behaviour.

This chapter lays the foundation for the further consideration of the role of pathological homogenisation in state-building and the development of international norms regarding such practices. It consists of three sections. The first considers the treatment of the state in mainstream theories of international relations and outlines an alternative approach that draws on critical and constructivist theories of international relations, emphasising the role of normative and ideational factors in the construction of the identities and interests of sovereign states and the shared social values of the 'society of states'. The second section surveys several prominent theories of state formation and examines how they account, if at all, for the pathological homogenisation that often accompanies state-building. The third section investigates the dimension of social life that is overlooked in most accounts of state formation – the role of culture and how this is bound up with the creation of legitimacy and changing criteria of collective identity.

State formation and international relations theory

The critical response to mainstream approaches to international relations

Mainstream theories of international relations take the identity of the state as given and explicitly bracket off consideration of the internal dimensions of state behaviour. For example, neorealist analyses deny the relevance of processes of state formation in understanding international politics. In this view, the anarchic structure of the international system drives states to pursue self-help in the absence of any supreme authority. In the classic exposition of this view, Kenneth Waltz rejects 'second image' explanations which take the internal structure of the state into account and argues that the anarchical structure of the international system forces states to act in certain ways regardless of their internal arrangements.[4]

Thus state-building and the construction of identity within the state are not relevant from this perspective. As long as the basic functions of statehood are performed – a central government which has control over the means of violence, over a defined population and over a defined territory – then 'a state is a state is a state'.[5] State interests are considered relevant but the most basic interests are assumed to be identical for all states and driven by the nature of the system: all states have an interest in survival in an anarchical system, which is best pursued through strategies of self-help based on zero-sum calculations. Neoliberal theorists, though interested in how states cooperate under anarchy, accept the realist model of states as self-interested, rational and unitary actors. As a consequence, they too explicitly bracket off the role of collective identity construction in state-building as they also take the identities and interests of actors on the international stage for granted.

Over the last two decades of the twentieth century mainstream approaches have been subjected to criticisms from a number of different perspectives. Once the state was 'brought back in' to both social theory and international relations theory in the 1980s, this opened up consideration of how states, rather than being pre-social 'facts', are constituted through social, political and cultural practices. From this perspective, the state is seen as a normative order, and it is intersubjectively constructed normative values that provide the unifying standards and symbols that legitimate authority and allow us to perceive the state as a unitary and sovereign actor. Thus, sovereignty 'is negotiated out of interaction within intersubjectively identifiable communities'[6] and it is this institution which legitimates 'the state' as an agent in international social life. As Michael Walzer notes, unity can only ever be symbolised,[7] but it is through the claim to sovereignty made on the state's behalf, and how this is articulated

---

[4] Kenneth N. Waltz, *Man, the State and War: A Theoretical Analysis* (New York: Columbia University Press, 1959); Kenneth N. Waltz, *Theory of International Politics* (New York: Random House, 1979). The only unit level factors Waltz takes into account are the 'capabilities' of states, though he insists that the 'distribution' of capabilities, which matters most, is a systemic factor.

[5] With apologies to Gertrude Stein.

[6] Thomas J. Biersteker and Cynthia Weber, 'The Social Construction of State Sovereignty', in Thomas J. Biersteker and Cynthia Weber (eds.), *State Sovereignty as Social Construct* (Cambridge University Press, 1996), p. 11.

[7] Michael Walzer, 'On the Role of Symbolism in Political Thought', *Political Science Quarterly* 82:2 (1967), 194.

and put into practice, both domestically and internationally, that a sense
of unity is created.

Despite many differences, the various critical approaches to international relations all share a concern with how identities and interests
are constructed, highlighting the importance of questions of inclusion/
exclusion and identity/difference in international relations. Building on
these insights, various constructivist scholars have investigated how normative change and identity construction proceeds 'on the ground'.[8]
Although constructivism is a loose term that covers many different approaches, most scholars associated with it share an interest in the empirical
exploration of *how* identities are constructed, *how* culture matters and *how*
this is relevant to international relations. As Martha Finnemore argues,
'[s]imply claiming that norms matter is not enough for constructivists.
They must provide substantive arguments about which norms matter
as well as how, where and why they matter.'[9] From this perspective, the
re-reading of canonical texts and the critique of the assumptions of mainstream theories of international relations by critical scholars of international relations raise interesting and important questions, but historical
and sociological work is necessary if they are to be answered. Below, I
trace briefly how the state was 'brought back in' to international relations theory, and what contributions critical theory and constructivism
have made to understanding the social construction of identities and
interests.

From the early 1980s critical theorists began to question the assumptions underlying realist discourse as well as the conclusions that realists
draw about international political life. Whether of the modernist or post-
modernist variety, critical theorists questioned the sharp boundary that
mainstream international relations draws between the domestic and international realms, and the assumption, particularly strong in American
neorealism, that scholars of international relations should be engaged in
value-neutral 'social science'.

An exemplar of early critical theory is Robert Cox's critique of realist
discourse as ideology, which echoes the earlier Frankfurt School critique
of 'traditional' theory based on a positivist social science which assumes
that it is possible to accumulate knowledge about human society by the
objective application of scientific method.[10] Cox distinguishes between

[8] Richard Price and Christian Reus-Smit, 'Dangerous Liaisons? Critical International
    Theory and Constructivism', *European Journal of International Relations* 4:3 (1998).
[9] Martha Finnemore, *National Interests in International Society* (Ithaca: Cornell University
    Press, 1996), p. 130.
[10] Robert Cox, 'Social Forces, States and World Orders: Beyond International Relations
    Theory', *Millennium: Journal of International Studies* 10:2 (1982), 128. Neither is such

'problem solving' and 'reflective' theories, arguing that the former is designed to make existing patterns work as smoothly as possible while the latter reflects upon theorising itself in order to consider the creation of alternative social frameworks. 'Problem-solving' theory is essentially conservative, Cox argues, as it accepts the status quo, whereas the theory that results from the reflective approach is critical in the sense that it steps back from the 'prevailing order' and asks how it came about. 'It is directed towards an appraisal of the very framework for action, or problematic, which problem-solving theory accepts as its parameters.'[11]

Cox argues that, contrary to the neorealist view that all states are functionally similar within the anarchical system of states, understanding international relations requires investigation of the different forms of state/society entities in history. He then goes on to focus on the role of production in state formation and the impact this has had on international relations, as social forces within states overflow state boundaries and the international system in turn acts back on states and their constituent societies. Although he makes a strong argument for reflective theory and for historical study of the constitution of states in the states system, his work is in the end another version of historical materialism, based as it is on the centrality of production. However, around the same time Anthony Giddens was arguing that a viable critical theory needs to be 'post-Marxist', and therefore able to recognise the shortcomings of Marxism as well as its strengths.[12] Given the complex nature of international relations, Giddens highlights the need for multidimensional accounts that recognise that there is no single dominant logic at work in the international system.

Echoing Giddens' doubts about single logic explanations, Andrew Linklater argues that the Marxist emphasis on production and class highlights only one of a number of axes of inclusion and exclusion in the contemporary international system, including race, gender and religion. For Linklater, it is the identification of unjust forms of exclusion and identifying the immanent possibilities for more inclusive political communities that should animate critical theory. Thus, 'in light of the wider human community' critical theorists should problematise the exclusionary

objectivity completely desirable as it denies important dimensions of human social, political and cultural experience. Max Horkheimer, 'Traditional and Critical Theory', in Max Horkheimer, *Critical Theory: Selected Essays* (New York: Free Press, 1972). See also Craig Calhoun, *Critical Social Theory* (Oxford: Blackwell, 1995), pp. 1–42; and Richard K. Ashley, 'Political Realism and Human Interests', *International Studies Quarterly* 25:2 (1981).

[11] Cox, 'Social Forces', 129.

[12] Anthony Giddens, *The Nation-State and Violence: Volume Two of A Contemporary Critique of Historical Materialism* (Cambridge: Polity Press, 1985), p. 336.

practices through which state sovereignty has been constructed.[13] To enquire into the justice of the criteria for membership within states, is 'to recognise that the nation-state is one of the few bastions of exclusion which has not had its rights and claims against the rest of the world seriously questioned'.[14] Thus, rather than accepting the state as a given in international relations, Linklater argues that critical theory should question the interpretations of the state and sovereignty that are so often taken for granted in mainstream international relations.

However, the explicitly emancipatory normative stance of this form of critical theory has been met with some scepticism from critical scholars influenced by postmodern social theory. They regard the 'emancipatory project' of 'modernist' critical theory as masking yet another attempt to impose new 'truths', which they regard as a form of domination. Despite this, though, there are many points of convergence between modern and postmodern forms of critical theory. For example, Richard Ashley, who rejected his earlier work based on Frankfurt School critical theory,[15] argues from a postmodern position (if that is possible) that it is the task of modern statecraft to defer the ever-threatening crises of political identity that face the modern state by constructing singular sovereign identities. It is only by deferring questions about such identities, he argues, that it has been possible to maintain a system of sovereign states, each of which is regarded as legitimate. This has entailed the displacement of threats to outside the state, constructing the external realm as fraught with danger. But the 'co-ordinated displacement of anarchic dangers [to the outside of the state]...is a task made ever more difficult to perform to the extent that the state system is universalised and to the degree that claims on space and time inscribed beneath the sign of man become ever more extensive'.[16]

Modernist critical theorists would have no disagreement with the substance of this argument that it has been the task of modern statecraft to impose a singular identity (and it is this that this study investigates), as they wish to challenge the definition of political community which remains bounded within the state. But Ashley is representative of the postmodern position when he asserts that the inscription of self-identity must *always* be defined at the expense of the other. The breakdown of received interpretations and the postmodern proliferation of meanings

---

[13] Andrew Linklater, 'The Question of the Next Stage in International Relations Theory: A Critical-Theoretical Point of View', *Millennium: Journal of International Studies* 21:1 (1992), 93.

[14] Linklater, 'The Question', 93.   [15] Ashley, 'Political Realism'.

[16] Richard K. Ashley, 'Untying the Sovereign State: A Double Reading of the Anarchy Problematique', *Millennium: Journal of International Studies* 17:2 (1988), 259.

is to be celebrated, according to this view, rather than perceived as a problem to be solved by the imposition of a new sovereign – and inherently oppressive – voice, in the name of stability. This position rejects any projects that seek alternative forms of political community that are more inclusive, or which seek to articulate how the boundary between self and other can be negotiated in more respectful ways. The position that Ashley and others take renders the normative goal of devising alternative political communities inherently problematic as it means the assertion of yet another form of domination.[17]

But there is a contradiction here between the theoretical concern with how boundaries have been drawn at the expense of the other and the political reality of marginalisation. The reformulation of boundaries to mark out unjust categories of insiders and outsiders, as recently seen in Bosnia, for example, will be resisted from any critical (or liberal) perspective. But the celebration of marginality carries the danger of trivialising the concrete reality of those who are truly marginalised in the contemporary world system, which despite many changes is still a system of sovereign states. As Walzer points out, '[s]tatelessness is a condition of infinite danger',[18] and though we may wish to contest the categories which make this so, the celebration of existence 'on the margins' overlooks the perilous political consequences of a truly marginalised existence for millions of people across the globe.[19]

Where Ashley argues that the crisis of representation uncovers the fact that all boundaries, normative or practical, are inscribed arbitrarily, modernist critical theorists contend that just as social practices and the normative structures they create are not unalterable, neither are they *totally* arbitrary. As Linklater argues, '[m]oral principles are neither immutable and universal nor are they arbitrary and groundless means of organising a meaningless reality'.[20] Thus despite the critiques of universalism as yet

---

[17] On postmodern critiques of relations of domination at work in what has been accepted as reasonable, just, progressive, and so on, see Stephen White, *Political Theory and Postmodernism* (Cambridge University Press, 1991), p. 7.

[18] Michael Walzer, *Spheres of Justice: A Defense of Pluralism and Equality* (New York: Basic Books, 1983), p. 32.

[19] On the charge that postmodernism can mean a retreat from practical politics, see White, *Political Theory*, p. 21. White draws a distinction between the postmodern 'responsibility to the other' and the modernist 'responsibility to act'. On the problems faced by such positions of analysing 'the transformation of power and social structure as it bears on practical action in the modern world', see Calhoun, *Critical Social Theory*, p. 116.

[20] Andrew Linklater, *Men and Citizens in the Theory of International Relations*, 2nd edition (London: Macmillan, 1990), p. 217. For a discussion of how postmodern international relations theorists draw parallels between the way in which the state and the discipline of International Relations both seek to impose sovereign identities, see Linklater, 'The Question', 88–92. In a critique directed at Michel Foucault, Jurgen Habermas argues that Foucault's failure to explain how normative choices could be validated through

another face of Western domination, modernist critical theory regards as
valid a minimal universalism, which seeks to recognise cultural difference
yet also recognises some shared principles of coexistence.[21]

As noted above, Linklater argues that critical theory should seek to go
beyond the Marxist emphasis on class-based exclusion. Notions of legitimate inclusion and exclusion, he argues, are 'constitutive not only of
society in the abstract but of individual and collective identity'.[22] As the
rationales of various forms of inclusion and exclusion come under scrutiny
Linklater identifies three dimensions of such an inquiry. These are 'normative, concerning the philosophical justifications for excluding some
persons from particular social arrangements while admitting others; sociological, concerning the workings and maintenance of systems of inclusion and exclusion; and praxeological, concerning the impact of systems
of inclusion and exclusion on human action'.[23] Taking these questions as
a starting point, this study traces the development of changing criteria of
inclusion and exclusion in a number of states. At the sociological level, I
take seriously Linklater's injunction to inquire into the 'origin and development' of modes of inclusion and exclusion. At the praxeological level
I address the pressing problem of the gap between changed norms of acceptable state behaviour and what action can be taken when states clearly
abrogate these norms. This is complex, for as Finnemore notes, there may
be 'tensions and contradictions among social values'.[24] This problem is
addressed in chapter 6. For the moment, it is the sociological dimension,
'concerning the workings and maintenance of systems of inclusion and exclusion', to which I now turn, and which brings constructivism into play.

Constructivism: the social construction of identities and interests

Critical theory of the Third Debate, had 'a distinctive metatheoretical or
quasi-philosophical profile', focusing on 'the epistemological, methodological and normative assumptions and implications of dominant rationalist
theories. In comparison, little effort was made to apply the conceptual
and methodological apparatus of either modern or postmodern critical
theory to the sustained empirical analysis of issues in world politics.'[25]
Constructivism takes up this neglected dimension of the critical project.

communicative means, meant that the dimensions of social interaction that are not
simply reducible to power relations were ignored. Jurgen Habermas, *The Philosophical
Discourse of Modernity* (Cambridge MA: MIT Press, 1987), p. 253. See Calhoun, *Critical
Social Theory*, pp. 97–131, for a discussion of these points.
[21] Linklater, *Men and Citizens*, postscript.   [22] Linklater, 'The Question', 82.
[23] Ibid., 78.   [24] Finnemore, *National Interests*, p. 82.
[25] Price and Reus-Smit, 'Critical International Theory', 262–3.

Richard Price and Christian Reus-Smit identify three core aspects of the constructivist approach. Like critical theorists of the Third Debate, constructivists pay attention to the 'importance of normative or ideational structures as well as material structures'; they assert that 'identities constitute interests and actions'; and that agents and structures are mutually constituted.[26] Thus, to the constructivist 'social realities are as influential as material realities in determining behaviour. Indeed, they are what endows material realities with meaning and purpose. In political terms, it is these social realities that provide us with ends to which power and wealth can be used.'[27] From a constructivist perspective, understanding the construction of identities and interests is the key to understanding political action and change in the international system. Thus constructivists seek to trace how intersubjectively constituted identities at both the domestic and international levels translate into political action. Furthermore, identities themselves come out of and are rearticulated in political practice – they are both motivations for, and outcomes of, action. Social agents and social structures are viewed as mutually constitutive, so as Alexander Wendt argues, while social structures influence the identities and actions of agents, 'social structures are only instantiated by the practices of agents'.[28]

Wendt draws a helpful distinction between the corporate and social aspects of state identities but he then goes on to argue that although corporate identities do indeed have histories, 'a theory of the states system need no more explain the existence of states than one of society need explain that of people'.[29] He argues that the domestic aspect of state identity construction can be bracketed off, as it is the interaction of states with other already existing states which constructs the social identity of states. This view rests on an isomorphism which assumes that individuals in society and states in the states system can be treated as like units, but the very fact that the corporate identity of the state is just that – corporate – and not an individual identity, means that we need to look at how this identity is constructed, how the 'we' to which Wendt refers is constituted and maintained. In this respect, Wendt's systemic constructivism differs little from the way mainstream theories of international relations bracket off identities and interests.[30] As a consequence, his

---

[26] Ibid., 266–7.   [27] Finnemore, *National Interests*, p. 128.

[28] Alexander Wendt, 'The Agent–Structure Problem in International Relations Theory', *International Organization* 41:3 (1987), 359.

[29] Alexander Wendt, 'Collective Identity Formation and the International State', *American Political Science Review* 88:2 (1994), 385.

[30] Wendt has reasserted this view more recently. Although he extends the discussion of collective identity to include 'type' and 'role' identities this does not solve the problem

conception of the relationship between agents and structures is 'relatively narrow', and his model of world politics remains static in the absence of any 'non-systemic sources of state identity – such as domestic political culture'.[31] This reliance on the systemic level alone undermines Wendt's constructivist approach so that he is only marginally better equipped to explain the constitution of states or the states system than neorealists.[32]

However, drawing on the distinction Wendt makes between the corporate and social aspects of state identities, we may characterise the use by political elites of pathological homogenisation in state formation as a means towards the goal of 'corporate state identity construction', and the development of international norms as a form of 'societal state identity construction'.[33] In direct contrast to Wendt, though, I argue throughout this book that the corporate and social aspects of state identity stand in a dialectical, mutually constitutive relationship. One crucial aspect of this relationship is investigated in the following four chapters, in which I trace the construction of corporate state identities, and how the practices by which corporate identities are constructed also constitute the boundaries between states as moral boundaries. In these practices, elites draw on the cultural and symbolic resources of their time and place in order to recast and reinvent collective identities within the state.

International norms do indeed arise out of the social interaction of states, but Wendt ignores the fact that it is through this interaction that the society of states evolves standards of legitimate corporate state behaviour.[34] International society thus plays an active role in state-building, as international principles of legitimate state action define, in part, how corporate state-building *should* occur. What is more, this is a two-way relationship. As the criteria of political legitimacy within states have changed, and with them the domestic principles which underpin *corporate* identity construction, so too have the international principles that structure the state system. As chapter 6 explains, international norms that set the standard of legitimate state behaviour can be understood as both a *response to* corporate state-building and *part of* societal state-building.

of his bracketing off of corporate identity in my view. See Alexander Wendt, *Social Theory of International Politics* (Cambridge University Press, 1999), pp. 193–245.

[31] Price and Reus-Smit, 'Critical International Theory', 268.

[32] It is worth noting that Wendt is probably the only systemic constructivist. This is an important point given that he is often taken as representative of constructivism as a whole, when most constructivists differ from him in regarding the domestic and international aspects of world politics as mutually constitutive.

[33] Wendt, 'Collective Identity Formation', 385.

[34] Ibid.; Cynthia Weber, *Simulating Sovereignty: Intervention, the State, and Symbolic Exchange* (Cambridge University Press, 1995), p. 5.

The empirical focus of much constructivist scholarship draws criticism from some critical theorists. They argue that constructivism forgoes a reflectivist orientation and becomes another form of 'problem solving theory' that is positivist, or at least overly rationalist. However, this project begins from the proposition that it is possible to pursue a more empirically based form of scholarship without losing or betraying a critical purpose.[35] It is constructivism that provides an approach through which the difficult questions posed by critical theory – questions about the construction of moral community through practices of inclusion and exclusion – can be investigated at the level of political action in a system of sovereign territorial states.

Theories of state formation

While international relations scholars have largely ignored processes of state-building, this is not true of scholars in other fields. Historical sociologists and institutional economists have devoted considerable attention to such processes. Unfortunately, though, they have tended to marginalise questions of homogenisation, and have neglected the role of culture and identity in state-building. The following section examines how materialist, institutionalist and power-based approaches account for early modern state formation and then goes on to briefly survey rational choice accounts of contemporary ethnic violence which, although not explicitly concerned with state-building, inevitably deal with ethnic violence in the context of state collapse and reformation.

Materialist explanations

Materialist explanations of state formation, such as that presented by Immanuel Wallerstein, treat the state as functional to the development of the capitalist world system. Wallerstein argues that the initial thrust of the fifteenth-century 'restorers of order' came out of the crisis of feudalism as they responded to the recessions, famines and plagues that beset Europe in the fourteenth century. By the fifteenth century widespread economic tightening resulted in peasant rebellions and internecine warfare, including wars amongst the nobility. Weakened by this, the nobility looked to kings to restore and maintain order.

While Wallerstein characterises the disorder of the fourteenth century as the outcome of economic pressures, the fifteenth-century construction

[35] See Price and Reus-Smit, 'Critical International Theory', for an overview of the different views in this debate. Also see Ted Hopf, 'The Promise of Constructivism in International Relations Theory', *International Security* 23:1 (1998).

of what was to become a new order – involving neither the total collapse of the world-economy or its transformation into a world-empire[36] – is understood as a prerequisite of economic resurgence. 'The capitalist world-economy seems to have *required* and *facilitated* this secular process of increased centralisation and internal control, at least within the core states.'[37] Thus 'strong states' were necessary for economic development and so we see the rise of centralising, mainly absolutist states in the early modern period. That states and the states system were seen as functional for economic resurgence and the growth of the world-economy is considered explanation enough, with Wallerstein adding little more to explain these developments.

In the early modern era, European monarchs strengthened their states, and their own position within them, through a number of means, including 'bureacratization, monopolization of force, creation of legitimacy, and homogenisation of subject populations'.[38] Increased bureaucratisation meant that economic policy decisions needed to be mediated through state structures. Thus by the sixteenth century, Wallerstein argues, kings fulfilled the role of 'managers of the state machinery'.[39] These 'managers' handled the processes of decision-making that became increasingly necessary as states became increasingly autonomous in the pursuit of their interests. States became 'actors with a special ability to pursue their economic ends'. Statism, the 'claim for increased power in the hands of the state machinery',[40] was the prevailing ideology of this world-economy.

Wallerstein's characterisation of the relationship between the economic and the political, reflected in his portrayal of the development of the world-economy and the formation and consolidation of states within this, gives deterministic precedence to economic factors. In this account political action takes place within the framework provided by states, which were formed in response to the needs of the world-economy, and which are structured differently according to their place in this world-economy. This economically reductionist account does not adequately reflect the complex inter-relation of the political and economic factors. It gives a very thin account of the political and strategic dimensions of the international system, and virtually ignores the cultural dimension of states and the system of states, consigning them all to the category of 'superstructural'.

---

[36] 'World-economies have historically been unstable structures leading either towards disintegration or conquest by one group and hence transformation into a world-empire.' Immanuel Wallerstein, *The Capitalist World-Economy* (Cambridge University Press, 1979), p. 5.
[37] Immanuel Wallerstein, *The Modern World-System*, vol. 1 (San Diego: Academic Press, 1974), p. 136, emphasis added.
[38] Ibid., p. 136.   [39] Ibid.   [40] Ibid., p. 147.

In his more recent work, Wallerstein continues to characterise the world-economic system as one in which decisions made on a world scale are economic, and political decisions are relevant only to the 'smaller structures' of states and the states system which exist within the framework provided by the world-economy.[41] In a nutshell, for Wallerstein: 'The interstate system is the political superstructure of the capitalist world-economy and was a deliberate invention of the modern world.'[42] Contrary to Wallerstein's argument, though, the 'small structures' of states did not develop only as a function of the world-economy. Rather, they developed through the transition to a new form of political organisation which restructured relationships – economic, political, cultural and social – both within these new political units and between them.[43]

Wallerstein does refer to the process of homogenisation, but in his account the homogenisation of populations, and the forced displacements which often attended it, are seen as functions of the demands of the growing world-economic system. Within this system, Wallerstein argues, it was in the economic interests of the monarchs to have 'ethnic' homogeneity amongst certain strata. Wallerstein dismisses the role of beliefs and ideas in historical change. For example, the role of religion within the emergent Spanish state is regarded as a legitimating rationalisation for economically determined action. While it may have been internalised by the actors, he argues, 'religious enthusiasm' was a rationalisation of economic interests. Because he regards belief systems as superstructural, there is no investigation of the relationship between this belief system and the construction of interests.

The decision to forcibly assimilate, expel or exterminate certain groups in the name of a homogenised identity cannot be explained purely in terms of the pursuit of material benefits. In all the cases examined in this study, decisions were made to target groups for expulsion or extermination in the knowledge that this would entail economic, and certainly in the later cases, political, costs. Wallerstein claims that the expulsion of the Jews of Spain in 1492 was part of an offensive across centralising states to push

---

[41] Immanuel Wallerstein, *Geopolitics and Geoculture: Essays on the Changing World-System* (Cambridge University Press, 1991). In particular see the chapter entitled, 'National and World Identities and the Interstate System'. Also see Immanuel Wallerstein, 'Culture as the Ideological Battleground of the Modern World System', in Mike Featherstone (ed.), *Global Culture: Nationalism, Globalization and Modernity: A Theory, Culture and Society Special Issue* (London: Sage, 1990).

[42] Wallerstein, *Geopolitics and Geoculture*, p. 141.

[43] As Zolberg argues, '[t]he system could not have gotten off the ground without the force Europeans could muster as a consequence of their achievement of a mode of political organisation that antedated the formation of the capitalist world economy'. Aristide Zolberg, 'Origins of the Modern World System: A Missing Link', *World Politics* 33:2 (1981), 262.

Jews into peripheral areas. He argues that the Jews of Spain played a role analogous to that of the urban bourgeoisie in other countries, and that non-Jewish merchants saw them as competitors, landowners saw them as creditors, and both groups put pressure on the Catholic Monarchs to expel them.[44] This does not, however, adequately account for the expulsion, as it does not explain why the monarchs allowed conversos (converts to Christianity from Judaism) who were in the same economic niche as the Jews, and who were able to 'prove' they were genuine converts, to stay. Nor does it account for the subsequent expulsion of conversos from the Church and positions in the bureaucracy. As chapter 2 demonstrates, these expulsions cannot be understood without some reference to the cultural context of the time, a context in which religion played a central role.

The same point can be made for the three other cases of pathological homogenisation considered in this book, all of which demonstrate that a narrow, economically deterministic conception of interests cannot explain the choices made by different regimes to forcibly homogenise their populations. Why, then, was a homogenised population deemed desirable as sovereign states emerged from the breakdown of heteronomous and imperial structures of authority? To answer this question a different understanding of 'interests' that recognises that they can be constructed in different ways, is necessary. This allows consideration of how the perceived need for an unambiguous unitary identity could become the highest priority of state-builders, despite the economic and political costs this might entail. This question will be taken up at greater length in the section below on the role of culture in political life, and will be returned to in each of the case studies on pathological homogenisation.

Institutionalist accounts

From an institutionalist perspective, state-building in early modern Europe is understood as the expression of the dominant forms of institutional rationality. Institutionalist accounts have much to tell us about the choices that state-builders made with regard to property rights and the sort of states that resulted from these choices. Like Wallerstein, institutionalists take the interests of state-builders for granted, assuming that leaders were motivated solely by the desire for economic gain. But, once again, this cannot explain the policies of pathological homogenisation pursued by state-builders, who either overlooked the economic costs of their policies, or made their decisions in the full knowledge that

---

[44] Wallerstein, *The Modern World System*, pp. 147–8.

they might entail high costs. To explain such decisions we must look at the social and cultural dimensions that institutionalist accounts, resting on the assumption of all interests as economic interests, largely ignore.

Douglass North and Robert Thomas argue that the modern state became the most viable form of political and economic organisation because it was the most efficient provider of private property rights.[45] In the earliest phases of state formation, military capacity was the most salient means of consolidating power. However, as rulers engaged in internal pacification and external expansion via war and dynastic marriage,[46] they needed increased revenue to maintain themselves, and they chose different options to do this. The key to the different paths of development in early modern Europe is the deals rulers struck to raise revenue: the concessions they made, who they made them to and how they made them.[47] Thus, the institution of private property rights developed out of the trading of privileges for revenue that occurred between rulers and their subjects, in particular the nobility and the rising merchant class.[48] Those rulers who instituted and enforced private property rights allowed economic efficiency and growth and provided a model of success, while those who continued to support monopoly rights blocked innovation, efficiency and longer-term growth. For example, England and the United Provinces became successful capitalist states, while the early front runners, such as Spain, declined because of the institutional choices rulers made. Thus, for North, the very early period of state formation prepared the ground for the later struggles over control of the institutional *form* of the state, which occurred in the seventeenth century, leading to the institutionalisation of private property.

North's *Structure and Change in Economic History* highlights how institutional forms can change. He focuses on the relationship between motivated individuals and changing social structures.[49] It is institutions which

---

[45] Douglass C. North and Robert Paul Thomas, *The Rise of the Western World: A New Economic History* (Cambridge University Press, 1973), p. 80.

[46] Ibid., p. 81.

[47] Douglass C. North, *Structure and Change in Economic History* (New York: W. W. Norton, 1981), pp. 66, 141.

[48] Ibid., p. 83.

[49] Ibid., p. 11. North identifies limitations in both neoclassical and Marxist explanations of structural change, arguing that neither approach accounts for important dimensions of human activity. On the one hand neoclassical economic theories assume that individuals will act out of easily defined and calculated self-interest and cannot explain altruistic behaviour. On the other hand Marxism makes assumptions about the identity of groups in the form of class, and does not account for the problem of free riders: those who do nothing to initiate or support change but stand to benefit from it. Too many free riders can undermine or block change that other actors are working towards.

mediate between agents and structures, he argues, as they serve to constrain the self-interested maximising behaviour of individuals. It is these 'constraints that make possible human organisation by limiting certain types of behaviour'.[50] In this view, rules and regulations are devised to constrain behaviour that works against the interests of principal actors. North includes the general ethical context as well as codified rules, so that ethical norms function to reduce 'enforcement costs'.[51] This is based on the assumption that in the absence of constraining institutions, individuals will engage in self-interested maximising behaviour. There has to be, 'some degree of individual restraint from maximising behaviour . . . hence the enormous investment that is made to convince individuals of the legitimacy of . . . institutions'.[52] There are two problems with this account. The first is the view of institutions and norms as merely constraining; the second is the assumption that all actors are self-interested, maximising individuals that underpins this view of institutional constraint. While institutions and norms do constrain actors, they are also constitutive of the interests, identities, expectation and behaviour of actors. They provide a framework within which action occurs and gains meaning. In other words, they allow actors to act in a meaningful way, instead of merely limiting what actions can be taken.

In trying to articulate the relationship between agents and structures in institutional change, North does acknowledge that perceptions are important in informing the choices that actors make. He asserts that a theory of ideology is necessary to explain how different perceptions of reality influence the reactions of individuals to an 'objective' situation and why individuals made the choices they did.[53] It is this last element, the recognition of ideology, at the level of theoretical intent at least, which distinguishes North's model from neoclassical analyses. It is not possible, he argues, to explain structural change without some notion of ideology that recognises the importance of agency. Structural change is driven by the activity of agents, as 'alterations in institutions involve purposeful human activity'.[54] There are three aspects of ideology that are stressed here. First, ideology as world view; second, the moral/ethical stance that is taken, or the normative judgements that are made; and third, how ideologies change as individuals alter them in response to perceived slippage between existing explanations and experience. Thus, there is a very strong sense of how institutions, which change over time, 'do not occur in a vacuum, but are the result of peoples' perceptions stemming from historically derived opportunities and values'.[55]

---

[50] Ibid., p. 61. [51] Ibid., p. 18. [52] Ibid., p. 19.
[53] Ibid., pp. 7–8. [54] Ibid., p. 58. [55] Ibid., p. 13.

Despite the importance of this insight, and of North's attempt to grasp the interaction of agency and structure, his theory of institutional change remains anchored in methodological individualism and assumes that individuals will act to maximise their interests defined in terms of wealth. This undermines the importance he ascribes to agents' self-understanding, as ultimately both the identity and the interests of basic actors are taken for granted. Because he takes 'interests' – that which motivates agents – as given, he presents no theory of interest formation. When there are a number (even a limited number) of organisational options open to actors, *why* do they choose the ones they do? If it is on the basis of 'interests', how are these interests constructed and interpreted, because clearly, actors have often chosen paths which seem 'inefficient' from the perspective of maximising economic self-interest. While North uses the term ideology in a number of senses, ultimately he gives priority to ideology as 'legitimising the rules of the game', which in the end is not so different from Wallerstein. He does not enquire into how 'the game', and 'the rules of the game', are constituted. As a result, this approach provides important answers to a particular set of questions about the sort of institutional choices state-builders made. It cannot, however, answer the questions that this study asks about the social construction of identities and interests, and about the role of such constructions in state-building. It does not provide resources for understanding the construction of corporate identities and the interaction of agents and structures in constituting not only 'the rules of the game', but also the game itself, as well as who is a meaningful participant in the game.

In a more recent institutionalist approach, Hendrick Spruyt challenges conventional international relations theory, arguing that instead of taking the existence of the territorial sovereign state for granted, the success of this institutional form must be explained.[56] Spruyt sees major institutional change as an unusual occurrence, for unless there are major benefits to outweigh the costs involved it will be blocked. The transformation to the modern state is one such institutional shift, although it was but one of a number of institutional responses that agents devised.[57] Spruyt compares the modern state with the other institutional forms that developed in late medieval and early modern Europe, namely city-states and city leagues. He also asks why the nation-state outlasted its competitors

---

[56] Hendrick Spruyt, *The Sovereign State and its Competitors* (Princeton University Press, 1994).

[57] The institutional outcome is thus not just the result of 'Darwinian struggles', but also of 'what actors themselves also find acceptable', and the impact of belief systems on this. Hendrick Spruyt, 'Institutional Selection in International Relations: State Anarchy as Order', *International Organization* 48:4 (1994), 553.

and became the universalised form of political organisation. This second question is usually overlooked by approaches that assume that because the sovereign territorial state became the dominant form its dominance was inevitable or necessary, as Wallerstein, for example, assumes, because it allowed the continued functioning of a larger economic system.[58] What then made the sovereign state so successful? The core of Spruyt's argument is that the nation-state outlasted its competitors because it could meet both the internal needs of centralised authority and administration, and the external need to be recognised as a legitimate actor that could make and keep agreements in the long term. At the centre of these capacities is the concept of territorial sovereignty. The territorial demarcation of the fixed boundaries of political authority meant that the reciprocal recognition of states as legitimate political actors was possible. Because states were compatible in this way they could make and keep long-term agreements and the success of this institutional form meant that others copied or defected to them.[59]

Spruyt accepts the important role of warfare in state-making but asks why the state was better than its competitors at waging war. Size and military capacity alone cannot explain this, as at times city-states and city leagues outstripped states on these criteria. What was crucial to military success, Spruyt argues, was institutional efficiency, and the key to effective institutional organisation was the presence of 'clear sovereign authority'. It is the presence or absence of such authority that accounts for 'variation between units'.[60] If we look at the competitors to the sovereign state we see a great many differences. City leagues had no internal borders, no hierarchy, no agreements on weights or currency, and diverse legal codes. Sovereign actors benefited from the leagues' lack of unity. Importantly, lack of a clearly defined sovereign authority made it hard for the leagues to *credibly* commit to international agreements.[61] Like city leagues, city-states had no internal hierarchy, lacked internal unity, and made no moves towards the rationalisation of economic practices or the unification of legal codes. However, they did survive for quite some time. Spruyt argues that this was possible because the city-states were represented by dominant cities and were thus able to behave like sovereign states – that is, as unitary actors, despite their internal differences – in their external actions, and were thus considered legitimate actors in the international system.[62]

---

[58] Spruyt, *The Sovereign State*, p. 5.   [59] Spruyt, 'Institutional Selection', 554–5.
[60] Ibid., 551. Early on city-states equalled and in some cases outstripped the revenue of emerging sovereign states.
[61] Ibid., 543.   [62] Ibid., 548–9.

Though Spruyt pinpoints 'clear sovereign authority' as what accounts for variation between these different political entities, he does not investigate the construction of corporate state identity as part of the consolidation and centralisation that successful state-builders embarked upon. While Spruyt has a more dynamic sense of the interaction of economic and other dimensions of social life, including belief systems, ultimately his account has little to say about the social construction of collective identities within states. He identifies clear sovereign authority as the important factor in the success of nation-states as an institutional form, but focuses on the role of reciprocal recognition between states. To conclude, institutionalist accounts thus contain a problem similar to that found in Wallerstein's, though in the case of institutionalist approaches this arises from their methodological individualism, namely, that interests are unquestioningly understood as economic interests.

Power-based explanations

There are a number of power-based explanations of state-building, which in different ways emphasise the role of violence in the development of sovereign states. Norbert Elias stresses the internal pacification that occurred through domestication of the nobility, a process he describes as the 'civilizing process'. Anthony Giddens and Michael Mann stress the military capacity of the modern state, particularly since the eighteenth century in the case of Mann. Charles Tilly stresses the role of war in state-making, beginning in early modern Europe, seeing early states as the contingent outcome of competition between monarchs for military ascendancy.

Elias traces the process by which monarchs gained control over the means of violence and taxation, both of which were necessary to further war-making. An important part of this process was the 'taming' of the nobility, which occurred over a long period. The means by which absolutist rulers gained ascendancy, through manipulating the balance of power between the nobility and the bourgeois, is exemplified, Elias argues, by Louis XIV's France. Through this 'royal mechanism', Louis successfully maintained his own position by controlling and manipulating the tensions between these competing groups.[63]

Elias has little to say directly about the pathological homogenisation of peoples in state-building. However, his work does have implications for understanding such practices. As Zygmunt Bauman notes, the civilising

---

[63] Norbert Elias, *The Civilizing Process*, vol. 2, *State Formation and Civilization* (Oxford: Blackwell, 1982), p. 200.

process that Elias illuminates should not be viewed as a progressive process towards less violence, but rather as a 'reconfiguration of violence', in which it is not so much 'eliminated' from the everyday, but 'evicted'. The civilising process is thus the 'concentration of violence under the control of the state, where it is used to guard the perimeters of national community and the conditions of social order'.[64] Bauman emphasises how this carries the potential for the state to turn on its own subjects or citizens, and how this can play a role in the constitution of corporate identity within the state, as political elites define those who belong within its boundaries and those who are 'strangers' to be expelled or annihilated.

However, like Elias, Bauman says nothing about the cultural dimension of corporate identity construction. Although Elias traces the complex social changes that were part of state formation, his account of the civilising process treats culture merely as the instrument of power. But cultural processes cannot be so easily subsumed within the workings of 'power'. Instead, the linkages between culture and power need to be investigated, as does the role of culture in constituting social norms. Simple conceptions of power which ignore how culture provides frameworks which give action meaning, cannot explain the constitution of identities and the practical choices that state-makers make in such processes. Thus such a conception misses an important aspect of the processes of pathological homogenisation.

According to Giddens, two factors drove the development of the state: changes in military technology, and the pressure of the states system as a primary 'source' and 'condition' of state formation.[65] He thus prioritises the international system as the structure that shapes states as agents. This is despite his avowed interest in providing a theory of structuration that takes into account the dual nature of structures as both the medium and outcome of social action.[66] As a result, his emphasis on military interaction, driven by new technologies, has much in common with realist explanations of international politics.

Although Giddens recognises the growing coincidence of population and territory, he does not directly discuss forced conversions or displacements. For example, in his discussion of Louis XIV as the epitome of the absolutist ruler, he says nothing about Louis' attempt to forcibly convert the Huguenot population to Catholicism, though he does give account of other aspects of internal pacification, in particular the pacification of

---

[64] Zygmunt Bauman, *Modernity and the Holocaust* (Cambridge: Polity Press, 1990), pp. 27, 107.
[65] Giddens, *The Nation-State and Violence*, pp. 104–10.   [66] Ibid., pp. 19, 26.

the communes and the rise of corrective punishment and treatment for criminals and those seen as deviant.[67]

Giddens acknowledges that the unity of the national state has a cultural dimension, regarding nationalism as 'the cultural sensibility of sovereignty, the concomitant of the coordination of administrative power within the bounded nation-state'.[68] He observes that the unity within the state cannot remain purely administrative, as the domestic coordination of activities presumes some cultural homogeneity. Here culture is understood as a function of the need for greater integration within the administrative unit that is the state. Unfortunately, this view strips the modern nation of authentic meaning, reducing it to a psychological phenomenon that feeds on the 'rootlessness of everyday life', merely providing a means by which society can be further penetrated by the state.

Giddens sees the modern nation-state that arises out of this administrative imperative as a 'conceptual community', in a way that traditional states were not. In this he ignores the constitutive role of culture, reducing it to the role of an instrument of domination used to meet the administrative needs of the nation-state, and overlooking the role that culture played in early modern state-building, which predated the age of nationalism. The absolutist state, of which Louis XIV's France is so often regarded as the epitome, was also a 'conceptual community' constructed out of the available cultural resources, which were religious. As I argue with reference to Louis's France in chapter 3, the role of culture cannot so easily be reduced to a function of administrative centralisation.

Like Giddens, Mann emphasises the military capacity of the modern state. He also identifies three other sources of social power – the economic, political and ideological – and acknowledges the important role that religion played in early modern or 'proto-national' states. However, he argues that since the eighteenth century military and political sources of power have been dominant. In this period ideological sources of power have been important primarily in relation to class and nationalism.[69] For Mann, religion 'produced' what he calls rudimentary proto-national states, bringing him closer to recognising the constitutive role that systems of meaning can play. But in drawing a distinction between the ascendancy of 'ideological power' in this phase and the ascendancy of military power in the later stage of nation-states, he underplays the role of actors in early state-building and their active use of the cultural resources available to them. Religion did not produce proto-national states, human agents did in interaction with the cultural structures of the time. And in

[67] Ibid., pp. 97–9.   [68] Ibid., p. 219.
[69] Michael Mann, *The Sources of Social Power*, vol. 2, *The Rise of Classes and Nation-States, 1760—1914* (Cambridge University Press, 1993), p. 35.

the later phase of nation-states, the idea of the 'nation' has hardly played a secondary or supporting role. Indeed the idea that it is the national principle that legitimates the existence of sovereign states, and provides the criterion for membership within the state, transformed Europe, and in time, the rest of the world.

Ultimately, Mann's concept of ideology as merely another aspect of power leaves no room for the constitutive role of culture. This is despite the fact that he rejects crude characterisations of ideology as nothing more than the legitimation of interests, arguing that 'calculations of interest were always influenced by all of the entwined sources of social power, and always involved norms – sometimes peaceful, sometimes violent – emanating from complex attachments to the "imagined communities" of class and nation'.[70] Mann argues that norms should not be conflated with power but his account of ideology as a power source does not explain the processes of identity and norm formation, processes that not only come out of, but also *create*, 'imagined communities'. While advances in communication allow the development of a specifically modern, abstract concept of the nation, other ideas of political and religious community have also been imagined. The construction of the sovereign state as a moral community to which some groups were entitled to belong and from which some groups should be removed predated the modern nation-state.

Tilly offers a nuanced power-based explanation of state formation which takes into account institutional developments and economic factors. In contrast to institutionalist approaches, Tilly pays more attention to processes of internal pacification in state formation. Tilly explicitly places such processes in the broader context of the delineation of the boundary between the internal and the external aspects of states, and he notes that homogenisation of populations often played a role in this pacification. Tilly does not reduce this process to a by-product of the development of capitalism, though he does give an account of the complex interaction between capital and coercion. Rather than assuming some telos of development of the state within the European capitalist world system, as Wallerstein does, he characterises the development of the state as a contingent outcome of the struggle for power between rulers in early modern Europe.[71] Like institutionalists, Tilly argues that although war and coercion were the driving forces behind the formation and early development of states, as states stabilised and grew they became less coercive as institutions developed and capitalists and rulers struck bargains

[70] Ibid., p. 50. This is in reference to the eighteenth century and after.
[71] Charles Tilly, 'War Making and State Making as Organised Crime', in Peter B. Evans, Dietrich Rueschemeyer and Theda Skocpol (eds.), *Bringing the State Back In* (Cambridge University Press, 1985), p. 170.

with one another. Yet unlike institutionalists, Tilly rejects the idea that processes of state-building were the outcome of rational choices by leaders. States emerged as the contingent outcome of the struggle for power, which pushed rulers to consolidate their realms in order to extract the funds necessary to fight wars.

Tilly identifies the homogenising drive of states as part of the process of internal consolidation and the concomitant differentiation of the internal and external aspects of the state. In the early modern period, states had to deal externally with the impact of other states and the pressure from the system of states as it began to take shape. These processes were inextricably bound up with the struggles over centralisation, pacification and the construction of single, sovereign identities, all of which were internal to states.[72] As they armed against external threats, 'the state's expansion of its own armed force began to overshadow the weaponry available to any of its domestic rivals. The distinction between "internal" and "external" politics, once quite unclear, became sharp and fateful. The link between war-making and state structure strengthened.'[73] Though much cultural diversity remained in Europe, '[i]n a large perspective, nevertheless, the European states-making process minimised the cultural variation within states and maximised the variation among states'.[74] Thus homogenisation was part of the consolidation of the coercive power of the state. Internal pacification is one of the more self-conscious aspects of state-building, according to Tilly. Although rulers did not set out to build states as such, they did consciously implement policies to standardise populations, and while united populations might present a threat if they were to turn on the rulers, this threat was outweighed by the benefits of homogenisation:

within a homogeneous population, ordinary people were more likely to identify with their rulers, communication could run more efficiently, and an innovation that worked well in one segment was likely to work elsewhere as well. People who sensed a common origin, furthermore, were more likely to unite against external threats. Spain, France, and other large states recurrently homogenised by giving religious minorities – especially Muslims and Jews – the choice between conversion and emigration.[75]

In addition to his rather unfortunate conflation of forced displacement with voluntary emigration, the account Tilly gives of homogenisation has little to say explicitly about the sorts of choices that were made by elites and how they were translated into practice. By what techniques and using which resources did rulers raise awareness of a 'common origin' and a

---

[72] Charles Tilly, *Coercion, Capital and European States, AD 990–1990* (Oxford: Basil Blackwell, 1990), pp. 25–6.
[73] Ibid., pp. 69–70.   [74] Ibid., p. 79.   [75] Ibid., pp. 106–7.

'common cause'? With reference to the early modern period, Tilly points to the forced assimilation or expulsion of religious minorities, but he does not investigate this any further.

It is only when discussing nationalism that Tilly explicitly refers to the use of cultural resources in the construction of collective identities, using the concept of culture in the sense of 'national cultures',[76] in a manner similar to both Giddens and Mann. But nationalist criteria of political identity do not represent the first appearance of cultural factors in the construction of state identity. To be sure, nationalism does represent the *self-conscious* use of the concept of culture as *national culture* in the way that Tilly highlights, but the use of culturally meaningful symbols to constitute political identities precedes the age of nationalism. Early modern monarchs also drew upon the cultural resources available to them as they consolidated their rule and in the pre-national era these resources drew on the prevailing religious world view. Sovereignty has always required legitimation, but the form this takes, and thus the normative content of sovereignty, has changed in great epochal shifts. Nationalist criteria of political identity, profoundly powerful as they are, represent a shift to a new principle of legitimacy and new criteria of inclusion and exclusion, rather than the first use of 'cultural' resources in defining corporate state identities.

In the early modern period a number of states drew on religious resources in the process of constructing corporate identities, and they targeted minority groups for punishment or expulsion. Political elites in Spain, England and France all drew on religious resources in constructing state identities. Referring to the role that Protestantism played in the formation of English political identity, Philip Corrigan and Derek Sayer argue that 'religion was not, in the seventeenth century, a disposable set of rationalisations, it was a vital element in the framework within which people thought: including thinking their politics'.[77] As they point out, religion provided the framework of social and cultural meaning of the time, within which rulers operated as much as the ruled and the 'conceptual and symbolic augmentation of the authority of the crown'[78] was as important as the material accumulation that accompanied state formation.

Tilly observes that the twentieth century saw an increasing number of refugees. He also identifies a shift from what he sees as an 'aberration'

[76] Charles Tilly, 'States and Nationalism in Europe 1492–1992', *Theory and Society* 23:1 (1994).

[77] Philip Corrigan and Derek Sayer, *The Great Arch: English State Formation as Cultural Revolution* (Oxford: Basil Blackwell, 1985), p. 77.

[78] Ibid., p. 47.

to a 'standard technique of government' in the politicides and genocides of that century. It is evident, though, that he sees no connection between the earlier processes by which rulers sought to create homogenised populations within their states and twentieth-century practices. This is curious, as his own work shows that the different forms of pathological homogenisation have been techniques used by state-builders since early modern times. It is in the twentieth century, as the state system has spread across the globe and there are fewer safe exits for targeted minority groups, that genocide and politicide have become a 'standard technique'.

Considered purely in terms of the state's coercive capacity, the different strategies of homogenisation – forced assimilation, expulsion and extermination – have been available as possible techniques of government from very early on in the history of the system of states. The interesting and still pressing question is why, where and under what conditions are particular techniques used, and against whom? What is the loyalty to, and the identification with, the sovereign that Tilly refers to? How is it constructed to represent the unity of the state and to legitimate control of increasingly complex societies? How do particular identities come to be understood as threats to be excised from the state? By what processes are those who are different transformed into political misfits? While Tilly certainly sheds more light on the processes of homogenisation than the materialist, institutionalist and other power-based accounts, he does not address these questions, as he does not explicitly attend to the symbolic and cultural aspects of these processes.

Before going on to consider the role of culture in corporate identity construction I now briefly turn to rational choice accounts of the late twentieth-century explosion of ethnic violence around the globe. Though by no means exclusively concerned with state-building, these accounts deal with events that have often occurred in the context of state breakdown and reformation, for example the ethnic cleansing that accompanied the breakdown of the former Yugoslavia, which I analyse as an attempt to build corporate identity through pathological homogenisation, in chapter 5.

Rational choice explanations

As Badredine Arfi notes, while rational choice explanations 'help us partially explain the strategic dilemmas of ethnic conflict and design possible ways to manage them', they do not take account of the way in which 'actors' social identities constitute their interests and strategies' and that the 'social environment is part of what constitutes actors' identities and interests'.[79] Rather, they take it as given that self-interested individuals rationally calculate what is in their material interest and act accordingly.

Russell Hardin exemplifies this approach in his oft-cited rational choice account of the causes of conflict between groups.[80] Hardin begins from the assumption that individuals make a rational choice to join ethnic groups in order to gain access to resources which, he argues, one group usually gains at the expense of another. This rests on the assumption that inter-group relations are inherently conflictual and zero-sum, but this is not necessarily so. However, as Arfi argues, whether inter-group relations are cooperative, neutral or aggressive depends on the social identities of those groups.

Although Hardin acknowledges that individuals make choices within the constraints of certain histories and the knowledge available to them, his account reduces the social situation of individuals to nothing more than the information they will take into account when calculating their individual preferences, based on predetermined interests. This omits the intersubjective processes through which both individual and collective identities are shaped. Individuals do not 'choose' freely but are constituted as agents, at least in part, by the social structures within which they exist and which provide a meaningful framework for action.

In the process of rejecting primordialist accounts of ethnic violence Hardin includes 'moral' understandings of group identification in the same basket as 'primordial . . . or irrational'.[81] In opposition to this, I contend that an understanding of the moral content of identities – particularly when sharp boundaries between 'us' and 'them' are being drawn – is central to an account that recognises the intersubjective nature of group identities, and that such an account provides an alternative to primordialist accounts that does not strip group identities of meaning and reduce them to 'interests', even though they are indeed socially constructed.

Why is this so important? When the boundaries between insider and outsider are being marked out in ways that are consequential for political membership – and in the context of the modern state this has often meant who will survive and who will not – there is a crucial moral dimension to this process. 'Outsiders' are often deemed as beyond normal moral

[79] Badredine Arfi, 'Ethnic Fear: The Social Construction of Insecurity', *Security Studies* 8:1 (1998), 157. In particular see David A. Lake and Donald Rothchild, 'Containing Fear: The Origins and Management of Ethnic Conflict', *International Security* 21:2 (1996); David A. Lake and Donald Rothchild, 'Spreading Fear: The Genesis of Transnational Ethnic Conflict', in David A. Lake and Donald Rothchild (eds.), *The International Spread of Ethnic Conflict: Fear Diffusion and Escalation* (Princeton University Press, 1998).

[80] Russell Hardin, *One for All: The Logic of Group Conflict* (Princeton University Press, 1995).

[81] Ibid., p. 20.

consideration and therefore their elimination is not, according to this logic, of moral concern to 'insiders'. There is, of course a particular rationality at work in such situations, but rational choice accounts cannot fully explain this.

For example, Hardin describes a young Croatian man who could 'rationally' go about his self-appointed business of killing Muslim civilians – men, women and children – even though he declared he didn't 'hate' them. 'He openly confesses to having nothing other than interests at stake' and these interests were defined in terms of being Croatian. When the conflict in the former Yugoslavia broke out the young man felt he had no choice. *'Perversely he had to leave his community altogether or he had to identify with it altogether.'*[82] Hardin's acceptance of the young man's account of his motivations does not allow for consideration of the interaction of agency and social structure at work as this individual became part of the process of defining what it means to be Croatian in the most exclusive way, and how the identity that was constructed led to a particular, murderous understanding of his interests.

As Yugoslavia disintegrated, extreme nationalists sought to reconstruct Croatian identity through drawing a sharp boundary between Croatians and non-Croatians. This was a *moral* boundary that made it possible for this young man to kill people towards whom he felt no personal animosity (unless he was a psychopathic individual who merely had a desire to kill), precisely because the moral category into which they had been consigned meant they did not matter, in fact their very existence, including that of children, posed a threat to his identity. Furthermore, despite Hardin's acceptance that the young man had only two choices, to either kill or leave his community, in fact he did have other options, difficult though these may have been as, clearly, although extreme nationalists had their supporters among the Croatian population not all young Croatian men decided to actively kill non-Croatians. Many Croatians did not accept the either/or, in/out dichotomy presented by extreme nationalists, even under conditions of insecurity. This was an intersubjective process that was deeply contested but one in which this particular individual, by his actions, became an agent working to further the most virulent, exclusive understanding of Croatian identity.

What occurred in the former Yugoslavia was a contest within the successor states, particularly in Croatia and Bosnia-Herzegovina – as well as between them – not only for territorial acquisition but also over the way in which the corporate identity of the new state should be constituted. As I demonstrate in chapter 5, this was a normative contest, in which strategies

---

[82] Ibid., p. 148. Emphasis in original.

of pathological homogenisation played an important role. This was by no means separate from the contest for power understood in material terms but it is not merely reducible to this.

Hardin is of course aware of the manipulation of identity at work in Yugoslavia, and he notes that 'beliefs must be manipulated into being'.[83] But this begs the question of how this is done: out of what are beliefs 'manipulated into being'? Ironically perhaps, what drops out of this account which places such emphasis on individuals choosing group affiliation is a sense of *agency*, because there is no sense of the way in which individual agents act within social structures that influence their identities and interests. Hardin gives no account of how social structures are themselves produced by agents and in turn how agents are both constituted by and act within these social structures.

David Lake and Donald Rothchild illuminate another aspect of ethnic violence that is left implicit in Hardin's account, the role of the state, arguing that ethnic conflict is most likely to occur under conditions of state weakness and loss of legitimacy. 'States that use force to repress groups, for instance, may appear strong, but their reliance on manifest coercion rather than legitimate authority more accurately implies weakness.'[84] Like Hardin, they take the self-interested maximising behaviour of individuals as a given. However, while Lake and Rothchild recognise the way in which ethnic identities, which have the potential to be exclusivist, can 'become politically salient', they do not assume that this necessarily leads to conflict between groups. As noted, state weakness or lack of legitimacy create the preconditions that may lead to a number of strategic dilemmas arising among contending groups: information failure (when information about intentions is not shared), problems of credible commitment to peaceful means, and, arising out of these, the development of a security dilemma as groups find it increasingly difficult to trust one another.[85] Under such conditions of rising distrust between different groups 'ethnic activists' or 'political entrepreneurs' may employ nationalist discourse which plays on shared history, myths and so on, to both stimulate and exacerbate conflict between groups.[86] While they recognise how national myths can be used by elites to 'force the appearance of conformity among their own group members', they contend that ethnic attachments are not the primary cause of such conflicts. Rather, when groups compete for limited resources, they look to alternative futures when 'calculating strategies' and will act preemptively to head off any perceived threats. Thus, collective

---

[83] Ibid., p. 147.   [84] Lake and Rothchild, 'Spreading Fear', pp. 43–4.

[85] Ibid., pp. 12–17. Lake and Rothchild draw on James D. Fearon, 'Rationalist Explanations for War', *International Organization* 49:3 (1995), as well as Hardin's *One for All*.

[86] Lake and Rothchild, 'Containing Fear', 20.

fear of the future, underpinned by the struggle for resources among individuals and the groups they constitute, drives such conflicts in their account.[87] As it is the state that controls access to resources, it is the state that becomes 'the object of group struggle. Accordingly, the pursuit of particularistic objectives often becomes embodied in competing visions of just, legitimate, and appropriate political orders.'[88] This was indeed the case in the former Yugoslavia which disintegrated in the wake of a major legitimacy crisis and sharp contest among elites as to how the federal state, and then its successor states should be configured.

However, was competition over resources enough to bring about the sort of systematic violence seen in Croatia, Bosnia-Herzegovina, and more recently Kosovo, where civilians were targeted for 'ethnic cleansing'? While this may certainly be part of the story it does not give us a complete explanation for these policies. To understand how such policies can even be considered as options we need to understand the identities of the actors involved. This includes the way in which these identities are constructed with respect to others. How the 'problem' of identity is 'solved' is an intersubjective matter that will affect policy choices such as whether the boundary between self and other is negotiated in a cooperative manner or is drawn through exclusion and violence. In the first four cases studied in this book, state leaders have drawn on strands within their own cultural contexts which, although contested, have been used to legitimate a sharp boundary between insiders and outsiders and they have been prepared to accept high costs in pursuing their policies.

What of the rationalist argument that ethnic violence arises when elites employ a rational policy to instrumentally construct corporate identities that allow them to legitimate their own positions? For example, V. P. Gagnon argues that ethnic violence in the former Yugoslavia was orchestrated by elites who were resistant to change and were intent on buttressing their own positions. Thus leaders created or channelled ethnic sentiments for instrumental reasons, focusing on short-term benefits for themselves rather than longer term costs. Clearly, leaders did use ethnic sentiment in an instrumental manner in the former Yugoslavia, but in his explanation of this Gagnon brackets off the processes through which group identities can change, contending that political action remained at the level of manipulative political discourse.

Gagnon argues that in Serbia nationalist discourse tied individual interest to a redefined collective interest in the 'survival of the Serbian people'. In constructing the threat posed by Muslims and Croatians, elites drew on

---

[87] Ibid., 21; Lake and Rothchild, 'Spreading Fear', p. 41.
[88] Lake and Rothchild, 'Spreading Fear', p. 45.

nationalist 'discourse' that has been part of shared national myth since the nineteenth century. 'Serbian conservatives relied on the particular idea of ethnicity in their conflictual strategy because political participation and legitimation in this region historically was constructed in such terms', that is, in terms of the right to national self-determination. This is true, but I would argue that this ethnic conception of national identity had genuine meaning for significant sections of the population, even if it was perverted and manipulated by elites. Despite Gagnon's wish to analyse this at the level of 'discourse', this cannot be separated from questions of intersubjectively understood identity. As Gagnon notes, elites used a strategy that drew on a 'framework that referred to familiar histori-cal events' even though these events were beyond the direct experience of most, resorting to the 'construction of terrible injustices, rather than merely appealing to a pre-existing feeling of solidarity'.[89] He argues that elites provoked conflict so that the individual interests of the population came to be constructed only with reference to the 'threats' posed to the community and this was used by elites to 'fend off domestic challengers who seek to mobilize the population against the status quo'.[90] Gagnon rightly argues that ethnicity or culture in themselves do not determine policies.[91]

However, I contend that the strategies that elites used to delegitimise dissent, and which made it increasingly difficult (though not impossible) to appeal to other concepts of the group identity without being charged as a traitor, were not only about 'maintaining the status quo' understood as holding onto power. Although in one sense this was an attempt to hold back democratic change it was also an attempt to radically reshape the political community within the rump Yugoslavia in a way that would both mark the boundaries of the new state and legitimate the author-ity of elites within it. In doing this Slobodan Milosevic and his Bosnian Serb allies drew *selectively* on the cultural resources that were available to them but they could not have done this if no such resources existed, and domestic culture, defined in ethno-national terms since the nineteenth century, provided a framework of meaning which allowed nationalist 'dis-courses' a normative purchase. As I demonstrate in chapter 5, the con-struction of the Serb nation as simultaneously victimised and heroic drew on the 'myth of Kosovo' that has been part of Serbian national culture since the nineteenth century. To emphasise a cultural dimension is not to

[89] V. P. Gagnon, 'Ethnic Conflict as Demobilizer: The Case of Serbia', *Institute for European Studies Working Paper* 96:1 (Ithaca: Cornell University, 1996), p. 12.
[90] V. P. Gagnon, 'Ethnic Nationalism and International Conflict', *International Security* 19:3 (1994/95), 132.
[91] Ibid., 136.

argue that conflict is natural between different cultures, or to essentialise what 'culture' is. But to focus only on 'discourse' begs the question of where such discourse comes from and, once again, raises the question of the relationship between agents and the social structures within which they exist and must act. Discourse can only 'frame political action'[92] if it has some way of resonating for at least a significant section of the population.

Both elite-based and group-based rational choice accounts make important contributions towards understanding the strategic aspects of ethnic conflict and, though this is not their intention, state-building through pathological homogenisation. However, the underlying assumption that political action is driven by rational, self-interested individuals pursuing predetermined interests paradoxically results in accounts in which actors lack agency and there is no account of the processes – social, political and cultural – through which agents interact with one another and, in turn, with the social structures that human agency both creates and changes. With this in mind I now turn to the relationship between agency and structure and the role of culture in collective identity construction.

The role of culture in corporate identity construction

Max Weber famously argues that the interests of social agents, both individual and collective, are given direction and meaning by prevailing world views. To be sure, 'material and ideal interests directly govern men's interests', but it is the prevalent 'world image' which provides the symbolic framework within which action takes place, and which Weber argues can lay the 'tracks' along which interests push action and within which action gains meaning.[93] In this conception, ideas are not the opposite of the material dimension, but are encoded in the material through social practices.[94] Thus, as R. B. J. Walker argues, 'to attempt to come to terms with culture now is to engage with questions of political practice'.[95]

Ann Swidler argues that rather than accepting the Weberian understanding of culture as 'laying the tracks' or directing ends, it is more fruitful to think of culture as providing a repertoire or a 'tool kit' upon which purposive agents can draw. In different circumstances, she argues,

[92] Gagnon, 'Ethnic Conflict', p. 31.
[93] Max Weber, 'The Social Psychology of the World Religions', in H. H. Gerth and C. Wright Mills, *From Max Weber: Essays in Sociology* (London: Routledge & Kegan Paul, 1970), p. 280.
[94] R. B. J. Walker, 'The Concept of Culture in the Theory of International Relations', in Jongsuk Chay (ed.), *Culture and International Relations* (New York: Praeger, 1990), p. 5.
[95] Ibid., p. 12.

agents will draw on different parts of their existing cultural repertoire, or what Pierre Bourdieu calls their 'habitus', to achieve their ends. 'Culture is not a unified system that pushes action in a consistent direction.'[96] This understanding, she argues, gives a clearer concept of culture as action or practices and of agents interacting with cultural structures and transforming them through their actions. It is in 'unsettled' times, which surely applies to the following case studies, that culture as the 'common sense', uncontested background and guide to action becomes problematic. In such circumstances, the cultural field becomes the ground of competing interpretations or ideologies,[97] the arena for normative contests.[98] In the struggle to create new meaning and new frames for action – new identities and interests – actors inevitably draw, albeit selectively, on elements within the existing cultural repertoire.

Although Swidler notes that in such struggles actors are the products of their cultural context, she tends to overemphasise their autonomy, as though actors select from a menu of cultural possibilities from which they are independent. This downplays how culture not only provides agents with the means to pursue their goals, but informs what those goals are and how agents themselves are constituted.[99] Yes, culture should be understood as practices if we are to move beyond the conception of culture as a static framework for action, a view which makes change difficult to explain. But this should not be at the expense of recognising those broader 'world views', the values which orient and give coordinated meaning to cultural practices, including the constitution of social identities and interests.

In a very different conception to Swidler's, John Meyer and others argue that culture provides 'far more than the *general values* and knowledge that influence tastes and decisions, it defines the *ontological* value of actor and action'. They argue that 'rules constituting actors legitimate types of action, and legitimated action constitutes and shapes the social actors'.[100] As Finnemore notes, this approach is not unlike Wallerstein's, as it assigns ontological primacy to structures over agents, though here it is the values

---

[96] Ann Swidler, 'Culture in Action: Symbols and Strategies', *American Sociological Review* 51:2 (1986), 277. Swidler cites Pierre Bourdieu, *Outline of a Theory of Practice* (Cambridge University Press, 1997), pp. 82–3.

[97] Swidler, 'Culture in Action', 282.

[98] Martha Finnemore, 'Norms, Culture, and World Politics: Insights From Sociology's Institutionalism', *International Organization* 50:2 (1996), 342.

[99] On alternative conceptions of the relationship between agents and structures, see Wendt, 'The Agent–Structure Problem'.

[100] John W. Meyer, John Boli and George M. Thomas, 'Ontology and Rationalization in the Western Cultural Account', in George M. Thomas, *et al.*, *Institutional Structure: Constituting State, Society and the Individual* (Newbury Park: Sage, 1987), p. 22.

of the world polity, rather than a capitalist world system, that constitute the crucial structure.[101]

In articulating the relationship between agents and structures, I do not attribute ontological primacy to social and cultural structures, as to do so underplays the role of agency. On the other hand, I do not assume that actors float outside their social and cultural context with exogenously given identities and interests that cultural resources merely provide the means to achieve. Rather, this is a mutually constitutive relationship in which cultural structures are the products of the practices and lived experiences of agents, and these in turn shape agents' identities and expectations as well as the means by which they seek to achieve their goals. In this regard, the role of culture in constituting actors and meaningful action is not sufficiently emphasised by Swidler. Actors do not merely make rational choices to use certain elements of the available cultural repertoire for given ends; they too are shaped by the cultural context in which they exist so that certain options appear possible and others do not. This is more than a matter of what skills are available in the cultural 'tool kit', though this is indeed important. Beyond what is in the 'tool kit' is the question of what constitutes identities and interests such that certain acts, that from outside a given society or state may seem unthinkable, become not only thinkable, but are put into practice.

On the other hand, the Stanford School's structural perspective understates the role that agents play in making and remaking the cultural, social and political context within which action occurs, both within states and in relations between states. Structures do have an enormous impact on identities but the precise relation between agency and structure will differ according to place and time. As Margaret Archer argues:

This is no bland confrontation in which actors survey the ideational array and unconstrainedly take their pick. For we are all born into and can only live embedded in an ideational context which is not of our own making. Our very knowledge about it, our vested interests in rejecting it and our objective capacities for changing it have already been distributed to us *before* the action starts ... [H]owever, there is the actual response of agency to this inherited cultural context and, in responding, actors can exploit their degrees of cultural freedom to great (elaborative) effect.[102]

Further elaboration of Bourdieu's concept of habitus is helpful in this regard. In Bourdieu's conception, 'the agent and social world is a relation between two dimensions of the social, not two separate sorts of being'.[103]

[101] Finnemore, *National Interests*, pp. 19–20.
[102] Margaret S. Archer, *Culture and Agency: The Place of Culture in Social Theory*, revised edition (Cambridge University Press, 1996), pp. xxv–xxvi.
[103] Calhoun, *Critical Social Theory*, p. 144.

Agents do not view their social context as an 'object constituted externally. The source resides neither in consciousness nor in things but in the relationship between two stages of the social, that is, between the history objectified in things, in the form of institutions, and the history incarnated in bodies, in the form of that system of enduring dispositions which I call habitus.'[104] From this point of view, not all actions can be understood as arising from the strategic use of cultural tools, as agents are shaped by and in turn interact with their social and cultural context in which they see 'only one or a few possibilities'.[105] This allows us to understand culture as practices which embody given value systems or world views, but which themselves may change in response to the innovations of agents. As Rogers Brubaker explains, the habitus is 'the system of internalized dispositions that mediates between social structures and practical activity, being shaped by the former and regulating the latter.'[106] Culture is thus both those shared meanings and values which provide a framework for action *and* the practices through which, over time, agents remake their own social and cultural context.

Culture and state-building

The rearticulation of political community from universal Church and Empire to territorially defined sovereign states was part of the transformation from the medieval to the modern world view, so well articulated by John Ruggie.[107] While the form of the territorial state is indeed one of the hallmarks of modernity, there was an intervening absolutist period, in which a hierarchical and dynastic form of authority remained dominant for some time, with competing claims between absolutist rulers who attempted to assert their precedence over one another. The cases studied in chapters 2 and 3 – fifteenth-century Spain and seventeenth-century France – thus exhibit distinctly pre-modern characteristics. All the same, these states made significant transitions towards the centralisation and consolidation of authority and the demand for a single corporate identity within state boundaries, which we now associate with modern states.

Ruggie's account highlights the symbolic and normative dimensions of this transformation, drawing on Foucault's term 'social epistemes' to

---

[104] Pierre Bourdieu, *In Other Words: Essays Towards a Reflective Sociology*, trans. M. Adamson (Cambridge: Polity, 1990), p. 190, cited in Calhoun, *Critical Social Theory*, p. 144.

[105] Calhoun, *Critical Social Theory*, p. 145.

[106] Rogers Brubaker, 'Rethinking Classical Theory: The Sociological Vision of Pierre Bourdieu', *Theory and Society* 14:6 (1985), 758. Also see Sharon Hays, 'Structure and Agency and the Sticky Problem of Culture', *Sociological Theory* 12:1 (1994).

[107] John Gerard Ruggie, 'Territoriality and Beyond: Problematizing Modernity in International Relations', *International Organization* 47:1 (1993).

refer to the particular configurations of meaning, signification and normative patterns that are dominant in different epochs: 'The demise of the medieval system of rule and the rise of the modern resulted in part from a transformation in social epistemology. Put simply, the mental equipment that people drew upon in imagining and symbolizing forms of political community itself underwent fundamental change.'[108] This is not to argue that social epistemes acted 'as some ethereal Zeitgeist', rather they took effect 'through specific social carriers and practices. Social epistemes affected outcomes via the mechanisms of social empowerment and delegitimation.'[109] How established meanings are challenged and new meanings gain legitimacy is illustrated in the changing content of the doctrine of sovereignty, which came to be associated with territorial rule.

As the Respublica Christiana fragmented, new forms of authority evolved which reflected a new model of social order, and indeed a new world view. In particular, the development of single point perspective allowed a distance between subject and object which had not previously been possible. In this 'reimagining' the world became a different place, which was to be understood and experienced differently by a differently constituted subject, culminating in the concept of the highly individuated self and the strict demarcation of the public and private realms, and also of the boundary between the internal and external dimensions of the state.[110] It is modern territorial rule, Ruggie argues, that expresses the 'consolidation of all parcelized and personalized authority into one public realm. This consolidation entailed two fundamental spatial demarcations: one drawn between the public and private realms and another drawn between the internal and external realms.'[111] Internally, sovereignty was expressed in the pacification of the monarch's realm; externally, it was expressed in the right of monarchs to make war.

Under heteronomous medieval political organisation, multiple identities were not especially problematic. This is not to say that at a local or civilisational level difference was not regarded with hostility often resulting in violence, hence the numerous pogroms against Jews, and the crusades. However, as sovereign authority became parcellised into increasingly clear-cut domains the existence of difference *within* became increasingly problematic, and was perceived as a threat to the unity of the realm and thus to the sovereignty of the monarch. Despite the fact that authority was still understood in dynastic terms, and there was certainly

---

[108] Ibid., 157.   [109] Ibid., 169.
[110] Also see R. B. J. Walker, *Inside/Outside: International Relations as Political Theory* (Cambridge University Press, 1993).
[111] Ruggie, 'Territoriality and Beyond', 151.

no concept of 'the people', the development of early conceptions of territoriality demanded that the dynasts' authority be reflected in unity within the state, which could only be articulated in terms of a demand for religious unity.

Ruggie rightly emphasises the importance of understanding the role of modes of differentiation in the transformation that occurred in early modern Europe. As he explains, 'Without the concept of differentiation ... it is impossible to define the structure of modernity in international politics – modes of differentiation are nothing less than the focus of the epochal study of rule.'[112] Part of the constitution of new modes of differentiation is the construction of new modes of inclusion in, and exclusion from, the political community. There are, of course, different ways of drawing this boundary but state-makers have often opted for strategies that are now regarded as pathological. In chapters 2 to 5 I am concerned with the practices of pathological homogenisation, by which elites sought to 'fix' sovereignty in both its internal and external aspects.[113] Thus in fifteenth-century Spain and seventeenth-century France rulers attempted to forge unified corporate political identities within increasingly centralised states. Even as these rulers challenged the universal authority of the Church, the cultural resources on which they drew in order to define homogeneous identities and legitimate their authority within their states were provided by the religious world view.

In the nineteenth century the age of nationalism ushered in a new form of political legitimacy both within and between states. As the national principle took hold state-builders turned to this new secular criterion of identification – which nonetheless displayed continuities with older religious world views – as they attempted to forge unified corporate identities within the boundaries of sovereign states. In chapter 4, I examine the early twentieth-century breakdown of the Ottoman Empire and the attendant genocide of the Armenian people, as the Young Turk regime sought to build a rationalised sovereign state from the remains of the dying empire.

The way in which human agents can transform the cultural context which frames their actions is demonstrated in this case. In the multinational Ottoman Empire religious criteria identified separate communities but these did not provide bases for political organisation. As the empire crumbled under both strategic pressure and the impact of the national

---

[112] Ibid., 152.

[113] Weber, *Simulating Sovereignty*, p. 3. For a discussion of the role of 'statecraft' in the constitution and maintenance of the state through the creation of boundaries, see Richard Devetak, 'Incomplete States: Theories and Practices of Statecraft', in John MacMillan and Andrew Linklater (eds.), *Boundaries in Question: New Directions in International Relations* (London: Pinter Publishers, 1995); also see Ashley, 'Untying the Sovereign State'.

idea, religious identities were not forgotten, but were transformed into new national criteria of identification, which now played a central role in political action oriented towards the creation of a modern state. In the hands of chauvinist nationalists who asserted that the modern, rationalised state they were creating should be a national state, this was to have grave implications for minorities, particularly the Armenian minority, within what would become the sovereign state of Turkey.

Thus, there is some continuity between the cultural resources that state-builders have used in the pre-national and national ages in that religious identities have continued to play a role in the constitution of secular national identities, but they have also undergone significant transformation. Behind both criteria of identification is the political entity towards which identification and differentiation is directed, and this is the territorially bounded sovereign state, understood as much more than a centralised administrative unit. For the modern state has from the beginning been constructed as defining a moral community, and elites have jealously guarded the state's monopoly on the right to define legitimate identity. In so doing, state elites have acted as agents in the constitution and reproduction of the state as a separate and bounded political unit within a system of such units.

Nationalism, legitimacy and state identity

Despite the centrality of the national idea as a legitimating principle in the contemporary international system, I contend that it is the process of state-building that is the consistent factor behind pathological homogenisation and its attendant expulsions, massacres and genocides. Through different epochs of state-building, first in the early modern period, then following imperial collapse in the wake of two world wars, and more recently following the end of the Cold War, state-builders have been concerned with how to conceive of *the state:* with how it should be 'personified' 'symbolized', and 'imagined'.[114]

As Ruggie argues, the significance of the shift to the modern territorial state is best seen 'through the lens of legitimations'.[115] Referring to the shift towards absolutist sovereignty that took place in the early modern era, Max Beloff notes that 'the modern idea of political sovereignty, the notion that over every man and every foot of ground, there must exist some single supreme authority was still something to be argued and

[114] Walzer, 'On the Role of Symbolism in Political Thought', 194.
[115] John Gerard Ruggie, 'Continuity and Transformation in the World Polity: Towards a Neorealist Synthesis', *World Politics* 35:2 (1983), 275.

fought over rather than the underlying presumption of all political action'.[116] In turn the proponents of the absolutist or dynastic principle
'argued and fought' against the proponents of the national principle, allied as it was with democratic ideas, though in the end they lost this
normative battle and the idea of popular, nationally defined sovereignty
gained ascendance.

It hardly needs to be noted that the nation and nationalism are subjects
of intense debate. The account I give in chapter 4 of the continuities
between the traditional Islamic world view of the Ottoman Empire and the
Turkish nationalism of the Young Turks, demonstrates how even as they
represented a break with the past, national identities also drew on older
cultural traditions and identities. Nonetheless, I argue that the nation
and the principle of nationalism as it is understood today are modern
notions that could not exist as they do without the existence of the state.
Thus, I accept Ernest Gellner's definition of nationalism as 'primarily
a political principle, which holds that the political and the national unit
should be congruent'.[117] This principle can be evoked against a state
which is seen as unrepresentative of particular national groups, but it
also provides powerful resources through which state-builders can define
corporate identity, delineate the boundaries of a new state and legitimise
their own rule.[118]

This argument contrasts with a body of literature that argues that national identities pre-date and indeed, in many cases, were behind the development of the modern state. For example, Adrian Hastings argues that
a medieval nation and nation-state existed in England, disproving claims
such as those I have just made.[119] Yet I contend that it is anachronistic to
regard earlier sentiments as equivalent to the self-consciously espoused
national identities we are familiar with today. For example, although it is
possible to identify a 'proto-nationalist' consciousness in Ferdinand and
Isabella's state-building and the way they wrested religious authority from
the Pope to the Spanish Catholic Church, importantly, this was not tied
to a popularly held national idea. Corporate identity construction was
part of the state-building process but the monarchs drew on an already
existing, religious, corporate identity and sought to forcibly homogenise
their subject population accordingly. This was also the case with France,
as I demonstrate in chapter 3.

---

[116] Max Beloff, *The Age of Absolutism 1660–1815* (London: Hutchinson, 1967), p. 20.

[117] Ernest Gellner, *Nations and Nationalism* (Oxford: Basil Blackwell, 1983), p. 1.

[118] Calhoun, *Critical Social Theory*, p. 252.

[119] Adrian Hastings, *The Construction of Nationhood: Ethnicity, Religion, and Nationalism*
(Cambridge University Press, 1997). Also see Liah Greenfeld, *Nationalism: Five Roads
to Modernity* (Cambridge, MA: Harvard University Press, 1992).

National identities, like other identities, are 'imagined' in ways that draw on shared cultures and histories, rather than being merely 'invented'.[120] But the national principle allied with, and directed at, the modern state led to the global ascendance of the national state as an organisational form. As Martin Wight argues,

> Until the French Revolution, the principle of international legitimacy was *dynastic*, being concerned with the status and claims of rulers. Since then, dynasticism has been superseded by a *popular* principle, concerned with the claims and consent of the governed. The sovereignty of the individual prince passed into the sovereignty of the nation he ruled. It will be noted that these principles of legitimacy mark the region of approximation between international and domestic politics. They are the principles that prevail (or are at least proclaimed) *within* a majority of the states that form international society, as well as in the relations *between* them.[121]

By the nineteenth century religion no longer unproblematically served as the basis for conceptions of community. This was the case even in the Ottoman Empire, as well as in the Christian world. For example, in chapter 4, I demonstrate how Turkish nationalism arose relatively late in the nineteenth century, in response to the nationalist claims that had been sweeping across Europe and across much of the Ottoman Empire. Anatolia came to be regarded as the *vatan* or 'fatherland' of the Turkish nation. As Anthony Smith notes, 'Turks in Anatolia before 1900 were largely unaware of a separate "Turkish" identity – separate that is, from the dominant Ottoman or the overarching Islamic identities – and besides, local identities of kin, village or region were often more important'.[122] The dominant religious identity of the empire, which was Muslim, was, under the influence of nationalist writers such as Ziya Gokalp, transformed into a virulent, exclusivist form of nationalism, which was behind the 1915 genocide of the Armenians.

While the national principle has become a structuring principle in the international system, the content of this principle has, in turn, changed over the course of the twentieth century. As chapter 6 illustrates, the racial definition of the 'national self' implicit in the standard of legitimacy current after World War I was amended to a non-racial conception in the wake of the Holocaust and decolonisation. Yet despite this, as the numerous ethno-national conflicts in the post-Cold War era have demonstrated, some regimes still attempt to link exclusive notions of national identity to the construction of a unitary sovereign identity, giving rise to a clash

[120] See respectively, Benedict Anderson, *Imagined Communities: Reflections on the Origin and Spread of Nationalism* (Oxford: Blackwell, 1983) and Gellner, *Nations and Nationalism*.

[121] Martin Wight, *Systems of States* (Leicester University Press, 1977), p. 153.

[122] Anthony D. Smith, *National Identity* (Reno: University of Nevada Press, 1991), p. 21.

between international and domestic norms of legitimate statehood. With this in mind, in chapter 5 I investigate the fragmentation of Yugoslavia and its attendant ethnic cleansing. Here a virulent form of nationalism served to justify pathological homogenisation, with the aim of building a Greater Serbia, or failing that a separate Bosnian Serb state within Bosnia-Herzegovina. That Serbs could exist within another sovereign state was not acceptable to Serb nationalists. This meant though, as Robert Hayden observes, that Yugoslavia had to be 'unimagined' before the ethnic cleansing that occurred there could take place. In Bosnia a process of cultural prescription was at work, where nationalists prescribed what 'the culture' should be, and simultaneously claimed that their preferred vision of community was descriptive of what already existed.

But the nationalist vision of a 'perfect match' between a national group – understood in the most exclusive sense – and the state rarely matches reality on the ground, and thus policies such as 'ethnic cleansing' are employed to *make* 'reality' fit the preferred vision. 'It is this lack of congruence between the present reality of life as lived and the objectification of life as it suddenly must be lived that produces the mortal horrors of ethnic cleansing.'[123] Although Hayden refers to the former Yugoslavia, his observation is relevant to all four cases of pathological homogenisation studied in this book, as each entailed a vision of how the political community within the sovereign state *should* be homogenised in order that it might symbolise the unitary, sovereign identity of the state.

Summary

As I have argued above, mainstream international relations theories have little to say about state-building or pathological homogenisation, having regarded such matters as 'not our area'. Likewise, most theories of state-formation have little to say about pathological homogenisation, and those that do acknowledge such practices see them as functional to the capitalist world economy, as in Wallerstein's account, or as part of the administrative centralisation of the state, as in Tilly's account. Like rational choice explanations, these accounts do not allow for the important role cultural and symbolic resources play in corporate identity building, and in turn the important role this plays in state-building. Cultural resources provide more than rationalisations of actions driven by assumed material

---

[123] Robert M. Hayden, 'Imagined Communities and Real Victims: Self-Determination and Ethnic Cleansing in Yugoslavia', *American Ethnologist* 23:4 (1996), 784. And as Calhoun notes, 'where nationalist rhetoric stresses oneness at the expense of a notion of a differentiated public, it becomes repressive not just of minorities, but of all citizens'. Calhoun, *Critical Social Theory*, p. 254.

or strategic interests. In order to understand how those who are different can become 'political misfits' who must be removed or obliterated one way or another, we need a more complex understanding of the processes by which state-builders are influenced by, and use, the cultural resources available to them.

This study investigates the role of pathological homogenisation in state-building through the consideration of four cases. The first two cases, the expulsion of the Jews and Moriscos from early modern Spain and the outlawing of Protestantism in seventeenth-century France, both precede the age of self-consciously espoused national identities. They illustrate how state-builders drew on the cultural frameworks of their times, which were primarily religious, in order to delineate the political community within the boundaries of the state as a shared moral community. As the dominant principles of political legitimacy have changed, so too have the criteria by which insiders and outsiders are distinguished. Since the democratic and nationalist revolutions of the late eighteenth century, the national idea has generated different criteria of community, but these are still directed towards delineating who belongs inside and outside the boundaries of the state. This is not to say that all national identities result in virulent practices. It is the most exclusive forms of nationalism, that understand national identities as primordial ethnic identities (notwithstanding their connection to religious identities), which are most likely to draw a sharp moral boundary between members and non-members, and it is these that are more likely to result in harsh policies towards those designated non-nationals. This is illustrated in chapters 4 and 5, which investigate pathological homogenisation in early twentieth-century Turkey as it emerged from the breakdown of the Ottoman Empire and late twentieth-century ethnic cleansing as new states emerged from the breakdown of Yugoslavia. As chapters 2 to 5 show, in all these cases the forging of symbolic unity entailed concrete practices that involved the forced conversion, expulsion, and in some cases, the extermination of minority groups. In chapter 6, I trace the development of norms of legitimate state action regarding minorities and consider this problem of practical politics in a world of sovereign states. In chapter 7 I examine the possible conditions under which contemporary state-builders will choose non-pathological forms of state-building, focusing on the Czech Republic and Macedonia.

2   The 'other' within Christian Europe: state-building in early modern Spain

In 1492 the 'Catholic Monarchs' Ferdinand and Isabella ordered the Jewish population of Spain to either convert to Christianity or leave the country. This order affected between 1.5 to 2 per cent of the population of Spain at the time and it ushered in a new conception of political life within the nascent state.[1] During the medieval period, as leaders elsewhere in Europe were sporadically expelling Jews, in Spain a period of relative tolerance existed, in which the Christian, Muslim and Jewish communities coexisted, albeit not without tensions. This chapter traces the breakdown of the medieval *convivencia*, and the rising tide of hostility towards both Jews and Muslims, and towards converts from these religions, known respectively as conversos and Moriscos. This hostility culminated in the reign of Ferdinand and Isabella with the establishment of the Spanish Inquisition in 1480 and the expulsion of the Jews in 1492. These events are the main focus of this chapter, as it was during this period that Ferdinand and Isabella laid the foundations of the modern Spanish state. Pathological homogenisation continued, however, with the expulsion of the Moriscos by Philip III in 1609, and I give a brief account of the cultural and social context in which this occurred.

After a brief introductory account of events in early modern Spain, I highlight the mutually constitutive nature of the construction of the corporate and social aspects of state identity that was taking place at this time. As noted in chapter 1, most explanations of state-building either ignore cultural factors, or see them as functional to some interest or identity that is taken for granted. I briefly review these accounts in light of the Spanish case before going on to trace in more detail the development of hostility towards various groups within Spain, and the expulsions of the

---

[1] Estimates of the numbers affected vary anywhere between 120,000–150,000 people. However, in a recent article Henry Kamen argues that though there has been general agreement on the figures involved, they have been overestimated. He argues that 'the Jewish population of Spain could not have exceeded 1.5 per cent of the total, which brings us to a figure of less than 80,000 persons as a maximum'. Henry Kamen, 'The Mediterranean and the Expulsion of Spanish Jews in 1492', *Past and Present* 119 (1988), 33.

Jews and Moriscos. In this I give an account of continuity and change in early modern Spain, and distinguish between earlier popular hostility towards religious minorities and the state-sponsored programmes directed towards creating a homogeneous corporate identity for the nascent state. I investigate how the monarchs drew on the available cultural resources in order to do this and the central role played by the Spanish Inquisition, which answered to the monarchs rather than to Rome, and was thus the first institution that had authority over all the realms that together constituted Spain. I then give an account of the expulsions of the Jews and the Moriscos.

The consolidation of territory and authority in Spain: Ferdinand and Isabella

The marriage of Ferdinand and Isabella in 1469, followed by Isabella's ascension to the crown of Castile in 1474, brought together the realms of Aragon and Castile for the first time. In 1480 the Catholic Monarchs established the Spanish Inquisition which was charged with finding heretics among Christian converts from Judaism, or, what was more likely by this time, their descendants. In January 1492, after ten years of war, the reconquest of Muslim Spain was completed with the conquest of Granada. This was followed a few months later on 30 March with the order that all Jews must either convert to Christianity or leave the country by the end of July.[2] John Lynch stresses that although Ferdinand and Isabella had the potential to be absolute monarchs, they were not. However, they laid the foundations for future claims to absolute authority. One important aspect of the shift towards absolutism that took place under their reign was the reorganisation of the relationship between the monarchs and their subjects, in which the monarchs had much more direct contact with their subjects and demanded greater uniformity amongst them.[3]

From the events of the late fifteenth century it is apparent that what would now be regarded as 'pathological homogenisation' played a central role in the state-making of Ferdinand and Isabella. When the last vestiges of the medieval *convivencia* were swept away with the expulsion of the Moriscos in 1609, the drive towards a homogeneous corporate identity within the state was complete. That this did not necessarily make a stronger state, and that it may in fact have contributed towards the economic decline of Spain, highlights the need to understand how these

---

[2] The Edict of Ferdinand and Isabella can be found in E. H. Lindo, *History of the Jews of Spain and Portugal* (New York: Burt Franklin, 1970 [1848]), pp. 277–80.
[3] John Lynch, *Spain Under the Habsburgs*, vol. 1 (New York University Press, 1981), p. 10.

state-makers understood their interests and how this influenced their policies, rather than to take their interests for granted.

Lynch identifies a 'proto-nationalist' consciousness in Isabella's determination to marry Ferdinand against strong opposition, and to bring together the conflicting kingdoms of Aragon and Castile.[4] The two monarchs inherited kingdoms torn by civil war and internal strife, which were struggling to recover from the economic recession of the previous century. They set about imposing internal order and consolidating and extending their political authority over both the nobility and the cities. In this endeavour they were extremely successful. Although they inherited strife, Isabella and Ferdinand left 'their successors the makings of a nation-state, unified, peaceful, and powerful beyond any in Europe'.[5] They went about this process of consolidation in a way that diverged from the policies of their predecessors, who since the ninth century had, in general, protected both Jews and conversos.[6] There is no evidence that Ferdinand in particular was anti-Semitic, and during the period when the Inquisition terrorised the conversos of Spain he retained many conversos and Jews at court. However, in order to build their own legitimacy amongst the cities and common people, the monarchs harnessed a rising hostility towards Jews and conversos that *did* have an anti-Semitic strand to it. This popular hostility was a complex amalgam of social, economic and religious resentment that had combined with racism since at least the mid-fifteenth century and was spurred on by a number of active propagandists, particularly within the lower levels of the Church.[7]

While there was continuity with medieval forms in the rule of the Catholic Monarchs, seen for instance in the constant round of travel that they embarked upon in order to impose their authority in person, there was also much reform and the beginning of a centralised state.[8] Ferdinand and Isabella did not totally integrate their kingdoms, but they did initiate the process of centralisation in the only way possible at the time, relying heavily on the symbolic resources available to them and understood by all their subjects, both high and low born – the resources provided by religion. As noted above, the resentment against Jews and conversos was not driven purely by religious factors: it was much more complex than this, but at the time the only way this resentment could

---

[4] Isabella's half brother King Enrique IV was against this match. To get around this Isabella and Ferdinand took the initiative and had themselves married when he was out of Castile.

[5] Lynch, *Spain Under the Habsburgs*, p. 1. It should be noted that all these terms are relative.

[6] There were some exceptions to this, but there was no systematic campaign across all realms, as seen in both the Inquisition and the expulsion of the Jews.

[7] See Benzion Netanyahu, *The Origins of the Inquisition in Fifteenth Century Spain* (New York: Random House, 1995).

[8] Lynch, *Spain Under the Habsburgs*, p. 37.

be coherently articulated, and policies which sought to harness this resentment implemented, was through religious means. By the time their
grandson Charles V came to the throne on Ferdinand's death in 1516,
Ferdinand and Isabella had provided what Lynch describes as 'the minimum conditions of order and unity',[9] and in doing so they were the
first to 'solve the problems of state-building', problems that involved the
pacification and control of their realms.

The year 1492 also brought the discovery of America, heralding the
expansion of the Spanish Empire. The transformation from realms at
odds with one another, and a Castile torn by civil wars in the first half
of the fifteenth century, to a relatively unified Spain ruling a vast empire
would not have been possible without the state-building of Ferdinand
and Isabella.[10] Although this was very much a proto-state by modern
standards, the scale of their achievement should not be underestimated.
As John H. Elliott argues:

> The conquest of Granada and the expulsion of the Jews had laid the foundation
> for a unitary state in the only sense in which that was possible in the circumstances
> of the late fifteenth century. At least in the minds of Ferdinand and Isabella, they
> helped impose a unity which transcended administration, linguistic, and cultural
> barriers, bringing together Spaniards of all races in common furtherance of a holy
> mission.[11]

Thus, it was during the reign of the Catholic Monarchs, which bridged
the fifteenth and sixteenth centuries, that the Spanish state 'developed
both an international existence and a corporate identity'.[12] This corporate identity was built in part through the combination – by no means the
total integration – of the kingdoms that each monarch brought to their
marriage. The corporate identity of the new state was built through the
demand for 'religious' homogeneity that in practice fused religious, cultural and racial identity. In fact, this took the place of any real attempt at
administrative integration of the realms. Lynch relates this to the 'concept
of unity held by the Catholic Monarchs'[13] which was based on political
unity through religious unity. 'In a country so devoid of political unity as
the new Spain, a common faith served as a substitute, binding together'
the subjects of the new state.[14]

This provided a broader identity that could transcend both regional
differences of culture and language and the lack of administrative integration. The new state was centred in Castile where there were fewer

---

[9] Lynch, *Spain Under the Habsburgs*, p. 37.
[10] John H. Elliott, *Imperial Spain 1469–1716* (Harmondsworth: Penguin, 1963), pp. 75–6.
[11] Ibid., p. 110.   [12] Ibid., p. 126.   [13] Lynch, *Spain Under the Habsburgs*, p. 19.
[14] Ibid., p. 108.

obstacles to centralisation, as the Cortes had been progressively domes-
ticated and were nowhere near as powerful as in Aragon, where there was
to be found, 'the most sophisticated and entrenched Estates structure
anywhere in Europe'.[15] The population of Castile was five or six times
greater and as a result Castile was much wealthier. Castilian dominance
over Aragon was not questioned by Ferdinand of Aragon, and Castilian
language and culture gradually expanded into 'Spanish' culture,[16] with
Castilian becoming the 'language of authority',[17] although there was no
attempt at economic integration. Thus, despite continuing regional differences and the tensions arising from the dominant role of the Castilian
language, a broader shared identity was being articulated in opposition to
Jews, Muslims and heretics. In the absence of administrative integration
and the existence of diverse regional cultures, the Spanish Inquisition, established by Ferdinand and Isabella to seek out heretics among conversos,
became 'the one unitary "Spanish" institution in the peninsular, an over-
wrought ideological apparatus compensating for the actual administrative
division and dispersal of the state'.[18]

The social and corporate identity of the Spanish state

It is true that the struggle between emergent states placed a 'premium on
a state's ability to tighten its internal political ordering, to structure rule
so as to make it more unitary, continuous, calculable, and effective'.[19] By
the same token, as Gianfranco Poggi notes, we can, if we wish, emphasise
the internal aspects of state development in the 'rulers' drive for more
effective and exclusive rule, and see the mutually defiant, self-centred
posture of all states towards one another as the *result* rather than the cause
of that drive'.[20] Here it is argued that this is a mutually constitutive process
in which the boundary between the internal and external aspects of the
state was constructed through internal homogenisation and interaction –
hostile or otherwise – with other states who were also in the process of
internal consolidation.

Within Christian Europe, the hostility between France and Aragon was
extended under Ferdinand's influence into a hostile Spanish policy towards France. Ferdinand's diplomatic efforts were directed towards the
encirclement of France through dynastic alliances. To this end, he was

---

[15] Perry Anderson, *Lineages of the Absolutist State* (London: Verso, 1974), p. 64.
[16] Elliott, *Imperial Spain*, p. 128.   [17] Lynch, *Spain Under the Habsburgs*, p. 4.
[18] Anderson, *Lineages of the Absolutist State*, p. 67.
[19] Gianfranco Poggi, *The Development of the Modern State: A Sociological Introduction* (Stanford University Press, 1978), pp. 60–1.
[20] Ibid.,

concerned with securing the Spanish frontier in the north, something he continued to pursue after Isabella's death in 1504, and it was his acquisition of Navarre in 1512 that 'completed the unification of Spain'.[21] Ferdinand gained a secure frontier to present to the rest of Europe, but he also gained subjects within that boundary who had some affinity with other Spanish subjects. Thus a contemporary account of Ferdinand's actions explained his seizure of Navarre in these terms: 'that people interested him because, being of Spanish tongue and customs, there was a *uniformity* with his other possessions; and, by extending his conquest to the mountains, he had *closed* the means of access to Spain'.[22] Echoing Lynch, Maravall sees at work in both Spain and France what he calls a clear and marked 'proto-national' sense, reflected in writings of the time, such as that referred to above. This is not to say the monarchs of the time had a national sense as it is understood today, 'but this does not preclude the fact that the policies of the great monarchs of the late XVth and XVIth centuries were based on a pre-national type of community consciousness'.[23] This demanded that the population within the state displayed some form of uniformity and built on what forms of identification already existed.

The question this raises is where did this 'new consciousness' come from? In the case of Spain this new sense of community arose against the backdrop of the rising popular resentment of those seen as 'aliens' or 'strangers', even if they had existed in Spain for a thousand years, as had the Jewish community, and even if they wished to assimilate into the Christian community, as did most conversos.[24] With respect to the reconquest of Granada, though the Ottoman Empire pressed on Europe, the crusade against Islam had been dead for well over a hundred years, but was revived by Ferdinand and Isabella.[25] Thus Castilians, Aragonese and others, despite their differences, shared in the effort to reconquer Granada for Spanish Catholicism, and they were brought together in a movement that denied entry into the Spanish community to Jews and Muslims, a community that was by definition Catholic. This created

---

[21] Lynch, *Spain Under the Habsburgs*, p. 36.

[22] Jose Antonio Maravall, 'The Origins of the Modern State', *Journal of World History* 6:4 (1961), 793. The words are those of Guicciardini, who travelled through Spain during Ferdinand's reign.

[23] Ibid., 795.

[24] For many years historians assumed that most conversos were false converts, but as Benzion Netanyahu convincingly demonstrates through exhaustive research of Jewish, converso and Old Christian sources, by the mid to late fifteenth century this was not the case. As he points out, most older accounts unquestioningly relied on the account left in the records of the Inquisition, which assumed the 'guilt' of all conversos, i.e. that they were all false converts. See Netanyahu, *Origins of the Inquisition*.

[25] Lynch, *Spain Under the Habsburgs*, p. 29.

problems, though, as there were large numbers of converts from Judaism, and their descendants, who declared their loyalty to Christianity and who argued that they too were loyal Catholic Spaniards.

Spain was unique in the process by which numerous converts were created in the late fourteenth and early fifteenth centuries, when many Jews were forcibly converted by being given the 'choice' to convert or die. This contrasted with elsewhere in Europe where all-out massacres were often the norm rather than mass forced conversions. Spain was also unique in that a racial doctrine of 'purity of blood', *limpieza de sangre*, was devised by the mid-fifteenth century in an attempt to block the assimilation into mainstream Christian society of large numbers of conversos. When this proved insufficiently effective, anti-conversos elements agitated for the establishment of an Inquisition to seek out heretics amongst conversos. Thus religion and race became entwined in a view which argued that conversos could not be accepted as true Christians on racial grounds, but then also sought to demonstrate that they were not true Christians on the ground of religious practice. The ongoing persecution of conversos by the Spanish Inquisition, and the expulsion of the Jews and later the Moriscos of Spain, was the outcome of the monarchs being influenced by and utilising this cultural resistance to the assimilation of these two groups. Difference, that in the medieval period, though not always comfortable, had been to some extent tolerable, now became intolerable within the new state.

Existing explanations

As I noted in chapter 1, Immanuel Wallerstein regards the development of independent sovereign states as a function of the world economic system. In this view, the religious justification of the expulsion of the Jews is seen as a rationalisation of economic interests. However, Wallerstein's account does not convincingly explain *why* the decision to expel the Jews was made, as it does not explain why the interests of the Spanish state were understood in this way at this time. Recent research on the expulsion of the Jews argues that by the time of the expulsion, the Jews were a dwindling community, which despite having some wealthy members hardly constituted either a major economic threat to its competitors, or enough of a prize for the crown to be motivated by a grab at Jewish assets.[26] Nonetheless, this was still an economically productive section of the society, so the decision must have been made with the ready acceptance

[26] Kamen, 'The Mediterranean'; Henry Kamen, *The Spanish Inquisition: A Historical Revision* (New Haven: Yale University Press, 1997); Netanyahu, *Origins of the Inquisition*.

of any losses that might occur. Wallerstein's assumption that all interests are driven by the desire for economic advantage forecloses further investigation of this.

In contrast to Wallerstein's view, Aristide Zolberg argues that the decision to emphasise 'religious unity as the foundation for the constitution of a modern state' was a *political* decision, about how to construct the corporate identity of the state, which was made with full awareness of the likely economic costs.[27] Furthermore, in the drive for a homogeneous identity within the boundaries of the state, Moriscos, or Spanish Muslims, who were forcibly converted to Christianity around 1500 (in abrogation of the terms of the capitulation of Granada), were persecuted throughout the sixteenth century and were finally expelled from Spain in 1609. The Moriscos filled a very different economic niche to the Jews (and conversos), as they were predominantly agricultural labourers. Once again, there was no economic benefit to be gained from the expulsion of these people, in fact this decision had a high economic cost. But the expulsion was viewed as 'necessary' in cultural and political terms, as the Moriscos were regarded as internal allies of the Ottoman Empire.

Institutionalist accounts also assume that interests were driven by economic factors. If the rulers of Spain did understand their interests only in terms of the maximisation of wealth, why did they make a choice to expel the Jews of Spain? If one accepts the older view that the Jews were an economically important segment of the community, the high economic costs of such an action would surely work against the expulsion on the grounds of economic self-interest. If one accepts the more recent view that the Jews of Spain as a group were not that wealthy, this again raises the question of what possible economic benefit could be gained from their expulsion. Clearly, there was more to the formation of the Spanish state and how the Catholic Monarchs understood their interests, and in turn the impact this had on corporate identity construction within the state, than explanations that rest on the assumption that all individuals are driven by economic rationality can show us.

Neither were the policies of the Catholic Monarchs an 'efficient' choice in terms of property rights, as there could be no confidence in the stability of property rights under such conditions. Although the Inquisition was established to target conversos, there were some cases of Old Christians also being targeted, even in its early days. In later centuries the Inquisition would turn its full attention to the Old Christian population. Despite their moves towards centralisation and rationalisation of the state, there is no

---

[27] Aristide Zolberg, 'The Formation of New States as a Refugee Generating Process', in Elizabeth Ferris (ed.), *Refugees and World Politics* (New York: Praeger, 1985), pp. 34–5.

evidence that the Catholic Monarch displayed any interest in innovative means of stabilising property rights, preferring to work with a system of monopolies.

As noted earlier, Charles Tilly most clearly addresses the role of the homogenisation of peoples in the pacification of emergent states. As Tilly argues, from the rulers' point of view the administrative and other benefits to be derived from a relatively homogeneous population outweighed the risks of a united population. And as he observes, a sense of commonality meant that peoples were more likely to unite against external threats.[28] Tilly notes that homogenisation in European states often took the form of forced assimilation or expulsion of minorities. And it is Tilly who notes the role that this internal homogenisation played in the differentiation of the internal and external aspects of the state, thus playing a role in the constitution of the international system.

However, Tilly does not explicitly attend to the symbolic and cultural aspects of this process and how closely they were tied to legitimation of the rulers. Nor does he make a connection, which is implicit in his work, between the homogenisation processes in the earliest phases of state-building in Western Europe, and the excesses of twentieth-century state-builders, committed in the pursuit of unitary state identity. It is, he argues, in the twentieth century that genocide and politicide have become a 'standard technique of government'. As argued in chapter 1, though, while assimilation, expulsion and genocide each represent different policies, there is a relationship between them, as they are all strategies that state-builders may use. The physical consequences of these policies have become increasingly dire, but all are directed at the removal of the independent existence of a particular group, whether through the cultural obliteration of assimilation, removal through expulsion, or outright annihilation. It is in the twentieth century, in an international system where fewer safe exits exist, and even fewer open points of entry into other states are available, that annihilation becomes a more thinkable option. Tilly's insights are a valuable entry point for this chapter, but the argument here is that the case of fifteenth-century Spain (like that of seventeenth-century France) is relevant when trying to understand the underlying processes that contribute to contemporary events, notwithstanding the many differences between the fifteenth and twentieth centuries. As noted above, the corporate identity building that occurred in early modern Spain took the place of any far reaching administrative integration. Thus, such homogenisation cannot be understood merely as a function of administrative

---

[28] Charles Tilly, *Coercion, Capital and European States, AD 990–1990* (Oxford: Basil Blackwell, 1990), pp. 106–7.

unification, but as a means that was more or less autonomous from these other aspects of state-building.

In conclusion, materialist accounts cannot explain the decisions that the monarchs made in favour of homogenisation through forced conversion and expulsion. Likewise, institutionalist accounts shed little light on these processes. Tilly demonstrates that such processes were often central to state-building but leaves out the cultural dimension and overlooks the continuities between earlier and contemporary methods of pathological homogenisation.

Despite the many currents that fed into hostility towards conversos and Jews in Spain, the cultural framework within which this could be articulated was religious. Benzion Netanyahu makes a compelling case for the emergence of European racism in fifteenth-century Spain and draws an interesting parallel between this and the racism that led to the Holocaust in the twentieth century.[29] In both cases, he argues, the desire of large numbers of Jews/conversos to assimilate to the dominant culture – and in so doing to claim equality – was met with a hostile response. In both countries, he argues, racial doctrine replaced religious doctrine in justifying discrimination, as in both countries 'religion no longer sustained an impassable division between groups'.[30]

Netanyahu is right to point to the rise of racial doctrine in fifteenth-century Spain, however the context within which this occurred was very different to that of nineteenth-century Germany, as the latter was a much more secularised society. In Spain in the fifteenth century the Catholic Monarchs wrested control of the state from both internal competitors and the universal authority of the Catholic Church. But this was by no means a secular society. At that time and in that place the resentment of the Jews and the conversos arose from, and was channelled through, a religious world view. As Philip Corrigan and Derek Sayer note, in this period, it was through religion that people 'thought their politics',[31] and it is the contention here that this is how they thought their social or economic resentment as well. This is not to imply that religion was merely a rationalisation of other 'interests'. In the fifteenth century it provided the backdrop, the shared cultural framework, of meaningful thought and action. Thus the monarchs too acted within this framework and it influenced the choices they made. I now turn to a more detailed examination

---

[29] Netanyahu, *Origins of the Inquisition*, pp. 1141–6. Netanyahu draws on, and engages with, the 'correspondence' between fifteenth and twentieth-century racism identified by Cecil Roth, 'Marranos and Racial Antisemitism', *Jewish Social Studies* 2:3 (1940). Marranos is another term for conversos or New Christians.
[30] Netanyahu, *Origins of the Inquisition*, p. 1053.
[31] Philip Corrigan and Derek Sayer, *The Great Arch: English State Formation as Cultural Revolution* (Oxford: Basil Blackwell, 1985), p. 77.

of the processes by which hostility towards Jews and conversos arose in fifteenth-century Spain, culminating in the expulsion of the Jews in 1492.

The Jews of Spain: forced conversion, assimilation and expulsion

Continuity and change

What distinguishes the actions of the Catholic Monarchs from those of their predecessors is the systematic nature of the policies they pursued. The Inquisition was set up in 1480 for the express purpose of tracking down false converts to Christianity. Although any heretic went in fear of the Inquisition, there was no doubt in the minds of Jews, Old Christians and conversos that the conversos were the target of its inquiries and it was popularly believed that they were false converts,[32] an assumption upon which the Inquisition acted. Likewise, although there had been local expulsions of Jews within Spain, the one commanded by Ferdinand and Isabella applied to Spain as a whole and, unlike many earlier orders, it was enforced. In this sense, these actions represent a break with the past. Yet at the same time the monarchs were responding to currents with long histories in Spanish society.

During the medieval period Spain was the only European country that retained a relatively high level of tolerance for Jewish communities. Medieval Spain was a relatively 'open society', with its tradition of *convivencia* under which three distinct monotheistic religious and cultural groups coexisted in relative harmony.[33] The pluralist culture of *convivencia* was particularly strong in Castile. 'The court of Alfonso X El Sabio (1252–1284) brilliantly reflects the religious and cultural cosmopolitanism of thirteenth century Castile, and Alfonso even called himself the king of the three religions.'[34] This toleration came about as a result of the Muslim conquest of large areas of Spain in the ninth century. Jews were initially held responsible for the Muslim conquest and were subject to massacres. However, the parts of Spain that remained under Christian

---

[32] Henry Kamen, *Spain 1469–1714: A Society of Conflict* (New York: Longman, 1983), pp. 38–42; Netanyahu, *Origins of the Inquisition*. As Netanyahu points out, the conversos were not seen as Jewish by the Jewish community. Though the first generation of converts were forced, by the mid to late fifteenth century it was clear in the minds of most Jews that most conversos indeed saw themselves as Christian, and hence they were regarded as traitors by many Jews, who as a consequence had little sympathy for the suffering of conversos at the hands of the Inquisition.

[33] This toleration was always relative and the different communities retained distinct characteristics. On the mutuality of religious dissociation see Jacob Katz, *Exclusiveness and Tolerance* (Oxford University Press, 1961), pp. 1–10.

[34] Edward Peters, *Inquisition* (New York: Free Press, 1988), p. 77.

control were in a state of economic blockade, with the Atlantic cut off by Islam. In the face of a sharp economic decline, it was quickly realised that the Jews provided a range of important economic services. Christian rulers thus came to protect the Jews, who not only provided services as tax farmers and tax collectors, but also provided much needed economic development through their international trade networks. '[T]he Jews provided essential services and skills in what was, for a long time, a frontier society with vast underpopulated regions.'[35]

More generally, in the earlier middle ages Jewish descent was not considered problematic. In the later middle ages under the influence of the Crusades and an increasingly militant Church, the term Jew gained increasingly pejorative connotations. Pope Urban II made the first call to Crusade in 1095, which marks the beginning of the hostility towards Jews that was to rise throughout the late medieval period in Western Europe. Forces taking part in the first Crusade in 1096 are known to have massacred Jewish communities in the Rhineland. Similar attacks that continued throughout the eleventh and twelfth centuries did not have official sanction. However, under Pope Gregory IX the Fourth Lateran Council of the Roman Church in 1215 set out mandatory guidelines on conduct towards Jews throughout Western Christendom. These guidelines, concerned with limiting social interaction between Christians and Jews, were imposed to varying degrees. While they did not advocate arbitrary attacks and mob violence, they represented an official policy that saw Jews as a threat to be marked out as different, and Jews were ordered to wear badges and sometimes hats, which clearly marked them as Jewish. This was accompanied by the policy that wherever possible they should be converted.[36] Across what was to become Spain, these rules were often ignored and Jews went about their business unmolested and unmarked.

Late medieval cosmology was changing though, and Jews came to be associated with magic. For example, '[I]n 1409 Pope Alexander V included Jews among practitioners of magic arts whom the inquisitors were to prosecute relentlessly.'[37] As John Edwards points out, much of the stereotyping of Jews involved 'the inversion of Christian practices and

---

[35] Stephen Haliczer, 'The First Holocaust: The Inquisition and the Converted Jews of Spain and Portugal', in Stephen Haliczer (ed.), *Inquisition and Society in Early Modern Europe* (London: Croom Helm, 1987), p. 7.

[36] John Edwards, *The Jews in Christian Europe, 1400–1700* (London: Routledge, 1988), pp. 14–16.

[37] Salo Baron, *A Social and Religious History of the Jews*, vol. 11, *Citizen or Alien Conjurer* (New York: Columbia University Press, 1967), p. 139. The original Papal Inquisition began in 1233.

values'.[38] The late medieval period saw an increasing concern with dev-
ils and demons, and the need for a Christian war against Satan. In this
context unbelievers were enemies of Christ, and allies of Satan, the devil
incarnate.[39]

By the fourteenth century, many sections of the Church were on the offensive against both Jews and Muslims, with the institution of mendicant
friars expressly concerned with conversion, despite the fact that this was
at odds with canon law. To add to the woes of Jewish communities, the
black death swept Europe in the mid-fourteenth century and Jews were
often blamed for this. This built on and in turn fed rising popular resentment often expressed in blood libels which accused Jews of atrocities
committed in the name of demonic practices. Across Western Europe:

[i]n general terms, the theological view of the Jews as obstinate adherents of a
dead religion, as inveterate enemies of Christianity, and as a threat to the rest of
the population, moved from the written texts of the theologians, the inquisitors,
and the lawyers, first into iconography and then into concrete accusations of
crimes, which on occasions led to further violence, robbery, and even deaths.[40]

Yet the kingdoms that were to become Spain went against the tide for
much of the medieval period and rulers in general protected Jews. However, by the fourteenth century the tide of popular hostility towards Jews
was on the rise there too. In Spain, as elsewhere, the disastrous late fourteenth century brought economic recession, famine and plague. The end
of the century brought a succession of riots, massacres and many forced
conversions to Christianity, 'culminating in the terrible pogroms of 1391
in Barcelona and elsewhere [in which] Jews were killed, driven into the
countryside, and forced to convert'.[41] This was followed by further mass
conversions in 1412 when laws were instituted in Toledo which made it
virtually impossible for most Jews to pursue their means of livelihood.
Estimates of the number of converts vary widely, but the number would

[38] Edwards, *The Jews*, p. 24.
[39] Baron, *Social and Religious History*, p. 135. Attitudes to Jews and to witches share some
common bases in late medieval cosmology/demonology. Hugh Trevor-Roper takes this
up in his discussion of the witch craze of the sixteenth and seventeenth centuries,
the first stirrings of which can be traced back to the late middle ages. Social fears were,
he argues, manifested and articulated in terms of the meaningful symbols of the time.
An obsessive belief in the devil was reflected in 'scapegoating of the devil's "agents"' –
witches or Jews. Hugh Trevor-Roper, 'The European Witch-Craze of the Sixteenth
and Seventeenth Centuries', in Hugh Trevor-Roper, *Religion, the Reformation and Social
Change, and Other Essays* (London: Macmillan, 1967), pp. 165–6. Trevor-Roper, p. 189,
argues that the cosmology which allowed demonology was not in fact rejected by the
Reformation, which explains why witchhunts were also strong in Protestant countries.
[40] Edwards, *The Jews*, p. 22.   [41] Peters, *Inquisition*, p. 82.

likely have been in the hundreds of thousands.[42] Though an accurate account of the numbers involved may never be possible, what is certain is that this presented Spain with a large segment of the previously 'alien' Jewish people who over the next few generations wished to assimilate into the Christian mainstream.

Over the next century many conversos (and some non-Christian families) rose to social and economic prominence, gaining positions within the royal administration and the Church. Many noble families intermarried with conversos, but many in the conversos' population retained a distinct cultural identity even as they sought to assimilate, and thus were not quickly absorbed as an unidentifiable part of the wider society. Attempts to assimilate were also blocked in large part by many (though not all) Old Christian families within the urban oligarchies who would not accept New Christians. They refused to accept that they had genuinely converted and practised as Christians or, indeed, that converts could in fact be legitimate Christians, the latter position flying in the face of Church doctrine.

In the early fifteenth century there was a rising tide of suspicion of conversos among the 'common people', encouraged by the tireless activity of some anti-converso campaigners,[43] which had its roots in the anti-Jewish sentiments that had led to the forced conversions in the first place. By the mid-fifteenth century the issue of 'race' was increasingly salient, with the doctrine of *limpieza de sangre* (purity of blood) used to justify discrimination against conversos on the grounds that they were of 'impure', that is, Jewish blood.[44] In 1449 in Toledo there was a popular uprising against the crown in which the conversos were the immediate target of social and economic resentment. Race played an important part in this. Jane Gerber cites an ordinance of that year in which conversos were described as 'infamous and ignominious, unfit, and unworthy to hold any public office or any benefice within the city of Toledo . . . ' As she goes on to argue:

> By this act, the very purpose of the pogroms of 1391 and subsequent conversionary movements – i.e., to convert the Jews and bring them completely and permanently into the Christian fold – was thwarted. The Conversos were now isolated as a new class, neither Jewish nor Christian, that was unassimilable and could not be redeemed.[45]

---

[42] See Netanyahu, *Origins of the Inquisition*, pp. 1095–102, for a discussion of the debates over these numbers. Netanyahu favours the higher estimates of 600, 000 people or more.

[43] See ibid., for detailed accounts of such campaigners in both the fourteenth and fifteenth centuries.

[44] Such views were always contested though and purity of blood statutes were not imposed everywhere. All the same, they had a 'socially corrosive effect'. Kamen, *The Spanish Inquisition*, pp. 230–54.

[45] Jane Gerber, *The Jews of Spain: A History of the Sephardic Experience* (New York: Free Press, 1992), p. 127; also see Netanyahu, *Origins of the Inquisition*.

Despite being revoked at this stage (the Toledo statutes were over-ruled by Pope Nicholas V as they went against Church teaching that 'all Catholics are one in body . . . ') purity statutes were to become more prevalent. Ironically, this race based doctrine was not supported by Ferdinand and Isabella. However, it was revived in subsequent reigns so that by the mid-sixteenth century '*limpieza de sangre* was an official requirement for entry to public office; thereafter all descendants of Jews were barred from holding positions of authority in the army, the university, the Church, and the municipality'.[46] Individuals needed certificates to prove 'cleanliness' which opened the way for much corruption and abuse to produce the required genealogies going back four generations. The Old Christians laid claim to 'Gothic blood' as descendants of the Visigoths, and thus claimed their own 'ethnic purity'. With the rise of this racial doctrine in the fifteenth century, anti-conversos saw little difference between Jews and conversos, except that, in their view, conversos had falsely gained privileges to which they were not entitled. However, despite their agitation, many conversos remained in positions of influence.

The Spanish Inquisition

The Spanish Inquisition was established to weed out heresy amongst conversos. In later centuries the attention of the Inquisition shifted to the Old Christian population in an attempt to buttress Catholic orthodoxy against the threat posed by the Reformation.[47] All the same, the Inquisition persecuted successive generations of conversos over the next 300 years, starting with the Spanish conversos in the fifteenth century, later turning to Portuguese conversos who came back into Spain in the sixteenth and seventeenth centuries, as well as the Moriscos in the sixteenth century. During the Reformation the threats from three sources – Jews/conversos (for these two were inextricably linked together no matter how much conversos protested that they were not Jews), Muslims/Moriscos and Protestants – were often cast as interrelated. But it was the perceived threat to the unity of the Catholic faith posed by 'false converts' from Judaism that was the catalyst for the Spanish Inquisition.

The argument that the conversos were actually 'Judaisers' was until recently a taken for granted assumption amongst many historians of the Inquisition, but as Netanyahu points out, this view was based on an unquestioning acceptance of Inquisition documents. Netanyahu argues that Hebrew documents of the time show that by the late fifteenth century the Jewish community had come to see conversos as renegades and

---

[46] Ibid., p. 128.   [47] Haliczer, 'The First Holocaust', p. 1.

apostates. Netanyahu argues that the stories of genuine conversion told by conversos, often discounted as self-serving, were most likely true and that most conversos genuinely identified themselves as Christian. The views of the Old Christians at the time were more complex, Netanyahu reports, with some accepting that most conversos were Christians, others unsure and some convinced that all conversos were false converts and therefore heretics. From this Netanyahu concludes that it is most likely that by the late fifteenth century, though some conversos may have secretly held to the Jewish faith, most were genuine converts who wished to assimilate into Christian society.[48]

Why then did the monarchs respond positively to calls for an Inquisition to be set up when their predecessors had resisted such pressure? For the Catholic Monarchs this presented a means of controlling the popular resentment against both Jews and conversos and directing it themselves rather than letting anti-Jewish, and particularly anti-converso, resentment be linked to resentment of the crown. Thus the monarchs set up the Inquisition in Castile and later extended it to other realms.[49] In 1478 they requested a Papal Bull establishing an Inquisition. On 1 November 1478, Pope Sixtus IV permitted the appointment of two or three priests over forty years of age as inquisitors. On 27 September 1480, the monarchs issued orders to establish tribunals in Aragon and Castile to try heretics. 'The royal decree explicitly stated that the Inquisition was instituted to search out and punish converts to Judaism who transgressed against Christianity by secretly adhering to Jewish beliefs and performing rites and ceremonies of the Jews.'[50] Royal commissions as Inquisitors were issued to the Dominicans in Seville. This choice in itself reflects the decision to take the part of those hostile to conversos, as the Dominican order was well known for such hostility. In mid-October of 1480 the Inquisitors went to work, and in early February of the following year, the first *auto de fe*, the public sentencing of convicted heretics, literally the 'act of faith', took place in Seville. On 11 February 1482, seven more Inquisitors were appointed including Tomas de Torquemada.[51]

Ferdinand and Isabella had already established a number of state councils and they now formed the *Consejo de la Suprema y General Inquisicion*

[48] Netanyahu, *Origins of the Inquisition*.
[49] Gerber notes that although early in their reign Ferdinand and Isabella protected their Jewish subjects, '[i]n retrospect it appears that several experiments in the treatment of Jews were proceeding simultaneously, not only expulsion, but also confiscation of property'. Gerber, *The Jews of Spain*, p. 132.
[50] Benzion Netanyahu, 'The Primary Cause of the Spanish Inquisition', in Angel Alcala (ed.), *The Spanish Inquisition and the Inquisitorial Mind* (New York: Columbia University Press, 1984), p. 3.
[51] Peters, *Inquisition*, p. 85.

(the Council of the Supreme and General Inquisition), with Torquemada installed as its president. Through the Inquisition the state took control of the Church in Spain, limiting the role of the papacy and usurping religious authority. On 17 October 1483, Torquemada was appointed Inquisitor-General of Aragon, Valencia and Catalonia. The Castilian and Aragonese Inquisitions were thus linked under a single authority whose head was directly responsible to the crown.

As the initial Inquisitor-General, Torquemada was the first individual to have authority that reached across Spain, as in principle Ferdinand and Isabella were each the ruler of their own separate realms.[52] Through this institution the Catholic Monarchs gained control of the judiciary and the Church which they used to further control and pacify their realms. The Inquisition helped build 'the power of the state by establishing an institution that, at least theoretically, was unconstrained by considerations of social status, wealth, or political influence'.[53] Given that the authority of the Inquisition, and of the crown itself, may in reality have been tenuous in many areas, spectacle played an important role in pacification and the creation of a unified corporate identity.

The *auto de fe* was the public announcement of the verdicts on cases tried by the tribunals of the Inquisition. Different forms were used, but the common aim of all *autos de fe* was exemplary, and 'a major role was played by the precise exposition of doctrine and public exposure of the transgression and the humiliation of the culprit'.[54] While it was not all that common, the public spectacle of the *auto de fe* with its 'fiesta like atmosphere', played an important role in buttressing the authority of the state and the legitimacy of the rulers.[55] This takes on greater importance if we consider that in the centralisation of the state this potent symbolic demonstration of authority was an effective means of control, as the spectacle worked as a threat through spreading fear of the potential retribution sanctioned by both the Church and the state. 'The intent

[52] During the age of Spanish expansion the Inquisition was also 'the only agency of government whose jurisdiction extended throughout all of the Spanish Empire'. Gustav Henningson, 'The Archives and the Historiography of the Spanish Inquisition', in Gustav Henningson and John Tedeschi (eds.), *The Inquisition in Early Modern Europe: Studies on Sources and Methods* (Illinois: Northern Illinois University Press, 1986), p. 54.
[53] Haliczer, 'The First Holocaust', p. 10.
[54] Maria Victoria Gonzalez de Caldas, 'New Images of the Holy Office in Seville: The *Auto de Fe*', in Alcala (ed.), *The Spanish Inquisition*, p. 268.
[55] Gerber, *The Jews of Spain*, pp. 131–2. Many who appeared at the *autos de fe* were sentenced to death, while those who were not carried a permanent stigma, as did their descendants. Penitents were required to wear a garment which marked them out as shameful. This garment, known as a *sanbenito*, was a sack, often with the family name inscribed upon it. When the sentenced expired or the penitent died, the *sanbenito* was placed on the wall of the local church for the whole community to see. Not surprisingly they disappeared from time to time. Peters, *Inquisition*, p. 94.

of the *auto de fe* was precisely to be what its name indicates, an act of faith, an act of public exaltation of triumphant Catholicism, a collective expression of the social rejection of heresy and of the public subjection to the strictest orthodoxy.'[56] Those sentenced to death or subjected to imprisonment and/or other punishments were overwhelmingly conversos. In the early years of the Inquisition around 2,000 people, mainly conversos, were burnt and many others suffered the social humiliation of trial and loss of property.

This hostility to conversos was to have important consequences for the Jewish community who, once the hunt was on to find heretic conversos, were accused of leading conversos astray. Their very presence, it seems, was a threat to the cohesiveness of Catholic identity within the new state. The existence of the Jewish community became increasingly unacceptable to many in Spain. For the monarchs, hostility towards the conversos could be managed through the Inquisition, which for all its depredations, could not wipe out all conversos. Hostility towards the Jews was another matter, though, and the targeting of this community for conversion or expulsion (which created even more converts) provided a further means of building their legitimacy.

The expulsion of the Jews of Spain

As we have seen, the pogroms and forced conversions of the fourteenth and early fifteenth centuries were not state sponsored, even though Ferdinand and Isabella subsequently established the Inquisition to apprehend and punish false converts. By contrast, the expulsion of the Jews was a systematically imposed policy implemented by the rulers of an emergent sovereign state. In 1492 Ferdinand and Isabella issued an edict giving the Jews of Spain four months to convert to Christianity or leave the country. The reason given in the edict was the perceived negative 'influence' of Jews on 'bad Christians', that is, conversos suspected of being false converts. Estimates of the number who left vary widely, but at least 80,000 people left during the Spring and Summer of 1492, while an estimated 100,000 people chose to convert and remain. Many who were expelled would return and convert due to the hardships they experienced

---

[56] Gonzalez de Caldas, 'New Images', p. 267. Of course public spectacle was not the sole province of those found guilty at the *auto de fe*, but the form of all secular punishments at the time. It was to the secular arm that the church 'relaxed' prisoners for public execution. On the use of torture and public punishment, and the transformation to other forms of punishment, see Michel Foucault, *Discipline and Punish: The Birth of the Prison* (London: Penguin, 1979). For an account that is critical of Foucault for his failure to explain historical change, see Peter Spierenberg, *The Spectacle of Suffering* (Cambridge University Press, 1984).

elsewhere, meaning that at least half the Jews of Spain chose to stay and convert, despite the pressures on conversos. The end result of the Catholic Monarchs' policy was an increased number of conversos within Spain and also within Portugal. The last forced conversion took place in Navarre in 1498, and with it the Jewish community of Spain as 'a legally constituted and recognized body came to an end'.[57]

This example of state formation straddles the late medieval and early modern periods. The incipient state developing under the aegis of Ferdinand and Isabella was in many respects medieval, but it also showed some of the hallmarks of the centralising, rationalising modern state. Ferdinand and Isabella's Spain had taken a step into the early modern period. What differentiates the Spanish expulsion from earlier expulsions in both England and France is first the sheer numbers involved, second that Jews had been in Spain for 1,000 years, and third, in contrast to the limited roles allowed Jews in both England and France, where Jews were restricted to money lending activities, the much more socially and economically differentiated role of the Jews in Spain. It was in fact 'a decision unprecedented in European history. Jews expelled by other countries in medieval times had been tiny minorities; in Spain, by contrast, they had for centuries been a significant, prosperous and integral part of society.'[58]

The scale of the conversions and expulsion and its psychological impact on Jewish communities everywhere is reflected in how it was regarded as a major catastrophe. Whilst across Western Europe in the medieval period, unification of 'host peoples often spelt ultimate disaster' for Jews,[59] it is in Spain that we see for the first time a centralised and sustained policy involving the forcible conversion or expulsion of a significant proportion of the population who fulfilled a range of social and economic roles.

Stephen Katz takes a different view of this. He asserts that the expulsion was the last in a long line of medieval expulsions, all based on the view that Christian states had the right to expel Jews.[60] In short, he understands the expulsion as part of a long-practised premodern resolution of the 'Jewish problem'. But what we see in the case of early modern Spain is a mixture of the medieval world view and the innovative actions of early modern state-builders: the state that the Jews were being expelled from was very different from previous states. Katz points to the ethical system of the

---

[57] Gerber, *The Jews of Spain*, p. 144.
[58] Henry Kamen, *Inquisition and Society in Spain: In the Sixteenth and Seventeenth Centuries* (London: Weidenfeld and Nicolson, 1985), p. 13.
[59] Baron, *Social and Religious History*, p. 199.
[60] Steven T. Katz, *The Holocaust in Historical Context*, vol. 1, *The Holocaust and Mass Death Before the Modern Age* (New York: Oxford University Press, 1994), p. 375.

Catholic Church which allowed the expulsion but not the killing of Jews and sees continuity with medieval practices. However, the pope did not support this expulsion, and in fact the papal states offered refuge to Jews. The important point here is that the Spanish case reflects a combination of continuity with the late medieval period as well as change, as the actions of the Catholic Monarchs pushed themselves – and the state they were building – into a new era. The Spanish expulsion was characterised by what Baron describes as a 'decisiveness and simultaneity of action' that was not to be found in the widespread but sporadic expulsions ordered by a range of rulers across western Europe.[61]

The Catholic Monarchs were able to wrest religious authority from the Catholic Church while avoiding a formal break. As the political and the religious spheres became increasingly distinct, the mediation between these spheres became the preserve of state rulers, as the state became identified as the realm of moral community. This could not be articulated, however, in any other than religious terms at this time. Although Jews had been subject to persecution, massacre and expulsion during the medieval period, the systematic nature of the policies of the Catholic Monarchs and the role they played in the construction of a corporate identity within the boundaries of the new state, make this a modern political act.[62]

The Moriscos of Spain: conversion, assimilation and expulsion

In 1492, when the city of Granada fell, the reconquest of Islamic Spain was finally achieved after ten years of war. Those Moors who survived the fall of Granada were before long forcibly converted to Christianity

---

[61] Baron, *Social and Religious History*, p. 240.

[62] In the case of the Jewish community, in medieval England this was a small community that had existed for only 200 years, arriving under the aegis of William the Conqueror. They had always remained a visibly different group, maintaining their links with French Jewry and continuing to speak French when the rulers took up the vernacular. They fulfilled an extremely circumscribed role as money lenders and a source of taxes for the monarchy. Their money lending activities made them the object of increasing resentment from their debtors, especially the barons, who in some cases used Crusades as a pretext to wipe out Jewish money lenders and, with them, their debts. They were subject to increasingly heavy and arbitrary taxes (and ransoms), and expulsions from many towns culminating in the general expulsion from England in 1290. Edward I was under pressure from estates and the bourgeoisie 'then in the throes of its struggle for extended parliamentary rights'. As in England the expulsion from France targeted a small minority who had been restricted to money lending and who had provided a means of finance for the monarchy. Once the community was bled dry they were of no further use and could be expelled. However the order for expulsion applied to royal France only and was ignored or only partially enacted in some regions, according to the disposition of local rulers. Baron, *Social and Religious History*, pp. 201–25.

under Ferdinand and Isabella, in abrogation of the capitulation signed in 1492. Conversions continued sporadically during the early sixteenth century until Charles V issued a decree in November 1525 ordering the conversion of all Muslims in Aragon and Valencia. From this point on the Muslim religion no longer officially existed in Spain, and as Christians the Moriscos were now subject to the Inquisition, beginning a period of persecution and social discrimination.[63]

These events set in motion relations of mutual hostility and tension which culminated in the expulsion of the Moriscos in 1609. The final drive towards expulsion was set in motion much earlier than 1609, but the attention of the reigning monarch Philip III was diverted by other matters for some time, especially the rebellion in the Low Countries. A peace treaty with the Netherlands was signed in 1609, which left Philip's army free to enforce expulsion as the solution to the 'Moriscos problem'.

Muslims in Spain: from Mudejars to Moriscos

Under Islamic religious law, *Mozarabs*, as those Christians and Jews living under Islamic rulers were called, were not regarded as equal to Muslims, but they were granted freedom of worship because they were recognised as 'peoples of the book'. This set the conditions for the medieval *convivencia* in Spain. But by the late medieval period this once influential model was waning. As the century turned, the approach of Bishop Juan Segovia (*c.* 1400–58), who had 'proposed peace and open forum' between Christianity and Muslims, gave way to calls for a crusade to 'eliminate the infidel'.[64] The fall of Granada in 1492 represented the culmination of growing hostility towards Islam in Spain, but the reconquest in itself did not 'eliminate the infidel'. In fact, it meant that the number of Moors in the territory now controlled by Spain had increased to around 500, 000 in a population of approximately 7 million.[65]

There was also a fundamentally different understanding of the nature of contractual agreements. In Islam, the *Shari'ah*, or God's law, was 'immutable and inviolate, binding for all times and beyond human powers to amend'.[66] Thus if *Mozarabs* were under the protection of God's law this was not subject to change or reinterpretation. By contrast, under Christian rule the treatment of minorities was not understood in the same way:

[63] Kamen, *Spain 1469–1714*, p. 173.
[64] Anwar G. Chejne, *Islam and the West: The* Moriscos (Albany: State University of New York Press, 1983), p. 5.
[65] Lynch, *Spain Under the Hapsburgs*, p. 30.   [66] Chejne, *Islam and the West*, p. 3.

the protection of minorities in a Christian environment was conferred by a treaty whose provisions were often influenced by political and military expediency and by other circumstances. Treaties were apt to change, and actually did, subject to the whims of rulers or to the ever-changing politico-military situation.[67]

So it was that the terms of capitulation which granted safety to *Mudejars* (Muslims living under Christian rule), and 'the preservation of their law, mosque, and religious foundations', following the fall of Granada in 1492 were violated before the fifteenth century was over.[68] This, Anwar Chejne argues, followed a pattern that the Catholic Monarchs had employed elsewhere whereby an initial appearance of implementing terms of capitulation was soon followed by a programme of mass conversions. Initially the conversion of the Muslims of Granada was sought through persuasion and education. However, as this met with little success, Ferdinand and Isabella sent Francisco Ximenez de Cisneros, archbishop of Toledo to Granada, and his policies prevailed.[69] Cisneros advocated enforced conversion, and his methods were in violation of the terms of the capitulations.[70] Among other things he procured the conversion of prominent members of the *Mudejar* community through imprisonment and ill treatment. The case of Zegri Azaator, who became known as Gonzalo Fernandez Zegri, is perhaps the most well known.[71]

The forced conversions and other inflammatory actions resulted in Muslim rebellion, and the murder of one of Cisneros' agents, which in turn resulted in harsh retribution from the monarchs. 'The risings gave to the Christian authorities the opportunity to rid themselves of the Capitulations of Granada, and to modify or rescind the Mudejar status of other Muslims elsewhere.'[72] By 1499 the 'effective end of Islam in Granada, at least of Islam as a public religion',[73] had been reached. The further decrees confirming this policy elsewhere in the lands of the crown of Castile did not come until 1501 and 1502, and in Aragon and Valencia it was not until the 1520s that forcible conversions were pushed through (against some opposition from a minority of the Christian aristocracy). It

---

[67] Ibid., p. 3.

[68] Ibid., p.6: 'The Granadans were granted generous terms guaranteeing their safety; the preservation of their law, mosque, and religious foundations; respect for their privacy; general amnesty for all prisoners; freedom to emigrate; freedom of travel and worship; and the use of their language and customs.'

[69] Gerber, *The Jews of Spain*, p. 124.

[70] 'In 1516 Cisneros not only insisted on forced baptism, but instituted an ordinance calling for the abandonment of Moorish dress and customs.' This was rescinded but it played an important part in perpetuating resentment. Chejne, *Islam and the West*, p. 7.

[71] L. P. Harvey, *Islamic Spain 1250 to 1500* (University of Chicago Press, 1990), pp. 331–3.

[72] Ibid., p. 334.   [73] Ibid., p. 335.

was in 1499 though, that the monarchs brought the *mudejar* compacts to an end in the key Muslim community, that of Granada.[74]

After the forced conversions, the term Moriscos (little Moors) came into use, 'placing them in a special category within the Christian faith'.[75] Like the conversos, the Moriscos were differentiated on the grounds of recent conversion, but also of race. The label Morisco reaffirmed that they were considered to be Arabs or Berbers and therefore inferior to Old Christians who, it was argued, had *limpieza de sangre*, or purity of blood. 'These claims of course cannot be justified as the Old Christians were as much a mixture as the Moors. In fact, it was almost impossible to distinguish one from the other at this juncture of history, notwithstanding claims to the contrary.'[76] The Moriscos were as 'Spanish' as anyone else, as were the conversos who were also subjected to the doctrine of *limpieza de sangre*, as were the Jews who were expelled in 1492. Despite this, by the late fifteenth century, and then throughout the sixteenth century:

> the Moriscos were singled out as a thorn in the side of the Spanish. Moriscan utterances, deeds, behaviour, customs, dress, food, and very manner of doing things were abominable and ought to be eradicated. Edict after edict was issued to correct or eliminate all features associated with Moriscos. As a people, they not only lacked purity of blood, but were crude and ignorant...In sum [the Morisco] was an undesirable stranger in his own land, denied the opportunity to adjust within the new religious order.[77]

Like the conversos before them, even those Moriscos who had genuinely converted were distrusted, the result being a widening gap of mutual suspicion between the two communities.[78] But many Moriscos were resistant to conversion, which provided another target of investigation for the Inquisition. Furthermore, as Lynch notes, because of their connections with the Ottoman Empire, the Moriscos were 'regarded as a security threat, [so] the role of the Inquisition here approached that of a police force at the service of the state'.[79]

The Moriscos and the Spanish Inquisition

Like converts from Judaism, once converted, Moriscos were subject to the Inquisition. This was decided finally during the reign of Charles V (1516–58) following a controversy over whether or not forced converts were actually Christians. As with the conversos, the Inquisition punished

---

[74] Ibid., p. 335.   [75] Chejne, *Islam and the West*, p. 7.   [76] Ibid., p. 7.
[77] Ibid., p. 8.   [78] See Ibid., ch. 2, for an account of Morisco self-image at this time.
[79] Lynch, *Spain Under the Hapsburgs*, p. 25.

any perceived transgressions severely. Although Charles V's successor Philip II (1555–98) attempted a more moderate policy towards Moriscos, the Church was hostile to them, and they were perceived as a threat to both the Church and the state throughout the sixteenth century. In great part this was due to the Old Christians' resistance to the assimilationist 'solution' and their refusal to accept Moriscos as part of Spanish society. Throughout the sixteenth century the Inquisition continued to try Moriscos for heresy. Those who argued in favour of a policy which demonstrated 'Christian charity' were ultimately not influential, as religious and political opposition to Catholicism increased in the Ottoman Empire and within Christendom itself. Heretics in general were linked and connections were drawn between the Moriscos and the Protestant heresy.

Though the Moriscos were the product of forced conversions like the conversos, and though they were expelled, as were the Jews, they filled a different, and much more restricted, economic niche to these groups. Though Jews had a range of occupations, they played a significant role in commerce, a role picked up by conversos on their expulsion, or continued by those who converted. Conversos had also played a significant commercial role and many had attained high offices and risen to prominence in Spanish society. By contrast, the Moriscos were mainly agricultural labourers, and as a consequence many landowners argued against their expulsion.

The Moriscos also differed from the Jews in that they could be linked to the very strong external threat presented by the Ottoman Empire, which was constantly pressing on Spain. They were directly linked to the empire by the religion they had been forced to publicly forgo and by their cultural practices. Forced to convert and then subjected to persecution, many identified strongly with the Ottoman Empire and displayed a strong desire to hold on to their own religious and cultural traditions. Thus when they rebelled in the mid-sixteenth century this strengthened the perception of their links to the Ottoman Empire and, by association, to Spain's opponents throughout Europe, so that 'when the Moriscos rebelled in 1568, their revolt formed part of a widespread, political and religious movement against the Hapsburgs and Catholic Christendom'.[80]

Yet the expulsion of 1609 occurred after the internal threat posed by Moriscos, and the external threat posed by the Ottoman Empire, had largely abated. A treaty was signed with the Ottoman Empire in

[80] Andrew C. Hess, 'The Moriscos: An Ottoman Fifth Column in Sixteenth-Century Spain', *American Historical Review* 74:1 (1968), 4.

1580, marking the end of large scale Christian–Muslim conflicts in the
Mediterranean. So it must be asked: why were they expelled? During the
second half of the sixteenth century internal economic problems meant
higher levels of discontent and mutual resentment among both the Old
Christians and the Moriscos,[81] and the sense of religious embattlement
was not easily forgotten. The Moriscos were still seen as a threat to
the unity of Catholic Spain, and were still regarded as a potential 'fifth
column', as the reversal of the reconquest might be attempted, or the
Moriscos might aid Protestantism in some way. As Hess notes, 'Philip II
and his Spanish officials raised a major issue involving international relations when they charged, in effect, that the Moors in Spain made up a
fifth column that aided both the Ottoman advance in North Africa and
the Protestant cause in Europe.'[82] The rising concern in Spain over the
spread of Protestantism increased the perceived threat of *any* deviation
from Catholicism.[83]

The expulsion of the Moriscos

The possible expulsion of the Moriscos was discussed as early as 1582,
but Philip II was unwilling to implement such a programme. However,
Philip III, who ascended the throne in 1598, was prepared to pursue
such a policy, though it was not until 1609 that he issued a royal decree
which ordered the expulsion of the Moriscos (with some few exceptions).
The orders were issued secretly to avoid resistance from the Moriscos,
but were intended to be systematically carried out all the same: 'Orders
were issued to landlords ... to deliver Moriscos working for them to the
port of departure, allowing them to carry portable things.'[84] Although
safe conduct was ordered for those who had to leave, many were robbed
and/or murdered. This well-organised expulsion continued until 1614.

   In this chapter I have stressed the important role of religion as the
meaningful cultural criterion by which corporate identity construction
took place. As I argued above, in Spain this was complex and interacted
with a racial doctrine not seen before in Europe. Given these conditions,
convivencia could not continue with the Muslims any more than it could
with the Jews of Spain. All other identities were to be subordinated to this
dominant religious identity. In the case of Spanish Muslims, an assimilatory solution was tried in the first instance, but once again this 'solution'
to corporate identity building was unsuccessful, as religious identity could
not easily be detached from a broader cultural identity. Thus expulsion
came to be seen as the solution.

---

[81] Ibid., 22.   [82] Ibid., 5–6.
[83] Chejne, *Islam and the West*, pp. 10–11.   [84] Ibid., p. 13.

There is debate over the numbers of Moriscos expelled but it is clear that a high proportion of the population were forced to leave. There is also debate over how they fared, but it is no exaggeration to say that large numbers perished one way or another, or arrived at their final destinations starving and destitute.[85] In response to a request from Philip III to consider whether or not children should also be expelled, the Church, in July 1610, raised the age limit for Morisco children entitled and compelled to remain in Valencia to seven, and a group of theologians recommended that:

> all Morisco children above the age of seven should be sold as perpetual slaves to Old Christians . . . The five theologians who signed this document argued that slavery was not only morally justifiable . . . but spiritually beneficial: these children would be less likely to become apostates, since their masters would ensure that they remained Roman Catholics for fear of forfeiting their right to retain them, and, as slaves rarely married, this would be another good method of ridding Spain of 'this evil race'.[86]

Taking very young children from their families was part of a policy of obliterating all traces of Islam from Spain, although this act was more controversial than the actual expulsion.[87] Biblical justifications were given along with the argument that the Moriscos posed a security threat, both in terms of their connections with the Ottomans (and also the French), and also 'in the broader social sense',[88] as some Moriscos were starting to climb the social ladder, and they had a higher birth rate. By 1614 the expulsion was virtually complete. 'However, there remained the preoccupation of cleansing the land of the remaining infidels and those who managed to return from exile . . . Even the word Morisco was decreed to be forgotten, for this use would constitute bad taste.'[89]

Like the expulsion of the Jews, this expulsion of as many as 300,000 people came at a very high human cost, causing 'thousands of tragedies'.[90] It also came at a very high economic cost for the Spanish state. In Valencia,

[85] Roger Boase, 'The Morisco Expulsion and Diaspora: An Example of Racial and Religious Intolerance', in David Hook and Barry Taylor (eds.), *Cultures in Contact in Medieval Spain: Historical and Literary Essays Presented to L. P. Harvey* (Exeter: Short Run Press, 1990), p. 12.

[86] Ibid., p. 13. It is interesting to note that within Spain no one argued for a policy of tolerance towards the Moriscos on egalitarian (though assimilatory) grounds as Las Casas did with regard to the Indians in the 1550s.

[87] Ibid., p. 14. A meeting of the Council of State of 1 September 1609 ordered that, 'all children aged ten or under should remain in Spain to be educated by priests or trustworthy persons whom they would serve until the age of twenty-five or thirty in return for food and clothing, and that even suckling babes should be given up'. Chejne, *Islam and the West*, pp. 12–13.

[88] Boase, 'The Morisco Expulsion', p. 15.   [89] Chejne, *Islam and the West*, p. 13.

[90] Kamen, *Spain 1469–1714*, p. 212.

despite the emigration of 14,000 landless Christians, 45 per cent of Morisco villages were still deserted in 1638 and the government was forced to embark on repopulation programmes. Aragon was also hit hard in the economic slump that followed. 'It was one of the most ill-considered policy acts of the century, carried out against the views of a large body of informed opinion in Spain, denounced by foreigners – Cardinal Richelieu condemned it as barbarous – and very quickly regretted on all sides.'[91] Thus ended the tradition of *convivencia* in Spain.

Conclusion

Catholic opinion was by no means monolithic throughout this period, and some voices were raised in protest at the decision to expel the Jews and later the Moriscos. This was not the only choice open to successive monarchs and their counsellors as they sought to build the state, but ultimately they opted for the path of forced homogenisation, through conversion and expulsion. Investigation of the cultural context within which these decisions were made shows that the level of popular resentment towards non-Christians or 'false Christians' had risen in the second half of the fifteenth century, providing both a potential source of disorder if left unchecked – the Catholic Monarchs may well have decided to use their authority to check this in a different way – and also a valuable and very powerful 'cultural resource' that the monarchs could draw on in order to build their own legitimacy, while gaining the support of both the cities and the common people. It also provided a valuable means of keeping the nobility compliant. Thus they turned what could have been a challenge to their authority into a means of legitimating it.

In the Spain of Ferdinand and Isabella we see the use of available cultural and symbolic resources – based on the world view provided by religion – to define the criteria for the corporate identity of an incipient, but nonetheless centralising, state. With this came a demand for a single political identity that had not existed in the same way in medieval times. The Spanish Inquisition and the acts of the Catholic Monarchs can be seen as orthodoxy reasserting itself, or as the reformulation of political identity within the boundaries of the sovereign state. Returning to Ann Swidler's remarks about how taken-for-granted cultures take on the quality of ideologies in times of instability,[92] in the case of Spain we see both the assertion of orthodoxy – which has not been 'necessary' before – *and*

[91] Ibid., p. 221. There were many critics of this policy, but this was ignored by many historians. Kamen, *The Spanish Inquisition*, pp. 228–30.

[92] Ann Swidler, 'Culture in Action: Symbols and Strategies', *American Sociological Review* 51:2 (1986), 282.

the gradual translation of Catholicism to fit within the bounds of the emergent state. It was *because* the ground was shifting, so to speak, that new criteria of political identity were needed, but this was so early that the available cultural or symbolic means of articulating this identity could only be religious, though clearly this was a complex amalgam of a number of elements. Hence the religious and political identities demanded by the sovereigns were tied together, as they were elsewhere in Europe for some time to come.

In the case of the Moriscos, despite their forcible conversion they continued to be linked to external threats, from both the Ottoman Empire and Protestantism. Spain had already experienced bankruptcy twice in the sixteenth century, yet the decision was made to expel the Moriscos, which undermined the economic strength of Spain still further. In the absence of institutional innovation and administrative unification, Spain continued along the path of constructing the unity of the state through expulsion of minorities – which is now regarded as a pathological form of identity building. As chapter 6 explains in more detail, at the international level it is possible to trace a shift from no normative content in the international response to the expulsion of the Jews, to the comment made by Cardinal Richelieu that the expulsion of the Moriscos was a 'barbarous' act. Before too long, however, Louis XIV would attempt to impose a uniform religious identity on the population of France. It is to this second example of pathological state-building in the prenationalist age that I turn in chapter 3.

3   State-building in early modern France: Louis XIV and the Huguenots

In 1685 King Louis XIV ordered the Revocation of the Edict of Nantes, and thus effectively outlawed Protestantism in France. The Edict was originally promulgated in 1598 by Louis's grandfather, Henry IV, in an effort to negotiate principles of coexistence between the then politically and militarily powerful French Protestants, or Huguenots as they were known, and the French monarchy. Despite a prohibition on Protestants leaving France, the Revocation, along with the persecution that preceded and followed it, resulted in an estimated 200,000 refugees fleeing the country. Yet at the time of the Revocation the Huguenot population no longer posed any political or military threat to the French state. This raises the question of why the monarch and his advisers would choose this path when any threat posed by Huguenots to the political stability of the state was long past. Why did they pursue a policy that caused more problems than it solved domestically, that was bound to alienate Protestant states across Europe, and that abrogated the terms of the Peace of Westphalia, which had been accepted across Europe? Though Louis XIV may have considered that this policy was in the interest of the state, this begs the question of how this interest was understood by him and his advisers. Why was the forcible imposition of religious uniformity seen to be in the interest of the state, in an age when the religious wars had passed but when the memory of their devastating effect on Europe, including France, was still strong?

In order to answer these questions, in this chapter the popular Catholic hostility towards the Huguenots during the sixteenth century is contrasted with the policies of Louis XIV in the period leading up to the Revocation of the Edict of Nantes in 1685. Unlike earlier popular hostility this led to a systematically imposed government policy of forcible conversion. According to the ideology of absolutism which informed Louis's project of state-building, the Huguenots represented a threat to the unity of the state. The resources that the regime of Louis XIV drew on, as they sought to articulate and defend the rights of absolute monarchy, were religious despite the new relation between the King and God that absolutism posited. This case exemplifies the demand for a singular identity made by the absolutist sovereign and state, for it is in this period that the King and the state become separable entities. It also illustrates, once again, the use of religious criteria of identification in constructing the corporate identity of the state and the legitimacy of the sovereign in this prenational era.

After a brief discussion of continuity and change in France in the sixteenth and seventeenth centuries, I revisit existing accounts of state formation with reference to Louis XIV's treatment of the Huguenots. I then give an account of how religion was an inextricable part of the cultural framework of sixteenth and seventeenth-century France, and trace the role this played in the factional fighting that threatened to tear France apart in the sixteenth century. This involves consideration of the introduction of Protestantism into France and two important events in the history of Protestantism in that country: the St Bartholomew's Day Massacres of 1572, and the promulgation of the Edict of Nantes in 1598. I then go on to discuss how, despite the process of secularisation that was occurring, religion remained the cultural resource that Louis XIV drew on to symbolise the completeness of his rule and thereby legitimate his authority. I then trace Louis's policy towards the Huguenots leading up to the Revocation of the Edict of Nantes in 1685. The treatment of Huguenots in the late seventeenth century will thus be situated within a distinct historical and cultural context, highlighting how the interests of the state were understood at that time, and illuminating how state-builders drew upon religious resources in constituting the corporate identity of the French state in the prenational era.

Continuity and change in absolutist France

The Edict of Nantes, promulgated by Henry IV in 1598, sought to stabilise relations between French Catholics and Protestants and set out principles of coexistence for the two groups after a series of bloody civil wars. Although it was not based on principles of toleration as we would recognise them today, it did give the Huguenots legal standing as a separate religious group within the French state. In a sense, the Edict was part of a policy of 'appeasement' adopted by Henry IV in an effort to both protect and pacify his former coreligionists, the Huguenots, in the short term, with the aim of bringing them back into the Catholic Church in the longer term. However, this policy involved no systematic persecution of the Huguenots. Henry IV used his authority as monarch and his skills as a negotiator to deal with this powerful group, attempting to build a state whose very existence had been threatened, before it was fully formed, by a series of devastating civil wars.

In contrast to Henry's policy, the Revocation of the Edict of Nantes in 1685 was part of a systematically implemented policy to forcibly construct the corporate identity of the state according to the criterion of Catholic religious identity. This was despite the fact that the Huguenots had remained loyal to Louis XIV when much of the country was in open revolt mid-century.

The 1685 Edict of Fontainebleau which revoked Henry IV's Edict of Nantes was the culmination of a period of intensified persecution of Protestants in France. The techniques of persecution used to force conversions included increasing legal restrictions which affected the daily lives of Huguenots, the use of *dragonnades* (enforced billeting of soldiers with Protestant families), and material inducements. Finally, in 1685, Protestantism was outlawed and exit by Protestants was declared illegal except for pastors who were expelled if they would not convert. The mass exodus that ensued (not to mention the false conversions) was not what Louis XIV had intended, and he tried to convince many of his subjects to return – as Catholic subjects of the Most Christian King – with little success. The result of this attempt at pathological homogenisation was a massive population movement in which hundreds of thousands were driven from their homes. It was this event that gave rise to the first use of the term 'refugee'.[1]

Liah Greenfeld traces the seemingly paradoxical development of an abstract notion of the state at the same time that the idea of the absolute ruler as a god reached its apogee under Louis XIV. The latter developed to such an extent that for some writers, loyalty to the King and piety became synonymous.[2] The beginning of this paradoxical process can be seen in the time of Henry IV, where the process of the secularisation of the state used the available cultural resources and symbols of the time, which were religious, but the referent of the symbolism shifted first towards the person of the sovereign, and then to the state. By Louis XIV's time nobles of the robe, who had already pushed aside the older nobility, gave way to the office of the intendant. This represented the beginning of the development of an impersonal bureaucracy working as an instrument of 'god like' absolutist rule.[3] The closer the absolutist ruler came to being regarded as a god, the further God receded.

---

[1] Michael Marrus, *The Unwanted: European Refugees in the Twentieth Century* (Oxford University Press, 1985), pp. 8–9.

[2] Liah Greenfeld, *Nationalism: Five Roads to Modernity* (Cambridge, MA: Harvard University Press, 1992), pp. 109–33.

[3] Ibid., p. 128. Also see Charles Godard, 'The Historical Role of the Intendants', in William F. Church (ed.), *The Impact of Absolutism in France: National Experience Under Richelieu, Mazarin, and Louis XIV* (John Wiley & Sons, New York, 1969).

As the reference point of shared meanings, however, religion remained crucial to both the age and the monarchy. Embroiled in disputes with Rome, Louis nonetheless remained a champion of orthodoxy, tolerating neither the Jansenists within Catholicism nor his Protestant subjects. Greenfeld argues that '[t]he religious policy of Louis XIV inevitably resulted in the disaffection of Huguenots. The latter represented a major source of independence in France, and it is understandable why the king would wish to suppress them.'[4] Greenfeld takes this as given and questions the brutal means used against the Huguenots rather than the goal of extirpating Protestantism from France. But the role of absolutist ideology in Louis' policies requires further investigation, because as already noted, by the late seventeenth century the reality was that the Huguenots posed no threat to the state. What they *represented* to the absolutist state is, as Greenfeld acknowledges, another matter. Only vestiges of their former power remained, transformed now into the financial sphere, so the question that must be asked is *why* should the King wish to suppress them? The answer to this question lies in the nature of the relationship between absolutism and the religious world view. This relationship may not be apparent at first glance, given the abstract notion of the state that was developing and the shift towards secularisation. Given this shift, why was religious affiliation of interest to the absolutist regime, and why were the Huguenots a 'problem' to be solved by Louis as a state-builder?

The cultural and ideological framework within which Louis operated meant that the King and his advisers either underestimated or discounted the negative impact of his policies. Far from achieving the desired unity, these policies caused many Protestants to flee, others to falsely convert, and many exiles to become outspoken critics of the regime. For while it is true that Huguenots were among the most vocal critics of Louis' absolutism, what Greenfeld does not sufficiently emphasise in her account of these events is that this was *after* the increased persecution of the 1680s and the Revocation of the Edict of Nantes in 1685.[5] While Greenfeld

---

[4] Greenfeld, *Nationalism*, p. 129.

[5] Ibid., pp. 129–31, Greenfeld cites an anonymous tract, usually attributed to Jurieu, which was written in response to Louis' policies and published in 1690, five years after the Revocation of the Edict of Nantes. This is not representative of Huguenot thought during Louis' reign up to the 1680s, when most Huguenots were loyal to the crown. The source that Greenfeld uses to make her point is perhaps the most radical of the critiques which followed the Revocation of the Edict of Nantes, as it draws on the constitutional thought of François Hotman, who a century earlier was responding to the Massacre of St Bartholomew's Day. (See below on the massacre.) On different Huguenot responses see Nannerl O. Keohane, *Philosophy and the State in France: The Renaissance to the Enlightenment* (Princeton University Press, 1980), pp. 314–18. The text attributed to Jurieu (though as Keohane and others note, this attribution is not entirely convincing), is *Soupirs de la France esclave, qui aspire après la liberté* [The Sighs of France Enslaved], 1690. An excerpt from this can be found in Church (ed.), *Impact of Absolutism*, pp. 101–9.

treats the motivation for the policies towards Protestants as clear cut, this is not the case with the policies towards Jansenists. 'The king's misplaced zeal in the persecution of Jansenists, the tactlessness with which he pursued centralization of authority into the innermost recesses of his orthodox subjects' consciousness, was potentially more damaging to absolutism than the alienation of the Protestant minority. Louis's motives in this case are harder to explain.'[6] The nature of absolutism was such that *any* perceived or potential deviation was a problem, and that while deviation within the Catholic Church was not to be tolerated, the Huguenots, as the most visibly different group in a society where religion continued to provide the cultural framework for all aspects of life, were even less tolerable.[7]

For Greenfeld, the ultimate significance of the treatment of the Huguenots by Louis XIV lies in the critiques of absolutist power that emanated from Huguenot exiles, in which the state came to replace the King as the central object of loyalty.[8] Thus, '[t]he alienation of the Huguenots was of momentous significance in the development of the French national idea'.[9] Louis' treatment of the Huguenots and the response it engendered was certainly a step on the path to national identity, as Greenfeld argues.[10] But the policy was also an attempt at building corporate state identity through pathological homogenisation, highlighting how state-building – in which the symbolic and cultural dimension of social life played an important role – preceded the development of a consciously nationalist French identity. Louis' method of building the corporate identity of the absolutist French state through a systematically imposed attempt to destroy the Huguenots as a group can be distinguished from the combination of factional disputes and religious differences that threatened to tear France apart in the sixteenth century. Louis' actions reflect the fact that by the late seventeenth century the monarchy was stronger, and certainly comparatively more stable, than in the sixteenth century when it had struggled to raise itself above factional squabbles. However, the demand for complete unity on the part of Louis' regime and the perception that any divergence from what the regime considered orthodox presented a threat to this unity, suggests that despite the appearance of strength, the monarchy was fragile in many respects, and that the 'conceptual

---

[6] Greenfeld, *Nationalism*, p. 130.

[7] On the threat posed to absolutism by Jansenism, see Alexander Sedgwick, *Jansenism in Seventeenth-Century France: Voices From the Wilderness* (Charlottesville: University Press of Virginia, 1977).

[8] Greenfeld, *Nationalism*, p. 132.   [9] Ibid., p. 129.

[10] Also see John Breuilly, *Nationalism and the State*, 2nd edn (University of Chicago Press, 1993), pp. 75–95. Unlike Greenfeld, Breuilly accords central importance to the prior development of the centralised modern state in the development of nationalism.

and symbolic augmentation of the authority of the crown' played an important role in constituting the absolutist French state.[11]

State formation and the Huguenots

As I argued in chapter 1, existing explanations of state formation have little to say about the role of pathological homogenisation in state-building. Immanuel Wallerstein's materialist account explains the Revocation of the Edict of Nantes and the exodus of Protestants that accompanied it, in economic terms, arguing that toleration only occurred when financial pressures made it necessary. According to this view, once Louis XIV had, at least for the time being, settled his foreign wars (and the need for funds to be diverted to them) he could turn his attention to the Huguenots.[12] Wallerstein does not see religious differences as significant in their own right, arguing that regionalism was more fundamental than schism to the Wars of Religion.[13] As a movement for regional independence, he claims, the Huguenots could have consolidated in the south and west of France: 'The liquidation of the Huguenots was then part and parcel of the drive to maintain the integrity of France as a state.'[14] It is true that there was a strong regional component to the struggles between the Huguenots and the crown in the sixteenth century, and that at this time they did pose a threat to the viability of the state. However, by the time Louis XIV made his decision in 1685, the possibility of a regional resistance movement in the south was long past, and the Huguenots had proved loyal to the crown throughout the mid-seventeenth-century uprisings known as the Fronde.[15]

Wallerstein does note, though, that the pressure towards states based on one religion was very strong in sixteenth-century Europe, because of 'the need to combat centrifugal forces', which he labels 'religio-regional strife'.[16] However, his materialist assumptions mean that he does not investigate this any further, and thus his account remains descriptive, and does not illuminate the relation between religious beliefs and state-building. It does not help us understand why Louis XIV should decide to take the action he did, regardless of any economic costs this might entail.

[11] Philip Corrigan and Derek Sayer, *The Great Arch: English State Formation as Cultural Revolution* (Oxford: Basil Blackwell, 1985), p. 77.

[12] Immanuel Wallerstein, *The Modern World-System*, vol. 1 (San Diego: Academic Press, 1974), p. 266.

[13] Ibid., p. 294.   [14] Ibid., p. 294.

[15] Church describes the Fronde, a series of uprisings against the crown, which occurred during Louis XIV's minority, as the 'most massive rebellion against absolutism in the [seventeenth] century'. Church (ed.), *Impact of Absolutism*, p. 6.

[16] Wallerstein, *Modern World-System*, p. 296.

That Louis could now turn his attention to the Huguenots if he wished does not explain why he perceived them as a problem or why he chose the policy he did.

Of the institutionalist accounts discussed in chapter 1, it is Hendrick Spruyt who identifies the importance of 'clear sovereign authority' to state-building. Of most interest here, Spruyt briefly canvasses the possibilities of extending his analysis to looking at why the state has been successful in global terms. He suggests that it may be that the territorially defined sovereign state as it developed in Europe was successful as it allowed exit from particular states so that it was possible to seek refuge and better environments elsewhere. Of such movements he says only that: 'the reasons behind each [movement] are complex, clearly both movements [referring to Huguenots from France and Jews from Antwerp] had large economic repercussions'.[17] Huguenots were not granted permission to leave France. Indeed they faced heavy penalties if they were caught attempting to do so. Spruyt is thus able to tell us about the consequences of population movements, but the reasons behind these movements, the reasons why particular groups were marginalised or expelled, and how these policies might be related to conceptions of sovereignty, are not explored.

As noted in chapter 1, most power-based accounts have little to say about practices of pathological homogenisation. Charles Tilly is the exception to this, as he observes that state rulers frequently embarked on programs to homogenise their populations. However, Tilly regards this as a function of the administrative centralisation of the state and he does not enquire into the cultural dimension of such practices. He identifies the threat that Protestants posed to centralising monarchies across Europe in the sixteenth and seventeenth centuries.[18] The base of the Reformation in city-states strengthened resistance to the centralising state, he argues.[19] With this storm raging across Europe, the centrifugal forces which already existed within France (which of course were not only religious), were given further impetus, and, Tilly argues, could have pulled France apart quite late on. 'Between the 1490s and the 1650s, the crown faced repeated challenges – challenges so severe that, well into the seventeenth century, France could easily have evolved into a composite empire of multiple languages, divided religion and tribute-taking warlords instead of the relatively unitary state it became.'[20]

---

[17] Hendrick Spruyt, 'Institutional Selection in International Relations: State Anarchy as Order', *International Organization* 48:4 (1994), 554.

[18] Charles Tilly, *European Revolutions, 1492–1992* (Oxford: Blackwell, 1993), p. 150.

[19] Charles Tilly, *Coercion, Capital and European States, AD 990–1990* (Oxford: Basil Blackwell, 1990), p. 61.

[20] Tilly, *European Revolutions*, p. 150.

The authorities in different states chose different options in dealing with Protestantism: crushing, tolerating or co-opting and promoting the new religion. This, and not the popular appeal of the new religion, he argues, is the key to where and how Protestantism was successfully institutionalised.[21] In France these conditions were explosive. Many French nobles converted to Protestantism in the sixteenth century while the crown remained staunchly Catholic, and thus the stage was set for an enduring conflict. The event which set the match to this conflagration was the dynastic succession crisis set off by Henry II's early death, which led to the Wars of Religion between 1562 and 1598. This crisis would only end with the accession of Henry IV to the throne at the end of the sixteenth century.[22]

It was Louis XIV, argues Tilly, who 'squelched' Protestant power in France forever, starting with a 'slow strangulation' and culminating with the Revocation of the Edict of Nantes.[23] However, as many historians of the period demonstrate, Louis XIV did not begin the strangulation of Protestant power. This had begun long before with the Edict of Nantes itself.[24] By the late seventeenth century there was no Protestant rebellion to speak of as their power had been smashed by the events of the late sixteenth and early seventeenth centuries.[25] After 1629 most of the Huguenot nobility had abjured and returned to the service of Louis XIII. During the reign of Louis XIV which followed, Huguenots remained loyal to the crown, with a steady trickle of unforced conversions as French Protestantism lost some of its vitality and Catholicism underwent an intellectual renaissance. By the mid-seventeenth century the image of Protestants as seditious rebels, which was so strong in the sixteenth century, had faded (though it was never entirely forgotten). Louis XIV did not need to 'squelch' them by this stage for political, military or economic reasons, and in fact his policy damaged the state, both domestically and internationally.

None of the accounts of state-building canvassed above can answer the question of why it was that Louis XIV and his advisers thought that this

---

[21] Ibid., pp. 152–3.   [22] Ibid., p. 153.   [23] Ibid., p. 156.

[24] For example see N. M. Sutherland, 'The Crown, the Huguenots, and the Edict of Nantes', in R. M. Golden (ed.), *The Huguenot Connection: The Edict of Nantes, its Revocation, and Early French Migration to South Carolina* (Dordrecht: Kluwer Academic Publishers, 1988).

[25] Rebellions in the late seventeenth and early eighteenth centuries, such as the Camisard uprising, were *responses* to Louis's policies. Andrew Lossky, *Louis XIV and the French Monarchy* (New Brunswick: Rutgers University Press, 1994), pp. 293–4. For an argument that an English national identity was emerging from the fourteenth century see Adrian Hastings, *The Construction of Nationhood: Ethnicity, Religion, and Nationalism* (Cambridge University Press, 1997).

policy was in the interest of the state. Why was this policy considered a necessary part of Louis' state-building? In order to answer this question, I now turn to the sixteenth century and give an account of the relations between Catholics and Protestants and the relationship between religious identity and factional affiliation at this time. This provides a background to understanding the continuities and changes between the sixteenth and seventeenth centuries, which allows investigation of how state identity and interests were understood and the role such understandings played in Louis' treatment of the Huguenots in the late seventeenth century.

Catholicism and Protestantism in sixteenth-century France

Following the Reformation, Christians turned on one another across Europe and minority groups within Christianity were targeted for persecution and sometimes expulsion in the quest for religious unity, which was as important to Protestant states as it was to Catholic ones. In the Netherlands, Catholics were not allowed to practice openly, though they were not actively persecuted as minorities were in many other countries.[26] In England, the demand for a unitary religious identity gathered force under the increasing centralisation of the state. Following the excommunication of Elizabeth I, to be Catholic in England was to commit treason. Though this was by no means permanent, a moulding of identity was taking place, so that by the end of the seventeenth century Catholics were a small minority in England and the emerging corporate identity of the state was Protestant.[27] In France, the Reformation had a convulsive effect that threatened to tear the state apart.

The Reformation in France

From the year 1517 when Luther nailed his Ninety-Five Theses to the door of the Castle Church in Wittenberg, the Reformation spread quickly into France, with the first Reformed Church founded in Paris in 1555. In

---

[26] John B. Wolf, *Louis XIV* (New York: W. W. Norton & Co., 1968), p. 215.

[27] In England, Catholicism came to be identified with the arbitrary powers of the Spanish and French monarchs, whilst Protestantism was associated with constitutional government in the minds of many. In a state that demanded greater conformity from its subjects a number of different groups were persecuted during the reign of Elizabeth. Catholics were persecuted, as were gypsies, puritans were not tolerated, and authors of 'seditious tracts and libels' were punished. Witchcraft was understood as an attack on the state as witches were thought to conspire together against 'the godly state'. Corrigan and Sayer, *The Great Arch*, p. 64. After the Glorious Revolution in 1688, English, Irish and Scottish Catholics followed James into exile; see also Marrus, *The Unwanted*, p. 6.

France, the relationship between the Reformed and the old religion was different to that in most other states. For example, in both England and Sweden the 'top down' imposition of Protestantism occurred with relatively little bloodshed, while in Italy and Spain the Reformation did not penetrate deeply. France, however, was much closer to Geneva and this geographical proximity was combined with a strong movement against the decadence and corruptness of the Gallican Church, resulting in 'a massive invasion of France' through French translations of German writings that were widely available due to the advent of the printing press.[28] Despite this there was to be no Reformation from above in France, the country of the 'Most Christian King'.[29] Instead, efforts were made to bring Protestants back into the Catholic Church. Yet the repression of Protestants did not work as it did in Catholic states like Italy and Spain, as there were too many Protestants in France, and once the nobility started to convert – which they quickly did in the mid-sixteenth century – there were too many well-organised, and importantly, well-armed, Protestants. In the mid-sixteenth century, control of the Huguenot movement was quickly wrested from the pastors into the hands of the Protestant nobility and French Protestantism became central to the factionalism and regional resistance to central authority that threatened to pull the kingdom apart.

This situation was exacerbated by the early death of Henry II in a jousting accident in 1559, which left the state in the hands of a succession of weak regency governments under Catherine de Medici, who struggled to reestablish the authority of the crown. This was both a result of, and left the crown vulnerable to, the vagaries of factional power struggles, in particular between the Catholic Guise family and Protestant nobles. This crisis of legitimacy was to throw France into a period of civil wars that lasted from 1562 until 1629, when, under Louis XIII, and building on reforms instigated by the government of Henry IV, the monarchy was able to reassert control. Thus the legitimacy of the crown was under constant threat as factional struggles became inextricably entwined with questions of religious belief.

In the sixteenth century religion defined the social world and the community, constituting 'a body of believers rather than the more modern

---

[28] *The New Cambridge Modern History, Vol. 2, The Reformation, 1520–59* (Cambridge University Press, 1958), p. 213. John Calvin himself was a Frenchman and '[his] special concern had always been the reformation of France'. George L. Mosse, *The Reformation* (Illinois: Dryden Press, 1963), p. 75.

[29] Mack P. Holt, *The French Wars of Religion, 1562–1629* (Cambridge University Press, 1995), pp. 192–3; Mark Greengrass, *The French Reformation* (Oxford: Basil Blackwell, 1987), pp. 21–4. Greengrass stresses the role of Strasburg as a model for French Protestants.

definition of a body of beliefs'.[30] Collective behaviour was of the utmost importance to sixteenth-century Catholics. 'Just as one might benefit from the prayers of others, so might one be threatened by their sins, which could bring down the wrath of God on an entire people.'[31] Although there is no doubt about the factional interests and power politics which were played out in this era, we cannot dismiss the religious component of French political life, and the ongoing civil wars that came out of religious disputes as mere rationalisations of economic or strategic interests. Religious identification played an important part in the constitution of the body social and the body politic and thus often shaped the understanding of just what the interests of different parties were.

Who were the Protestants?

Following the Reformation, identification as Protestant, especially for the earliest converts, was a matter of choice, rather than ascribed membership. As Janine Garrisson points out, in the mid-sixteenth century when Protestantism started to spread through France, publicly converting to Protestantism meant a break with the traditions of the past 'whose gravity many who took the step failed to appreciate'.[32] When the majority adhered to Catholicism, this step put those who became Protestants outside the body social, and on 'the margins of French society... To belong to another church, to practice another faith, was in effect to found an alternative society with its own social groups and ranks, its own hierarchies of age and sex, and its own power structures.'[33]

Who converted? Well-educated, skilled artisans and educated professionals such as lawyers and doctors were drawn to Protestantism. Though Barbara Diefendorf focuses on Paris alone in *Beneath the Cross*, her findings give a general sense of those who were attracted to Protestantism across France.[34] Some Parliamentarians converted, at least until there were purges in the late 1550s and 1560s.[35] Lower level officials and many merchants also converted, particularly printers and booksellers.[36] Craftsmen were also an important group while peasants were not generally attracted to the reformed religion, only converting when their lord did so. This class, by and large 'remained loyal to Catholicism. Often

---

[30] Holt, *The French Wars*, p. 2.
[31] Barbara Diefendorf, *Beneath the Cross: Catholics and Huguenots in Sixteenth-Century Paris* (New York: Oxford University Press, 1991), p. 37.
[32] Janine Garrisson, *A History of Sixteenth-Century France, 1483–1598: Renaissance, Reformation and Rebellion* (New York: St. Martin's Press, 1995), p. 284.
[33] Ibid., pp. 284–5.   [34] Diefendorf, *Beneath the Cross*, pp. 110–12.
[35] Garrisson, *A History*, p. 287.   [36] Ibid., p. 287.

they nourished a profound hatred for the Protestants – townsfolk and villagers, iconoclasts and desecrators – enough, on several occasions, to lead to massacres.'[37]

Importantly, the new religion was taken up by many nobles, a factor which was central to the path it would take in France.[38] As nobles changed religion, the area over which they held dominion tended to change religion as well, although the principle *cujus regio, ejus religio* was not generally applied.[39] There were also two other groups that were important to the spread of Protestantism. These groups, who 'stood outside traditional social classification' were women and the young, 'who, irrespective of their family background or trade, were passionately involved with the Protestant adventure'.[40] It was the young in particular who took vigorous action, publicly singing psalms in French, and who were responsible for Huguenot iconoclasm.

Despite the enthusiasm of new converts, the new religion was proscribed by law, with the result that converts had to be prepared to lose social and financial standing.[41] Once the costs became clear many individuals with something to lose returned to the Catholic Church. There was also very strict discipline within the Protestant Church, which some members found too difficult: the Protestant Church, like the Catholic Church, was sure it held the one truth. Heretics were to be banished, though some concessions were made to forgive those who returned to Catholicism under pressure. Although there was some recognition of the need for secrecy in the face of sanctions against Protestants, the practice of taking part in Catholic rituals was strongly rejected. This, of course, would mark Protestants out, making them easy targets of both repressive law enforcement and popular hostility.[42]

Given the significant social and personal costs involved, why did so many convert? First it is important to reiterate that many people were not fully aware of the costs. Garrisson argues that Protestantism answered not only religious needs but also spoke to 'social and cultural realities'. Protestantism was, she argues, 'predominantly the religion of a culturally advanced minority. It was an ethically demanding religion of the book

---

[37] Ibid., p. 289. There was no hard and fast rule for which area would have a high percentage of converts and which would not. Holt, *The French Wars*, p. 37.

[38] Garrisson, *A History*, p. 286.

[39] The exception was Jeanne d'Albret (Henry of Navarre's mother) who suppressed Catholicism in the principality of Bearn, and made Protestantism the state religion in 1565. Garrisson, *A History*, pp. 286, 271. Also see Holt, *The French Wars*, pp. 38–41.

[40] Garrisson, *A History*, p. 289.   [41] Diefendorf, *Beneath the Cross*, p. 118.

[42] Ibid., pp. 119–21.

that called men and women to a deeper spirituality and a new and austere morality.'[43] In the face of disgust with a decadent Catholic Church that did not meet their spiritual needs, and a venal Church hierarchy that was bound to the crown,[44] the turn to Protestantism was a logical step for many who not only wished for a different relationship to God, but also (and inseparably from this) for a different kind of society.[45]

The hostility of the crown towards Protestants in France was crystallised by the affair of the Placards in 1534. Printed placards attacking the Catholic Mass were posted around Paris (including the door of the King's bedchamber).[46] This was a pivotal point in relations between the state and the Reformed Church, as the intemperate, indeed vitriolic, attack on Catholicism was regarded as treasonous.[47] Because of the concept of sacral kinghood in France, this attack on the Mass was also seen as an attack on the monarchy, and because of the constitutive role of the Church in French society, as an attack on the body social itself. It is from this point in 1534 that Protestants were seen as rebels as well as heretics,[48] and it was this event that started Francis I's campaign against Protestants 'in earnest'.[49] At the time, Francis I told Protestant princes that he was not against Protestantism as such, but was against the subversion of French society.[50] Yet from the vantage-point of the monarchy in sixteenth-century France, Protestantism was inherently threatening to established authority, and had to be eradicated. This was something that both Francis and his son Henry II set out to do.[51]

---

[43] Garrisson, *A History*, p. 291.

[44] Holt, *The French Wars*, pp. 12–14; Howell A. Lloyd, *The State, France, and the Sixteenth Century* (London: George Allen & Unwin, 1984), pp. 120–1, 125.

[45] On the relation between social and political instability and religious dissidence, see Lloyd, *The State, France*, pp. 118–19. Lloyd also notes that the European witch-craze was at its height in the sixteenth and seventeenth centuries.

[46] Donald R. Kelley explains why the Mass was such a target for Protestants. They took issue with the idea of the real presence of God in the church and clergy. The Mass in which the host was taken to be not symbolic of, but the real body of Jesus, just as the wine was the blood of Jesus, was anathema to Protestants, who saw this as blasphemous. For them the divine was separate from the corporeal. Donald R. Kelley, *The Beginning of Ideology: Consciousness and Society in the French Reformation* (Cambridge University Press, 1981), p. 394.

[47] In part this read: 'I call on Heaven and earth to bear witness to the truth against this pompous and vainglorious papal Mass, by means of which (if God sends no remedy soon) the world will have been utterly lost, ruined, overwhelmed, and devastated...' Cited in Garrisson, *A History*, p. 99.

[48] Holt, *The French Wars*, p. 20.

[49] Kelley, *The Beginning of Ideology*, pp. 14, 15–16; Garrisson, *A History*, p. 99.

[50] Kelley, *The Beginning of Ideology*, p. 18.

[51] Francis I called for retribution against all 'Lutherans'. The 25-year-old John Calvin was one of many to flee the persecution that ensued. Holt, *The French Wars*, pp. 20–2.

Religion and faction

In France, the sacred nature of kingship had been recognised since 751 when the title of the 'Most Christian King' was bestowed on the reigning monarch.[52] Since then the King's coronation oath had stressed his duty to act as protector of the Church, which included protecting the Church from heresy.[53] However, in the mid-sixteenth century, the Huguenots did not see themselves as treasonous, following as they did the reasoning of both John Calvin and Theodore de Beza that loyalty to the King was of utmost importance. This created an irresolvable contradiction for many Huguenots – how to be loyal to both the King and their religion – that led many of them to accept martyrdom as the only resolution.[54]

Taking seriously his coronation oath as protector of the Catholic faith, Henry II was determined to wipe out Protestantism in France. But his early death in 1559 brought these plans to an end, destabilised the monarchy, and inaugurated an era of civil wars. The nobility played a central role in the unrest that followed Henry II's death.[55] While joining the Reformed Church meant social marginalisation for those of lesser rank, members of the nobility were not prepared to sacrifice their political positions for religious principles and neither were they prepared to hand power willingly to the staunchly Catholic family of Guise. Hence the turn to arms taken by the Huguenot nobility as the only 'practical solution' they could see.[56] An intense struggle over who was closest to (and thereby controlled) the King and the King's advisers followed Henry's death. During the short-lived reign of Francis II the Guises had control, but they were displaced on his death, when Catherine de Medici acted as regent for her son Charles IX in his minority. This was merely the beginning of a struggle that was to continue throughout the sixteenth century.

At different times both the Protestants and the Catholic League took control of towns in opposition to central authority.[57] Both the contending religions were part of the centrifugal factional tendencies that could have pulled the state apart. In her capacity as regent, Catherine de Medici attempted to mediate between the contending factions. Her January 1562 Edict of Saint-Germain allowed 'limited but legal recognition of the

---

[52] This title had been used since 751 when it was applied to Pepin the Short. It was confirmed by the Pope in 1469 and thereafter became a standard designation of the King of France in all diplomatic documents. Lossky, *Louis XIV*, p. 12.

[53] Ibid., p. 7. The King was not a priest, but was not regarded as a layman either, p. 11.

[54] Garrisson, *A History*, p. 291.   [55] Ibid.   [56] Ibid., p. 292.

[57] Ibid., pp. 340–1: 'The First War of Religion was entirely typical in the way the town acted as focuses for both military strategy and religious fanaticism.'

Huguenots' in an attempt to avoid civil war.[58] This was not success-ful, as any concessions granted to the Huguenots incited strong Catholic resistance. The Parlement of Paris was the first to reject the Edict, as judges saw the Huguenots as a threat to the social and political order, and they stressed the King's obligation to drive out heresy.[59] They reluc-tantly registered the Edict after two formal letters commanding them to do so. But violent reaction against this Edict had already started, leading to civil war, the first of the religious wars that would plague France in the sixteenth century.[60]

With the beginning of the religious wars the nobility took control of the Huguenots from Calvinist pastors, thus significantly politicising the new religion.[61] Many conversions occurred and troops were raised through the client networks of the nobility. 'The result was a growing power base of rural nobles (estimated to be as many as one-third of all the lower nobility in the provinces), who, whatever their motivation, responded to the vocal appeals from the Calvinist churches for protection.'[62] Coups in a number of towns followed, from without and within, which were often followed by outbursts of iconoclasm.[63] As a result, Catherine de Medici turned to Catholics for support, involving the crown directly in the war, but this was a war that neither side was able to win, resulting in the peace declared in the Edict of Amboise of March 1563. However, the peace was rejected by the Parlement and the Catholic population at large as, like the previous Edict of Saint-Germain, it recognised some rights for Protestants. Various Parlements were eventually forced to register it though, and the King's presence was used to enforce it on a tour throughout France. Despite this attempt to impose a solution that recognised some Huguenot rights, violence continued throughout the country, with attacks on Huguenots commonplace.[64] Holt characterises this as a 'cultural clash' in which Catholics of all levels were uncomfortable with the concessions the crown made to the Huguenots, because they took issue with Protestantism as a religion and as a way of life, and rejected the critique of their own way of life implicit in Protestantism. Catholic Confraternities were founded which stressed Catholic community and solidarity against Huguenots.[65] These often took local action against Protestants, such as evictions and forced abjurations. Given the situation, in which religious differences were so enmeshed with factionalism, and in which for all intents and purposes the crown acted as one faction among others, this conflict

---

[58] Holt, *The French Wars*, p. 47.   [59] Ibid., p. 48.
[60] There were Wars of Religion in 1562–63; 1567–68; 1568–69; 1572–73; 1574–76; 1578–79; 1579–80; 1585–98. See Tilly, *European Revolutions*, p. 155.
[61] Holt, *The French Wars*, p. 51.   [62] Ibid.   [63] Ibid., p. 54.
[64] Ibid., p. 62.   [65] Ibid., p. 68.

could not be resolved and was played out until the end of the sixteenth century:

> [t]he first civil war that ended with the Edict of Amboise on 19 March 1563 set a pattern that would be repeated seven times over the next four decades: a military campaign in which neither side could defeat the other comprehensively, followed by a compromise peace that the crown could neither administer nor enforce. The inevitable result was the continuation of the civil wars.[66]

It is not the intention here to give a detailed history of the Wars of Religion in France, but rather to highlight the interrelationship of religious and factional differences throughout the sixteenth century, which were exacerbated by a weak monarchy and resulted in a civil war. There were two pivotal events in the relationship of the Huguenots to the French state in the sixteenth century. These were the St Bartholomew's Day Massacre of 1572 and the Edict of Nantes, promulgated by Henry IV in 1598 in an attempt to restore some order to the realm. It is to these events I now turn.

The St Bartholomew's Day Massacre

Though Catherine de Medici had pursued a policy of mediation between the Protestant and Catholic factions, by the end of the second War of Religion in 1568, Charles IX and his mother, frustrated with the lack of success of this policy, took harsher measures against the Huguenots. However, this resulted in the third civil war which lasted from 1568 to 1570, exhausted the treasury, and concluded with concessions to Protestants. Once again, the concessions made to Protestants by the Peace of Saint-Germain in August 1570 were incomprehensible to many Catholics.

The general population was much more involved in this third war, in which they had paid a high price, as they suffered the depredations of armies on both sides. The outcome of this was that the connection between Protestantism and social disorder was strengthened in the minds of much of the populace. Under the Treaty of St Germain Protestants returned to the towns they had left during the war, and sought to take up any official positions they had vacated. The restitution of real estate and moveable property that had been taken from Protestants in the third war was ordered, and the Reformed religion was legally practised in city centres for the first time. This resulted in an upsurge of violence against Protestants. The suffering and extreme hardship that civil war and disorder brought to the populace was heightened by crop failures,

---

[66] Ibid., pp. 55–6.

and the threat of famine made the general population extremely respon-
sive to the calls of religious and local authorities to take action against
heretics.[67]

It was in this context of unresolved religious tensions, in a country
already beset by high levels of social disorder and hardship, that the marriage of the Protestant Henry of Navarre to the Catholic Marguerite de
Valois took place in Paris on 18 August 1572.[68] The marriage of her
daughter, arranged by Catherine de Medici in an effort to allay tensions,
brought the Protestant nobility to Paris. It was while they were gathered
to celebrate the marriage that the massacres began. Mack Holt identifies a
series of four events, which are together called the St Bartholomew's Day
Massacres.[69] The first event was the failed attempt on the life of Admiral
Coligny, the leader of the Huguenots, on 22 August. The Huguenot nobility were angry at this attempt and some threatened vengeance if the
attempt was not punished.[70] The second event was the massacre of the
Protestant nobility, beginning with the murder of Admiral Coligny on
the night of 23–24 August 1572.[71] Generations of historians have sought
to identify the author of the massacre and to understand the motivation
for it. The blame has been placed in different quarters, though Catherine
de Medici is most commonly held responsible.[72] Whoever was responsible, it seems that this was a 'preemptive strike' to wipe out the Huguenot
leadership and forestall the retaliation which had been threatened after
the first attack on Coligny. This explanation makes sense in light of the

[67] Garrisson, *A History*, pp. 352–3.

[68] Diefendorf, *Beneath the Cross*, pp. 83–8; Emmanuel Le Roy Ladurie, *The Royal French
State 1460–1610*, trans. Juliet Vale (Oxford: Blackwell, 1994), p. 231.

[69] This account combines Holt's identification of the four separate events which made up
the massacre with the accounts given by a number of authors. Estimates of the numbers
killed in the massacres vary. Garrisson argues that a conservative estimate would be
around 5,000 people murdered across the country, 'at least 2000 of them in Paris alone
(representing 1 percent of its population), with some fifty noblemen assassinated in
the government operation'. Garrisson, *A History*, p. 358; Diefendorf estimates 'several
thousand', *Beneath the Cross*, p. 99; Tilly estimates that as many as 13,000 may have
died, Tilly, *European Revolutions*, p. 155.

[70] Admiral Coligny was injured by this attack, losing the index finger of his right hand
and having a bullet removed from his left arm. Robert M. Kingdon, *Myths About the
St. Bartholomew's Day Massacres, 1572–1576* (Cambridge, MA: Harvard University
Press, 1988), p. 28.

[71] Garrisson, *A History*, p. 356.

[72] However, N. M. Sutherland claims that this does not make sense given that de Medici was
trying to mediate the differences between the various parties by arranging this marriage
in the first place. See N. M. Sutherland, *The Massacre of St. Bartholomew and the European
Conflict 1559–1572* (London: Macmillan, 1973), pp. 312–46. Garrisson has it that the
Guises carried out the orders of the King's Council. Garrisson, *A History*, p. 278. The
one point that historians do agree on is that it is unlikely that the truth will ever be
known. Also see Holt, *The French Wars*, pp. 83–4.

increasing use of assassination in sixteenth-century France as a means of dealing with powerful enemies. To wipe out a man of power and influence was to strike an important symbolic as well as physical blow to his faction.[73]

The third event was a consequence of these killings. As news of the murders spread, a wave of killings swept across Paris where the ordinary people indulged in 'an orgy of slaughter'.[74] Although not intended by the crown, a general massacre was ignited by the words of the Duke of Guise, who as he left the scene of Coligny's murder said that it had been done at the King's command. These words, as Diefendorf puts it, 'transformed private passions into public duty'.[75] The fourth event that Holt identifies is the wave of provincial massacres set off by the violence in Paris.[76] The twelve provincial cities where massacres occurred had significant Huguenot minorities, which posed 'the same spectre of contamination of the body social as in the capital', whereas neither Catholic or Protestant strongholds were the scene of massacres.[77]

A number of historians have taken note of the character of the massacres which often included the mutilation of corpses, starting with that of the murdered Admiral Coligny. This highlights that the clash between the two religious groups was a cultural clash, and drew on available cultural symbols, such that the violence echoed the rituals of the Catholic Church and the legal system. As noted earlier, at this time religion was understood as the means by which a 'body of believers' were held together, and this led to both Catholics and Huguenots seeing each other as pollutants of the body social. However, while Huguenots were given to violent iconoclasm, and certainly were responsible for the death of many priests, there was nothing in their actions to rival the St Bartholomew's Day Massacres.

---

[73] Garrisson, *A History*, pp. 277–8. Henry III would use the same method to rid himself of the Guise brothers in 1588.

[74] Ibid., p. 357. As with all such 'popular' massacres, it is difficult to know exactly how many took part and how many approved. While most Catholics saw Protestants as pollutants, not all Catholics agreed with the massacres, and some sheltered friends and neighbours. Diefendorf notes that though this was a popular massacre it is probable that, at least in Paris, 'a minority – probably a relatively small minority – of Parisian citizens actively participated in the massacre. Roaming the city in small, fierce bands, they assaulted suspected Protestants in the streets, searched them out in their homes, and demanded entry to houses where they might be hiding, while the largely passive majority remained behind closed doors, afraid either to participate in or to protest against the activities of their peers.' Diefendorf, *Beneath the Cross*, p. 105.

[75] Diefendorf, *Beneath the Cross*, p. 99.   [76] Holt, *The French Wars*, p. 82.

[77] Ibid., p. 92. Kingdon notes that it is significant that all the towns to which the massacres spread had 'strong and powerful Protestant minorities', who had at times seized control of the town, and in some cases subjected their towns to iconoclasm. They were thus the target of resentment and massacres. Kingdon, *Myths About*, p. 41.

Natalie Zemon Davis, in her important article 'The Rites of Violence', shows how closely the 'rites of violence' enacted throughout France at this time followed the purificatory traditions of the Church.[78] Davis argues that the violence arose out of the culture of the time and used the symbols and forms of that culture. Thus Admiral Coligny's body was dragged through the streets in mimicry of the punishment meted out to criminals.[79] Further, '[t]he religious significance of destruction by water or fire is clear enough. The rivers that receive so many Protestant corpses are not merely convenient mass graves, they are temporarily a kind of holy water, an essential feature of Catholic rites of exorcism.' On the desecration of corpses she argues that burning or drowning 'was not cleansing enough. The bodies had to be weakened and humiliated further.'[80] The violence thus must be understood in the context of the world view of sixteenth-century Catholics. Heresy was a pollutant of which the community should be cleansed, doing away with 'the dirty and diabolic enemy'.[81] In the popular imagination natural events such as floods, and particularly a solar eclipse in 1571 were interpreted as signs of God's anger, so action to restore order to the social world was necessary.[82]

The popular massacres, though a response to the original killings, were in no way an intended outcome of government policy. As Holt notes, '[t]hat this general massacre was clearly fomented by popular religious tensions rather than any political decision by the elites at court is clear from the non-noble Huguenot victims targeted by Parisian Catholics'.[83] Diefendorf rightly asserts that a grave political miscalculation on the part of the crown occurred. With tensions running so high, Catherine de Medici and Charles IX should have realised that the city of Paris could explode into popular violence.[84]

Although those who took part in the massacres may have believed they did so with the sanction of the King, this was not so. The killing of the Protestant nobility was a clumsy attempt by the crown to dispose of the leaders of a troublesome faction in an effort to undermine it. This was not intended to be a general massacre of all Protestants, but at least

---

[78] Natalie Zemon Davis, 'The Rites of Violence', in Natalie Zemon Davis, *Society and Culture in Early Modern France* (Stanford University Press, 1975), p. 176. Davis takes issue with an earlier argument of Janine Estebe [Garrisson] that the violence had a class basis and came from 'the primitive soul of the people'. She argues that it was not only a matter of attacks on rich Huguenots, as although many wealthy Huguenots were killed, so too were many of modest backgrounds.

[79] See also Diefendorf, *Beneath the Cross*, p. 103; Holt, *The French Wars*, p. 87.

[80] Davis, 'Rites of Violence', p. 179.   [81] Ibid., p. 157.

[82] Holt, *The French Wars*, p. 89.   [83] Ibid., p. 85.

[84] Diefendorf, *Beneath the Cross*, p. 96.

some in the general population took this as permission to deal with those who they saw as polluting the body social, and a bloodbath resulted. Given the extremely difficult economic conditions the populace had to endure, and the constant call to rid the realm of heretics that rang out from Catholic pulpits, this eruption of violence is entirely explicable in retrospect. However, the assassination of the Huguenot leadership and the massacres that followed were not based on any coherent policy on the part of the crown. On the contrary, these acts came out of a knee-jerk reaction to the intemperate threats made by Huguenot nobles after the attempt on Coligny's life. This response was based on a miscalculation of the threat posed by the Huguenots, and on a miscalculation of the possible consequences.[85] It was not a systematic approach to dealing with a whole minority group perceived as a problem. It was the response of a weak monarchy that was threatened by a powerful noble faction and that used a common, though unsavoury and, in the long run, not particularly effective, method to deal with the perceived threat. As Davis argues, despite the high levels of violence in sixteenth-century French society, the violence of religious riots is distinguishable from action taken by political authorities, 'at least in principle'.[86]

Aftermath

The St Bartholomew's Day massacres sparked off the next in a long cycle of civil wars underpinned by the Protestants' claim that it was legitimate to challenge the authority of a monarch who had broken both natural and common laws.[87] The eighth, and final, civil war began in June 1584 when Henry of Navarre became heir to the throne when King Henry III's only surviving brother died.[88] This was anathema to the Catholic League, led by the Duke of Guise, and his brother, the Cardinal of Guise.[89] This

---

[85] Holt, *The French Wars*, p. 84.   [86] Davis, 'Rites of Violence', p. 153.

[87] During the first three Wars of Religion the Huguenots were primarily concerned with the power that the Catholic Guise family had over the crown. However, as Garrisson notes, after the massacres the Huguenot's arguments were 'more aggressive, more direct and more innovative'. The crown itself now came under scrutiny. Divine right was now called into question. For example, Beza now argued that sovereignty belonged to the people and sovereignty by popular consent meant that the sovereign was bound by obedience to divine and natural law and also the common good. 'Therefore rebellion against a sovereign who violated the laws of both God and man was authorized by God.' Garrisson, *A History*, p. 292.

[88] Henry of Navarre, forced to convert and held captive after his fellow Protestants were massacred in 1572, escaped in 1576 and immediately returned to Protestantism, taking up the leadership of the Huguenots.

[89] The Catholic League had an important popular component, as societies for the protection of Catholicism sprang up across the country. It was also a vehicle by which powerful nobles could challenge the king. The League represented one of three 'factions', the

led to challenges to the legitimacy of the crown from the Catholic side
as, 'the Leaguers took over their enemies' former arguments, proposing
the supervision of the administration by the Estates General and inciting
rebellion against a government of favourites who they considered to be
too lax towards heresy'.[90]

The Duke of Guise recruited mercenaries from Germany and Switzerl-
and, while in Paris arms were secretly procured by the clandestine Catholic
Society of the Sixteen. By this time most of the royal forces had joined
either the League or the Protestants. 'So the only way to preserve the
State was to make a deal with the more dangerous enemy, in this case the
League. The Treaty of Nemours (July 1585), by which the crown itself
in effect subscribed to the League, represented a temporary triumph for
the Guise and their followers.'[91] This meant the introduction of harsh
anti-Protestant policies. But, once again, and despite King Henry III's
own personal piety, this was not the result of any coherent policy on
the part of the crown, but was the outcome of a crown at the mercy of
a powerful faction.[92] This was seen again three years later when, after
being forced to flee Paris when it was overrun by the League, the King
signed the anti-Protestant Edict of Union, in which he vowed to extirpate
heresy and that Henry of Navarre would not succeed him as King. With
his back to the wall, Henry III's method of dealing with the challenge
to royal authority posed by the League was to have the Guise brothers
assassinated five month later in December 1588. This action galvanised
the League, which until then had not been a really coherent organisation,
made it more popular[93] and brought the wrath of the Church down on
the King.

In turn this response pushed the King back towards Henry of Navarre,
whom he recognised as heir to the crown. Protestant rights were restored,
and a combined campaign to regain Paris was planned. When Henry III
was assassinated in 1589 the heir to the crown was Henry of Navarre,
who came to rule as Henry IV. Although he was Henry III's legitimate

---

others were the crown itself and the Huguenots who were joined by moderate Catholics
or 'politiques'. On the League, see Holt, *The French Wars*, p. 130; Le Roy Ladurie, *The
Royal French State*, pp. 214–25; Garrisson, *A History*, pp. 297–318. On the relationship
between the Leaguers and more moderate Catholics, or 'politiques', see Diefendorf,
Beneath the Cross, pp. 174–7; Garrisson, *A History*, p. 327. Note the Leaguers' belief
that 'Agreement in religion is the only solid basis of any State: there can be no real unity
without it. This and not any theory of sovereignty in the Estates or the "people", is
the essential declaration of the League.' J. W. Allen, *A History of Political Thought in the
Sixteenth Century* (London: Methuen, 1960), p. 347.

[90] Garrisson, *A History*, p. 313.   [91] Ibid., p. 376.
[92] Moderate Catholics, were worried by this development, as it was so clearly an encroach-
ment on the autonomy of the French crown.
[93] Lloyd, *The State, France*, p. 141.

successor under Salic law, and had been explicitly recognised as such by Henry III,[94] his legitimacy was not accepted by much of the country. Once again, Paris led the way as it had in the St Bartholomew's Day massacres and in the popular rejection of Henry III.[95] On the other hand, Huguenots, always wary of Henry of Navarre's connections to the crown, were now increasingly suspicious of the possibility that he might abjure Protestantism.[96] Moderate Catholics supported Henry, as they considered that if he would abjure, France would have a legitimate, adult monarch who could bring some order and stability to the country.

Before Henry IV could be crowned he had to fight on two fronts. France was at war with Spain, and he also had to fight to wrest control of much of the country back from the League. He was not without allies in this struggle, however, as he had support from England, the Protestant German princes, the Netherlands and Venice.[97] There was a stalemate between League and royalist forces between 4 August 1589 and 17 May 1593.[98] Henry's religion was the stumbling block for the League, yet he could not easily walk away from Protestantism. A number of Reformed states were his international allies, and the support he gained from southern and mid-western France was tied to his role as the Protestant leader. However, he had promised to protect the Catholic faith when Henry III died. As time wore on competitors for the throne multiplied and the moderates who had supported Henry became increasingly restive, as he did not seem inclined to convert.[99] However, gradually the scales tipped in Henry's favour as the widespread desire for order after decades of civil war started to outweigh opposition to his rule. Internal strains in the League started to show, especially under the pressure of the siege of Paris, and there was also a reaction against the reign of terror to which the League subjected Paris.[100]

---

[94] Ibid., pp. 328, 383.

[95] Ibid., p. 317. In the 1590s Henry's army laid siege to Paris. This resulted in a high number of deaths, a conservative estimate being 30,000 in a population of 200,000. These figures are from Garrisson, *A History*, p. 388. Le Roy Ladurie's estimate is higher: 45,000 dead out of a population of 220,000. *The Royal French State*, p. 235.

[96] In the 1570s some Huguenots were wary of Henry of Navarre, who as a prince of the blood could not be expected to be sympathetic to the republican arguments of Huguenot theorists of this time. N. M. Sutherland, *The Huguenot Struggle for Recognition* (New Haven: Yale University Press, 1980), p. 287.

[97] Garrisson, *A History*, p. 385; Le Roy Ladurie, *The Royal French State*, p. 233.

[98] Garrisson, *A History*, p. 385. The League formally recognised the Cardinal of Bourbon as King Charles X on 4 August. This elderly man was held in captivity by Henry IV, and died in May 1590.

[99] Garrisson, *A History*, pp. 386–7.

[100] Like the Huguenot nobles, the nobles who led the League also betrayed their non-noble followers. Lloyd, *The State, France*, pp. 141–2.

Henry of Navarre was a consummate propagandist, a talent that would stand him in good stead as monarch. When his army beat the League's larger, Spanish backed army at the battle at Ivry in March 1590, the victory was proclaimed as a victory for 'the French' who had protected their country from foreigners.[101] Fighting off an army backed by Spain, Henry could portray himself as a 'just sovereign' and focus a growing sense of loyalty to the French crown on his own person. But Henry could only do this as a Catholic monarch, and so he abjured Protestantism in July 1593 and was crowned at Chartres in February 1594.[102] Paris submitted to his authority in March of that year and other towns followed.

It was Henry IV who finally gained some control over the factionalism that threatened to pull France apart. Yet in 1594 his authority was far from complete. He was thus engaged in the gradual extension of his authority, which he pursued through a combination of force, negotiation and payments to various parties. The Edict of Nantes, which marked the end of the eighth civil war, was part of this process. On the one hand, the Edict was to some extent extorted by pressure from powerful Huguenot nobles.[103] On the other hand, it was a means by which the King could attempt to set the framework for future peace.

The Edict of Nantes of 1598

Like many edicts of pacification before it, the Edict of Nantes was an attempt to stabilise relations between the Catholic crown and Protestants. Though it has sometimes been portrayed otherwise, the Edict did not set up France as a multireligious state. Although it was a 'legal acceptance of confessional disunity',[104] there was no moral acceptance of this, and the Edict reiterated that France was a Catholic state, and that Huguenots should be reconciled to Catholicism eventually. The Edict was not concerned with toleration as we would understand it today, but was aimed

---

[101] Garrisson, *A History*, pp. 388, 330. The allegiance of the League could be called into question as not only were they backed by Philip II of Spain, but their loyalty was to what they saw as a universal Catholicism, rather than a particularly French Catholicism. Henry used the most extreme terms to attack the League: 'His propaganda team did not hesitate to vilify the League's Spanish allies in the most racial terms; despite their extreme Catholicism, they were accused of being both quasi-Muslim and quasi-Jewish.' Le Roy Ladurie, *The Royal French State*, p. 236.

[102] Le Roy Ladurie, *The Royal French State*, p. 234.

[103] Sutherland, 'The Crown', p. 29. The Treaty of Vervins, marking (temporary) peace with Spain was signed on 2 May of the same year.

[104] Richard M. Golden, 'Introduction', in Richard M. Golden (ed.), *The Huguenot Connection: The Edict of Nantes, its Revocation and Early French Migration to South Carolina* (Dordrecht: Kluwer Academic Publishers, 1988), p. 10.

at laying the foundation for a 'durable and Established peace' and wiping out the memory of the religious wars.[105]

Henry justified his compromise with the Huguenots in terms of the well-being of the state, which was a departure from earlier edicts of pacification, none of which had 'explicitly adduced "the state" as a reason either for accommodating or for restricting Protestant practices'. In the Edict of Nantes we see the emergence of 'the idea of the state as an entity separate from ruler and ruled'.[106] Addressing the Parlement of Paris Henry claimed that the ruler was entitled to obedience, 'for no other consideration than that of my quality'. But there was a 'further consideration' to be taken into account in his case: 'If the obedience was due to my predecessors, as much or more devotion is due to me, especially as I have established the State ... I have re-established France', despite the actions of those who had done their utmost 'to ruin the State'.[107]

Henry IV chose not to establish the state through attempting forcible conversions, massacres or expulsions. As a former Protestant, he retained some sympathy for his former co-religionists and was not inclined to treat them harshly. But the concept of the state that he articulated was one in which all subjects owed their loyalty to him as their monarch and to the state he had restored to order. In this there was little room for recognition of the separate corporate identity of the Huguenots.

Protestants actively sought the Edict once Henry had abjured. His abjuration, and the truce he signed with the Catholic League five days later, seemed like a betrayal to the shocked Huguenots, and his accession to the throne by no means solved the Huguenots' problems.[108] The legal position of the Huguenots was 'chaotic and their actual position unfavourable' when Henry IV came to the throne.[109] Though Henry III had declared an armistice with Protestants, the concessions he made to them at this time were not known to most Catholics and certainly not to the parlements, and besides, the successive edicts had resulted in some confusion.[110] In 1595 demands for a completely new Edict were heard, but at this time

[105] Preamble to the Edict of Nantes, in Golden (ed.), *The Huguenot Connection*, p. 87. Also see Sutherland, 'The Crown', p. 31. 'Peace was the purpose of the Edict, not toleration, which was neither a virtue nor an ideal.'

[106] Lloyd, *The State, France*, p. 145.   [107] Ibid.

[108] Sutherland, *The Huguenot Struggle*, pp. 283, 299. The Huguenots revived the 'Protestant state' as a defensive measure. However, the threat of invasion by Spain, via the Spanish Netherlands, was of most concern to Henry at this time. With Spain's backing of the League also diverting Henry's attention, the Protestants became aware that the threat of force was the only way to get his attention (pp. 306–7).

[109] Ibid., p. 293.

[110] Ibid., pp. 292–3. Different drafts of the armistice were shown to Protestants and the Parlement of Paris. The one shown to the Parlement was 'fanatically Catholic in tone'.

Henry was not in a position to make concessions to Protestants, as he was waiting for absolution from the Pope, and was also negotiating the submission of the League to his authority.[111] However, by 1596, despite being engaged in a war with Spain, Henry was no longer able to ignore the Protestant demand that their civil and legal status be reviewed.[112] Despite the fact that Henry was forced to make these concessions, he still controlled the timing and form of the Edicts.[113]

The Edict of Nantes, which came out of this struggle, was actually four documents, consisting of ninety-two general articles, fifty-six secret articles, and two royal *brevets* (acts of grace). Two sets of articles were the Edict proper, registered by the parlements. The two *brevets*, issued separately, were thus not presented to the parlements for registration, resting solely on Henry's authority.[114] The Edict ordered the restoration of Mass to all places, and the return of all property to the Catholic Church in those places where it had been taken over by Protestants. Protestants were granted full liberty of conscience, though where they could actually practise their religion was limited. Worship was restricted to all places where Protestantism had been allowed in 1596 and up to August 1597, and in all places of worship allowed in previous Edicts of pacification.[115] Protestants were also granted full civil rights along with Catholics, and were eligible to all posts and offices (clause 27). The Edict also renewed judicial protection, and established bipartisan chambers of parlements to judge cases against Huguenots (clauses 40–4 49–52, 65). In practice there was much resistance to the rights granted to Protestants and so they remained dependent on the good favour of the King.[116] Clause 82 of the Edict prohibited Protestant political assemblies at either the national or regional level. The secret articles allowed colloquies, but only for religious purposes. Despite this, in practice, religious meetings were also political meetings until the reign of Louis XIII.

The fifty-six secret articles explained the previous ninety-two, and dealt with exceptions and gaps in the law, and with the practise of Protestantism

---

[111] Sutherland, *The Huguenot Struggle*, pp. 309–10.

[112] Mark Greengrass, *France in the Age of Henry IV* (Harlow: Longman, 1984), p. 76.

[113] Sutherland argues that as Henry was not unsympathetic to the Protestant cause, he would have taken measures to ensure the security of Protestants in any case, but would have wanted to do it as part of the legitimate authority of the crown. But he was forced into it as the price of peace. This was also why the Edict of Nantes partially accepted the Protestant 'state within the state'. Sutherland, *The Huguenot Struggle*, p. 312.

[114] Sutherland, *The Huguenot Struggle*, p. 328. Both the Edict of Nantes and the Edict of Fontainbleu which revoked the Edict of Nantes are reprinted as appendices in Golden (ed.), *The Huguenot Connection*, pp. 86–139.

[115] Sutherland, *The Huguenot Struggle*, p. 330. The privileges of the nobility were maintained as Protestant worship was allowed in all Chateaux of about 3,500 seigneurs.

[116] Greengrass, *France in the Age*, p. 77.

in places which had previously been covered by Catholic League Edicts. The two *brevets* were the most important part of the Edict for the Protestants, as these granted them some limited military and political status.[117] What went into the *brevets* were those concessions that impinged on the King's authority, and those which had no hope of being registered by Parlement.[118] The first one, issued on 3 April 1598, was very brief and promised through a 'secret agent' to provide funds for Protestant pastors. The secrecy was a means of overcoming Catholic opposition to such payments.[119] The second *brevet*, issued on 30 April 1598, was much longer. It guaranteed that Protestants were to retain for eight years from the publication of the Edict (15 February 1599) all the towns they held in 1597, which added up to around 200 towns, half of which were garrison towns. The King also agreed to contribute towards the upkeep of Huguenot garrisons, though these payments were never made in full. He also undertook to appoint Protestants to offices, which went beyond merely allowing them to take up offices if they were offered. Persons of rank were permitted to practise as Protestants at court, as long as this was done 'privately and silently'.[120]

Despite much that has been written about the independence granted to Protestants by the Edict of Nantes, these *brevets* made the Huguenots dependent on Henry's goodwill as they were the personal promises of one King and were not binding on his successors. In effect Henry bought the loyalty of the Huguenot nobility just as he bought the loyalty of the League, and 'bound them more closely to the monarchy rather than separating them from it'.[121] At best, they made the Huguenots one estate of the realm among many, albeit a more marginal and potentially more vulnerable one.[122] It took almost a year for the Edict to be passed by a reluctant Parlement, but it was finally registered on 25 February 1599. No party regarded this outcome as entirely satisfactory, but it was nonetheless, according to Sutherland, 'a sane and reasonable compromise'.[123] As noted above, the Edict was not about toleration, but about trying to restore some minimal order to a state that had come very close to being torn apart by civil war. Yet Henry IV's newly restored order was not to last very long as he was assassinated by a supporter of the Catholic League in 1610.

---

[117] Ibid.   [118] Sutherland, *The Huguenot Struggle*, p. 331.

[119] Ibid., p. 330.   [120] Ibid., p. 331.

[121] Greengrass, *France in the Age*, p. 78. Sutherland argues that the Edict destroyed their political power. See Sutherland, 'The Crown'.

[122] Greengrass, *France in the Age*, p. 79.   [123] Sutherland, *The Huguenot Struggle*, p. 332.

Louis XIII and the end of Huguenot power

Upon Henry's assassination in 1610, Marie de Medici became regent on behalf of her son Louis XIII. This meant a resurgence of League power, as those closest to the regent were pro-papacy, though they were more moderate than in the past. It meant that many of Henry IV's councillors lost their positions. One result of this was the reactivation of the Huguenot movement as a political force, something the Edict of Nantes was intended to prevent.[124] However, within a few years of reaching his majority, Louis XIII asserted his own authority (at the age of seventeen in 1617), exiled his mother, and imprisoned and later executed her chief adviser. He then restored many of Henry IV's advisers to their former positions.

Louis XIII was not sympathetic to the Huguenots, who under the Edict of Nantes, and in particular the *brevets* which had been reaffirmed in 1611 (and which they had interpreted to suit themselves), still retained some vestiges of political and military organisation. Militant Huguenots were now few in number, though, with most Huguenots remaining loyal to the crown during both the regency and reign of Louis XIII. But there were enough militants among the nobility, on whom the Huguenots were still dependent, to cause problems for the crown.[125] Louis met this challenge with force and between 1620 and 1630 the remaining military power of the Huguenots was destroyed.

The Edict of Alais which ended the Huguenots' quest for ascendancy recognised the articles of the Edict of Nantes, but not the *brevets*, the very parts that had left some remnants of Huguenot political and military independence, even though this had been tied to the goodwill of the King. The Huguenots thus lost any advantages that had been gained from the Edict.[126] 'In effect, this final peace underscored the ideal of Catholic accord and unity spelled out in the Edict of Nantes, but it totally destroyed the corporate existence of the Huguenots, leaving them as heretics in a Catholic world.'[127] This can be seen as continuous with the Edict of Nantes, which had also sought to achieve 'one faith, one King, one law'.

Louis XIII could have revoked the Edict of Nantes in 1629, but the good opinion of Protestant powers was too valuable in the eyes of this

---

[124] Holt, *The French Wars*, p. 175.

[125] Holt describes how the repoliticisation of the Huguenot movement was tied to an aristocratic rebellion against the crown during Louis XIII's minority. *The French Wars*, pp. 174–9.

[126] Greengrass, *France in the Age*, p. 78.   [127] Holt, *The French Wars*, p. 187.

regime. It was Cardinal Richelieu who pointed out that he 'needed to treat the Protestant princes of the empire with consideration'.[128] But since removing the *brevets* destroyed what tattered remnants of Huguenot political and military power were left, revocation cannot have been of primary importance, especially as there were other matters at hand. French involvement in the Thirty Years War meant that the King and government were more concerned with blocking Habsburg hegemony over Europe. 'For the next thirty years, until the Peace of the Pyrenees in 1659, all France's energies had to be devoted to the prosecution of the foreign war, whenever they were not diverted to fight open rebellion at home, as during the Fronde.'[129] Moreover, after 1629 relations between the Catholic and Protestant communities eased somewhat as the Huguenots were no longer automatically considered seditious.[130]

Once the Huguenots were disarmed and defeated as a political force, the Catholic faith could be restored publicly as the faith of the realm. Thus the Huguenots, though they remained a fairly stable and sizeable community, were no longer regarded as a threat to the state or as pollutants of the body social as they had been in the previous century.[131]

Louis XIV and the pursuit of unity

As we have seen, by the 1630s the Huguenots no longer represented a political or military threat to the French monarchy, yet at the end of the seventeenth century Louis XIV systematically imposed a policy of forced conversion on the Huguenot community. This section investigates why, according to the ideology of absolutism, the Huguenots were seen as a threat to the integrity of the French state.[132] Central to this is the relationship between the ideology of absolutism, the prevailing framework of shared understanding and symbols, and Louis's strategy of state-building.

---

[128] Francois Bluche, *Louis XIV*, trans. by Mark Greengrass (Oxford: Blackwell, 1990), p. 413.

[129] Lossky, *Louis XIV*, p. 5.   [130] Sutherland, 'The Crown', p. 30.

[131] Holt, *The French Wars*, p. 187.

[132] While some argue that Louis was never truly absolutist, the way in which his rule is characterised here rests on the commitment of Louis and his officials to the ideology of absolutism. This is not to claim that a totalitarian control analogous to that reached by some twentieth-century regimes was ever attained, or indeed imagined as possible. The penetration of civil society was very weak by comparison to contemporary democratic states. However, under the rule of Louis XIV the French state definitely saw a step forward in the centralisation of administrative and military capacity and a strengthening of the authority of the crown. For a perspective which stresses the first point see Roger Mettam, *Power and Faction in Louis XIV's France* (Oxford: Basil Blackwell, 1988). For a perspective that recognises the role of the ideology of absolutism in the struggle between centralising and centrifugal forces in France, see David Parker, *The Making of French Absolutism* (London: Edward Arnold, 1983).

Louis XIV and the ideology of absolutism

Louis XIV became King of France in May 1643, at the age of four years and eight months. His personal reign began in 1661 on the death of Chief Minister Mazarin when he stated his intention to rule without a chief minister. Louis was trained from his earliest years by Mazarin and schooled in the ideology of the God-given legitimacy of absolute rule. Yet he was also well schooled in possible challenges to such legitimacy, as it was during his minority that the Fronde broke out.[133] The Fronde was a series of three uprisings between 1648 and 1653. Harsh tax-gathering methods in a context of dire economic hardship and famine, brought on by failed harvests in 1648–51, led to popular uprisings and then the Parlements and the nobility rising up against the crown. Though widespread, these uprisings were not well organised, and were controlled under the direction of Cardinal Mazarin. There was some continuity with previous conflicts in these uprisings, seen for instance in how the nobility took the death of Louis XIII and the ensuing regency government as a sign of weakness and an opportunity to rebel. Yet the Fronde differed from the conflicts of the previous century, as none of the uprisings represents the intersection of religious division and political factionalism which had threatened to tear France apart then. Throughout this period the Huguenots remained loyal defenders of the divine rights of absolute Kings, as Mazarin readily acknowledged.[134]

As David Parker notes, the absolute authority of the monarch was asserted so vigorously precisely because of the centrifugal tendencies that threatened to pull the French state apart,[135] although the precise source of these tendencies had changed since the sixteenth century. Absolutism was thus very much a response to a series of crises, of which the Fronde was the first in Louis XIV's reign. In fact there was a gap between the image and the reality of absolutism. Parker argues that what we call absolutism was 'a pragmatic, frequently *ad hoc* and contradictory attempt to *restore* royal authority in the context of a rapidly changing world'.[136] Similarly, Peter Burke argues that by the end of the seventeenth century rulers had lost an important part of what Pierre Bourdieu terms 'symbolic capital': 'In short, kings were losing their symbolic clothes.

---

[133] Holt, *The French Wars*, p. 16. The term 'Fronde' means a fight with slings, an allusion to the fight between David and Goliath, in which the high and mighty are brought down. Richard Bonney, 'Cardinal Mazarin and His Critics: The Remonstrances of 1652', in Richard Bonney, *The Limits of Absolutism in* ancien règime *France* (Aldershot: Variorum, 1995).

[134] Wolf, *Louis XIV*, p. 384. The role of Huguenot financiers in supporting the crown may also explain this policy at this time.

[135] Parker, *The Making of French Absolutism*, p. 146.   [136] Ibid., p. 90.

They were becoming demythologized and demystified.'[137] Therefore, 'it might not be unreasonable to apply to this period the famous phrase of Jurgen Habermas, "legitimation crisis"'. This is not to claim that rulers lost all legitimacy, but that 'one important mode of legitimation was losing its efficacy... The king's problem was that he was a sacred ruler in an increasingly secular world.'[138] The King continued to carry out the usual sacral rituals such as touching the sick but a new method of legitimation was needed. Burke identifies a new strategy, appearing from about 1680, which sought to deify the king himself.[139] The device of the sun was still used to represent the King, as it always had been, but it was not as important as it had been in the past. Gradually, references to antiquity declined and the King's own actions, rather than myths, were represented in works of art and on the many medals produced during Louis' reign.[140] As Burke suggests, it could be 'that the great effort which the French government put into the representation of Louis XIV, the sheer number of medals, equestrian statues, tapestries and so on (especially in the second half of the reign), was a response to a crisis, or more exactly to a series of crises'.[141] Apart from the first crisis of the Fronde, in the later part of Louis' reign political difficulties began to accumulate as French armies were less successful than previously as much of Europe allied against Louis's expansionist policies. Constant warfare in turn rendered the financial problems of the realm more serious. Thus, Burke argues the increased investment in heroic images of the King – as King, not as some mythological personage – reveals a crisis of representation. This propaganda was needed exactly *because* the legitimacy of the King was not taken for granted, but had to be created, or 'fabricated'.

However, to emphasise the cracks in the absolutist edifice is not to underestimate the extent to which the centralisation of state administration and control over the means of violence continued under Louis. The military was rationalised under the instruction of war minister Louvois, building the most powerful army in Europe.[142] The administrative reach of the state was increased with the delegation of further powers to provincial intendants. These were officials, created by Catherine de Medici and first used systematically under Louis XIII and Richelieu after 1630. They were commissioned directly by the King to gather information and to implement his policy: in particular to oversee the collection of taxes. Their

[137] Peter Burke, *The Fabrication of Louis XIV* (New Haven: Yale University Press, 1992), p. 129.
[138] Ibid., p. 130.   [139] Ibid., p. 131.   [140] Ibid.   [141] Ibid., p. 132.
[142] Richard Bonney, 'Absolutism: What's in a Name?', in Bonney, *The Limits of Absolutism*, p. 108.

powers and their numbers were increased under Louis XIV. Yet the intendants were not a threat to the power of the crown, as they were dependent on the crown for their positions. The use of intendants meant that there was now a kind of provincial official to assist with state-building, who could develop ties of patronage to their own advantage but were nonetheless loyal to the crown.[143]

Yet the absolutist state did not have an administrative or policing capacity that came anywhere near those of contemporary states. Thus the symbolic construction of a unitary corporate identity remained an important means of legitimating absolutist rule and building the absolutist state. To this end, the regime drew on the broad cultural framework of seventeenth-century society which, no less than in the sixteenth century, was provided by religion. This was despite the contradictions between religion and the scientific world view that Louis encouraged as a patron of the arts and sciences. To legitimate his rule, a 'social and political cement' was necessary. Therefore the ideal of unity embodied in 'one King, one law, one God' became increasingly important, rather than less so, in the absolutist context:

In modern societies with their temporal secular orientation, this ideal of unity of spirit can be attained by education and propaganda vaguely subsumed under the heading of 'nationalism'. Seventeenth-century society still believed in God, in Heaven, in Hell; it made the church the custodian of the words for good and evil, and very naturally it regarded the religious beliefs and institutions as having paramount importance as cement for that society.[144]

The Church also served as a practical means of disseminating government policy to the populace at large and acted as an agent of social control.[145] By maintaining the fear of the disastrous consequences of disobedience, local communities would to some extent police themselves. However, Huguenots, with their separate religious communities were outside the framework within which the social body was defined and therefore outside the framework through which political control, in part, operated. In this process of communicating with and controlling the population through the Church, no less than in the flood of representations of the King as heroic, we see a growing concern with the control of each individual subject. Although there is certainly no sense of 'the people' in the nationalist sense to be found in the age of absolutism, we see an emerging demand for the loyalty of all subjects as part of a single population. Thus a unified 'homogeneous' population became a requirement of a monarchy concerned with order and control.

[143] Ibid., p. 114.   [144] Wolf, *Louis XIV*, p. 383.   [145] Lossky, *Louis XIV*, pp. 36–7.

The persecution of Huguenots and the Revocation
of the Edict of Nantes

Despite Mazarin's acknowledgement of Huguenot loyalty during the Fronde, in 1657 – before Louis XIV began his personal reign and while Mazarin was still chief minister – the King's Council forbade Protestants gathering in the colloquies which brought together a number of parishes to discuss common affairs. This broke the intermediate level of the Protestant communication network. As a result, from the beginning of Louis' personal reign, what was left of organised Protestantism, which was the religious aspect, was seriously undermined.[146] After 1661, the process continued, breaking down centralised communication and cutting Huguenot communities off from one another.[147]

Pressure on the Protestants was building despite the fact that the theological differences between Catholics and Protestants were nowhere near as significant as they had been in the previous century. Indeed, for a time there was an 'amicable Protestant–Catholic dialogue', but this ended with the rise of religious controversy in the 1670s. Less liberal Catholics accused Protestants of fomenting civil war in the sixteenth century and argued that seventeenth-century Protestants were tainted by association. This led to heated debates as Huguenots sought to defend themselves against these accusations. Despite their protestations of loyalty to the crown, the Huguenots were once again associated in the French imagination with republicanism, and their cause was not helped by the examples of republicanism to be found in Protestant England, the Swiss Cantons and the United Provinces.[148] This view was blind to the differences within Protestantism, and discounted Huguenot loyalty to the French crown. It read republican intentions into the republican organisational structure of the Protestant Church (which was in practice dominated by the 'aristocratic principle').[149] 'In other words, the Revocation attempted to abolish a *religious* heresy, because it was thought to harbour a political heresy: the Reformed religion was seen as a potential threat to monarchy.'[150] In general, the Catholic clergy were still as hostile as ever

---

[146] Ibid., p. 197.   [147] Wolf, *Louis XIV*, p. 384.   [148] Bluche, *Louis XIV*, p. 402.

[149] Elisabeth Labrousse, 'Understanding the Revocation of the Edict of Nantes From the Perspective of the French Court', in Golden (ed.), *The Huguenot Connection*, pp. 51–2.

[150] Ibid., p. 50. Labrousse shows that in the late seventeenth century the Huguenots came to be regarded as schismatics rather than heretics, and this meant that they could be compelled to join the Catholic Church again. This involved 'a good deal of sophistry', she argues, and meant that the measures against Protestants could be presented as merely the withdrawal of the King's favours, rather than the aggressive sanctions they actually were. Louis could then be portrayed as 'the father of his people' rather than as a despot. Labrousse, 'Understanding the Revocation', pp. 56–7.

to the Huguenots and continued to petition the King to abolish the Edict of Nantes, or at least to come up with the most restrictive interpretations of it. The irony of this is that some authors argue that left to its own devices French Protestantism may well have faded out, as by the mid-seventeenth century there was a decline in the intellectual vitality of French Protestantism and a revival of Catholicism.[151]

Another important factor in the increasingly harsh treatment of Huguenots was the deteriorating relationship between Louis and the papacy, which led Louis to assert himself as the 'Most Christian King'. In 1683 Louis failed to take part in the defence of Vienna against the Ottoman Empire, once again calling into question his loyalty to the universal Church. The action against the Huguenots helped Louis gain the support of the French Church in his effort to assert his own authority against Rome. In his effort to assert the independence of France and the French Church from papal authority, 'Louis could point to such measures as evidence that he was engaged in a Catholic crusade inside France. On the whole there was considerable popular support for most of these measures.'[152] Thus the conversion of the Huguenots provided another means of 'vindicat[ing] his claim to be the Eldest son of the Church ... Never mind Pope Innocent XI's remark that the king of France sought *one* religion, not *true* religion, for his realm, or the pontiff's disapproval of forced conversions, most of which were not sincere.'[153]

In the early stage of Louis's personal reign policies vacillated between the use of force and remission.[154] The *dragonnades* (the practice of quartering troops in the homes of Protestants) were first used early in Louis's personal reign, though in restricted areas, and Protestant temples built after 1596–97 were destroyed. From around 1669 until 1678 there was some breathing space for the Protestants as Louis was most preoccupied with the war against the Dutch. The Treaty of Nymwegen in 1678 marks the turning point towards the most overt policies intended to rid the French state of the Huguenots through their conversion to Catholicism. Persecution was stepped up in a number of ways. A stricter interpretation of the rights of Protestants under the Edict of Nantes was imposed, and they were excluded from royal favour and patronage.[155] Due to increasing regulations, it was virtually impossible for Huguenots to go about their normal business without breaking one law or another.

---

[151] Ibid.
[152] Lossky, *Louis XIV*, p. 218. See also Wolf, *Louis XIV*, p. 171; and H. G. Judge, 'Louis XIV and the Church', in John C. Rule (ed.), *Louis XIV and the Craft of Kingship* (Columbus: Ohio State University Press, 1969).
[153] Judge, 'Louis XIV', p. 219.   [154] Golden (ed.), *The Huguenot Connection*, pp. 16–17.
[155] Judge, 'Louis XIV', p. 242.

'Academies were closed, churches burned, rights withdrawn.'[156] This was combined with financial inducements that took the form of tax relief for those who abjured, which in turn created the problem of false abjurations amongst a poor population. From these policies, which were severe enough, there was a shift to outright violence.

From 1681 the *dragonnades* were used more widely. This harsh policy is usually attributed to the war minister of the time, Louvois. Whole towns are said to have converted at the news that the *dragonnades* were approaching. Those Huguenots who refused to convert suffered at the hands of the soldiers:

Seventeenth century soldiers were drawn from the bottom of the social heap; even when their officers attempted to keep them in some sort of discipline, they were dangerous to any population with which they lived. These soldiers quartered on Huguenot families were given much freedom to misbehave so that their unwilling hosts would 'see the light quickly'.[157]

Some authors argue that the reality of these practices was kept from the King by Louvois, but given Louis' 'hands on' approach to policy it is hard to believe that he did not know about them.[158] These policies could not be implemented without widespread cooperation from clergy and officials who competed with one another to report (often incorrectly) that they had secured the most conversions, leading the King to believe that a genuine mass conversion was underway.[159] Why a King who prided himself on his grasp of the affairs of state, and used his personal authority to best advantage, would believe that force – a policy that had failed in the past – would be effective can only be explained in terms of the ideology of absolutism and the high value it placed on order and unity. Thus, 'in the ideology of absolutism, the Edict of Nantes signified for France, a humiliating weakness',[160] a weakness that must be remedied through the forced conversion of the entire Huguenot population, estimated to be around 1 million people.

[156] Keohane, *Philosophy and the State*, pp. 312–13.
[157] Wolf, *Louis XIV*, p. 392. Billeting of troops had proved an effective method of bringing provincial estates to heel earlier in the reign. See Parker, *The Making of French Absolutism*, p. 124.
[158] Wolf, *Louis XIV*, p. 393. Soldiers billeted in Huguenot homes were instructed 'to use whatever rough measures might aid the process of conversion'. Keohane, *Philosophy and the State*, p. 313.
[159] Wolf, *Louis XIV*, p. 407.
[160] Keohane, *Philosophy and the State*, p. 312. The quote here is from Elisabeth Labrousse's introduction to her edition of Pierre Bayle, *Ce que c'est que la France toute catholique*, p. 9.

Considering that so many Protestants abjured after the use, or threatened use, of *dragonnades*, we might ask why Louis bothered with the Revocation of the Edict of Nantes? One answer that is often proposed is that given the scale of conversions the economic incentives granted in the form of remission of taxes produced inequalities between Old and New Catholics which the Revocation would wipe out. The Edict of Nantes was also regarded as a 'dead letter'. The policies of the previous six years had resulted, according to those intendants and clergy who tried to outdo each other in the number of conversions they claimed, in few, if any, Protestants remaining in France. Thus the Revocation of the Edict of Nantes, promulgated in the Edict of Fontainebleau of October 1685, was considered to be merely a legal recognition of something that had already occurred.[161]

The Edict of Fontainebleau abolished the practice of Protestantism throughout France (with the exception of Alsace, with its Protestant population, that Louis had annexed). It ordered the destruction of all Protestant churches and that all Protestant pastors who refused to convert should leave the country within two weeks. Emigration of other Huguenots was prohibited on pain of the galleys for men and confiscation of property for women. No Protestant meetings of any kind were allowed, nobles were forbidden to practise or allow the practice of the Protestant religion, on pain of confiscation of all property, and all children were to be baptised in Catholic churches.[162] Despite the high number of conversions at this time, many were false conversions and the Protestant Church, rather than ceasing to exist, went underground. In July 1686 capital punishment was ordered for those Huguenots found to be meeting secretly in so-called '*desert* assemblies', a measure which in itself reflected the failure of the Revocation of the Edict of Nantes.[163] Bringing the Protestants into the Catholic Church by force was not as simple a task as the Catholic clergy assumed – as Henry IV had recognised in the 1590s. In fact, many in the clergy misunderstood the nature of Protestant faith and the resistance to conversion, seeing only 'stubbornness',[164] something which Henry IV, born into Protestantism, did not do. It is estimated that about one fifth of French Protestants, making up about 1 per cent of the population, or around 200,000 people, fled in the wake of the

---

[161] 'Since there were no longer (in the eyes of the law) any Huguenots remaining in the kingdom, the legislation granting them privileges had no longer any legal rationale.' Bluche, *Louis XIV*, p. 405.

[162] A translation of the Revocation of the Edict of Nantes can be found in Golden (ed.), *The Huguenot Connection*, pp. 135–9.

[163] Labrousse, 'Understanding the Revocation', p. 56.   [164] Ibid., p. 60.

persecution leading up to the Revocation and after the Revocation itself. This was despite harsh penalties for those caught trying to emigrate, as explained above.[165] The exiles went mainly to neighbouring Protestant territories.[166]

Although the Revocation was popular within France at the time, and like all the other 'heroic' actions of the King, was commemorated by medals, poems and sermons from the clergy, in the longer term it did the royal image more harm than good. For the persecutions, and then the Revocation, turned loyal subjects into opponents of the crown. Rather than rooting out the political dissent with which Protestantism had been equated, the Revocation caused dissent where none had existed before, and critiques of Louis flooded France. In fact, the Revocation was 'a gift' to the enemies of Louis who set about attacking it in medals, prints and pamphlets. This hostile work inverted the work of the pro-Louis propagandists and parodied the heroic images of Louis to highlight what they saw as the King's vanity.[167] Thus the 1690s saw the beginning of the dissipation of the myth of the King as god.

It was the Huguenots in exile who were the 'most outspoken' critics of the regime after 1685 and who had an important influence on later revolutionary thought. Pierre Bayle's criticisms focused on the policies of Louis, rather than absolute monarchy itself. He acknowledged the concept of the interest of the state, but asked what interest could possibly be served by attacking obedient subjects, arguing that 'intolerance, in fact creates the problem that it is meant to solve'.[168] Thus Bayle developed a position on religious tolerance that was radical for the time. In turn, Jurieu drew a distinction between absolute power and limitless power (despotism), rejecting the latter 'because it supposes a "kind of idolatry" with respect to the prince and a reduction of the people to a state of servitude, in itself illegitimate'.[169] Thus Jurieu could support William and Mary ousting James in England, and advocated that Huguenots should

---

[165] Although Wolf notes that there seems to have been a policy of giving property to Catholic relatives, this was still confiscation. In the absence of Catholic relatives, property was the crown's to dispose of as it wished. Wolf, *Louis XIV*, p. 398.

[166] Around 70,000 people went to the United Provinces, 30,000 to 40,000 went to Germany, 40,000 to 50,000 went to Great Britain, 20,000 to Switzerland, 2,000 to Denmark and other parts of northern Europe; between 1,500 and 2,000 Huguenots eventually went to the American colonies. Golden (ed.), *The Huguenot Connection*, pp. 22–3.

[167] Burke, *The Fabrication*, pp. 143–4.

[168] Elisabeth Labrousse, 'The Political Ideas of the Huguenot Diaspora (Bayle and Jurieu)', in Richard M. Golden (ed.), *Church, State and Society under the Bourbon Kings of France* (Lawrence: Coronado Press, 1982), p. 242; Keohane, *Philosophy and the State*, pp. 314–15.

[169] Labrousse, 'The Political Ideas', p. 250.

join William's army in the hope that Louis XIV would be overthrown. The author of the *Soupirs*, 'an aristocratic and conservative tract', argued for the return of the liberties of the French which had been quashed under Louis XIV. This outspoken critic of absolutism equated Louis' rule with tyranny and charged that he had oppressed all Frenchmen equally, which reduced those of all stations to the same low level. The 'mythical version' of French history put forward in this document had a strong appeal, and '[i]t proved very powerful in France between 1685 and 1750 because it assured groups best placed to work for alternatives to absolutism that they had the sanctions of the past behind them. They were not revolutionaries or usurpers, but men claiming their rightful ancient part in government.'[170]

With the Revocation, Louis simultaneously asserted his role as the 'Most Christian King', by which he hoped to gain the Pope's approval, and France's independence from the papacy. However, the Pope was less than enthusiastic about Louis' actions.[171] The Revocation had a negative economic impact through the loss of many educated, skilled and hard-working subjects, who were assets to the societies that granted refuge. It caused administrative chaos as the civil records of Protestant communities were lost. Added to this was the loss of many well-trained soldiers, sailors and officers who offered their services to other powers.[172] Forced conversions meant that many individuals committed sacrilege, a factor overlooked by those members of the clergy who forced Protestants to take part in Catholic Communion.[173] Many converted falsely and then proceeded to avoid attending Mass, contributing to 'the spread of anticlericalism and even of unbelief [secularisation] in the eighteenth century'.[174] Importantly, false converts felt little loyalty to the regime and many were now much more sympathetic to France's adversaries. In 1688 the government ordered the disarming of all converts, though nobles were allowed to keep some weapons. Such orders were given periodically until 1714. In effect, the government created a problem where none had existed before, and through their policies created 'a distinct and separate class of potentially disloyal subjects who had to be watched'.[175] In the longer term, as we have seen above, the treatment of the Huguenots sowed the seeds of the critique of absolutist rule that was one strand in the development of

---

[170] Keohane, *Philosophy and the State*, pp. 316–18. Keohane notes that the attribution of the *Soupirs* to Jurieu is not entirely convincing. Also see Labrousse, 'The Political Ideas', pp. 253–4.

[171] Keohane, *Philosophy and the State*, p. 313.

[172] Lossky, *Louis XIV*, p. 227, estimates 8,000 to 9,000 sailors, 500 to 600 officers, and 10,000 to 12,000 soldiers 'who were much better trained than those in foreign armies'.

[173] Labrousse, 'Understanding the Revocation', pp. 60–1.

[174] Lossky, *Louis XIV*, p. 226.   [175] Ibid., p. 227.

French revolutionary thought, which eventually destroyed absolutism in France. For the Huguenot population that remained in France and went underground, it would be another hundred years before an open debate on toleration would take place in their country.[176]

Conclusion

In this chapter I have investigated the role of pathological homogenisation in the construction of corporate state identity in absolutist France. Imbued with the ideology of absolutism, the regime of Louis XIV attempted to forcibly convert Huguenots, when force had not won converts in the past, but had led France into a series of devastating civil wars, and importantly, when the Huguenots no longer posed any political or military threat to the state or the monarchy. As we have seen, absolutism was a doctrine that sought to assert the rights of the monarchy in response to a number of crises of legitimacy, not least of which was that the sacral character of kingship was disintegrating. As an absolute monarch, Louis XIV demanded complete obedience to both the monarchy and the state, which were indivisible.

Despite the process of secularisation that was under way, the religious world view still provided the criteria through which identification and obedience could be demanded and given. In this view, there was no room to consider the complexities of Huguenot loyalty to both their religion and the crown, and as a result the arguments of those Huguenots who defended the rights of absolute monarchy did little good for the Huguenot cause. In terms of the ideology of French absolutism, in which the Catholic world view provided the dominant cultural reference points, Huguenots did not fit but should, and could, be 'made to fit', thereby imposing order and making manifest the completeness of Louis XIV's rule.

There is much continuity between sixteenth and seventeenth-century France. Religion still played a central role in constituting the social world and the monarchy faced many crises. Yet, as we have seen, in the sixteenth century religious difference became entwined with a political factionalism that retained many feudal aspects. In this situation, a series of regency governments faced repeated assaults on their legitimacy from both Protestant and Catholic factions, and the royal party itself often descended into factional politics – the St Bartholomew's Day massacres being a notable outcome of this state of affairs. The crises Louis XIV faced in the second

---

[176] Geoffrey Adams, *The Huguenots and French Opinion 1685–1787: The Enlightenment Debate on Toleration* (Waterloo: Wilfrid Laurier University Press, 1991).

half of the seventeenth century were of a different nature. The Fronde was a series of widespread uprisings against economic hardship and the assertion of absolutist authority. These uprisings reached across all classes of French society, with the nobility once again seeing an opportunity to assert itself against the monarchy in the absence of an adult monarch. But these uprisings were not religiously motivated. Indeed, the Huguenots remained loyal throughout this period. Further crises were brought about by Louis' expansionist policies which resulted in a series of military defeats and financial hardship for the state. As Lossky notes, France was secure when Cardinal Mazarin died, but 'Louis destroyed this within the first ten years of his personal reign', that is, after 1661.[177] Concerned with the hegemonic aspirations of Spain, France under Richelieu and Mazarin had set about blocking these, but by the 1670s states across Europe allied to block what were widely regarded as Louis' hegemonic aspirations. Louis' self-interested pursuit of his own goals at any cost was highlighted for European powers by his failure to take part in the successful defence of Vienna against the Ottoman Empire in 1683. In this context, the enforcement of religious unity became increasingly important to Louis, for it symbolised the legitimacy and strength of his authority both internally and externally. Internally, unity represented order and obedience to the crown, externally, his actions were meant to highlight the social legitimacy of the French state. However, the terms in which this action was legitimated were in reference to the now disintegrated Catholic Respublica Christiana, rather than the minimal principles of toleration articulated at Westphalia, which are discussed in chapter 6. Furthermore, the contradictions in Louis' policies were apparent to the Pope and the rulers across much of Europe. Though the persecution of Huguenots and their conversion to Catholicism was seen by Louis as simultaneously vindicating his role as the 'Most Christian King' and asserting France's independence from the papacy, forced conversions were no more acceptable to Rome in the late 1680s than they had been in 1492 when Ferdinand and Isabella gave the Jews of Spain a choice between conversion or expulsion.

Louis sought to justify his actions with reference to the outdated, or at least strongly contested norm that a sovereign could do as they wished with religious minorities within their state. This was widely rejected across Europe just as his dynastic claims to the Spanish throne and his hegemonic aspirations in general, were rejected. In trying to solve a crisis of legitimacy Louis and his officials drew on the available, traditional, cultural reference. Thus we see Louis using religious criteria to legitimate government control of a *defined* population within the territorial

---

[177] Lossky, *Louis XIV*, p. 60.

boundaries of the sovereign state. There was no sense of popular national identity at this time, indeed it was in response to absolutism that this would later arise. In the late seventeenth century, the notion of a national identity that went beyond the monarchy, or at most the political classes, 'would have been offensive to those in authority or routinely participating in politics. In the political rhetoric of the period the idea of the nation, if it appeared at all, was subordinated to religious and monarchical principles.'[178] Yet, we see in the seventeenth century an attempt by the regime of Louis XIV to define the corporate identity of the state with reference to the imposition of the absolutist order over the population as a whole.[179]

As Louis XIV sought to assert France's preeminent position in Europe through military means, he also sought to construct a 'strong' state within France, understood in terms of obedience and loyalty to the state. However, just as his ambitions led to alliances against him, thwarting his quest for 'glory', so too the path he chose to enhance the domestic legitimacy of his rule and to build the corporate identity of the state, though popular within France at the time, was rejected across Europe and soon came to be seen as a huge political error and a religious crime by many.[180]

In the sixteenth century, up until the reign of Henry IV and the promulgation of the Edict of Nantes in 1598, we see hostile and often violent popular responses to attempts by the monarchy to come to some accord with Protestants. In the seventeenth century the popular hostility towards Huguenots still existed, and without this the regime could not have devised and attempted to implement its policy of forced conversions. However, in contrast to the events of the sixteenth century this was a consciously devised *government* policy, imposed as systematically as the penetration of the state at that time would allow, and in which state controlled agencies (local intendants, the army and even the clergy) were employed. This is not to deny some haphazard aspects to this policy and its implementation, particularly if compared to the practices of pathological homogenisation that became all too familiar in the twentieth century. But in contrast to the massacres of Protestants in the sixteenth century, which were set off by factional politics and driven by outbursts of popular Catholic rejection of Protestantism, the programme of Louis XIV was

[178] Breuilly, *Nationalism and the State*, p. 76.
[179] Absolutism was not just about a new and more effective form of administration, but was also concerned with 'new controls over social, economic, professional, religious and other elements of the life of the people'. Church (ed.), *Impact of Absolutism*, p. 5. But the absolutist regime was not concerned with the costs its policies and pursuit of 'glory' imposed on subjects.
[180] Bluche, *Louis XIV*, p. 406.

one in which the regime sought to remake the population within the state according to an absolutist doctrine which stressed the value of order and which had a very clear conception of how that order should be defined. At the time of the Revocation of the Edict of Nantes, the regime could only draw upon the available cultural framework, which was religious. In chapter 4 I turn to the first of two case studies which trace policies of pathological homogenisation that have drawn upon self-consciously 'national', rather than strictly religious criteria of identification.

4   Pathological homogenisation and Turkish state-building: the Armenian genocide of 1915–1916

Chapters 2 and 3 investigated examples of pathological homogenisation pursued through policies of forced conversion or expulsion. In both of these cases, although state-builders sought to destroy the collective identity of the targeted minority, and caused great suffering in the process, they were not intent on the physical destruction of all members of the targeted group. This was, however, the intention of those responsible for the Armenian genocide of 1915–16. The Committee of Union and Progress (CUP) that came to power in the Ottoman Empire in the revolution of 1908 was animated by a chauvinist strand of Turkish nationalism, and was intent on building a rationalised and homogeneous Turkish national state. Accordingly, minority groups, of whom the Armenians were the largest and most vulnerable, were to be removed from Turkey. This is the first of two cases, therefore, that consider how pathological homogenisation has operated in the age of nationalism.

With the ascension to power of the conservative Sultan Abdul Hamid II in 1876, reform was blocked in the Ottoman Empire until the early twentieth century, when the so-called Young Turks came to power.[1] The Young Turks, though initially concerned with reforming the Empire in order to save it, ultimately sought to remake the remains of the crumbling Ottoman Empire into a centralised, modern and national state, one that would stand as an equal among European powers. This carving out of a homogeneous national state from the remains of a multinational Empire was to have a tragic impact on the Armenian people, who in the early twentieth century were still subjects of the Ottoman Empire. The result of the territorial losses suffered by the Empire in the nineteenth and early twentieth centuries was that by 1914 'the largest Christian national group left in the Ottoman empire . . . were the Armenians, most of whom lived

---

[1] Bernard Lewis argues that Abdul Hamid was a reformer, pushing through many bureaucratic reforms. While it is true that he did implement reforms, particularly those which would buttress his own hold on power, the point still stands that he was an essentially conservative ruler who blocked social and political reform. Bernard Lewis, *The Emergence of Modern Turkey* (Oxford University Press, 1962), p. 174.

in the eastern portions of Anatolia'.[2] And by this time, with the truncation of the Empire, especially in Europe, and the growth of Turkish nationalism in the later nineteenth century, Anatolia had become increasingly significant for Turkish nationalists as their historical *vatan* ('fatherland' or 'homeland'),[3] and it came to play a central role in the idea of a Turkish national state. Turkish nationalism, as it developed in the second half of the nineteenth century, was largely a response to the nationalist claims that had swept across the Empire. There were both liberal and authoritarian strands to this nationalism, but it was the most authoritarian and chauvinist strand that animated the regime that came to power in 1908.

The Armenian genocide occurred in a well-developed international system, into which the Ottoman Empire had been inexorably drawn since the seventeenth century. In the nineteenth century, Ottoman membership of the European society of states was conditional on Ottoman acceptance of the shared standards of 'civilised' behaviour, which in the case of the Empire, meant equal treatment of minorities. However, these values clashed with the world view and values that underpinned Ottoman imperial rule. Under duress, the weak Empire acceded to the European standards of legitimate state behaviour, at least 'on paper'. In reality, the promised reforms were rarely put into practice. The role of external pressures was certainly important, but if we are to understand the path that the Young Turks took in their efforts at state-building we must look also at the internal cultural resources available to these state-builders, and how they interpreted them as they sought to remake the Empire into a strong and sovereign entity that would be seen as an equal by European powers. The Armenian genocide was not inevitable, but internal and external factors interacted in such a way as to make this an attractive means for the Young Turk regime to pursue its goal of creating a homogeneous national state.

Thus this chapter focuses on the deportation and genocide of the Armenian people which occurred during World War I.[4] This was a

[2] Ulrich Trumpener, *Germany and the Ottoman Empire 1914–1918* (Princeton University Press, 1968), p. 200.

[3] David Kushner, *The Rise of Turkish Nationalism 1876–1908* (London: Frank Cass, 1977). Kushner discusses how the concept of an essentially Turkish Anatolia developed in the second half of the nineteenth century. Though the Ottoman Empire had started from this area, for most of the life of the expansionist Empire it was regarded as of no particular significance. On the further development of the concept of Anatolia as the Turkish *vatan* under the Kemalist regime, see p. 101.

[4] With its focus on genocide this chapter steps into a new area. This is a huge field of scholarship in itself, with its own debates and controversies. To focus on the Armenian genocide and its role in state-building is in no way intended to deny the uniqueness of

centrally planned and administered programme that followed a similar pattern across the provinces of Turkey in which Armenians were to be found.[5] The chapter illustrates how this policy and its implementation can be traced to the modernising intent of the Young Turks and their desire to remake the crumbling Empire into a rationalised, centralised modern state. Yet though they were modernisers, the Young Turks drew on a complex amalgam of traditional attitudes and a growing sense of national identity that refused to accept non-Muslims as equal subjects of the Empire. This process of state-building entailed rethinking the criterion of membership of the political community, and increasingly the idea of a homogenised population – a Turkish population within a Turkish state – gained potency. As Gerard J. Libaridian observes:

The legitimation of power on the basis of ethnic, cultural, and religious identity of the population acquired a dynamic significance for old empires and new states. For the Young Turks, who engineered and supervised over the transitional stage, the creation of a new Turkish nation-state out of the old Ottoman Empire passed through the path of the homogenization of the population.[6]

This was the case despite the imperial ambitions of the Young Turks. They envisaged a renewed Empire – but this vision was of a pan-Turkic Empire ruled by Turkey, thus they displayed a mixture of Turkish nationalism and imperialism. It was Mustafa Kemal (Ataturk), leader of the Republic of Turkey that was formally recognised at Lausanne in 1923, who clearly and explicitly articulated the idea of a homogeneous Turkish national state, and finally rejected the idea of Empire.[7] But it was the Young Turks who laid the groundwork for the homogeneous state with their programme of clearing Anatolia of Armenians. Thus the Young Turks were a transitional regime, because, although the national idea was most explicitly articulated by Kemal, the Young Turks were the first to implement a programme of homogenisation and Turkification.

this genocide, or indeed that of the World War II Holocaust. The intention here is to illustrate how genocide is one, extreme, strategy of pathological homogenisation through which state-builders seek to construct a unitary corporate identity.

[5] Leo Kuper notes that the Armenian genocide shares with the German genocide against the Jews, 'centralized planning and bureaucratic organization'. Leo Kuper, *Genocide: Its Political Use in the Twentieth Century* (New Haven: Yale University Press, 1981), p. 105.

[6] Gerard J. Libaridian, 'The Ideology of the Young Turk Movement', in Permanent Peoples' Tribunal, *A Crime of Silence: The Armenian Genocide* (London: Zed Books, 1985), pp. 37–8.

[7] Roger W. Smith, 'Denial of the Armenian Genocide', in Israel W. Charny (ed.), *Genocide: A Critical Bibliographical Review*, vol. 2 (New York: Facts on File, 1991), pp. 103–4. It was this regime that was behind the compulsory exchange of populations between Greece and Turkey in the 1920s, on which, see chapter 6.

The chapter begins with a brief overview of theories of state formation that consider the question of genocide. I then go on to discuss different explanations of the genocide, this time from those scholars who specialise in the area. I inquire into whether the Armenian genocide was a continuation of imperial policies that had resulted in massacres during the nineteenth century, or whether it represented a break with the past. I argue that the genocide was aimed at fundamentally reshaping the remains of the Empire into a homogeneous national state. In order to better understand how this could come about, I trace the development of Turkish nationalism during the nineteenth century and the influence of the most chauvinist strand of nationalism on the CUP, and in particular on the views of the anti-liberal clique which seized control of the government from 1913. I then give an account of the genocide of 1915–16, through which the Young Turks sought to build a Turkish corporate identity within the state, which in turn buttressed their own, always precarious, legitimacy. The genocide occurred during World War I, which presented the regime with an opportunity to put into action their plans to solve the 'Armenian question' by casting the Armenians as an internal security threat while the Great Powers were engaged with their own conflicts. In both the conception and execution of the genocide, the CUP drew upon the religious and cultural resentment of Armenians that existed within the Empire. Through the use of propaganda and mass rallies they inflamed such sentiments to the point where the obliteration of a whole community became widely accepted. How the CUP drew on the cultural resources available to them in legitimating the genocide is a central theme of the chapter.

The genocide of the Armenians has been denied to this day by successive Turkish governments, with the exception of the short-lived imperial government that existed between the end of World War I and the ascendance of the Kemalist nationalist regime in the early 1920s.[8] Despite

---

[8] For example see Salahi Ramsadam Sonyel, *The Ottoman Armenians: Victims of Great Power Diplomacy* (London: K. Rustem & Brother, 1987). Sonyel looks to the role of the Great Powers in the Ottoman Empire and sees the Armenians as revolutionaries and traitors. He follows the so-called 'provocation thesis', which argues that Armenian revolutionaries were responsible for any government response. Sonyel's view echoes that of Stanford J. Shaw and Ezel Kural Shaw, who combine justification of the genocide with denial that it actually happened. Stanford J. Shaw and Ezel Kural Shaw, *History of the Ottoman Empire and Modern Turkey*, vol. 2 (Cambridge University Press, 1977). Also see Foreign Policy Institute, Ankara, 'The Turkish Argument: The Armenian Issue in Nine Questions and Answers', in Permanent Peoples' Tribunal, *A Crime of Silence*, pp. 132–67. The historian Bernard Lewis does not deny that over a million Armenians died during the reign of the CUP, but he places it in the context of a clash of two national groups fighting over a single territory – Anatolia. While there were Armenian nationalist groups, this position ignores the fact that this was not a battle between two

this denial, there is a mass of evidence to show that the genocide oc-curred.[9] Like many scholars, I take the genocide of the Armenians as an established historical fact,[10] and focus on the role of this premeditated extermination of over a million people in state-building in the midst of a collapsing Empire. This was a massive displacement of people, which was portrayed as a deportation measure, made necessary by internal security conditions in a state of war. In reality it was a 'relocation to nowhere'. As we shall see below in more detail, those who were not summarily executed – women, children and the elderly – were death marched to the Syrian desert and the Mesopotamian valley. For those who survived the marches, no arrangements had been made and those who were not exe-cuted on government orders died from starvation, disease and sporadic attacks by a number of groups.

Explaining genocide and state formation

Of the accounts of state formation reviewed in chapter 1, only Charles Tilly's deals with the Ottoman Empire in its last days.[11] By the nineteenth

---

equal forces. On the contrary, the Armenian people, including women and children, were methodically exterminated. Lewis, *Emergence of Modern Turkey*, p. 350. For further discussion and sources see Smith, 'Denial of the Armenian Genocide', pp. 63–85.

[9] Scholars have long been denied access to Ottoman archives. In the late 1980s access was granted to some archives by the Turkish government, but it appears that the material was limited and the government took a very selective approach to who was allowed to study the material. See Vahakn N. Dadrian, 'Ottoman Archives and Denial of the Armenian Genocide', in Richard G. Hovannisian (ed.), *The Armenian Genocide: History, Politics, Ethics* (New York: St. Martin's Press, 1992); Vahakn N. Dadrian, 'Documentation of the Armenian Genocide in Turkish Sources', in Charny (ed.), *Genocide*; Christopher J. Walker, 'British Sources on the Armenian Massacres, 1915–16' and Tessa Hofmann, 'German Eyewitness Reports of the Genocide of the Armenians, 1915–16', both in Per-manent Peoples' Tribunal, *A Crime of Silence*; Arnold Toynbee (ed.), *The Treatment of Armenians in the Ottoman Empire: Documents Presented to Viscount Grey of Fallodon, Sec-retary of State for Foreign Affairs, with a Preface by Viscount Bryce* (London: Hodder & Stoughton, 1916), presents eyewitness accounts of the genocide. For an exhaustive ac-count of acknowledgements of the genocide, see Vahakn N. Dadrian, 'Genocide as a Problem of National and International Law: The World War I Armenian Case and Its Contemporary Ramifications', *Yale Journal of International Law* 14:2 (1989), 224–5. This covers the military trials of those responsible for the genocide held in Turkey in 1919, the United Nations recognition of the Armenian genocide in August 1985, recognition by the UN Commission on Human Rights in 1986, and by the European Parliament in June 1987. At this time the European Parliament stipulated that Turkey must recognise the genocide in order to become a member of the European Community (as it was then).

[10] As Yves Ternon notes, the debate over this matter is a 'false controversy'. Yves Ternon, 'Report on the Genocide of the Armenians of the Ottoman Empire, 1915–16', in Permanent Peoples' Tribunal, *A Crime of Silence*, p. 124.

[11] Charles Tilly, *Coercion, Capital and European States, AD 990–1990* (Oxford: Basil Blackwell, 1990); Michael Mann has nothing to say about state-building processes in

century this once great multinational Empire was so weakened that it was regarded as 'the sick man of Europe'. Throughout the nineteenth century the Empire lost much of its territory to a diverse range of nationalist claims from first its Christian, and later its Muslim subjects. As Tilly explains,

In southeastern Europe, the Crimean, Austro-German, and multiple Russo-Turkish wars each precipitated a further disintegration of Ottoman control and the formation of new national states under strong international influence: Greece, Serbia, Rumania, Bulgaria, Montenegro. The Crimean War's settlement (1856), moreover, recast the Ottoman Empire as Turkey, a new state in something resembling the European format.[12]

Although Turkey may have resembled a European state from the outside, the reality was more complicated. Internally, what remained of the Empire did not resemble a European state, for it was still constituted by a number of segmented religious communities, or millets. There was widespread internal resistance to the standards that the Great Powers attempted to impose on the Empire, particularly that all minorities should be accorded equality and this resistance, in great part culturally based, had an important influence on the path that internal state-building took in the next fifty years. To understand this, we must once again look at the cultural aspects of state formation. As the Empire broke down leaving Turkey as its successor state, the political transformation was accompanied by changes that challenged the whole social and cultural framework of the Empire, and which in turn generated different strategies of resistance from within.

As we saw in chapter 1, Tilly observes that it is in the twentieth century that 'politicides' and 'genocides' have become a 'standard technique of government' rather than 'the rare and appalling aberration they once seemed'.[13] As I argued there, this contradicts what his own work shows, namely, that different forms of pathological homogenisation have been used by state-builders since the inception of the system of states.[14] This also leaves unanswered the question of how such techniques can become 'standard techniques': not all state-builders use such methods, so under

the Ottoman Empire, except to note how the empire was crumbling in the nineteenth century, and how state infrastructures had the usually unintended effect of creating nation-states. Michael Mann, *The Sources of Social Power*, vol. 2, *The Rise of Classes and Nation-States, 1760–1914* (Cambridge University Press, 1993), p. 491.

[12] Tilly, *Coercion, Capital*, p. 169. Also see Roderic H. Davison, 'Nationalism as an Ottoman Problem and the Ottoman Response', in William Haddad and William Ochsenwald (eds.), *Nationalism in a Non-National State: The Dissolution of the Ottoman Empire* (Columbus: Ohio State University Press, 1977).

[13] Tilly, *Coercion, Capital*, p. 202.

[14] Ibid., p. 202. Although there is no doubt that, as Tilly points out, the numbers killed by their own state have dramatically increased this century.

what conditions are means such as genocide used, and importantly, how can such strategies come to be seen as legitimate both by rulers and by majority populations? For genocide, like the forced conversions or mass expulsion we have already encountered, does not occur in a social vacuum. To understand how genocide can become a 'thinkable' option for those in power, we must turn to work that deals specifically with genocide.

Leo Kuper argues that it is a liberal assumption that 'there are powerful moral inhibitions against the slaughter of one's own kind'. In all cases of genocide, indeed in all the cases investigated in this study, a process has to take place by which the victims are clearly marked as 'other' and therefore outside the community within which sanctions against violence still hold, a process through which they are marked as 'not of one's own kind'. 'Since the victims are not human, the inhibitions against their slaughter cease to be operative.'[15] This process is much easier when a community has long been decreed as outside what Helen Fein describes as 'the sanctified universe of moral obligation'.[16] She notes how genocide does not occur in a social or cultural vacuum. From this it can be deduced that though a prohibition of violence towards 'one's own kind' may in fact still be in place, what is crucial is the social and cultural construction of who is and is not of 'one's own kind'. Genocide must be preceded by a process by which those who are to be 'eliminated' are placed in a different moral category; 'leaders could not have chosen annihilation . . . had not the victims been previously defined as basically of a different species, outside of the common conscience and beyond the universe of obligation'.[17] Fein notes how in the Ottoman Empire conditions were such that non-Muslims were already considered to be outsiders. They were tolerated peoples of the book, but this toleration came at some cost. Their 'lives were to be protected in exchange for their accommodation to civil discrimination, ritual subordination, powerlessness and oppression'.[18] Thus non-Muslim communities were never seen as equal to Muslims and the heterogeneous Empire worked by keeping the different religious communities separate. Kuper argues that as the Empire broke down and national identities became increasingly pertinent '[t]he plural society provide[d] the structural base for genocide'.[19] Plural society in this context denotes a society with 'persistent and pervasive cleavages' between different sections of the society and in which differentiation is reflected in political or practical inequalities despite equality before the law, as was the case with the Armenians.[20]

---

[15] Kuper, Genocide, p. 85.
[16] Helen Fein, Accounting for Genocide (New York: The Free Press, 1979), p. 4.
[17] Ibid., p. 8.   [18] Ibid., p. 5.   [19] Kuper, Genocide, p. 57.   [20] Ibid., p. 58.

Building on the work of Fein and others, Robert Melson identifies a connection between what he calls 'total genocide' and revolution. Melson highlights how revolution provides the structural conditions in which genocide can occur, as was the case in Armenia and in Nazi Germany. He argues that:

[n]ational upheaval is an abrupt change in the political community, caused for example, by the formation of a state through violent conflict, when national boundaries are reformed, or after a war is lost. Thus, lost wars and the resultant battered national pride sometimes lead to genocide against groups perceived as enemies.[21]

This concept of national upheaval comes closest, Melson argues, to the notion of revolution he employs. The upheaval of the 1908 revolution and its aftermath was certainly an important factor in understanding the Armenian genocide. However, from the perspective of this study, the focus is on the profound transformation that was taking place at this time which was the 'backdrop' against which the revolution occurred: a process of nation-state *creation*. The revolution that took place in the dying days of the Ottoman Empire was itself part of the process in which the multinational Empire finally disintegrated, and from the remnants of which a new form of political organisation – the territorially defined, sovereign nation-state – was emerging that brought with it a reformulated concept of political community. As Melson argues, genocide occurs when states and societies are in crisis or under stress. Again, this does not pay enough attention to how in the case of the Armenian genocide the *kind* of state that was emerging is at issue. The Ottoman Empire was a multi-national suzerain state, the core of which transformed into a territorially bounded sovereign nation-state. The genocide occurred as this transition was under way and it was conceived as a means to the end of carving an exclusively Turkish national state out of the remains of Empire.[22]

The leaders of the CUP were not content to merely reform an already existing state. Rather, they were intent upon building something new, though this would not be explicitly recognised by the different regime in power after World War I, or by the international community at Lausanne in 1923. Nonetheless, the CUP were state-builders and they laid the foundation for the Republic of Turkey as a 'homogeneous

---

[21] Robert Melson, *Revolution and Genocide: On the Origins of the Armenian Genocide and the Holocaust* (University of Chicago Press, 1992), p. 15.

[22] Melson does acknowledge the collapse of the multinational Empire and the turn to Turkish nationalism. Robert Melson, 'Provocation or Nationalism? A Critical Inquiry into the Armenian Genocide of 1915', in Frank Chalk and Kurt Jonassohn (eds.), *The History and Sociology of Genocide: Analyses and Case Studies* (New Haven: Yale University Press, 1990), p. 277.

nation-state'.[23] As Melson notes, '[r]evolutions destroy not only the institutions and power of the old regime, they also undermine the legitimacy
of the state and place in question the identity of the community itself.
Revolutions, therefore, provide the structural opportunities for ideological vanguards to come to power and impose their view on society.'[24] In
fact, the legitimacy of the old regime was fatally weakened throughout
the nineteenth century, where to use Habermas' phrase once again, a
legitimation crisis had accompanied the crumbling of Empire. The revolution in the twentieth century was the point where the old regime finally
gave way, and power shifted to the revolutionary regime, although, as we
will see, the preeminence of the CUP was by no means certain in the
early years of the revolution. From Melson we gain an understanding
of the important role of social and political upheaval in genocide, and
how such upheaval provides an opportunity for the imposition of a vision
of a new order,[25] and hence as he shows, a new system of legitimation
which brings with it new criteria of identity in the reformed political
community.

Continuity and change

Some authors view the genocide of the twentieth century as a repeat, on
a massive scale, of the massacres of Armenians which occurred under
Sultan Abdul Hamid II in the nineteenth century. For example, in an
important article Vahakn N. Dadrian stresses the continuity in attitudes
towards Armenians who were regarded as of lower status than Muslims,
in both the nineteenth and early twentieth centuries.[26] Dadrian also
argues that in the nineteenth-century massacres the Sultan intended to
exterminate the Armenians as a solution to 'the Armenian question'.[27]
While there were important continuities in religious and cultural attitudes towards the Armenians, attitudes which provided a cultural basis
from which violence against Armenians could be legitimated in both
cases, there were also important differences between the two events. In
the nineteenth century, though massacres took place, there was no attempt to remove *all* Armenians – whether by expulsion or murder – from

[23] This is a national myth, which still has some purchase in Turkey today. However, like
most other nation-states Turkey is not completely homogeneous.

[24] Melson, *Revolution and Genocide*, p. 18.

[25] Libaridian acknowledges his paraphrase of Fein when he discusses the 'Turkish design
for a new order'. Gerard J. Libaridian, 'The Ultimate Repression: The Genocide of the
Armenians, 1915–1917', in Isidor Walliman and Michael N. Dobkowski (eds.), *Genocide
and the Modern Age: Etiology and Case Studies of Mass Death* (New York: Greenwood Press,
1987), p. 208.

[26] Dadrian, 'Genocide as a Problem', 254.   [27] Ibid., 244.

the Empire. In both cases, the cultural framework was still provided to a large extent by a religious world view which, under certain circumstances, legitimated violence towards non-Muslim minorities. Yet through the massacres of the Armenians the Sultan sought to impose an imperial view in which the Armenians should stay in their 'second class' place. In the case of the genocide, the religious world view was still important, but it had been transformed under the impact of nationalism, so that what were once religious communities were now understood as 'nations'. The traditional view that Armenians had their place as second-class subjects of the Empire gave way to the view that in their demands for legal equality the Armenians had forgone the right of protection. In this view, the Armenians should not be 'put back in their place' within the Empire – there was in fact no 'place' for such a group within the national state that the CUP and their supporters were intent on building. Popular hostility towards the Armenians was aggravated by mass rallies and propaganda which stressed the threat posed by the Armenians to the *Turkish* state.

Thus the genocide was an attempt to extirpate the Armenians from Ottoman Turkey in line with a vision of a homogenised national state in which the corporate identity was to be Turkic and Islamic. This policy can be distinguished from the massacres under the conservative Abdul Hamid, massacres that must be understood in the context of attempts to preserve traditional forms of authority and hierarchy, made in an effort to bolster a crumbling, but nonetheless, multinational Empire. The Sultan sought to keep those of lower status in their place, and was prepared to use violent means to do this, but he was not attempting their wholesale removal from the Empire. However, as Dadrian argues:

The Armenian Genocide was a direct consequence of the social-political system that existed in Ottoman Turkey during the years leading up to World War I. Because of certain intractable components, most notably religious beliefs which could not be reconciled with conceptions of Armenian equality, the Ottoman system was subjected to unabating external and internal pressures . . . The genocidal nature of the Turkish response was in part conditioned by Ottoman traditions and theocracy. The norms and the associated corpus of the Ottoman customary and common law for subject nationalities and minorities not only allowed, but in many instances encouraged, such a drastic response as a form of crisis management. Thus, what was considered deviant by external, international standards was considered normal and functional by domestic Ottoman desiderata.[28]

While the role of traditional attitudes in supporting the genocide of 1915–16 was certainly important, in themselves they do not, however,

---

[28] Ibid., 381.

satisfactorily explain the conception and decision to carry out a centrally administered programme of extermination. This programme was – in both its object of exterminating the Armenian population and its centrally administered execution – different from the massacres perpetrated by Sultan Abdul Hamid. As Melson highlights, the genocide occurred in a context of profound upheaval, and those responsible for it were not concerned with maintaining the status quo. At the heart of this process was the process of state-building, pursued through a policy of Turkification, and the identification of a Turkish national identity with the 'Turkish Fatherland' in Anatolia, the very territory where most Armenians were to be found. As Richard Hovannisian argues:

[T]he major difference between Abdul-Hamid and his Young Turk successors was that he unleashed massacres in an effort to maintain a state structure in which the Armenians would be kept in their place without the right to resist corrupt and oppressive government, whereas the Young Turks were to employ the same tactic on a grander scale to bring about fundamental and far-reaching changes in the status quo and to create an entirely new frame of reference which did not include the Armenians at all.[29]

This new frame of reference was a national, territorially defined, sovereign state. As I have argued above, this does not mean there were not many important continuities with the past, continuities of cultural attitudes that both influenced how the leaders of the CUP viewed Armenians, and which they drew on to gain support for their actions, and their rule. Thus the hostility and resentment that had made the nineteenth-century massacres possible still existed in the twentieth century and played an important part in the genocide. But as Hovannisian so clearly points out, these resentments were channelled within different political frameworks, one concerned with maintaining the imperial status quo and the other concerned with building a modern sovereign state.

Despite my disagreement with Dadrian's view of the goal of the nineteenth-century massacres, his work on the continuity of hostile attitudes towards Armenians is an important contribution towards understanding the genocide. It helps answer the question posed by Gerard Chaliand and Yves Ternon of why the Young Turk regime embarked on the elimination of the Armenian population of Turkey against 'their interests'. As Chaliand and Ternon ask: 'What overwhelming necessity drove the Young Turks to commit this crime and, against their short and long term interests, to bear responsibility before history?'[30] Part of the answer

---

[29] Richard G. Hovannisian, 'The Armenian Question, 1878–1923', in Permanent Peoples' Tribunal, *A Crime of Silence*, p. 17.
[30] Gerard Chaliand and Yves Ternon, *The Armenians: From Genocide to Resistance*, trans. Tony Berret (London: Zed Press, 1983), p. 19.

lies in the continuity of attitudes which Dadrian highlights. 'Although Islam is a religious creed, it is also a way of life for its followers, transcending the boundaries of faith to permeate the social and political fabric of a nation.'[31] This is, however, only part of the answer. Certain strands in this world view were translated into a chauvinist form of nationalist ideology, which in turn provided a means of legitimation for an authoritarian regime. This ideology then provided the range of possible options for this regime as they set about the *modern* project of state-building. Thus the inheritance of attitudes that Dadrian identifies certainly contributed to the genocide. But this needs to be combined with an understanding of the essentially modern nature of the project of state-building and nationalist politics in which the CUP were engaged. Fein's explanation of genocide in terms of 'the state's design for a new order',[32] and how it may appear 'as a rational choice to the perpetrator',[33] is most apt here. Below I seek to explain just how the genocide could seem like a 'rational choice' and what led the CUP to choose this most 'pathological' form of creating a unified national identity within the state they were intent on building amidst the ruins of Empire.

The end of Empire: nineteenth-century reform and reaction

Armenians in the Ottoman Empire

By the early twentieth century there existed a strong national consciousness amongst the Christian Armenians whose traditional homeland straddled Russia and Ottoman Turkey. In the nineteenth century, with the spread of general education and literacy, Armenian society underwent a renaissance in the cultural, economic and political spheres. However, despite the aims of some Armenian nationalists, independent statehood was not the goal of the Armenian majority. Rather, they wished to claim the equal rights that had been accorded them by the Ottoman Empire under pressure from the West. As Christians, the Armenians had always been second-class subjects in the Ottoman Empire, but they had lived under conditions of relative tolerance compared to the treatment of non-Christians by many Christian states.[34] As the Empire became weaker the

---

[31] Dadrian, 'Genocide as a Problem', 230.
[32] Fein, *Accounting for Genocide*, p. 7, cited by Libaridian, 'The Ultimate Repression:', p. 206.
[33] Fein, *Accounting for Genocide*, pp. 7–8.
[34] Robert Melson, 'A Theoretical Inquiry into the Armenian Massacres of 1894–1896', *Comparative Studies in Society and History* 24 (1982), 498; Roderic H. Davison, 'Turkish

Armenians were treated more harshly. The religious minorities in the Ottoman Empire had traditionally had some autonomy under the millet system, by which the leaders of each community were responsible for their community and directly answerable to the Sultan. 'This derived not only from the corporate nature of the Empire, but also from the Sacred Law itself, which regulated Muslim behaviour, and the relationship of *dhimmi* [protected non-Muslim peoples of the book] to Muslim.'[35] The two main Christian millets were the Armenian and the Greek Orthodox, the latter including 'Serbs, Bulgarians, Rumanian, and the inhabitants of southern Albania. Significantly, these national differences carried no particular meaning for the Ottoman government – not that is, until the nineteenth century – when nationalism began to foster new political identities.'[36] However, in the nineteenth century, rather than recognising nationalities the Ottoman government recognised new millets, many of which were splinter groups.[37]

Despite this relative tolerance, non-Muslims were always regarded as second-class citizens in the eyes of Muslims, and especially in the eyes of more conservative Muslims. 'Despite some local autonomy, millets were responsible for a *cyzia*, or tax and their members were excluded from military service. Both the tax and the exclusion were seen as signs of their inferiority.'[38] Compelled by the Great Powers, who were concerned about the treatment of minorities in the Empire, in 1839 and 1856 declarations of the equality of all the Sultan's subjects were made. However, in practice, these reforms were obstructed.[39] They were unpopular with a number of groups, including nationalists among the minority groups who wanted independence or autonomy, and so rejected the idea of being imperial subjects, even subjects with equal rights to all others. The ecclesiastical hierarchs who were the communal elites under the millet system also resisted the concept of equality, as it affected their status. Likewise, according to traditionally minded Muslims it was unthinkable that there could be equality between the different religious

---

Attitudes Concerning Christian–Muslim Equality in the Nineteenth Century', *American Historical Review* 59:4 (1954), 844.

[35] Melson, 'A Theoretical Inquiry', 497. Also see Dadrian, 'Genocide as a Problem'.

[36] Melson, 'A Theoretical Inquiry', 498. Davison notes that 'It is significant that the meaning of the word millet itself began to change in the nineteenth century, almost imperceptibly, until in the twentieth it came to mean nation and nationality. Religion and nation, sect and nationality, were thoroughly confused and intertwined.' Davison, 'Nationalism as an Ottoman Problem', p. 33.

[37] These were predominantly Catholic splinter groups, though a Protestant millet was recognised in 1850. The important non-Christian millet was the Jewish millet. Davison, 'Nationalism as an Ottoman Problem', pp. 36–7.

[38] Melson, 'A Theoretical Inquiry', 497.

[39] Lewis, *Emergence of Modern Turkey*, pp. 73–125.

communities. As peoples of the book, both Christians and Jews were to be accorded some respect, but ultimately they were infidels, and infidels who had been conquered. Therefore equality between these groups and Muslims was an affront to the social order in the eyes of many Muslims.[40]

Reform in the Empire

Although the Empire was under external pressure to reform, by the nineteenth century there was also recognition among some Ottoman elites that the weak Ottoman state could not compete with the modernising West unless it reformed itself. For a time in the mid-nineteenth century, the reformers were in the ascendant, and a period of reform (1830–76) known as the *Tanzimat* (meaning 'reordering') ensued.[41] The reformers believed that Europe was powerful and the gap between the Ottoman Empire and Europe was increasing because of the European capacity to innovate. They argued that if the Empire were to survive it must overcome stagnation and internal corruption, and take on policies of reform and innovation. Among other things this resulted in a programme of 'Ottomanisation' which required that the first loyalty of all subjects, no matter what their communal affiliation, should be to the Empire. Though the *Tanzimat* was aimed at reforming the Ottoman Empire in order to save it, it actually 'undermined the principle of legitimacy of the Ottoman state by constituting a breach with Islamic law and centuries of Ottoman tradition'.[42] The secular and universalist principle of the equality of all subjects, who all owed equal loyalty to the Empire, contradicted the traditional millet system, based on particularist ethno-religious identities, and thus 'centuries old norms and institutions' were undermined.[43]

Internal resistance to the reform programme and continued external pressure on the Empire combined to lead to further deterioration. In effect, the reforms destroyed the last vestiges of traditional limits on the power of the Sultan without putting any effective new institutions into place, creating for the first time a situation of absolute imperial power.[44] Despite reforms on paper, most institutions which could mediate between the Sultan and his subjects 'had been abrogated or enfeebled, leaving the

[40] Davison, 'Turkish Attitudes'.
[41] See Roderic H. Davison, *Essays in Ottoman and Turkish History, 1774–1923: The Impact of the West* (University of Texas Press, 1990).
[42] Stephan H. Astourian, 'Genocidal Process: Reflections on the Armeno-Turkish Polarization', in Hovannisian (ed.) *The Armenian Genocide*, p. 56.
[43] Astourian, 'Genocidal Process', p. 57.
[44] Lewis, *Emergence of Modern Turkey*, pp. 122, 166–8.

sovereign power with nothing but the paper shackles of its own edicts to restrain it'.[45]

The 'growth of autocracy' did not go unquestioned, however. The rise to power in 1861 of the despotic Abdul Aziz was a spur to Ottoman critics of the regime, mainly writers and poets, who were influenced by European ideas (and particularly influenced by French thought) and who argued that there should be constitutional limits on the powers of the sovereign.[46] Although they would have a great impact on later generations, these so-called 'Young Ottomans' had little impact on the government at the time. To make matters worse, the increasingly dire financial problems of the Empire were exacerbated by the extravagances of the profligate Sultan Abdul Aziz, and a series of loans from European powers pushed the Empire further into debt until it was declared bankrupt in 1875. The brutal suppression of an insurrection that spread from Bosnia-Herzegovina to Bulgaria in the same year, and the murder of both the French and German consuls by a mob in Salonika in 1876,[47] combined with bankruptcy to bring the Empire nothing but discredit in the eyes of Europe. From 1881 the Empire was placed under direct financial supervision by European powers.[48]

Throughout the nineteenth century the Great Powers tried to force change on the Ottoman Empire. This usually meant demanding reforms and threatening intervention if the reforms were not implemented. This gave rise to resentment and covert resistance on the part of the Empire, which, despite the threats of intervention, was in practice rarely challenged by the Great Powers. Great Power intervention helped Greece gain independence, but in the case of Armenia, the Great Powers asserted the rights of minorities, and petitioned the Sultan on their behalf, but rarely went further than this, leaving the Armenians in an extremely vulnerable position. This vulnerability was heightened with the deposition in 1876 of Sultan Abdul Aziz and, after the brief reign of Murad V (May–31 August 1876),[49] the ascension of Abdul Hamid II.

---

[45] Ibid., pp. 131–2.   [46] Ibid., p. 132.

[47] Ibid., p. 156. An estimated 12,000 Bulgarians were killed by Ottoman troops in May 1876, some after they had surrendered.

[48] Hovannisian, 'The Armenian Question', p. 12.

[49] Murad V had been an intelligent and active supporter of liberal ideas. For this he had paid by being kept secluded and under constant surveillance by Sultan Abdul Aziz. Under these conditions, combined with the impact of alcohol abuse, by the time he became Sultan in May 1876 he was in the process of mental breakdown. The violent death of Abdul Aziz, and the murder of a number of cabinet ministers, was the final straw which pushed him into final breakdown. He was deposed on the grounds of mental incapacity on 31 August 1876, and his younger brother Abdul Hamid became Sultan. Lewis, *Emergence of Modern Turkey*, pp. 158–9.

Abdul Hamid came to power having declared some sympathy for liberal ideas and constitutional government, but once sure of his own position he quickly dispensed with any such pretence, and in 1878 suspended the short-lived Ottoman constitution which had been promulgated in 1876. This conservative Sultan rejected outright even any lip-service to the reform programmes of his predecessors and the demands of the Great Powers, declaring, 'I made a mistake when I wished to imitate my father, Abdulmecit, who sought to reform by persuasion and by liberal institutions. I shall follow the footsteps of my grandfather, Sultan Mahmut. Like him, I now understand that it is only by force that one can move the people with whose protection God has entrusted me.'[50] With the suspension of the constitution in 1878, Abdul Hamid II implemented a highly centralised, autocratic and personal form of control of the Ottoman Empire. From the perspective of a conservative head of the Islamic community, as well as head of state, the Sultan regarded the demands of the Armenian communities that promised reforms be implemented as a sign that the Armenians were traitors.

Reaction in the Ottoman Empire under Sultan Abdul Hamid II

Armenian representatives had been involved in the negotiations leading to the 1878 Treaty of San Stefano, which followed the humiliating defeat of Turkey by Russia in the Russo-Turkish war. This treaty was not accepted by England due to the territorial concessions it made to Russia, and so in mid-1978 the Congress of Berlin was convened at which a reformulated treaty, the Treaty of Berlin, was drafted. This watered down the provisions made for the autonomy of Armenians in the previous treaty and gave back to the Ottoman Empire areas in eastern Turkey which included many Armenian communities. The very presence of Armenian representatives at San Stefano and Berlin made them suspect in Abdul Hamid's eyes. Though at times it was politic for the Sultan to appear to give way to the wishes of the Great Powers, in reality from the beginning of his reign he was resistant to both what he saw as external interference in Ottoman affairs, and any claims made by his subjects, which were seen as subversive. That the Armenians, once known as the 'loyal millet', would go outside the Empire and deal with the Great Powers, and Russia in particular, made them traitorous in his eyes.[51] As a result, after the Treaty of Berlin, the Ottoman treatment of Armenians became harsher, prompting the

---

[50] Quoted in Melson, 'A Theoretical Inquiry', 500.

[51] Toynbee notes how the reforms proposed by the Armenians 'rankled' with Sultan Abdul Hamid. Toynbee (ed.), *Treatment of Armenians*, pp. 622–3.

formation of Armenian secret political societies in the 1890s. However, most of these groups were not pursuing the idea of a separate Armenian state. 'Rather, they sought cultural freedom and regional autonomy, equality before the law, freedom of speech, press, and assembly, unhindered economic opportunity, and the right to bear arms.'[52] The majority of Armenians wanted reform rather than independence from the Empire,[53] a view reflected in the policies of the Armenian Revolutionary Federation or Dashnaktsuthuin (the so-called 'Dashnaks'), who advocated political and social reform within the Empire. The only exception to this was the Hunchakian party, which advocated an independent Armenia.

Over the course of the nineteenth century, the legitimacy of the traditional organisation of Ottoman society had been undermined by the external pressure from the Great Powers, the claims of nationalist independence movements that had resulted in the loss of most of the Empire's Balkan provinces by the end of the nineteenth century, and by the changes wrought by the attempted reforms of the *Tanzimat* period. From the perspective of many Turkish Ottomans, these changes were not legitimate, and they posed a direct threat to the integrity of the Empire as they understood it. Despite the fact that most Armenians advocated reform rather than national independence, their demands that reforms be put into practice were not seen as legitimate. In a sense, the European interventions in the Empire on behalf of minorities caused more problems than they solved for the Armenians. They fed the burgeoning sense of national distinctiveness and inherent rights, which in turn pushed the Armenian community to make repeated claims that legal reforms should be put into practice. But these claims resulted in increased resentment towards Armenians, rather than the implementation of the reforms that existed on paper. As Stephan H. Astourian notes, the resistance to real reform, and the 'fictional nature of the constitutional laws' in the Empire are highlighted by the ongoing debate of 1908–14 over whether or not non-Muslims should be granted full equality – equality that on paper they had long been granted.[54] In the late nineteenth century, as Armenians took their new legal rights for granted and acted accordingly, such

---

[52] Hovannisian, 'The Armenian Question', p. 16. Hovannisian notes that the right to bear arms was not unusual at the time.

[53] There were three important nationalist parties, 'favouring a lesser or greater degree of autonomy or self-determination'. The Hunchaks were socialists influenced by Russian revolutionary thought. Melson notes that it is hard to measure the extent of support to any exact degree, but considers that on the whole 'the influence of these parties was limited'. Melson, *Revolution and Genocide*, p. 50. Also see Roderic H. Davison, 'The Armenian Crisis 1912–1914', *American Historical Review* 53:3 (1948), 484–5.

[54] Astourian, 'Genocidal Process', p. 63.

behaviour represented a threat to the traditional order, according to which *dhimmis* were inherently unequal and dependent on the goodwill of their 'hosts'. For these people to assert that they had equal status as Muslims meant they had forgone the right to goodwill and protection from their hosts.

At this point, it is perhaps worth reviewing the factors which combined to build amongst Turkish Muslims a perception of the threat posed by the Armenians, which was out of proportion to the 'actual' threat they posed, but which nonetheless was extremely significant for the treatment of Armenians by Sultan Abdul Hamid.[55] Under the traditional millet system Armenians were not, and *could not* be, equal to Muslim Ottomans. Though Armenian nationalism did not result in a secessionist movement, the demand for equality in itself posed a threat to the old order. That this old order had already been undermined made the perception of threat, and the need to reassert the old order, all the more acute.[56] Thus, the reforms promised by Sultan Abdul Hamid at the Berlin Conference in 1878 were never implemented, and the Armenian demands for reform were resented as an illegitimate imposition on the authority of the Sultan and also as a religious and cultural affront by many Muslims. The geopolitical position of the Armenians exacerbated their vulnerability. As they existed on the boundary with the rival Russian Empire which was expanding as the Ottoman Empire was contracting, the Armenians were seen as connected to Russia, and as a potential fifth column for this powerful foe. The nineteenth-century 'renaissance', fed by general education and rising literacy amongst Armenians, led to a general upsurge of cultural, political and economic activity. This took place at a time of decline in the Ottoman Empire, and made the Armenian community an object of resentment which fed a stereotype of the grasping and cunning Armenian. As with all stereotypes this view ignored the historical reality behind communal differences. The stereotype allowed resentful Ottomans to overlook the fact that trade and commerce had traditionally been looked down on by Ottomans, so these roles were fulfilled by Armenians, Greeks and other minorities. It also overlooked the fact that for most Armenian peasants (as for other peasants) life was increasingly difficult during the nineteenth century as the Empire disintegrated and repression grew.[57] It is in this context of imperial breakdown and authoritarian repression, which nonetheless failed to stem the political, social

[55] The following discussion is based on Melson, 'A Theoretical Inquiry'.
[56] Ibid., 494–509.
[57] In the nineteenth century Armenian peasants were subjected to violence and land usurpation which the state ignored. Astourian, 'Genocidal Process', p. 66; Davison, 'Turkish Attitudes'.

and cultural changes that many found bewildering, that the massacres of 1894–96 must be understood.

The massacres of 1894–1896

Between 1894 and 1896 'tens of thousands' of Armenians were massacred in the Ottoman Empire.[58] Melson defines massacre as 'the intentional killing by political actors of a significant number of relatively defenseless people'.[59] Such acts can be distinguished from genocide in that massacre has more restricted goals. 'Genocide is a kind of massacre which seeks physically to eliminate or extirpate a communal group from the social structure. In this sense, genocide is a kind of revolution.'[60] Massacre, in contrast, is generally a 'policy initiative of limited scope', used either to maintain the status quo against upwardly mobile groups, or in revolutionary situations to remove obstacles to change.[61] The massacres which occurred in the late nineteenth century, during the reign of Sultan Abdul Hamid, clearly fall into the former category. They were not aimed at the total elimination of the Armenian population from Turkey, but represented an effort to put the Armenians 'back in their place', which according to the traditional millet system was as loyal and subservient second-class subjects of the Sultan.[62] From the point of view of the Sultan, the massacres also served as 'a sort of ambassadorial note to the European powers to refrain from intervention in the domestic affairs of Turkey'.[63]

The massacres began in 1894 when villagers in Sassoun resisted the attacks and demands for taxes made by local Kurds. The Kurds appealed to the Sublime Porte claiming that the Armenian villagers were engaged in rebellion and sedition.[64] A combined force of the Ottoman army and Kurds put the town under siege, and when the Armenians finally surrendered, several thousand were massacred.[65] The European powers were

---

[58] Melson, *Revolution and Genocide*, p. 43. Toynbee estimated that more than 100,000 men, women and children were massacred. Toynbee (ed.), *Treatment of Armenians*, p. 624.

[59] Melson, 'A Theoretical Inquiry', 482.   [60] Ibid., 483.   [61] Ibid., p. 484.

[62] As we have seen in chapter 3, massacres are not always the result of a 'policy initiative' as they can result from mob violence. In drawing these distinctions between massacre, partial genocide and total genocide, Melson acknowledges that 'from the point of view of the victim it makes very little difference whether he or she is being tortured and killed in a "massacre", a "partial" or a "total" genocide'. However, in terms of what this means for the groups of which individual victims are a part, there is a difference: 'From the perspective of group survival, however, it of course does make a difference whether the killers are intent on annihilating a group or some parts of it'. Melson, *Revolution and Genocide*, p. 29.

[63] Kuper, *Genocide*, p. 116.   [64] Toynbee (ed.), *Treatment of Armenians*, pp. 624–6.

[65] Hovannisian, 'The Armenian Question', p. 16.

outraged by this atrocity, but only Russia, France and Great Britain were prepared to address the Sultan on this matter, calling again for reforms in the treatment of Armenians.[66] The Porte claimed that any killing was justified as it was a response to insurrection. However, witnesses and sympathetic Europeans argued that there was no insurrection, and that villagers had sought to defend themselves in the face of attacks by Kurds.[67]

In response to the protests of the Great Powers, the Porte appointed a commission of inquiry, but 'it refused to hear Armenian testimony'.[68] Further, some of those who took part in the massacres were decorated. Once again, 'following testimony from the consular delegates, the European powers exerted pressure on the Porte to institute reform that had been agreed upon in the treaties of San Stefano and Berlin in 1878 but which had never been implemented'.[69] Reforms were to take effect in October 1895, but before this could happen a wave of massacres of Armenians spread across the Ottoman Empire. This wave began as a response to a procession of Armenians in Constantinople, organised by the Hunchak party. The march was organised as a way for Armenians to publicly claim the rights accorded them under the promised reforms, reforms which the Great Powers were insisting should be enacted. The procession was attacked, with many killed. Following this, massacres spread across the Empire, but they were worst in 'the six vilayets [administrative provinces] of Erzerum, Bitlis, Van, Harpout, Sivas, and Diarbekir, where reforms had been slated to go into effect'.[70] To exacerbate matters still further, on 24 August 1896 some members of the Dashnak party embarked on a siege of the Ottoman Bank in Constantinople. This was intended as protest against the massacres that had occurred, and as a way of attracting the intervention of the Great Powers on behalf of the Armenians. The siege did serve to highlight the plight of the Armenians, and the revolutionaries escaped, but the Armenian people paid a high cost for this action, which 'was followed by the wholesale massacre of Armenians in Constantinople, where it is estimated that six thousand perished'.[71] These events illustrate how European pressure, with no real intervention in support of the Armenians, merely made matters worse for them.[72]

Why was massacre chosen as a way of putting the Armenians 'in their place'? Massacre had been used before in Bulgaria and also against Armenians in the Empire. It was more destructive than repression by

[66] Ibid.   [67] Melson, *Revolution and Genocide*, p. 45.   [68] Ibid.   [69] Ibid.
[70] Ibid., p. 46.   [71] Ibid.
[72] Ibid., p. 47. The numbers killed are subject to debate. Those who argue in favour of the 'provocation thesis' tend to underestimate the numbers. Melson's estimate is of anywhere between 2 per cent and 12 per cent out of an estimated 2.5 million Armenians in the Empire at that time.

police, as it damaged the fabric of communities, which would take much longer to recover.[73] And it sent a clear message to Armenians that despite legal reforms, in practice, the traditional beliefs about the place of non-Muslims in Ottoman society still held firm and the position taken by the conservative sultan who 'was not prepared to move in the direction of authentic equality and liberty'.[74] In such a situation, where legal changes had not penetrated very far, and in a society resistant to the notion of the equality of all subjects, there was what Dadrian describes as a 'lethal disjunction' between public and common law.[75] The reforms that granted equality under law had been imposed on the Empire from outside, but within the Empire there was no acceptance of such equality. With their demands for reform, the Armenians had 'broken contract' as Ottoman subjects and therefore, from the Muslim point of view, Muslims had the right to kill them and to take their property. In a manner reminiscent of the way in which Catholics in sixteenth-century France 'cleansed' the body politic through the 'rites of violence' that accompanied the St Bartholomew's Day massacres, and thus attempted to restore the Catholic order of things, Dadrian notes that during the nineteenth-century massacres Armenians were often killed according to Muslim rites of slaughter.[76] In these acts we can see a ritual intended to restore the 'proper' order of things in the Empire.

In these massacres we see the continuity of traditional beliefs and practices having a violent impact on Armenian communities, in great part as a reaction to legal reforms imposed on the Empire by the European powers. However, the Empire was by no means static and change was occurring within Muslim circles, despite Abdul Hamid's attempts to hold it back. By the end of the nineteenth century, Turkish nationalism, which played an important role in both the fall of Abdul Hamid and a few years later the Armenian genocide, was on the rise. It is to this that we now turn.

Turkish nationalism, the Young Turks and the Revolution of 1908

Turkish nationalism in the nineteenth century

During the second half of the nineteenth century the idea of a Turkish national identity developed and spread within the Ottoman Empire.

---

[73] Ibid., p. 64.   [74] Ibid., p. 65.   [75] Dadrian, 'Genocide as a Problem', 244.
[76] Natalie Zemon Davis, 'The Rites of Violence', in Natalie Zemon Davis, *Society and Culture in Early Modern France* (Stanford University Press, 1975); Dadrian, 'Genocide as a Problem', 243.

Though Europeans had used the words earlier, 'Turk' and 'Turkey' were not found in Ottoman writings until the nineteenth century. Prior to this, if the words had any meaning at all in the Empire it was to designate linguistic affiliation. From the first half of the nineteenth century, however, Western European concepts, such as 'nation, freedom, homeland, equality', began to filter through to some members of the elite.[77] Turkish nationalism was also, in no small part, a response to the national claims of subject peoples in the Ottoman Empire.[78] Sultan Abdul Hamid sought to head off both non-Muslim and Muslim nationalism by emphasising the Islamic character of the Empire and strengthening institutions which buttressed Islamic customary law. However, his policies failed and along with the non-Turkish nationalisms that sprang up across the Empire a Turkish national consciousness also emerged.[79] By the end of the nineteenth century much territory had been lost by the Empire, and by World War I Turkey would lose all its remaining European territories and meet strong resistance from Arab nationalists. These events in turn further reinforced Turkish nationalism.

The nineteenth century saw a burgeoning of Turkish social and cultural clubs, such as 'The Turkish Hearth'. The club's journal, *Turkish Homeland*, was widely read and it contributed to the spread of the idea of Turkish national identity.[80] However, many Turkish nationalists were destined to spend much of their time in exile during the reign of Abdul Hamid. Whilst some were exiled within the Empire, others made their way to European cities, in particular Paris, where they absorbed European literary and political ideas which they then reformulated into their own programmes of reform for the Ottoman Empire. The slogan of this group of reformers, who launched the Society of Union and Progress, and its newspaper, *Meshveret*, was 'order and progress'. Henceforth, the members of the society were known as the Young Turks.[81] The Young Turk movement attracted both Turks and non-Turks 'who were united in their opposition to the personal rule of the Sultan'.[82]

Opposition to the Sultan's rule brought together groups with diverse views of the Empire. The most important difference, which came to light

---

[77] Kushner, *Rise of Turkish Nationalism*, p. 3.

[78] For the period preceding the fall of Sultan Abdul Hamid see Kushner, *Rise of Turkish Nationalism*. For an account of the earlier influences on Turkish nationalism, such as European Orientalists and Turks from the Russian Empire, see Erik J. Zürcher, *Turkey: A Modern History* (London: I. B. Taurus & Co., 1993). Also see Ernest Edmondson Ramsaur Jr, *The Young Turks: Prelude to the Revolution of 1908* (New York: Russell & Russell, 1957).

[79] Kushner, *Rise of Turkish Nationalism*, p. 4.   [80] Ibid., p. 13.

[81] Chaliand and Ternon, *The Armenians*, pp. 29–30.

[82] Kushner, *Rise of Turkish Nationalism*, p. 6.

at the First Congress of Ottoman Liberals held in Paris in 1902,[83] was between liberals and integralists. The liberals, led by Prince Sabaheddin (the Sultan's nephew), and supported by non-Turks such as the Armenians, argued that the Empire must reform itself along Western lines to produce a decentralised, democratic state. They accepted a concept of Ottomanisation which was based on equality of all subjects within the Empire. The integralists, though in favour of modernisation and the return of the constitution, rejected liberalism as a basis for a reformed Ottoman Empire.[84] They argued the case for a strong, centralised state and a unified Empire. This group, led by Ahmed Riza, were much more 'Turkist' in their orientation, and were driven by a conviction that as minority nations broke away and the Great Powers pressured the Empire, whose Turkish subjects laboured under a tyrannical ruler, it was the Turks who 'needed sympathy' rather than condemnation.[85] When this group used the term 'Ottomanisation' they meant a homogenisation process by which all Ottomans would become Turks. Riza 'used the word "Ottoman" freely in connection with individual inhabitants of the Empire, Moslem and Christian, as did Sabaheddin, but in Riza's vocabulary the word did not connote so much an individual with supra-national citizenship as a person who, if he was not already a Turk, must be hammered into a reasonable likeness of one'.[86]

Young Turk nationalism

One of the most important influences on Turkish nationalism, and in particular on the Committee of Union and Progress (CUP), was the writer Ziya Gokalp.[87] Influenced by the work of Emile Durkheim, which he interpreted to suit his own vision, Gokalp presented an organic conception of Turkish society, notable for its 'rejection of minority rights and

---

[83] Ramsaur Jr, *The Young Turks*, pp. 64–75.
[84] See Ibid., pp. 21–50, on the Society in Europe in the late nineteenth century and how Abdul Hamid was able to undermine it.
[85] Ibid., p. 93.   [86] Ibid., p. 92.
[87] The name Ziya Gokalp was one of a number of pen names used by the author, which from about 1911 became permanent. Uriel Heyd notes that the name 'is an old Turkish name found in the genealogical tree of the ancestors of the Ottoman Sultans'. Uriel Heyd, *Foundations of Turkish Nationalism: The Life and Teaching of Ziya Gokalp* (London: The Harvill Press, 1950), p. 33. Gokalp was a member of the Central Committee of the CUP during the genocide of the Armenians. After World War I he denied that massacres, let alone genocide, had occurred, but acknowledged that he approved of the 'expulsions' of the Armenians. Heyd, *Foundations of Turkish Nationalism*, p. 37. He was put on trial by the military tribunal which investigated the genocide in 1919. Exiled to Malta, he returned to Turkey in 1921. On other thinkers who influenced the development of Turkish nationalism see Kushner, *Rise of Turkish Nationalism*, pp. 12–24.

individual liberties implicit in liberal nationalism, and in its glorifying the ascriptive and "primordial sentiments" of the majority group'. In this, 'it had certain affinities to *Volkism* and racism as well'.[88] Gokalp's work helped translate older conceptions of religiously based communal differences into the framework of national identities, using millet to mean *nation*.[89] Furthermore, he rejected the traditional concept that all Muslims formed a single millet, further transforming the meaning of an old concept. However, though he replaced the idea of an overarching religious community with a conception of different nations, there was some continuity with the past, as his collectivist notion of the supremacy of the society over the individual echoed the Islamist tradition.[90] And there was no doubt, according to Gokalp, that although the Turkish nation should be Islamist, the nation was paramount. He based these ideas on his reading of Durkheim, but 'rather arbitrarily' substituted 'nation' for Durkheim's conception of 'society'. As his biographer notes, 'For Durkheim's *society* he substitutes *nation*, which for the French sociologist is only one of the various social groups to which modern man belongs. Consequently he transfers to the nation all the divine qualities he had found in society, replacing the belief in God by the belief in the nation: nationalism has become a religion.'[91] As Heyd goes on to note, 'this deification of national society has most far reaching consequences' as whatever 'society desires is morally good'.[92] Heyd is silent on the Armenian genocide, but as will be seen below, the consequences of this reasoning were to be drastic for the Armenian community. He does note, however, that 'The danger involved in this conception is evident. If there are no higher values than the good of a particular society, then society is not subject to any moral obligations regarding its relations to other societies. Through identifying the ideal society with the nation, Gokalp is logically bound to approve of extreme nationalism which denies all international obligations.'[93] We might add that such a conception also denies any obligations to internal groups which are not part of 'the nation'. Gokalp's work highlights the process, common to many elites who were influenced by, and who reacted against, the West, through which Turkish nationalists gained an increasingly strong sense of the value of their own national culture and of the need to protect this culture, whilst they borrowed from Western Europe the necessary 'techniques and inventions

---

[88] Melson, 'Provocation or Nationalism?', p. 280.
[89] Heyd, *Foundations of Turkish Nationalism*, p. 61.   [90] Ibid., p. 55.
[91] Ibid., p. 57. Also see Heyd on Gokalp's rejection of Western individualism and the concept of an international society, pp. 123–6. See also Zürcher, *Turkey*, pp. 134–6.
[92] Heyd, *Foundations of Turkish Nationalism*, p. 58.   [93] Ibid.

common to all mankind and which constitute the means of progress'.[94] Gokalp's work also shows how in seeking to assert a strong and cohesive collective identity – indeed as this case shows, in seeking to *construct* such an identity – an extreme exclusivist strategy may be taken. Thus, the Armenians, already non-Muslims within the Ottoman Empire, were now also non-Turks within the Turkish national homeland, and thus doubly excluded from 'the universe of moral obligation', to return to Fein's phrase. How this moral exclusion was translated into a policy of genocide and how this was put into practice, is what I turn to next.

The Revolution of 1908 and the development of chauvinist nationalism

The revolution of 1908 came from within the Empire, driven by young officers of the 3rd Army stationed in Macedonia. These officers were affiliated with the CUP, which had been operating as a secret society within the Empire, but the CUP that won power in 1908 was not the CUP of the nineteenth century. As Ramsuar notes, the name was taken on as a sign of respect for earlier activists and does not denote strict continuity.[95] It is arguable that the revolutionaries of 1908 were not really revolutionaries at all, as they were merely intent on reinstating the constitution of 1876 which had been suspended by Abdul Hamid. The truly revolutionary aspect of the CUP would emerge after 1909,[96] but in the meantime the constitutionalist aims of 1908 engendered widespread popular support, including that of the Armenian population.[97]

Sultan Abdul Hamid was not deposed by the revolution of 1908, as the conservative elements in the rank and file of the army would not have found this acceptable. It was only after an attempted counter-revolution in 1909 that the Sultan was finally deposed and his brother installed as Sultan. Martial law was imposed at this time, the constitution was suspended and a state of siege declared.[98] Tension grew between the

---

[94] Kushner, *Rise of Turkish Nationalism*, p. 89.

[95] Ramsaur Jnr, *The Young Turks*, p. 94.

[96] Feroz Ahmad, *The Young Turks: The Committee of Union and Progress in Turkish Politics, 1908–1914* (Oxford University Press, 1969), p. 16.

[97] The Armenians supported the Young Turks, as 'reformists and revolutionaries', and they 'envisaged a new, progressive government for their common homeland'. Hovannisian, 'The Armenian Question', p. 17. Also see Davison, 'The Armenian Crisis', 482; and Toynbee (ed.), *Treatment of Armenians*, p. 626.

[98] At this time there were two massacres of Armenians in Ardana, with between 20,000 and 30,000 killed. Dadrian sees these as a 'rehearsal' for the genocide to come. Vahakn N. Dadrian, *The History of the Armenian Genocide: Ethnic Conflict from the Balkans to Anatolia to the Caucasus*, 2nd edn, revised (Providence: Berghahn Books, 1997), pp. 179–84.

CUP and the military, but the rise of opposition to the CUP, both from within its own ranks and from conservative and traditionalist elements, served to push the military and CUP closer together again. Because of opposition to their plans and policies, the CUP spent much of the period between 1908 and 1913 in the struggle to either retain or claw back power, which was constantly shifting so that it often seemed that the power and influence of the CUP had been smashed. However, by 1914, following the parliamentary elections of 1913–14 in which the CUP was the only party to contest the elections, the party gained effective political control of the Ottoman Empire.

At the time of the revolution against the Sultan in 1908 the CUP had few coherent policies beyond getting rid of Abdul Hamid and installing a constitutional government. As a consequence, once in power, they floundered for the next few years. But they were animated by a desire to reform the Empire, the reasoning being that a modernised Empire would be stronger and have a better chance of survival.[99] The group that had taken control of the CUP were by no means Westernisers, but nationalists concerned with reforming what remained of the Ottoman Empire into a centralised modern state. In the name of modernisation, followers of the CUP were installed in a range of institutions, from the army to the replacement of the entourages of the imperial family with CUP followers (and the regulation of the conduct of the imperial family). They were installed in provincial administrations and consolidated their own organisation, which despite attempts at reform still operated very much as a secret society. By 1914 the CUP had gained a stranglehold on political power.[100] 'When Parliament reconvened on 14 May [1914] all the strings of political power were in the hands of the CUP. The opposition parties were no more, the Committee had a majority in Parliament, the military was under control, and all sources of internal conflict and friction seem to have been removed.'[101]

CUP members were drawn from a broad socioeconomic range, so the party could not operate within the older political framework of the Empire. They needed a 'new focus of interests' that was not based on social position or economic class. The initial policy of Ottomanisation was replaced by a policy of pursuing 'religious and national unity', and the problem of how to organise parties along new lines was solved by replacing a system of different parties 'with the all-embracing CUP'.[102] The CUP developed a mass following, so for the first time in the history

[99] Pierre Vidal-Naquet, 'By Way of a Preface and by the Power of One Word', in Permanent Peoples' Tribunal, *A Crime of Silence*, p. 3.
[100] Ahmad, *The Young Turks*, pp. 144–60.   [101] Ibid., p. 150.   [102] Ibid., p. 162.

of the Empire politics had a populist element. The party mobilised urban crowds through mass meetings, but remained oligarchic rather than representative. 'The very idea of mobilizing the masses was revolutionary for the politics of the Empire. Yet the Committee never had any intentions of broadening the power structure to include or even serve the urban workers or the peasants.'[103] This populist appeal would be important during the Armenian genocide, as ordinary people would be exhorted to take part in the massacres – and would also be threatened with severe punishment if they assisted Armenians.

When they first came to power the CUP had an official policy of Ottomanisation and equal treatment for all minorities within the Empire.[104] This was policy in word only as their interpretation of Ottomanisation was never liberal, and by 1914 the CUP had become increasingly and overtly nationalist to the point that the regime could be identified as 'chauvinist nationalists'. As Lewis notes, the question of what was to be done to save the Empire had been debated since the sixteenth century, but debate reached its highest pitch in the nineteenth century, with Ottomanisation, Islamisation and Turkification all put forward as possible unifying principles. As Lewis explains, though Ottomanisation remained the official policy for many Young Turks, Ottomanism was no more than 'an impossible fantasy'.[105] They recognised that the Ottoman Empire was not a nation but a system of domination and hegemony, and saw their task according to this vision:

The task of the loyal members of the dominant group was to defend that group – its supremacy, or, failing that, its very existence – against the dangers that threatened it.

One of the most pressing of these dangers was uncertainty as to the very nature of that group. Were they Muslims, or were they Turks? Most of them, clearly, were both, but the question of whether the Muslim community or the Turkish nation was to be the basis of identity and the focus of loyalty was one of the most hotly debated of the time. Much would depend on the answer – the social and cultural policies of the state, its international friendships and alignments, even, it might be, its territorial limits.[106]

The Committee of National Defence, set up soon after the Balkan War broke out in 1912, was 'possibly the first explicit official use of the term national' in Turkey.[107] This built on the populist trend of politics at the time, 'and sought to substitute the identity of the nation for the old Ottoman and Islamic identity, though', Ahmad argues, 'the nation was

---

[103] Ibid.   [104] Heyd, *Foundations of Turkish Nationalism*, p. 129.
[105] Lewis, *Emergence of Modern Turkey*, p. 228.   [106] Ibid., pp. 228–9.
[107] Ahmad, *The Young Turks*, p. 162.

still not labelled "Turkish"'.[108] However, it is clear that the 'nation' under discussion was implicitly Turkish by this time, and this was the basis of corporate identity building pursued by the CUP. That this would happen was not a foregone conclusion, but in the context of a number of wars, a growing sense of the isolation and vulnerability of the Empire,[109] and increasing internal uncertainty, the most radical and chauvinist members of the CUP gained power and set about buttressing that power by any available means. One of the most potent was to be the reinforcement of a Turkish national identity – centred on Anatolia as the Turkish homeland – through the expulsion and genocide of the Armenian population.

It was during the four years following the suspension of the Ottoman constitution in 1909 that the Young Turks turned to *overtly* chauvinist policies. As Hovannisian notes, '[i]t was during this period that the concepts of Turkism and exclusive nationalism captivated several prominent Young Turks, who began to envisage a new, homogeneous Turkish state structure in place of the enervated and exploited multinational Ottoman Empire'.[110] It was around the same time that the policy which led to genocide began to take shape.[111] In February 1911, Mehmet Talat, one of the principle architects of the Armenian genocide, at that time Minister of the Interior, was 'sacrificed' by the CUP in order to placate its critics. On Talat's replacement an immediate change in policy was noted. 'Towards the provinces and the non-Turkish elements the principle of centralization was quietly withdrawn, while the capitulations were not attacked with the same vigour as before.'[112] In his discussion of this change, Feroz Ahmad does not explicitly discuss what Talat's policies were, but they can be seen in the changes that were made when he was temporarily out of power. 'These changes were recorded in a circular to provincial governors in which [it was] pointed out that the fundamental policy of the Porte was that all Ottomans should enjoy the benefits of liberty and justice, the object being "to attain unity and thus efface the discord of nationalities which was the greatest wound in the State".'[113]

By early 1911 the defeat of the CUP seemed complete, as the only two remaining CUP members of Cabinet resigned on 8 May, and Talat resigned as President of the party. But the declaration of war against

---

[108] Ibid.   [109] Davison, 'The Armenian Crisis'.

[110] Hovannisian, 'The Armenian Question', p. 18.

[111] Vahakn N. Dadrian, 'The Secret Young-Turk Ittihadist Conference and the Decision for the World War I Genocide of the Armenians', *Holocaust and Genocide Studies* 7:2 (1993), 179.

[112] Ahmad, *The Young Turks*, p. 86.

[113] Ibid., pp. 86–7. At this time Talat was elected President of the Parliamentary Party in order to 'take him out of the limelight'.

Turkey by Italy in late September of 1911 gave the CUP a new lease of life.[114] They won the 1912 elections with a landslide result.[115] This was possible as the electoral system favoured their base of support in the provinces, and they had more experience than the newly organised Liberal Union. From this position in government they passed legislation which restricted the press and prohibited public meetings. At the new parliament which opened on 18 April 1912, the new Cabinet 'now took on a decidedly Unionist colouring'.[116] It was from this point that the Central Committee of the CUP came into its own as a ruling force, quashing any dissent within its own party. 'The [CUP] had come a full circle: in 1908 the Committee had invested all the hopes of the revolution in the legislature; after four short years it was reverting to the old situation by handing back the power to the executive.'[117] By the middle of 1912 revolt was stirring and the country was again without government.[118] The Sultan briefly took charge, and a new Cabinet, hostile to the CUP, was put in place, but in 1913 a new coup occurred in which the most chauvinist nationalists within the CUP seized power. From then until the end of World War I the government was dominated by a triumvirate, 'composed of Ibrahim Enver, minister of war; Talat, minister of internal affairs and subsequently grand vizier; and Djemal, military governor of Constantinople and later minister of the marine'.[119] What Ahmad describes as the '[b]rutalisation of political life' was an important aspect of the political revolution in Turkey at this time. Having seized power, the CUP intended to hold onto it, and to this end 'repression and violence became the order of the day'.[120] Dissent often cost people their lives, as the CUP brooked no criticism of their policies. Thus the regime took a turn towards authoritarianism, no less so than the Sultan who had preceded them. But in this case the authoritarian policies were directed towards developing a modern rationalised state.

The Empire was, however, in a precarious position. With the growing list of territorial losses that had beset the Empire since 1908, the CUP became even less tolerant, with the last vestiges of pluralism fast disappearing. While the Young Turks had never had much sympathy for the claims of minorities within the Empire, the series of disasters that the Empire faced resulted in an increasingly hardened attitude towards minorities. On 5 October 1908 Bulgaria proclaimed its independence. The next day Austria annexed Bosnia-Herzegovina, which it had occupied since 1878. In 1911 the Italians captured Libya, and in 1912 the Balkan

---

[114] Ibid., pp. 90–1.   [115] Ibid., pp. 100–5.   [116] Ibid., p. 104.   [117] Ibid., p. 105.
[118] Ibid., pp. 106–8.   [119] Hovannisian, 'The Armenian Question', p. 18.
[120] Ahmad, *The Young Turks*, p. 163.

Wars erupted, in which the 'Balkan states effectively eliminated Turkey from Europe'.[121] The loss of all this territory 'in effect destroyed the multinational and multireligious character of the Ottoman Empire'.[122] When Muslim Albania and Macedonia seceded it became apparent that even a pan-Islamic Empire, advocated by some, would not work.[123]

Even in the era when a programme of Ottomanisation was put forward, what the Young Turks meant by this was not an acceptance of a supranational identification of all subjects with the Ottoman Empire in a manner consistent with diverse national identifications. On the contrary, their interpretation of Ottomanisation 'came close to Turkification of the non-Turkish elements'.[124] Though the Committee for National Defence made the first public reference to Turkish identity, a policy of Turkification was adopted at a secret meeting at the 1910 Congress of Young Turks in Salonika. In public pronouncements, Ottomanisation was labelled a failure, on the grounds that minorities were resistant to it. It was to be replaced by a policy which would strive for unity through 'material and educational development of the Empire', in order to create a 'community of interests'. But, at the same time, Talat addressed a secret conclave in Salonika and advocated a policy of 'Turkification'. Many sources are silent or evasive on what was actually said at this secret meeting. For example, Ahmad notes that Talat overemphasised the power and authority the CUP had in Istanbul, and he mentions that Talat spoke in 'harsh terms', but he does not actually tell us what Talat said.[125] Despite one publicly avowed policy, another was taking form amongst some members of the CUP, and there was a power struggle taking place within the CUP, in which Talat, Enver and others who took the most chauvinist approach, would eventually triumph. Lewis documents a report made by the British acting Consul in Manastir, which related the speech made by Talat. The report claimed that Talat argued that attempts to Ottomanise the 'Ghiaur' [a derogatory term used to denote non-Muslims] and to 'convert them into loyal Osmanli' had failed. 'There can therefore be no question of equality, until we have succeeded in our task of Ottomanizing the Empire.' Lewis then goes on to quote the words of the British Ambassador at the time, Sir Gerald Lowther, who reported: 'That the Committee have given up any idea of Ottomanizing all the non-Turkish elements by sympathetic and Constitutional ways has long been manifest. *To them "Ottoman" evidently means "Turk" and their present policy of "Ottomanization" is one of pounding the non Turkish elements*

---

[121] Melson, 'Provocation or Nationalism?', p. 277.   [122] Ibid.

[123] Ibid., p. 279. The revolt of Arab subjects of the Empire would come later. During the war the Arabs and Indian Muslims fought on the British side.

[124] Ramsaur Jnr, *The Young Turks*, p. 133.   [125] Ahmad, *The Young Turks*, p. 85.

in a Turkish mortar....'[126] Jacob Landau also notes the resolutions passed at the annual conventions of the CUP 'promoting the Turkish language for assimilation of non-Turks in the Empire'. Although the deliberations of the CUP were secret, as the remarks made by Lowther show, enough information leaked out to give consular officials a fairly clear idea of the policies that were being formulated. 'In the second annual convention, which met in Salonica in November 1910, it was decided that the Turkish language be employed in all schools throughout the Empire, aiming at denationalisation of all non-Turkish communities and instilling of patriotism among Turks.'[127]

The secret decisions made at the CUP convention in 1911 'were reportedly even more extreme: universal advancement of the Turkish language' and organisation of Turks in other, now independent states and in all states with Muslim populations, in order to form lines of communication between them and the CUP.[128] This illustrates the coexistence of Turkish nationalism and pan-Turkism in the CUP. Libaridian notes that it was a problem for the Young Turks that they still had not given up the idea of Empire and so needed a broader ideology than exclusive Turkish nationalism.[129] Prior to World War I, we can see these different strands of thought and the struggle between different elements within Turkish political life, but by the time the war broke out the CUP was entrenched, and within the CUP power was in the hands of an overtly chauvinist group which was hostile to all minorities within Turkey, and particularly hostile towards the Armenians. Bringing into reality Talat's vision of a 'homogeneous' Turkey would require 'the liquidation in one form or another of the existing heterogeneous elements',[130] and the most numerous and most vulnerable at this time were the Armenians. As Chaliand and Ternon observe:

Like the Jews at the time of the Second World War, the Armenians were then a particularly vulnerable minority. Religious hostility towards them as towards all non-Muslims (gyaurs) in the Empire was profound and the Young Turks were to exploit it; people were to be massacred, in the name of religious intolerance, to advance an ultranationalist and racist goal. In addition, they inflamed the traditional hostility of the majority group by accusing the group marked out for

---

[126] Lewis, *Emergence of Modern Turkey*, p. 214, emphasis added.
[127] Jacob M. Landau, *Pan-Turkism in Turkey: A Study in Irredentism* (London: C. Hurst & Co., 1981), p. 47. As Dadrian notes, 'Austrian, French and British intelligence sources in that city [Salonika] confirmed the occurrence of this meeting and the authenticity of the speech.' Dadrian, 'Genocide as a Problem', 254.
[128] Dadrian, 'Genocide as a Problem', 48.
[129] Libaridian, 'The Ultimate Repression', p. 207.
[130] Dadrian, 'Genocide as a Problem', 254.

massacre of treason. Like most minorities, the Armenians had no sister-state to defend their interests and found themselves at the mercy of a government settling what it is customary to call 'internal affairs'.[131]

With the outbreak of World War I the Armenian community implored the government to choose a policy of neutrality, knowing that involvement in the war would be disastrous for Armenians as it would mean another Russian–Turkish war. The CUP sealed a secret agreement with Germany in August 1914, with the creation of a 'new Turkish realm' on their minds. In October 1914 Turkey attacked Russian naval installations, bringing it openly into the war. This was the end of the remotest possibility of reform within the Empire. 'Rather, the Young Turk leaders were drawn to the newly articulated ideology of Turkism, which was to supplant the principle of egalitarian Ottomanism and give justification to violent means to transform a heterogeneous empire into a homogeneous state based on the concept of one nation–one people.'[132]

Speeches made by Enver and Talat at the time reflect this concept of the nation and the concomitant moral exclusion of Armenians from the Turkish nation-state. This was also reflected in the conversations that Talat, in particular, had with the American Ambassador to the Ottoman Empire, Henry Morgenthau, who records Talat asserting that the treatment of Armenians was a matter 'internal' to Turkey. The arguments that Morgenthau made on behalf of the Armenians, based on humanitarian grounds, were flatly rejected. Ambassador Morgenthau reported that 'when the Turkish authorities gave the orders for these deportations, they were merely giving the death warrant to a whole race; they understood this well, and in their conversations with me, they made no particular attempt to conceal the fact'.[133]

The extermination of the Armenians did not present a moral problem to Talat, as in his view they had no rights. As we have seen in the other cases in this study, however, a few individuals cannot devise and implement a policy towards a substantial number of people, in a social or cultural vacuum. In his discussion of genocide Kuper agrees with those authors who stress the important role of elites in perpetrating genocide, but with the important addendum 'that whatever the responsibility of elites, they are working with social forces present within the society, and not creating a genocidal situation out of a vacuum or transforming a harmonious equilibrium into a genocidal conflict'.[134]

---

[131] Chaliand and Ternon, *The Armenians*, p. 115.
[132] Hovannisian, 'The Armenian Question', pp. 19–20.
[133] Morgenthau, pp. 308–9, cited in Kuper, *Genocide*, p. 112.
[134] Kuper, *Genocide*, p. 50.

I have sought so far to demonstrate the conditions of profound social and political upheaval that existed as Turkey moved towards the genocide of the Armenians. The once great Empire was crumbling under the combined weight of its internal weakness and external pressure from the Great Powers, who hovered anxiously, waiting to lay claim to the pieces.[135] Under these conditions the conservative Sultan Abdul Hamid II attempted, through massacre and repression, to reimpose the traditional social framework, provided by the Islamic world view, in which non-Muslim minorities accepted their secondary status as guests of their Muslim 'hosts'. But as we have seen, by the late nineteenth century, the Sultan's repression did not serve to strengthen the Empire but once again brought the attention of the Great Powers to bear on the treatment of minorities. However, the interventions of the Great Powers caused more problems than they solved for the Armenian community in the Ottoman Empire. Although the Great Powers continually asserted the legitimacy of the principle of equality, they could, or would, do little beyond these assertions to assist the Armenians, whose claims were met with increasing hostility and massacres.

Unlike Sultan Abdul Hamid, the CUP that came to power in 1908 were not only intent on reforming the Empire, but also sought to transform it into a modern state that could compete with other European states. In this they too used repression as a means of achieving their goals, but where the Sultan had sought to keep Armenians 'in their place' the CUP devised a policy to solve the 'problem' of the Armenians by removing all of them from the 'Turkish heartland' of Anatolia. Why did the CUP choose to do this through a programme of extermination rather than a mass expulsion? To expel the Armenians to other places within the Empire was not an acceptable option as they would still want equal rights, something that the CUP, no less than the Sultan, was not prepared to grant them. It would be even less acceptable to push them over the border into Russia as this would mean a hostile population on the other side of the border with a hostile neighbour.

Beyond these reasons, there is also the question of the cultural attitudes towards the Armenians, attitudes that arose out of older religious conceptions, that made their extermination both thinkable and do-able. As I have noted above, during the nineteenth century Turkish nationalism developed in such a way that the old idea of millets as religious communities was translated into the idea of national communities. In this

---

[135] On the conflicting pressures as the Great Powers squabbled amongst themselves and jostled for influence in the Ottoman Empire prior to World War I, see Davison, 'The Armenian Crisis'.

transformation, though they were now seen as a 'nation', the Armenians were definitely not seen as equal. In fact, their claims to equality were offensive to many Muslims. In the early twentieth century, these attitudes, though disconnected from any deep religious commitment on the part of the members of the Central Committee of the CUP who were either atheist or agnostic,[136] still informed their resistance to treating the Armenians as equal subjects of the Empire. These religiously based attitudes also informed the general attitude towards the Armenians of many ordinary subjects of the Empire, for whom religious identity was still primary, even as it was being translated into national identity. Thus in terms of the emerging Turkish national identity, the Armenians could not be equal, and their demand for equality was an affront which meant that they were no longer worthy of protection. Indeed, they were truly 'beyond the bounds of moral obligation' for many if not all Muslim subjects of the Empire. It was in this context that the genocide could be put into practice.

The genocide of the Armenian people: 1915 and after

Dadrian notes that the nature of the crime of genocide 'requires conspiratorial secrecy by the perpetrators, who wish to avoid personal implication'. He goes on to argue that the decision to implement a policy of genocide follows a weighing up of perceived costs and benefits, and therefore 'requires both an operational blueprint and a plan of concealment and cover up'.[137] The implementation of a genocidal policy also depends on opportunity, and in the case of the Armenian genocide, the outbreak of World War I provided this, as the Great Powers were taken up with their own engagement in the conflict.[138] One of the central aspects of this genocide was how a process of deflection occurred in order to 'cover the tracks' of the CUP's policy. Though it was organised by the government, it was to appear as a spontaneous communal outburst.[139] The CUP incited the population by emphasising the religious differences between Muslim

---

[136] Dadrian, 'Genocide as a Problem', 232.
[137] Dadrian, 'The Secret Young-Turk', 173. In this article Dadrian presents a document dubbed 'The Ten Commandments' by British authorities, in which a ten-point plan for the implementation of the genocide was set out. The exact dating of the document is uncertain, but it seems to be from around December 1914–January 1915, just before the genocide began. As Dadrian observes 'The Ten Commandments is part of a draft plan to dislocate, deport, and destroy the Armenians of the Ottoman Empire,' 174.
[138] Indeed, Dadrian claims there is some evidence to show that the CUP's decision to enter the war was 'substantially influenced', by their desire for a chance to 'solve' their internal problems. Dadrian, 'Genocide as a Problem', 256.
[139] Ibid., 176.

and Armenian subjects which, as we have seen, retained a high level of salience in the Ottoman Empire. The genocide was declared a *jihad*, a holy war against the infidels, which was a deliberate means of inflaming religious feeling and part of a propaganda campaign which ensured the participation of many ordinary Turks in the deportations and massacres of the Armenians.[140]

The deportation, which is how the action against the Armenians was characterised, was administered by the Interior Ministry headed by Talat. This was despite the fact that the War Ministry was responsible according to the hastily promulgated Temporary Law of Deportation, which was pushed through Cabinet in May 1915 when the deportations and killings had already started.[141] '[T]he Interior Ministry and its subsidiary offices, including the provincial centres of administration, security, police, and gendarmerie forces, actually organized and administered the deportations.'[142] A central role in the genocide was played by the 'Special Organisation', a unit formed especially to deal with the 'Armenian problem', and made up almost entirely of criminals, many of whom were released from prison specifically for this purpose. Though the publicised role of the Special Organisation was in intelligence and counterespionage, it was in fact set up to help implement the genocide. 'Equipped with special codes, funds, cadres, weapons, and ammunition, they functioned as a semi-autonomous "state within the state." Their mission was to deploy in remote areas of Turkey's interior and to ambush and destroy convoys of Armenian deportees.'[143]

There is a dearth of sources on direct orders for the genocide, which should come as no surprise given the care taken at the time to cover the tracks of the operation. There is a great deal of circumstantial evidence though, and some evidence of the orders that were given still exists.[144] One of the reasons that such orders are difficult to trace is that they went through the Special Organisation and were often given verbally.

---

[140] Kuper, *Genocide*, p. 118. The government also used print media to wage a propaganda campaign against the Armenians. Dadrian, 'Genocide as a Problem', 264.

[141] Dadrian, 'Genocide as a Problem', 273.

[142] Ibid.

[143] Ibid., 274. On the use of chettes (irregular troops), the Special Organisation and the Turkish police (gendarmerie), see also the findings of Permanent Peoples' Tribunal, *A Crime of Silence*, p. 215.

[144] Dadrian's whole body of work stands as a painstaking effort to document all sources relating to the orders for genocide, the implementation of the policy, and the trials which occurred in 1919. In particular see 'The Turkish Military Tribunal's Prosecution of the Authors of the Armenian Genocide: Four Major Court-Martial Series', *Holocaust and Genocide Studies* 11:1 (1997). Though these trials were undermined by both unrepentant Turkish bureaucrats and the rise to power of the nationalist Kemalists, the documents arising from them are a valuable source of information on the genocide.

In effect, the government was giving orders on two levels, 'public orders for propaganda purposes, and private orders, to accomplish its real
intentions',[145] and much incriminating evidence was destroyed after the
war.[146] However a great number of eyewitness accounts exist, gathered
from survivors and witnesses who were citizens of both Turkey's opponents and its allies. In particular, there exist a number of eyewitness
accounts from Germans who were in the Ottoman Empire at the time as
'diplomats, engineers (in the construction of the Baghdad railway), busi-
nessmen, missionaries, doctors, nurses, teachers and soldiers, and [who]
were thus able to a greater or lesser degree to gain some insight into political and social conditions in the country'.[147] As allies of the Empire
the Germans had greater freedom of movement. Generally sympathetic
to Turkey, many witnesses had lived there for many years, and watched
the growth of chauvinist nationalism and the unfolding genocide with
horror.[148]

The order of things: outline of a genocide

The genocide was characterised by the systematic nature of the killings.
Provincial and local administrations played an important role. Local
branches of the CUP, and also of associated clubs such as 'Turkish
Hearth', meant that a network of command and implementation criss-
crossed the country, coordinated by the use of the telegraph. For it is
modern technology that allows the scale and systematic implementation
of killing that become familiar during the twentieth century. The local
branches of the Turkish Hearth 'became the catalyst of genocide, exerting
pressure where necessary on reluctant officials, inflaming the hatreds of
the populace with tales of Armenian treachery and atrocity, and in general
activating the genocidal process'.[149] Although the genocide was centrally
planned and administered, '[i]t proceeded, however, appreciably by in-
direction, that is to say not by massacres from the centre, but by setting
in motion the genocidal process, as a low-cost operation with extensive
reliance on local social forces'.[150]

[145] Walker, 'British Sources'. Amongst other accounts Walker cites two from Arab officers
of the Ottoman army, who speak of 'secret orders', pp. 56–7.
[146] Ibid., p. 57.
[147] Hofmann, 'German Eyewitness Reports', p. 61. The collection of eyewitness accounts
brought together in Toynbee (ed.), *Treatment of Armenians*, is drawn on by most later
accounts.
[148] In Germany, despite the efforts of some German citizens, there was complete censorship
on reporting events in Turkey or Armenia until 1917, and close screening of reports
until October 1918.
[149] Kuper, *Genocide*, pp. 118–19.   [150] Ibid., p. 119.

The implementation of the policy of genocide began in January 1915 with the disarming of Armenians in the Turkish army, who were then put into labour battalions until they were taken out in groups of eighty to one hundred and executed.[151] This was followed on the night of 23–24 April 1915 with the arrest of hundreds of intellectuals and leaders of the Armenian community in Constantinople. They were deported to Anatolia where they were put to death.[152] Before the deportations took place all able-bodied men in towns and villages were rounded up. They were ordered to assemble at the local government building and then marched to the outskirts of the town or village and executed. The manner of execution varied according to location, though the programme of organised executions was the same.[153] They were shot, hacked to death, and in some cases taken out to sea and drowned. The disarming of the remaining Armenian population took place at the same time.[154] Throughout the whole process Armenian property was seized by the government.[155]

On 24 May 1915, aware of what was happening, the Entente powers called for Turkey to stop this assault on the Armenian population 'on the grounds of humanity and civilisation'.[156] The Turkish response was to issue the May 1915 general decree on the deportation of Armenians, which 'tried to justify, as necessary war-time precautions, measures which, in fact, had already been introduced at the end of March in Cilicia and the province of Erzurum'.[157] Talat declared that the Armenians 'were untrustworthy, that they could offer aid and comfort to the enemy, and that they were in a state of imminent nationwide rebellion, [he] ordered their deportation from the war zones to relocation centres – actually the deserts of Syria and Mesopotamia'.[158] The Armenians were portrayed as pro-Russian (though this was not borne out in fact) and as the greatest threat to Turkey's security. However, in reality, the Armenians were not to be driven out from war zones alone, but from the whole Empire with the exception of the cities of Constantinople and Smyrna, the two major cities closest to Europe with the highest concentration of foreign diplomats and merchants, who could act as witnesses.[159]

---

[151] Hofmann, 'German Eyewitness Reports', p. 70.
[152] As Hovannisian notes, many of these were personal associates of the Young Turks. Hovannisian, 'The Armenian Question', p. 20.
[153] See the findings of Permanent Peoples' Tribunal, *A Crime of Silence*, p. 216.
[154] Melson, *Revolution and Genocide*, p. 143.
[155] Dadrian, 'Genocide as a Problem', 267.   [156] Ibid., 262.
[157] Hofmann, 'German Eyewitness Reports', p. 72. On 1 March 1915 the government suspended Parliament, ensuring that any opposition to their policies would not get a hearing. Dadrian, 'Genocide as a Problem', 273–4.
[158] Hovannisian, 'The Armenian Question', p. 20.
[159] The resolve of the German General Liman von Sanders, who threatened to turn his troops on anyone who took action against Armenians, was also behind the survival of

After the proclamation of the deportation law the deportations accelerated. Women, children and older men were deported from their homes and driven into the desert, either into Syria along the Euphrates or into Mesopotamia. They were subjected to rape and murder along the way, with many girls and young women being carried off and never seen again. The Armenians were attacked by members of the army, the Special Organisation, bands of Kurds and in some cases the local Muslim population. Many children were taken to be brought up as Muslims. Many died along the way from starvation, exposure or mistreatment, and many, particularly women, threw themselves and their children into the Euphrates as the only way to avoid further suffering.[160] Those who departed to Mesopotamia had some chance of survival, whereas those who were taken along the Euphrates into Syria had no chance. '[T]he Armenians were driven ever onward towards Deir-el-Zor; approximately 200,000 reached their destination. Between March and August 1916, orders came from Constantinople to liquidate the last survivors remaining in the camps along the railway and the banks of the Euphrates.'[161] Despite these policies there were still some Armenians left in Turkey. Some were hidden by Turkish or Kurdish friends, or saved by resolute officials who were brave enough to risk their own lives by defying the orders from the government. But the Armenian presence in the Ottoman Empire was destroyed with more than a million people killed. In 1915, when the genocide began, in the light of changing international norms of legitimate state behaviour, the Allies pleaded with the Ottoman government to stop what they were doing. At the same time, they also promised that justice would be done at the end of the war, and that the Allied governments 'will hold personally responsible . . . all members of the Ottoman government and those of their agents who are implicated in such matters'.[162] Despite some attempts to bring the perpetrators to justice, this promise was not kept.

The CUP was deposed in late 1918, and under allied pressure a domestic trial of those held responsible for the genocide was mounted in 1919.[163] At this time the blame for the genocide was placed squarely at

the populations of Symrna and Adrianopolis. Permanent Peoples' Tribunal, *A Crime of Silence*, p. 218.

[160] For the accounts of survivors and eyewitnesses see Toynbee (ed.), *Treatment of Armenians*, for example, document number 12, p. 25, which is an account given by a German nurse. Also see Hofmann, 'German Eyewitness Reports', pp. 72–3, for an account of Lepsius' chronology of the deportations, and Donald E. Miller and Lorna Touryan Miller, 'Women and Children of the Armenian Genocide', in Hovannisian (ed.) *The Armenian Genocide*.

[161] Permanent Peoples' Tribunal, *A Crime of Silence*, p. 217.

[162] Dadrian, 'Genocide as a Problem', 262.

[163] Dadrian, 'The Turkish Military'. Talat, Enver and Djemal were sentenced to death in absentia.

the feet of the CUP rather than on the Turkish state as a whole. While it is true that the CUP were the instigators of this policy, it is also true that it could not have been carried out without the acquiescence of large numbers of the population. This is not to deny that some Turks tried to shelter Armenians, but this response of looking for an easy scapegoat highlights the lack of national self-reflection on this issue.

The domestic trials of 1919 were in effect sidelined, and once the nationalist regime of Mustafa Kemal came to power, they seemed intent on denying that the genocide had ever occurred. They were aided in this by the path of international politics between 1918 and 1923, when Turkey was recognised as an independent sovereign state. During the genocide Talat rejected the right of other powers to interfere in a matter which, he argued, concerned the security of Turkey's borders. His attitude 'implicitly relied upon the rule of international law that "the state is entitled to treat its own citizens at discretion."'[164] As we shall see in chapter 6, while this view was not universally endorsed at the time, it did prevail and moral abhorrence towards the genocide was not translated into effective international action. Once Kemal came to power, the new regime rejected the right of the Allies to impose any conditions on them, and asserted the sovereignty of Turkey. In the scramble for influence as the Empire finally collapsed, the principles of legitimate state action haltingly articulated at this time, were lost.[165]

Conclusion

In this chapter I have investigated the role of pathological homogenisation – in this case through genocide – in early twentieth-century Turkey. Animated by virulent nationalism, the Young Turk regime set about systematically exterminating the Armenian population as the Ottoman Empire collapsed. I have contrasted the World War I actions of the Young Turks with those of Sultan Abdul Hamid II in the late nineteenth century. The Sultan used massacres of the Armenian population in an attempt to repress their demands for equality and as a way of letting the Great Powers know that he had no intention of complying with their demands. He thus attempted to put the Armenians back in what had been the traditional place of non-Muslim minorities in the Empire. That is, they were tolerated as long as they accepted institutionalised discrimination. In contrast to the Sultan's actions, those of the Young Turks were

[164] Dadrian, 'Genocide as a Problem', 278.
[165] Dadrian, *History of the Armenian Genocide*, pp. 304–5; Permanent Peoples' Tribunal, *A Crime of Silence*, p. 221.

not directed towards keeping the Armenians 'in their place'. This regime sought to construct a homogeneous national state in which there was no place for Armenians. Indeed, the extirpation of the Armenians played an important role in the construction of a supposedly homogeneous population within Turkey: it was an initial 'clearing of the ground' – both literally and symbolically.

As I have demonstrated, there were many continuities between the Ottoman Empire of the late nineteenth and early twentieth centuries. In particular, the cultural framework, provided by the Islamic world view, which had underpinned the political organisation of the Empire, still played an important role. During the late nineteenth century, in the hands of nationalist writers such as Gokalp, the term 'millet' came to designate 'nation' rather than a religious community. Throughout this transformation, however, the social categories of insider and outsider, superior and inferior that the term millet carried remained salient for many Muslims. Thus, although Turkish nationalism now differentiated between the Turkish and Armenian nations, there was great resistance to the concept that the Armenians could attain equal status within the Empire. In this way the earlier concept of toleration of non-Muslim peoples of the book as long as they accepted institutionalised discrimination – and the other side of this which was a total rejection of any moral obligations towards them if they broke this norm – was still important in informing attitudes towards Armenians, well into the twentieth century. During the nineteenth century, with their claims to equality the Armenians had, in the eyes of the Sultan and many of his Muslim subjects, 'broken contract'. Likewise, in the twentieth century their claims to equal rights were treated with hostility and they came to be seen by the Young Turk regime as a 'problem' to be dealt with by extreme measures.

Although the leaders of the Young Turk regime were not particularly religious themselves, their hostility towards the Armenians had its origin in the religious/cultural attitudes that were widespread in the Ottoman Empire at the turn of the century. They in turn played on and exacerbated these attitudes in the wider community in order to legitimate and to implement the genocide. But where did the idea that it was necessary to remove *all* Armenians from Turkey, and that this should be done through extermination rather than expulsion, come from? The answer lies in the fact that the Young Turks were intent on carving out a homogeneous national state in a context of imperial breakdown and war. They were surrounded by independent states that had once been part of the Empire, and by Great Powers, particularly Russia, that they saw as predatory. To expel the Armenians into any of these territories was unthinkable. Yet according to the chauvinist nationalist view of the Young Turks, as long as the Armenians existed inside Turkey, particularly in what had come to be understood as the Turkish 'fatherland' of Anatolia where most Armenians lived, they posed a numerous and highly visible threat to the unity of the Turkish national state.

Thus, through the policy they embarked upon, the Young Turks sought to construct a cohesive Turkish national identity. At the same time they sought to deflect any challenges to their authority. Accusing the Armenians of treason and claiming that they posed a security threat, any Ottoman subject who spoke up on their behalf, or who sought to protect Armenians, as some did, could be labelled as traitors. Thus, this authoritarian regime appealed to Turkish national identity to bolster their own precarious legitimacy. As Kuper observes, however, genocide does not take place in a social vacuum. The genocide could only even be conceived of, and could only be put into practice because of the prevailing attitudes towards Armenians which cast them as outsiders with no rights.

Like the Sultan before them, the Young Turks rejected the pleas of the Great Powers to modify their treatment of the Armenian minority. However, where the Sultan sought to reestablish the Empire on its traditional base, and despite the fact that they had not entirely let go of imperial and pan-Islamic ambitions, the Young Turks were intent on building a modern, rationalised state in what was left of the Empire, a state that Europe would have to take seriously. To this end, they asserted the principle of sovereignty over internal matters. In doing this they had picked up one of the fundamental principles animating the system of states, and also picked up the dynamic of inclusion and exclusion at work in the states system, with the national principle now providing the criterion for membership within states.

As we have seen, by the late nineteenth century the national principle of political legitimacy that had swept across Europe started to take effect inside the centre of the Empire, within Turkey itself. In the early twentieth century, as the Young Turks sought to build a 'strong' state in Europe, they also sought to construct a 'strong', that is, homogeneous state in Turkey. In this we see a complex mixture of the new national principle that now provided the criterion for membership in the political community, and older, traditional religious attitudes that informed how the new principle was understood. But it was not only the principle of political legitimacy and membership of political community that had changed. As the Empire collapsed the Young Turks turned their attention towards a different form of political organisation, so successful in Europe: the sovereign, territorial state. It was this they were intent on building and they used the means that seemed to them most likely to achieve their end.

5 'Ethnic cleansing' and the breakup of Yugoslavia

This fourth case study brings us into the late twentieth century and the processes of state disintegration and reformation in the former Yugoslavia. Through the events in the former Yugoslavia – particularly in Bosnia between 1992 and 1995 and more recently in Kosovo during the late 1990s – the world is now familiar with the euphemistic term 'ethnic cleansing'. The practices covered by this term highlight how pathological homogenisation is still an attractive strategy for some would-be state-builders. This is particularly so in the absence of democratic institutions and, as was the case in the former Yugoslavia, such strategies may be directed at staving off democratic change. Ironically, the principle of self-determination, born with the democratic revolution and now a structuring principle of the international system of states, can be seen at its most awry and destructive in the former Yugoslavia. As Robert Hayden notes, '[t]he logic of "national self-determination" in Yugoslavia not only legitimates homogenisation of the population but has also made that process so logical as to be irresistible. The course of the war has followed this logic of establishing the nation-state by eliminating minorities.'[1] Such readings of national self-determination are of course at odds with international standards of human rights and legitimate statehood and I trace the tensions in the international system in more detail in chapter 6. In this chapter I focus on attempts to eliminate significant sections of the population from areas of the former Yugoslavia in the name of national homogeneity.

These policies were implemented through a number of means, including systematic mass murder, the systematic rape and impregnation of women and girls, torture and the mass deportation of civilians. It also included the systematic destruction of sites of cultural, historical and religious significance in an attempt to obliterate the past which did not accord with history as nationalists were intent on rewriting it. Thus, '[a]fter all

---

[1] Robert M. Hayden, 'Imagined Communities and Real Victims: Self-Determination and Ethnic Cleansing in Yugoslavia', *American Ethnologist* 23:4 (1996), 795.

the mosques in the formerly Muslim-majority city of Zvornik were systematically destroyed, the warlord Branko Grujic declared, "There never were any mosques in Zvornik"'.[2]

While atrocities were committed by all sides in the former Yugoslavia, I am primarily concerned with the policies of the Serbian government under the leadership of Slobodan Milosevic, and its Bosnian-Serb clients under the leadership of Radovan Karadzic, which stand out as examples of a systematically implemented policy to change the constituent population of Bosnia-Herzegovina by force in the name of a 'Greater Serbia', and thus reconstruct the boundaries of Serbia both symbolically and physically.[3] It is these measures that this chapter investigates, followed by a short epilogue on events in Kosovo and Serbia in the second half of the 1990s, culminating in the 1999 NATO bombing campaign against Serbia, Slobodan Milosevic's fall from power in late 2000 and his subsequent extradition to the Hague in late June 2001.[4]

Throughout, I am interested in answering the following questions: what was the relationship between the symbolic construction of otherness, and the cultural resources it drew upon, and the implementation of a programme of pathological homogenisation? What role did these practices play in state-building as the multinational Yugoslavia collapsed, and why did the governments of Serbia and Croatia and the Bosnian Serbs choose this path to state-building? In order to answer these questions, I begin with a brief account of the construction of the first and second Yugoslavias after World War I and World War II respectively, and consider aspects of continuity and change in these developments. I then go on to provide an account of the collapsing legitimacy of communism in Yugoslavia during the 1980s and the rise of a virulent strand of ethnic nationalism, for the break-up of Yugoslavia was preceded by the delegitimation of the structures and institutions of the existing multinational Yugoslav state.[5]

---

[2] Michael Sells, 'Religion, History, and Genocide in Bosnia-Hercegovina', in G. Scott Davis (ed.), *Religion and Justice in the War Over Bosnia* (New York: Routledge, 1996), p. 25. As Sells goes on to note (p. 26), this not only destroyed the evidence of 500 years of Bosnian Muslim civilisation in this town, but it also obliterated five hundred years of coexistence between the two major groups in the area, Muslims and Serbs.

[3] On the commission of atrocities by all parties to the conflict, see Steven L. Burg and Paul S. Shoup, *The War in Bosnia-Herzegovina: Ethnic Conflict and International Intervention* (Armonk: M. E. Sharp, 1999), pp. 171–81. On the radicalisation of, and retaliation by Bosnians, see Norman Cigar, *Genocide in Bosnia: The Policy of 'Ethnic Cleansing'* (College Station: Texas A & M University Press, 1995), pp. 137–8.

[4] Milosevic first appeared before the International Criminal Tribunal for the Former Yugoslavia on 3 July 2001, on charges of crimes against humanity.

[5] Dennison Rusinow, 'The Avoidable Catastrophe', in Sabrina Petra Ramet and Ljubisa S. Adamovich (eds.), *Beyond Yugoslavia: Politics, Economics, and Culture in a Shattered Community* (Boulder: Westview Press, 1995), p. 17.

The breakdown that occurred was the second time that Yugoslavia had broken apart. Though some commentators have characterised this breakdown as inevitable, it only became so in the late 1980s when the inability or refusal of politicians from Yugoslavia's different constituent republics to deal with mounting economic, political and social problems – themselves the product of the incompatibility of the communist system and change – sealed Yugoslavia's fate. As Dennison Rusinow notes, what was inevitable was that violence would likely accompany any breakup. However, the scale of this violence was beyond prediction. The magnitude of this violence is 'comprehensible only as the result of deliberate incitement and exploitation, by the same politicians, of historical or personal memories of ancient and recent wrongs and stereotypes'.[6] Thus culture, history and memory became violent instruments in the hands of self-serving elites who opened old wounds, created new grievances, and incited fear and violence in order to reap benefits, which were inevitably personal rather than for the general population and the state as they promised. Such benefits were also inevitably short term, leaving another legacy of destruction and violence for future generations to inherit. Despite their claims to be the bearers of national pride, they caused massive destruction to their own people as well as others. As Paul Shoup notes with reference to Serbia, 'A government dedicated to democratic principles in Serbia – even if it was nationalist – would have chosen a different path in settling its differences with Croatia, if only because it would have the interests of Serbia more at heart.'[7] But for these nationalist rulers pathological homogenisation based on a nationalist criterion of identification provided an alternative to democratisation.

What I seek to illuminate in this chapter is the relationship between the clearly cynical use of nationalist symbols and imagery by nationalist elites and the emotional purchase that these have for at least some sections of the population. For example, although Slobodan Milosevic manipulated, encouraged and exacerbated cultural stereotypes and resentments, he did not create them. These were the cultural resources he found at his disposal, if democratisation and economic reform, with the attendant possibility of losing authority, was to be avoided. It is in this context that I investigate the development of the 'myth of Kosovo' and Milosevic's skilled use of this in his rise to power as a nationalist leader. I then discuss how the myth of Kosovo legitimated the form of pathological homogenisation known as 'ethnic cleansing' that was practised in

[6] Rusinow, 'The Avoidable Catastrophe', p. 14.
[7] Paul Shoup, 'Titoism and the National Question in Yugoslavia: A Reassessment', in Martin van den Heuvel and Jan G. Siccama (eds.), The Disintegration of Yugoslavia, Yearbook of European Studies, vol. 5 (Amsterdam: Rodopi, 1992), p. 71.

Bosnia-Herzegovina between 1992 and 1995, and how this proceeded. Finally, I return to events in Kosovo in the late 1990s. Through discussion of these events I trace the relationship between the manipulation of symbolic and cultural resources, and political action in the form of pathological homogenisation used as a strategy of state-building.

Mass killing returns to Europe in the late twentieth century

As with the other cases in this study, for the events that so recently took place in the former Yugoslavia to occur, a process had to take place by which victims were clearly marked as outsiders, 'not like us', and not of the community within which sanctions against violence still held. In this way, as Leo Kuper notes, '[s]ince the victims are not human, the inhibitions against their slaughter cease to be operative'.[8] In chapter 4 I observed that genocide does not occur in a social or cultural vacuum, and that though a prohibition of violence towards 'one's own kind' may in fact still be in place throughout such a period, what is crucial is the social and cultural construction of who is and is not of 'one's own kind'. The delineation of the categories of 'us' and 'them' was an important factor in the ethnic cleansing that occurred in the former Yugoslavia. As we saw in the case of the Armenian genocide, this process is much easier when a community has long been decreed outside what Helen Fein describes as 'the sanctified universe of moral obligation'.[9] In Bosnia-Herzegovina, media campaigns which stressed the lack of humanity of non-Serbs and the threat they posed to Serbs, preceded the physical expulsion, rape and murder. These drew in the case of Muslims on the historic loss of Kosovo to the Ottoman Empire in the fourteenth century, and in the case of Croatians on the World War II atrocities committed by the Ustasha regime. As Fein observes with reference to earlier genocides, 'leaders could not have chosen annihilation . . . had not the victims been previously defined as basically of a different species, outside of the common conscience and beyond the universe of obligation'.[10] To modify this somewhat for this context, we might say the leaders could not have implemented their decision to pursue ethnic cleansing, if they had not first been able to convince at least a sizeable proportion of their population that the victims were simultaneously less than human and posed a mortal

---

[8] Leo Kuper, *Genocide: Its Political Use in the Twentieth Century* (New Haven: Yale University Press, 1981), p. 85.

[9] Helen Fein, *Accounting for Genocide* (New York: The Free Press, 1979), p. 4.

[10] Ibid., p. 8.

threat to the existence of their own community. In turn, this community was defined through the existence of this threat. For the whole process of expelling non-Serbs and creating a 'homogeneous' state was also about constructing a unitary identity for Serbs, convincing *them* that they were one people, simultaneously heroic and victimised by non-Serbs within Yugoslavia (and also by the international community), and thus united against overwhelming odds. To repeat, this is not to argue that Serbia alone implemented discriminatory policies,[11] or to deny that atrocities were committed on all sides, but it is to argue that Serbian actions were part of a systematically implemented government policy, which aimed at the homogenisation of the population through 'ethnic cleansing' or the 'forced unmixing of peoples' who for as long as they lived intermixed were a living refutation of the nationalist ideologies which arose in Yugoslavia. Thus, as Hayden argues:

extreme nationalism in the former Yugoslavia has not been only a matter of imagining allegedly 'primordial' communities, but rather of making heterogeneous ones unimaginable. In formal terms, the point has been to implement an essentialist definition of the nation and its state in regions where the intermingled population formed living disproof of its validity: the brutal negation of social reality in order to reconstruct it . . . It is this reconstruction that turns the imagination of community into a process that produces real victims.[12]

It is this reconstruction of political identity through strategies of pathological homogenisation, and the central role this played in reconstituting sovereign states amid the breakdown of Yugoslavia, that is the focus of this chapter.

History and myth in the disintegration of Yugoslavia

The first Yugoslavia

The multinational state of Yugoslavia was a product of the momentous changes which occurred following World War I and the crumbling of both the Austro-Hungarian and Ottoman Empires. The Kingdom of the South Slavs, as it was known, was constituted under Serbian hegemony. The Kingdom was torn apart during World War II and reconstituted as the Federal Republic of Yugoslavia after the war under the rule of Josip Broz Tito and the Yugoslav League of Communists. The brief discussion

---

[11] On the institutionalisation of discriminatory citizenship rules in the Yugoslav successor states, see Robert M. Hayden, 'Constitutional Nationalism in the Formerly Yugoslav Republics', *Slavic Review* 51:4 (1992).
[12] Hayden, 'Imagined Communities', 783–4.

of the 'first' and 'second' Yugoslavias which follows highlights how the cultural and historical 'repertoire' on which nationalists drew in the late twentieth century has its roots in nineteenth-century nationalism.

In the nineteenth century, although the European powers focused on Russia and the disintegrating Ottoman Empire, the 'national question' was just as important in the South Slav region that came to be known as Yugoslavia. However, the quest for national equality on the part of many South Slavs was not of high importance to Western European diplomats who regarded them as irrelevant to the concerns of the Great Powers.[13] Ivo Banac argues that Western statesmen had little real understanding of the national question in Eastern Europe as the paths of national development had been so different in the East and West. In particular, the West had no 'shared history of subjugation to foreign rulers',[14] as in Eastern Europe. In the case of Yugoslavia its constituent parts were split between the Ottoman and Austro-Hungarian Empires. Indeed, under the dual monarchy, parts of Croatia came under different rulers. The kingdom of Serbia was first to loosen imperial ties, gaining autonomy from the Ottoman Empire in 1830 and independence in 1878.

From its inception after World War I Yugoslavia was riven by internal conflict. This was not, however, the result of some natural state of affairs in relations between South Slavs, but the product of different histories and loyalties under different imperial rulers, and the development of competing national ideologies in the nineteenth century, as in other parts of Europe. The Illyrian movement in Croatia was pan-Slavic in orientation, and most of these 'awakeners' were prepared to forgo their own dialect and put forward the Stavokian dialect, spoken in both Croatia and Serbia, in the interests of linguistic unity. In contrast to this, Serbian nationalism was from the beginning assimilationist in orientation. The Orthodox Church cultivated the idea of a separate Serbian national identity well into the nineteenth century and on gaining independence from the Ottoman Empire in 1878 Serbia was able to develop autonomous state institutions, with particular emphasis placed on the development of Serbian military forces. In the late nineteenth century, the idea of a Serb national identity was secularised when it was tied, in the minds of nationalists, to the use of a Serbian language rather than to the Orthodox Church. The chosen language was once again the Stavokian dialect, but rather than a pan-Slavic interpretation of the widespread use of this dialect, Serbian nationalists considered anyone who spoke this to be Serbian. Thus a

[13] Ivo Banac, *The National Question in Yugoslavia: Origins, History, Politics* (Ithaca: Cornell University Press, 1984), p. 11.
[14] Ibid., p. 12.

Greater Serbia could be traced (so it was argued) around the contours of all those who were 'really' Serbs by dint of their language. This assimilationist view was to inform the later attitude of Serb elites towards a unified Yugoslavia.

In the late nineteenth century the pan-Slavic view of Croatian identity was challenged by a nationalist ideology that argued that Croatia constituted a separate nation and was thus entitled to its own state, in what amounted to an inversion of the 'Greater Serbian' idea into the idea of a 'Greater Croatia'. However, this differed from Serbian nationalism as it was exclusionary rather than assimilationist. In response to Greater Serbianism, this version of Croatian nationalism was explicitly defined in terms of the exclusion of Serbs and a sharp distinction was drawn between Catholic Croatians and Orthodox Serbs. This exclusivist Croatian nationalism also envisaged that Greater Croatia would encompass Serbia. The distinction made between Croats and Serbs was a cultural one, which used religion as the marker of difference, but allowed for the possibility of conversion of Serbs to Catholicism. However, religion was not used as a cultural marker in the same way with Slavic Muslims, whose religious affiliation was ignored and who were regarded as Croats. As the Slavic Muslims made no national claims at this time, they did not pose a threat to Croatian identity in the eyes of Croat nationalists.[15] It was this exclusivist conception of Croatian statehood *vis-à-vis* Serbs that informed the actions of the World War II 'Independent State of Croatia'.

At the end of World War I, when it became evident that the Austro-Hungarian Empire was on the verge of collapse, negotiations began between a number of national groups over the constitution of a unitary South Slav state. The National Council of Croats, Slovenes and Serbs, representing the lands controlled by Austria-Hungary until the end of the war, argued for unification on the basis of equality for all the constituent parts of the new state. This was not the form of unification envisaged by the Serbian government, who regarded the role of Serbia as paramount. In negotiations at the end of 1918, pressured by the spectre of imperial collapse and the vulnerable position in which this would leave some nations, the unification of the South Slav lands was agreed upon, despite the lack of guarantees of the rights of non-Serbs. In effect, the National

---

[15] Bette Denich, 'Dismembering Yugoslavia: Nationalist Ideologies and the Symbolic Revival of Genocide', *American Ethnologist* 21:2 (1994), 372–4. On the important role of the Orthodox and Catholic Churches in both Serbian and Croatian nationalism see Pedro Ramet, 'Religion and Nationalism in Yugoslavia', in Pedro Ramet (ed.), *Religion and Nationalism in Soviet and East European Politics*, 2nd edn (Durham: Duke University Press, 1989), pp. 302–23.

Council handed over control of Croatia, Slovenia and Bosnia-Herzegovina to the Serbian government under the increasingly authoritarian regent, later King, of Serbia, Alexsandar. The government took an assimilationist view that all non-Serbs were now part of Greater Serbia.

Renamed the Kingdom of Yugoslavia in 1929, post World War I Yugoslavia represented the first attempt to construct a centralised state in the wake of imperial breakdown. However, Serb assimilationism meant that this was done in a manner which resulted in the routine violation of the rights of non-Serbs. Serbian law was imposed across the Kingdom without consultation, and Serbian political institutions and culture, which were much more militaristic than elsewhere, were imposed on Croatia and Bosnia in particular. This was attended by abuses of power, such as systematic beatings of the population. Education was centralised, and a single currency was brought about through the devaluation of the (Austro-Hungarian) crown against the (Serbian) dinar, robbing Croatian peasants of savings and changing the economic balance in Serbia's favour.[16] Such events fed anti-Serb Croatian nationalism and encouraged the development of the underground Ustasha (uprising) movement, which used terror in pursuit of an independent Croatia and which was responsible for the assassination of King Alexsandar in 1934.[17]

In January 1929, King Alexsandar proclaimed his 'personal regime', ushering in an era of dictatorship and police terror. Though officially following a policy of Yugoslavian unitarianism, in practice he pursued a policy of Serbianisation.[18] Serbia did not recognise Bosnia-Herzegovina as a distinct province, as in a manner parallel to that of Croatian nationalists, the prevailing Serbian view was that Slavic Muslims were 'really' Serbs. In effect, Bosnia-Herzegovina was 'partitioned out of existence' as different districts were joined to areas of Croatia, Serbia and Montenegro, in order to ensure Serb majorities in each of these wherever possible. Following the assassination of the King in 1934, the governing base was broadened somewhat, but this was soon followed by increased repression, and from 1939 the dismemberment of Bosnia-Herzegovina continued. In a manner that seems familiar from the perspective of the late twentieth century, Bosnia-Herzegovina was divided between Croatia and Serbia on the basis of which of the two groups had a majority in a particular area. How the Muslims saw matters, indeed the very existence of an

---

[16] The above is based on the account in Banac, *The National Question*.
[17] Denich, 'Dismembering Yugoslavia', 374.
[18] Ivo Banac, 'Bosnian Muslims: From Religious Community to Socialist Nationhood and Postcommunist Statehood, 1918–1992', in Mark Pinson (ed.), *The Muslims of Bosnia-Herzegovina: Their Historic Development from the Middle Ages to the Dissolution of Yugoslavia* (Cambridge, MA: Centre for Middle Eastern Studies, Harvard University, 1994), p. 138.

independent identity shared by Slavic Muslims, was overlooked: 'The division was effected by discounting the Muslims altogether . . . the Muslim plurality made no difference.'[19]

From these events it is clear that post World War I state-builders either ignored, or attempted to repress non-Serbs. Banac argues that the Yugoslav intellectuals who set up the original Yugoslavia 'looked upon themselves as engineers who would pull a passive backward country into modernity, if need be by force'.[20] In this they ignored cultural and historical differences, and their efforts to impose their policies provoked great resistance. As we have seen in the previous case studies, this was not the first time that centralisation and homogenisation were sought through the imposition of the religion or culture of a dominant group. This also alerts us to the fact that the bases of the conflict that erupted in the late twentieth century are to be found in modern political processes, that is, in the first attempt at building the Yugoslav state in the wake of imperial breakdown – that took the form of an attempt at pathological homogenisation – which can be traced to the rise of nationalist ideologies in the nineteenth century, rather than to inherent 'ancient hatreds' between the different ethnic groups.

Yugoslavia differs from the other cases in this study, however, in that no constituent group had a clear majority, and the number of national groups also added to the complexity of the situation. Given these conditions, Serbian hegemonic aspirations faced intense resistance. The failure of the government to take into account cultural and historical differences and to treat each constituent group with equality and dignity could only be destabilising in such a multinational political entity which purported to be a modern state rather than an empire. 'Instead of creating a powerful modern state, the intellectual makers of Yugoslavia paved the way for instability, dictatorship, and foreign intervention.'[21] Indeed, the first Yugoslavia was not to survive for long, as it was invaded and partitioned during World War II, and was torn apart by civil war. However, this attempt at state-building through assimilating all South Slavs to the dominant Serb state institutions and political identity set up a dynamic of competing national claims and counter claims that would, as Banac argues, be a continuing source of instability.

In April 1941 Yugoslavia was invaded by the Nazis. A puppet government was installed in Croatia and Bosnia-Herzegovina 'became an integral part of the collaborationist Independent State of Croatia'.[22] This did not mean autonomy for Bosnian Muslims, however, as the Ustasha

---

[19] Ibid., p. 140.   [20] Banac, *The National Question*, p. 225.
[21] Ibid., p. 225.   [22] Banac, 'Bosnian Muslims', p. 141.

saw them as Croats of Muslim confession. Though the Ustasha wooed the Muslims with displays of respect, there was never any real sharing of power.[23] As in recent times, during the war there were atrocities on all sides of the ideological and communal divides. In Croatia, the Nazi-backed Ustasha, drawing on the anti-Serb sentiments that had been part of Croatian nationalism since the late nineteenth century, embarked on a programme which included forced conversions to Catholicism, expulsions into Serbia, and the physical extermination of Serbs as well as other non-Croat groups such as Jews and Gypsies.[24] As Bette Denich notes, the population was taken by surprise when the 'metaphors of purification' which stressed a Croatia 'cleansed' of Serbs, were taken literally and translated into a policy of extermination.[25] In Kosovo and other Albanian areas which had been merged with Nazi controlled Albania, Serb and Montenegrin minorities were targeted. The Serb population of Bulgarian-occupied Macedonia (around 100,000 people) was pushed across the border into German-controlled Serbia. 'Moslems from Bosnia, Germans and Hungarians from Vojvodina were recruited to fight the Nazi war in the Balkans.'[26] The actions of those Muslims who took part in attacks on Serbs associated all Muslims with the Ustasha in the minds of many Serbs, despite the fact that Muslims 'were caught on all sides of the battle lines', some fighting with the Ustasha, others with the partisans, while Muslims were massacred by both the Ustasha and Chetniks.[27]

On the Serb side, there was a Yugoslav government in exile, but 'its voice, however, was invalidated by its "Royal Army in the Homeland" which took the notorious name of Chetniks', who, driven by Serb counter-nationalism and intent on restoring the prewar Yugoslav government, sought vengeance against those they regarded as 'Croat, Moslem, Albanian etc., "traitors", clearing away all renegade nationalities from "Serb" territory'.[28] In a programme which mirrored the Ustasha programme for a nationally homogeneous Greater Croatia, the Chetniks proposed a homogeneous Greater Serbia via post-war population exchanges. However, although the Chetniks committed atrocities in the name of reprisals, they did not have a centralised programme which could be described as genocidal at this time.[29] Nonetheless, we can see at this time the shift from an assimilationist to an exclusive view of Serbian national identity in which non-Serbs should be removed from Serb territory.

[23] Ibid., p. 142.   [24] Denich, 'Dismembering Yugoslavia', 374–5.
[25] Ibid., p. 375. The memorialisation of Jasenovac, the best known of the extermination sites, proved a powerful symbol for resurgent Serb nationalism in the late 1980s.
[26] Branka Magas, *The Destruction of Yugoslavia* (London: Verso, 1993), p. 26.
[27] Sells, 'Religion, History', p. 34.   [28] Magas, *Destruction of Yugoslavia*, p. 26.
[29] Denich, 'Dismembering Yugoslavia', 375.

The second Yugoslavia

Despite the rhetoric of contemporary nationalists, the diffuse loyalties
in these conflicts defy easy categorisation. Though many Croats did take
part in Ustasha massacres of Serbs, so too many Croats fought on the side
of Josip Tito's anti-fascist partisans. Likewise, Serbs fought as Chetniks,
but others fought as partisans, and not all Bosnian Muslims took part
in the massacres of Serbs. This jumble of cross-cutting allegiances and
the legacy of extreme violence across both communal and ideological
boundaries was the inheritance of the second Yugoslavia. Such an inheritance will always be difficult, but if there is no process of national
reconciliation this leaves wounds improperly healed, which can be easily
opened again. There was certainly no such process of reconciliation in
Tito's Yugoslavia. Instead, Communist Party control was imposed on the
country, and very little real discussion of the war occurred beyond the
memorialisation of the partisans as heroes. Yet, at the same time, with
the exception of Bosnia-Herzegovina, the republics of Yugoslavia were
each constituted as the republics of their majority nations. The combination of a taboo on any frank discussion of the war or of national
differences, and a federal system that was decentralised along the lines of
republics defined in terms of their majority nations, meant that no attempt
was made to come to terms with the past or to rethink the ethnic basis
of national identity in the republics. This set up the conditions of mutual
distrust and lack of knowledge or understanding (even of their own history), conditions which nationalists could exploit and which ultimately
made possible the destruction of Yugoslavia.[30]

Under Tito, nationalism was disavowed and the Communist Party
sought to create a new Yugoslavia, represented in the slogan 'brotherhood
and unity', meaning the unity of equal nations. Class conflicts and loyalties were stressed rather than national identities[31] and Yugoslav unity was
drawn against the threat of outside intervention, first from the West and
later from the Soviet Union. In practice, the Titoist regime did not ignore
national affiliations, but sought to find some way of managing representation of the different groups (at least at the elite level) whilst asserting
the final authority of the party. In the end though, the federal structure of
post-war Yugoslavia did nothing to alleviate national animosities. From
the beginning, with the exception of Bosnia-Herzegovina, the constituent

[30] Shoup, 'Titoism'. Or as Sabrina Petra Ramet, commenting on the different nationalist
revivals, puts it: 'At the most fundamental level, the peoples of Yugoslavia lost the ability
to understand each other – because they do not understand each other's values and concerns, or each other's perceptions.' Sabrina Petra Ramet, *Balkan Babel: Politics, Culture
and Religion in Yugoslavia* (Boulder: Westview Press, 1992), p. 30.
[31] Ramet, *Balkan Babel*, p. 51.

republics were designated as the republics of each majority nation. Titoism did not challenge the nineteenth-century definition that equated *narod* or 'nation' with 'people' defined in terms of ethnicity. The result of this was that despite the rejection of nationalism at one level, at another, 'nation' retained an ethnic connotation and this conception of national identity remained as a building block of the federal state. Despite the reality of mixed populations in most republics, each 'nation' retained 'an ambiguous hegemonic status in its "own" republic'.[32] Thus the constituent republics were institutionalised as the republics of and for ethnically defined national communities. The exception to this was Bosnia-Herzegovina, although the Muslims of Bosnia-Herzegovina were finally recognised as a nation in 1968.

In the immediate post-war centralised federal system, Serbs were dominant. However, in 1962 Tito joined reformists who were pushing for decentralisation, in part as a way to counter the power held by Serbia in the centralised system. The Serbian security service resisted these moves and was purged by Tito in 1965, after which 'Serbian predominance in the federal agencies was increasingly challenged, as were the strong-arm methods in dealing with the non-Serbs.'[33] As a result, non-Serbs gained some ground, including within Serbia, where the ethnic Albanians of Kosovo, are the majority population in that area. The Yugoslav constitution of 1974 furthered the decentralisation process. At the time, the constitution 'seemed to provide political stability (using cautiously crafted practices of ethnic quotas, strict rotation of cadres, and the universal enjoyment by constituent republics of the right to veto federal legislation)'.[34] As before, the republics were constituted as the republics of majority nations, while minority groups within Yugoslavia whose nationality was not of the constituent republics, such as the Hungarian or Albanian minorities, were referred to as 'nationalities'. It was at this point that the regions of Kosovo and Vojvodina within Serbia were granted autonomous status, though not complete sovereignty.

In the wake of efforts at decentralisation in the 1960s there was an upsurge of nationalism in Croatia. Associated with this is the figure of Franjo Tudjman who eventually rose to power in Croatia in 1991. In the 1970s, Tudjman, a historian, embarked on an effort to change what he regarded as the privileged status of Serbs in Croatia,[35] for which he spent time in

[32] Denich, 'Dismembering Yugoslavia', 375.
[33] Ivo Banac, 'The Fearful Asymmetry of War: The Causes and Consequences of Yugoslavia's Demise', *Dædalus* 121:2 (1992), 147.
[34] Ramet, *Balkan Babel*, pp. 38–9.
[35] Because Tudjman considered that this privilege was based on the view that Serbs had been the specific targets of the Ustasha during World War II, it was necessary to show

jail as Tito quashed Croatian nationalism. Up to and during the 1970s the Yugoslav state was buttressed by an economic boom (based on borrowing which would cause problems when the loans became due in the 1980s), with political stability provided by Tito as the final arbiter of disputes.[36] However, despite the attempt to develop institutionalised practices of negotiation and arbitration to mediate the competing claims of the different republics, the ultimate reliance on Tito's authority to hold the system together was destabilising in the longer term. Decentralisation increased over time as a great deal of autonomy devolved to the constituent republics and the autonomous regions of Kosovo and Vojvodina. In effect, the communists allowed regional pluralisation, which took the form of administrative decentralisation, as a substitute for political liberalisation. Though eager for greater administrative autonomy, the Communist Party elites within the different republics were not interested in relinquishing their own authority in the interests of pluralism. The communists argued that the introduction of multiparty democracy would lead to 'fratricidal war in Yugoslav conditions. In order to maintain this fiction, Yugoslav politicians stoked the fires of inter-ethnic distrust by constant commentaries on the ethnic genocides of World War II.'[37] Thus, national differences came back on to the agenda as a means through which the often mutually hostile elites could buttress their own positions.

The weakening of the central government after Tito's death in 1980 allowed the parties in Serbia, Slovenia and Vojvodina to 'further liberalize their policies in the spheres of culture, the media, and even religion', though with very different results.[38] Liberalisation allowed plays such as 'The Pigeon Cave' by the nationalist playwright Jovan Radulovic to be performed in Serbia in the early 1980s. The title refers to a cave in the

---

that this had not been the case. He therefore argued that the total number of victims was lower than generally accepted and that most of these victims were non-Serbs such as Jews, Gypsies and anti-fascist Croats. In his view, though the Ustasha regime was certainly criminal, it did not differ significantly from the criminality of wartime Chetniks or the Partisan use of terror. 'This explanation of the Ustashe terror is, in Dr Tudjman's work, embedded in a general philosophy of history according to which mass terror and genocide are permanent features of human history.' Tudjman's philosophy of history and his revisionist history of the Ustasha can be seen as part of an attempt to remove the stigma of genocide from Croatia, as the Serbs were not specifically targeted by the Ustasha, and, in the broader view, neither is genocide itself unique. 'Anyone who argues to the contrary, Dr Tudjman claims, is a Serb nationalist attempting to denigrate the Croat nation.' Aleksandar Pavkovic, *The Fragmentation of Yugoslavia: Nationalism in a Multinational State* (London: Macmillan, 1997), p. 93.

[36] Ramet, *Balkan Babel*, p. 23. This also extended to quelling the stirrings of nationalist interpretations of Yugoslav history, yet Tito's actions in trying to dampen the power of Serbia while still pushing unitarism fed this. See Ivo Banac, 'The Dissolution of Yugoslavia Historiography', in Ramet and Adamovich (eds.), *Beyond Yugoslavia*, p. 42.

[37] Ramet, *Balkan Babel*, p. 23.   [38] Ibid., p. 11.

Krajina region which contains the remains of Serb villagers who were murdered by the Ustasha during World War II. For, as Denich points out, the Ustasha did not succeed in their aims and at the end of the war, Serbs who had survived returned to their homes in Croatia and Bosnia-Herzegovina with traumatic memories which were not acknowledged or dealt with in Tito's Yugoslavia.[39] After Tito's death, discussion of the past, denied under his regime, became increasingly acceptable, and in the hands of nationalists the emphasis was on past losses and the wrongs done to their people. This played an important part in the creation of pathological vengefulness, which contributed towards the justification of ethnic cleansing. 'The Pigeon Cave' was eventually banned again under pressure from Croatia but it and other works like it were an indication of the responses to liberalisation that occurred in the absence (or crushing) of moves towards democratisation. Around the same time the media took up investigations into aspects of the past which were previously untouchable, such as massacres committed by the communist partisans at the end of World War II.[40]

The destruction of Yugoslavia

The delegitimation of the Communist Party in Yugoslavia

After Tito's death in 1980 a Serbian campaign branding the 1974 constitution, and Tito himself by implication, 'anti-Serbian' gained momentum only to gain further impetus after Slobodan Milosevic came to power.[41] The main Serbian complaint was against the recognition of the autonomous regions of Kosovo and Vojvodina within Serbia under the 1974 constitution. In 1989 a general strike begun by miners and supported by the general ethnic Albanian population was held in Kosovo in response to the implementation of repressive laws by the Serb regional government prohibiting demonstrations. Early demonstrations had occurred from the early 1980s in response to the tough social and economic conditions and increasingly harsh measures taken by the authorities in Kosovo.[42] There was little sympathy for ethnic Albanians in Serbia, as the demands of ethnic Albanians were seen as an affront to Serbian sovereignty and were met with yet more repression. There is no doubt that the autonomy asserted by Kosovo under the federal system was problematic for Serbia. Though formally part of Serbia, Kosovo and

---

[39] Denich, 'Dismembering Yugoslavia', 375.   [40] Ibid., 378.

[41] Serbian questioning of the constitution was first heard as early as 1977, even though they remained 'reliably Titoist'. Ramet, *Balkan Babel*, p. 11; also see Pavkovic, *Fragmentation of Yugoslavia*, p. 103.

[42] Noel Malcolm, *Kosovo: A Short History* (London: Macmillan, 1998), pp. 334–56.

Vojvodina both had their own votes in the federal presidency, and could thus vote against Serbia. But first the federal government of Yugoslavia, and then the government of Serbia, both took a heavy handed, adversarial approach to dealing with this problem that served to escalate tensions.[43] Demonstrations and riots in Kosovo prompted Serbian calls for an end to Kosovo's autonomy, which in turn provided a means of attacking Tito's federalism. The Serbian elite characterised the threat posed by ethnic Albanians in Kosovo as a threat to the existence of Serbia itself. The popular mobilisation that resulted 'was innately anti-Albanian, but also anti-Titoist, and anti-Yugoslav'.[44] The important role of the 'myth of Kosovo' in laying the ground for ethnic cleansing in Bosnia-Herzegovina will be investigated in more detail below.

How did the Yugoslav federal system come to lose legitimacy so quickly? To return to the early years of this process, 1979 to 1983 saw a sharp change in the fortunes of Yugoslavia. The death of Vice-President Evard Kardelj in 1979 was followed by the death of President Tito in 1980. Meanwhile, relations between ethnic Albanians and Serbia were deteriorating as the country faced an economic slump, with matters further exacerbated by mismanagement at the federal level and a number of corruption scandals.[45] The sharp decline in living standards, and severe hardship for many, led to increasing social fragmentation, reflected in a soaring crime rate. In a context of extreme social unrest and uncertainty about the future,[46] the communist system increasingly lost legitimacy in the face of the apparent inability – and often the outright unwillingness – of communist politicians and officials to change.

In the face of such hardship, social disintegration and uncertainty, the 'certainty' offered by nationalists became increasingly attractive, and it was the various nationalist parties that won the free elections held in the constituent republics of Yugoslavia during 1990. Though the nationalists did not win by huge margins, the first past the post system used in the elections ensured that in Slovenia, Croatia and Serbia the nationalist parties of the respective republics gained the most seats. In Bosnia-Herzegovina a three-way split between the Muslim, Croatian and Serbian parties resulted in a short-lived coalition government.[47]

---

[43] For further background on Kosovo see Malcolm, *Kosovo*; and Sabrina Petra Ramet, 'Why Albanian Irredentism in Kosovo Will Not Go Away', in Sabrina P. Ramet, *Social Currents in Eastern Europe: The Sources and Meaning of the Great Transformation* (Durham: Duke University Press, 1991), pp. 173–94.

[44] Banac, 'Fearful Asymmetry', 149.   [45] Ramet, *Balkan Babel*, p. 39.

[46] Ibid., p. 23. Such anger was expressed through demonstrations such as that in August 1989 in Montenegro, when 30,000 people protested against poverty and hunger.

[47] In the elections held in Croatia in April–May 1990, the six-party coalition of the Croatian Democratic Bloc, led by Franjo Tudjman and his Croatian Democratic Union (HDZ), using populist mobilisation similar to that employed by Milosevic in Serbia, won

Prior to the elections the differences between the republics were becoming more pronounced. Revisionist history was on the rise, particularly in Croatia and Serbia,[48] and the 1974 constitution was the subject of intense debate, sparked by the publication of a series of critical articles in the weekly newspaper, *Borba*. Following this debate a commission was set up 'to review the political system and prepare recommendations for reform' and to submit a report to the 13th Congress of the Yugoslav Communist Party.[49] Federal Party officials stressed recentralisation despite strong regional differences on the subject and continued resistance from the Slovenian party.[50]

But the seemingly triumphant party was undermined by both nationalism and the resistance to political change that was part of the communist system. While federal president Markovic attempted to implement economic reforms and then failed in his attempt to transform his personal popularity into electoral success,[51] a number of formerly communist politicians transformed themselves, seemingly overnight, into nationalists. Although the Communist Party had a monopoly on political power, it was divided into eight regional organisations with sharp differences over policy. Attempts at recentralisation met resistance from national groups used to self-government under the decentralised system and this conflict came to a head as the legitimacy of the party crumbled in the late 1980s, along with the economic and social fabric of Yugoslavia. By this time many intellectuals had turned against the federal system, especially

44 per cent of the vote which translated into 58 seats in the Croatian Diet. In the most powerful Socio-Political Chamber of the Diet the HDZ won 54 out of 80 seats. Thus the first past the post system allowed the HDZ to win an absolute majority in the Diet without winning an absolute majority of votes. Elections in Bosnia-Herzegovina were held in November 1990 and the results reflected the shift to ethno-nationalist identification in Yugoslavia. Alia Izetbegovic's Party of Democratic Action (SDA), a Muslim party, won 37.8 per cent of the vote (with 43.5 per cent of the population Muslim), Karadzic's Serb Democratic Party (SDS) won 26.5 per cent of the vote (with 31.3 per cent of the population Serbian), and the HDZ won 14.7 per cent of the vote (with 17.5 per cent of the population Croatian). In Serbia multiparty elections were held in December 1990. The first past the post system meant that with 45.8 per cent of the vote Milosevic's Serb Democratic Party won 77.6 per cent of seats in parliament. Direct elections for president reflected Milosevic's high personal popularity, as he gained 65.35 per cent of the vote. Pavkovic, *Fragmentation of Yugoslavia*, pp. 111–19.

48 Banac, 'The Dissolution', pp. 48–51.
49 Ramet, *Balkan Babel*, p. 16.   50 Ibid., p. 18.
51 Pavkovic, *Fragmentation of Yugoslavia*, pp. 101–2. Markovic attempted to do this with negligible networks of community support and had trouble gaining access to the media. An attempt to set up a federal television station was short lived. On this see Mark Thompson, *Forging War: The Media in Serbia, Croatia and Bosnia-Hercegovina*, Article 19 (London: International Centre Against Censorship, 1994). On the rise of revisionist history in Croatia, particularly with reference to the activities of the Ustasha, see Denich, 'Dismembering Yugoslavia', 375–8.

in Serbia. Ramet notes that up to a point the intelligentsia had assumed that any overhaul of the system would put them in a role of partnership rather than opposition to the party. Yet, she argues, a caveat is necessary here, for the 'defection of the intellectuals had already begun', so that by 1987 many were working not to reform the system but to overthrow it.[52]

The SANU memo of 1986

This shift in the position of intellectuals is reflected in the infamous memo from the Serbian Academy of Arts and Sciences (SANU) of 1986. As Banac notes, this memo was novel in that it questioned Yugoslavia as the 'optimal solution for the Serbs',[53] whereas in the past Serbs had pushed for the unification and further centralisation of Yugoslavia. The memo reflects an elite concerned to maintain their own position and willing to use the available symbolic means at their disposal to do this, such as unresolved recent history and national stereotypes. Thus communist intellectuals turned into nationalists and joined hands with the anti-communist Orthodox Church.[54] The SANU memo also 'effectively inverted the Croatian [nationalist] platform, suppressed fifteen years earlier' under Tito.[55] There was, however, no Tito to suppress this form of virulent nationalism, and it was not to remain in the intellectual sphere, as it soon found a political advocate in Slobodan Milosevic.

The memo, presented to the Yugoslav and Serbian national assemblies, claimed that what was happening in Kosovo, which was interpreted as the 'gradual surrender of Kosovo and Metohija to Albanians', constituted treason. The memo claimed that Tito had 'pursued consistent discrimination against the Serbs and Serbia',[56] and that within the autonomous region of Kosovo the human rights of the Serb minority were being systematically violated. It claimed that genocide was taking place in Kosovo, forcing a Serb exodus from 'ancient hearths'.[57] Though seemingly made in passing, the memo made a very strong claim that the Albanian leaders in Kosovo sought an ethnically pure region.[58] As Branka Magas comments:

[52] Ramet, *Balkan Babel*, p. 19.
[53] Banac, 'The Dissolution', p. 55; Sells, 'Religion, History', pp. 32–3.
[54] On the role of intellectuals under Eastern and Central European communist regimes see Zygmunt Bauman, 'Intellectuals in East-Central Europe: Continuity and Change', *Eastern European Politics and Societies* 1: Spring (1987).
[55] Denich, 'Dismembering Yugoslavia', 371.   [56] Banac, 'Fearful Asymmetry', 150.
[57] Cited in Magas, *Destruction of Yugoslavia*, p. 49.
[58] 'Editors of Praxis International Defend Their Position on Kosovo'. Magas, *Destruction of Yugoslavia*, p. 57. Also see Sells, 'Religion, History', p. 33.

[t]he fact that it was signed by a highly representative section of the Belgrade intelligentsia and professional middle class (including Orthodox priests and re- tired army officers) suggests the consolidation in the Yugoslav capital of a political gravitational centre outside the Party and to its right, promising a rerun of the nationalist upsurge in Croatia in the late 1960s – but now in the very different context of the mid-1980s.[59]

The claims in the memo have since been shown to be absurd. For example, despite the claims that Serbian women were being systemati- cally raped in Kosovo, Kosovo actually had the lowest level of rape of any of the Yugoslav republics, reflecting its generally lower crime rate.[60] However, as Mark Thompson notes, '[t]he memorandum set the tone (at once self-pitying, morbid and vengeful) of nationalist discourse ever since, and it has been widely regarded as the blueprint of the expansion- ist designs upon Croatia and Bosnia which were revealed in 1991 and 1992'.[61] Further illuminating the role of intellectuals in the upsurge of nationalism, Banac observes that the Serbian historiography that came after the SANU memo went beyond revisionism, becoming 'an agency of an aggressive national aggrandizement, clearly in service of Milosevic's political programme'.[62] The centrepiece of this programme was the at- tainment of a dominant role for a rejuvenated Serbia within Yugoslavia or, failing that, carving out a Greater Serbia from the remains of Yugoslavia. A central element in the attempt to put such a programme into practice was the rise to power of Slobodan Milosevic.

In 1986 Slobodan Milosevic replaced his mentor Ivan Stambolic as chair of the Central Committee of the Serbian Communist Party, while Stambolic became President of the joint presidency of Serbia. Stambolic had himself argued in 1981 that '"a unified and strong Serbia" was a pre- requisite to a strong Yugoslavia',[63] but by 1987 he and Milosevic differed over how to handle Kosovo, with Milosevic preferring a more coercive policy. Stambolic and his followers were ousted following a 'fully tele- vised, ritualistic bashing' of one of Stambolic's aides.[64] Milosevic quickly set about consolidating his own position, with a purge of the Belgrade party and the installation of his own followers, predominantly central and south Serbs. Stambolic was dismissed from the presidency in December

---

[59] Magas, *Destruction of Yugoslavia*, p. 53.
[60] The allegations of rape were not borne out by official statistics which show a much higher rate of rape in Serbia than in Kosovo. Such unfounded allegations were 'ultimately insidious' though as they were accepted by many Serbs. Sells, 'Religion, History', p. 32.
[61] Thompson, *Forging War*, p. 54.   [62] Banac, 'The Dissolution', p. 55.
[63] Ramet, *Balkan Babel*, p. 26.   [64] Pavkovic, *Fragmentation of Yugoslavia*, p. 103.

1987.[65] Attacks on Tito in the media were then stepped up, furthering the delegitimation of the federal system. Milosevic also replaced his opponents in the autonomous provinces with individuals loyal to him. Likewise, he purged the communist elites of Serbia and Montenegro,[66] replacing them with his supporters.[67]

Nationalism and state-building

Under conditions of systemic change or breakdown nationalist criteria of identity can provide meaning and a sense of certainty. For elites, such a discourse provides new legitimating myths as old ones crumble. This is especially the case in situations such as the former Yugoslavia, where we see the manipulation via the media of the sense of threat posed by those designated as 'other' and the articulation of conceptions of a homogeneous Serb, Croat or Slovenian identity. Although this occurred to differing extents in the republics, the focus here is on Serbian nationalism, in both Serbia and in Bosnia-Herzegovina and the role it played in attempts to build a Greater Serbian state as Yugoslavia crumbled. Through a consistent barrage of news reports insisting that Croatians and Bosnian Muslims were intent on destroying Serbs, and the use of footage that portrayed Serbs as victims (not always, but often, incorrectly) this sense of threat was created and perpetuated. The corollary of this was that it was imperative for Serbs to be united, and so any dissent amongst Serbs themselves, which of course there was, could be targeted as disloyal, a betrayal of all Serbs. Thus an exclusive, unitary national identity, which was predicated on a notion of a homogeneous Serb state for Serbs, and that characterised non-Serbs as 'the enemy', was simultaneously constructed by elites, cultivated through populist politics, and imposed upon any dissenting Serbs.[68]

Slobodan Milosevic 'quickly sensed an opportunity in Serbian fears',[69] which had been raised by nationalist discourse in Serbia throughout the 1980s. Thus the authoritarian party apparatchik was transformed into an authoritarian demagogue, who, buttressed by support from the middle-class intelligentsia, used staged mass rallies combined with a stranglehold

---

[65] Stambolic has been missing, presumed dead, since 25 August 2000. His disappearance occurred in the context of numerous murders of high profile people in Serbia, a crackdown on the media and opponents of the government in the run up to the September 2000 elections in which Milosevic finally lost power.

[66] Pavkovic, *Fragmentation of Yugoslavia*, pp. 101–2.   [67] Ramet, *Balkan Babel*, p. 21.

[68] V. P. Gagnon, 'Ethnic Conflict as Demobilizer: The Case of Serbia', *Institute for European Studies Working Paper* 96:1 (Ithaca: Cornell University, 1996).

[69] Banac, 'Fearful Asymmetry', 151.

on the media to build his own support. If Milosevic picked up on nationalism in an opportunistic way, what caused the groundswell of nationalism in the first place? As I have sought to show above, a number of factors came into play. First, the decreasing legitimacy of the Communist Party led to a sense of political instability as the federal system crumbled along with the party itself. Hence the 'certainty' offered by nationalism became more attractive to many. Part of the reason for the Communist Party's loss of legitimacy was the inability or unwillingness of many sections of the party to respond to the economic problems facing Yugoslavia which caused extreme hardship. The demands of the ethnic Albanians of Kosovo for greater autonomy and for greater social and economic rights gave Serbian nationalists a weapon to use, which they willingly did. To be sure, extreme nationalism is not the only alternative under conditions of profound change, but in Serbia extreme nationalism was triumphant. It must be stressed, however, that this does not mean that there was no opposition to such policies. But in the absence of democratic institutions an authoritarian leader was able to consolidate his rule to such an extent that opposition became increasingly difficult, at least until Milosevic's final fall from power in late 2000.

In the transition from communist multinational state to a national state, constructed along the most exclusivist lines, the possibilities for the development of civil society in Serbia were foreclosed and the nationalist option was presented as legitimate by those in power, which in turn buttressed their own legitimacy. The pro-democratic opposition in Serbia was quashed by Milosevic and illegal means were used to crush the huge anti-government demonstrations held in 1991, thus ensuring that he remained in power. Milosevic argued that he championed 'an effective modern state',[70] but his interpretation of this meant a strong centralised authoritarian state, rather than a democratic one and, ultimately, his policies resulted in a vastly weakened state. This echoes the views of all the leaders in the case studies surveyed above, that a strong state demands complete unity. The 'strength' of such a state, whether it be absolutist France, the late Ottoman Empire or Milosevic's vision for Serbia/ Yugoslavia, comes from state control achieved through repressive policies and the construction of a unitary corporate identity, which is drawn from the available cultural reference points. Whether defined according to religious, national or ethnic criteria of identification and differentiation – or some combination of these – the designated criterion of acceptable identity becomes the only one congruent with membership in the political

---

[70] Ramet, *Balkan Babel*, p. 33.

community. Thus Milosevic's nationalism was underpinned by the idea of a 'Greater Serbia', or 'one state for all Serbs', and the corollary of this, that it was unacceptable that Serbs should exist as a minority in another sovereign state.

The legitimacy built on such foundations must inevitably be buttressed by, at the very least, the awareness of the possibility of overt force. Those who advocate such a 'strong' state are inevitably compelled to buttress their control with force and elites work hard to create what they claim exists – a unitary sovereign state. The symbolic augmentation of authority plays a central role under such conditions. Thus the capacity to draw on and manipulate the symbolic and cultural resources that are meaningful is of the highest importance to such regimes, both as a means of popular mobilisation (and demobilisation of opponents) and for the rationalisation of the violence that is necessary to maintain their rule.

Although nationalism was on the rise throughout Yugoslavia in the 1980s, it was Milosevic's 'bare faced Serbian nationalism' which was the 'catalyst' that took Yugoslavia from 'crisis' to war.[71] Though Milosevic had to quash dissent, there was also a high level of support for him amongst the Serbian population. His measures to end the autonomous status of Kosovo and Vojvodina were 'enormously popular among Serbs'. However, what made many Serbs love him, made him 'hated and feared in Croatia and Slovenia'. In 1989 Milosevic attempted to build a base of support among non-Serbs by talking about an 'anti-bureaucratic revolution', but this failed in the face of scepticism about his motives.[72] Milosevic's strategy was popular because it restored many to the positions of respect that they had lost under the communist regime. He allowed the acknowledgement of nationalist artists, writers and intellectuals, and permitted the revival of the Orthodox Church. His repressive policies in Kosovo and Vojvodina made him a national hero in Serbia, and with the opposition crushed he had gained very high levels of popularity by the end of 1989.[73]

The 1990 election of nationalist governments in most republics meant the end of Yugoslavia, as the conflict between different nationalist claims degenerated into war. The problem stemmed from the fact that the principle of national self-determination had been interpreted in Yugoslavia as the right to self-determination of the nation (*narod*) within each republic. As we have seen, this was based on an ethnic definition of nation and meant the majority group within each republic, not all citizens. As Hayden puts it, 'the winning message in each republic was one of classic

[71] Ibid., p. 36.   [72] Ibid., p. 27.   [73] Ibid., p. 29.

nationalism: Serbia for Serbs, Croatia for Croats, Slovenia for Slovenes, and Macedonia for Macedonians'.[74] In Bosnia-Herzegovina the vote was split to reflect the three main ethnic groups, with Ante Markovic's Alliance of Reform Forces of Yugoslavia, 'the most important party standing for a civil state of equal citizens', garnering only 5.6 per cent of the vote.[75]

The nationalists who came to government throughout 1990 did so on platforms that claimed the necessary congruence of the ethnically defined nation and the state. As Hayden notes, '[a]lthough this formulation was hardly new to European history, it did have sinister implications for minorities in states that were suddenly defined as the nation-states of their respective ethnic majorities. By definition, anyone not of the majority ethno-nation could only be a citizen of second class.'[76] Where reality did not fit this model of statehood, policies were implemented that attempted to *make* reality 'fit' the model, thus the policy of 'ethnic cleansing' to bring about the desired population in a given territory. In the case of Slovenia, with its relatively homogeneous population, the implications were less severe than in more mixed areas.[77] Bosnia-Herzegovina, with its heterogeneous population, was most vulnerable to such policies. Before we go on to consider the policy of ethnic cleansing in the former Yugoslavia and its most tragic outcome in Bosnia-Herzegovina, we first need to understand the symbolic manipulation that preceded the physical expulsion that took place. For as Fein argues, before such acts can be committed the 'other' must first be expelled from the realm of moral obligation and rendered 'not like us', and therefore not subject to the same rules of conduct that exist within a community. To do this, nationalists have to use the available symbolic and cultural repertoire. In the case of Serbia, the 'myth of Kosovo' proved a very effective rallying point, one that was used to draw a sharp moral boundary between Serbs and the Muslim ethnic Albanians of Kosovo, and, by implication, all Muslims in Yugoslavia. This powerful and emotive imagery was combined with the cry that the rise to power of Franjo Tudjman in Croatia meant the 'return of the Ustasha', with the implication that all Croats were enemies of all Serbs. In the late twentieth century, one of the most important means to spread this message, along with mass rallies, was the use of the electronic and print media. It is to this symbolic manipulation and its effects that I now turn.

[74] Hayden, 'Imagined Communities', 787.
[75] Ibid.   [76] Ibid., 787.
[77] Though here too, as Hayden points out, the 'constitutional nationalism' that granted a different set of rights to Slovenians over other groups in the country, works against the principles of democracy. Hayden, 'Constitutional Nationalism'.

Chauvinist nationalism and symbolic manipulation

In terms of the absolute conception of sovereign identity that extreme nationalists espouse, the existence of a large culturally and religiously different group poses a threat to the coherence of the absolute identity that is being claimed and is therefore deemed intolerable. By the 1980s the ethnic Albanians of Kosovo outnumbered Serbs by nine to one. Though forming a majority within Kosovo, the Albanians constitute a minority within Serbia. On the other hand, the Serbs, a minority within Kosovo, claimed that any autonomy granted to Kosovo was an infringement of their rights as members of the majority nation of Serbia. Under such conditions, the claim that the Albanians of Kosovo posed a threat to Serbs and Serbia could easily be inflamed further, as it was throughout the 1980s. This culminated in Slobodan Milosevic's appropriation of this perceived threat, in order to effect his climb to power.[78] The use of the myth of Kosovo, combined with the reinterment of Serb war dead killed by the Ustasha, also paved the way for the characterisation of non-Serbs in a way that legitimated the policy of ethnic cleansing.

As a number of authors note, while these recent conflicts have often been represented as 'ancient hatreds', they cannot be traced back further than the nineteenth century,[79] although there are different analyses of the path and causes of conflict since then. For example, Banac dismisses claims that the violence was religiously based, although he acknowledges that religion had some role in the conflicts. For him the causes are primarily ideological and political.[80] What this view overlooks, though, is how the ideological and the political draw on the cultural, of which religious identities are part. On the other hand, Michael Sells characterises nationalism in the former Yugoslavia as 'religious nationalism' in which fundamentalist versions of Christianity and nationalism 'reinforce one another and merge'.[81] Thus, Sells sees the violence as religiously motivated. While nationalists certainly drew on religious symbolism to both motivate and justify violence, Sells is silent on the final object of such discourses and the practices that they legitimated, which was control of sovereign states defined in terms that legitimated the authority and position of nationalist elites. So while the relationship between religious

---

[78] Indeed, Banac points out that the shift of many Serbian intellectuals towards nationalism was gaining momentum by the 1980s and they backed Milosevic. This was despite the fact that they were anti-centralists and Milosevic had built his career 'as an orthodox Titoist ready to use "administrative measures" against dissidents'. Banac, 'The Dissolution', p. 55.

[79] Banac, 'Fearful Asymmetry', 147.   [80] Ibid., 147.

[81] Michael Sells, *The Bridge Betrayed: Religion and Genocide in Bosnia* (Berkeley: University of California Press, 1996), p. 89.

and national identification is crucially important to understanding the violence in the former Yugoslavia, and Sells' work makes an important contribution to understanding this, the two forms of identification should not be collapsed into one another.

In an approach closer to that of this study, Ramet ties religion and politics together as both deriving from culture, broadly defined. Notions of otherness have been constructed and reinforced with reference to complex cultural markers in which religious and ethnic identities, interpreted through the matrix of nationalist ideologies, are claimed as ancient, 'authentic' and superior. Such claims are legitimated through the designation of others as simultaneously inferior and threatening. Because the violent, and complex, recent past was not adequately dealt with under Tito, it was 'available' for nationalists to manipulate as part of the construction of the identities they claim to be so ancient. 'Different memories, set atop unhealed wounds, provide the seedbed for deep bitterness, resentments, and recurrent desires for revenge.'[82] Nonetheless, the violence would not have occurred in the way it did without the symbolic manipulation, interventions and arming of the Bosnian Serb and Bosnian Croat armies by elites who had, particularly in the case of Serbia, the formidable resources of the state at their disposal and were interested in maintaining and, if possible extending, their control over those resources.

To argue that nationalists draw on the available cultural repertoire or framework is not to argue that a culture is inherently violent. Cultures are complexes of practices and beliefs which are contested and can change, particularly in times of crisis. There are, for example, different strands to Serbian culture and different possibilities that exist within the myth of Kosovo, but the nationalists who triumphed under Milosevic were able to pick up on strands of resentment and claim the 'truth' of their interpretation of the categories 'Serb' and 'non-Serb'. And if necessary they were prepared to forcibly impose their version on dissenters. Elements of the nationalist view obviously had emotional resonance for many Serbs as Yugoslavia crumbled around them, causing great uncertainty about the future.[83] Thus it is no surprise that Milosevic's party's slogan during the 1990 elections was 'with us there is no uncertainty'. The slogan on the banner behind Milosevic and other officials at the 600th anniversary of the battle of Kosovo in 1989 read 'Only Unity Saves the Serb'.[84] All the same, the nationalist version was contested and nationalists had

---

[82] Ramet, *Balkan Babel*, p. 41.

[83] Not all though. See Ivan Torov, 'The Resistance in Serbia', in Jasminka Udovicki and James Ridgeway (eds.), *Burn This House: The Making and Unmaking of Yugoslavia* (Durham: Duke University Press, 1997); Gagnon, 'Ethnic Conflict'.

[84] Sells, *The Bridge Betrayed*, pp. 86–7.

to work hard to get the population to accept, or at least acquiesce in, their version. They did this through the use of emotive symbols, which picked up on threats to Serb collective identity, mass rallies, and almost complete control of the media, which continually reinforced these messages. It was also hard for activists against the wars in Croatia and Bosnia to gain wider support in the absence of a tradition of civil disobedience and the 'absence of the spirit of protest in the culture as a whole'.[85] At the same time, those brave enough to express their dissent were labelled as traitors, and therefore to be put in the category of 'non-Serbs' if they did not realise where their loyalty *should* rest and act accordingly.[86]

The Kosovo myth

As many commentators have noted, Kosovo is an important symbol to the Serb community, regarded by many as a 'Serb Jerusalem', a place of the 'archetypal founding event in Serb romantic mythology'. This event was the death of Serb Prince Lazar when Kosovo fell to the Ottoman Empire in 1389, a battle in which his opponent, the Ottoman Emperor Murat, was also killed. Kosovo is also the centre of great works of religious architecture and the ancient seat of Serb leadership.[87] The idea of removing the majority ethnic Albanian population from Kosovo has arisen at various times during modern Serbian history, usually in times of crisis, but there has never been complete accord on this. In the nineteenth century, when ethnic Albanians were treated as hostile and expelled from Serbia following the Congress of Berlin, there were critics of this policy within Serbia. At that time, as now, there were those who argued for a less coercive way of dealing with large minorities. However, then as in the late twentieth century, the most hardline approach was taken.[88] Willem Vermeer also notes that the tendency to speak of Kosovo as the 'cradle of the medieval Serbian state or the Serbia "people" is historically incorrect, as the original Serbian lands were to the west of Kosovo.[89] Furthermore, ethnic Albanians have been a majority in Kosovo 'as long as people can remember'.[90] Despite this, the fact remains that Kosovo is a significant site in Serb culture because it has been *understood* as the 'cradle' of Serb

---

[85] Torov, 'Resistance in Serbia', p. 261.   [86] Gagnon, 'Ethnic Conflict'.

[87] Sells, 'Religion, History', p. 31; Malcolm, *Kosovo*, pp. 58–80; also see Sells, *The Bridge Betrayed*.

[88] Willem Vermeer, 'Albanians and Serbs in Yugoslavia', in van den Heuvel and Siccama (eds.), *The Disintegration of Yugoslavia*, pp. 102–3.

[89] Vermeer, 'Albanians and Serbs', p. 105. In this regard Vermeer is particularly critical of the SANU manipulation of the known historical record, 'to conform to the political demands of society', p. 104.

[90] Vermeer, 'Albanians and Serbs', p. 104.

culture, and this symbolism has been claimed and used by nationalists. Thus 60,000 Serbs signed a petition against what they argued was the 'fascist genocide [of Serbs] in Kosovo', despite the lack of any concrete evidence that genocide was actually occurring there.[91]

The important symbolic role of Kosovo in Serb culture meant that it could easily be 'appropriated and radicalized' by nationalists in order to create a sense of Serb unity in the face of threat and also to 'create an ideology that allowed genocide'. The nationalists used 'the martyrdom of Prince Lazar at the battle in Kosovo in 1389 as a central component of the ideology of "ethnic cleansing".[92] Although this was not often declared outright, it would occasionally break through in a forthright expression such as 'the hands of the Muslims who are with us are stained and polluted with the blood of their ancestors... namely those who did not embrace Islam'.[93] This had serious implications for all Muslims as 'betrayers of Serbs', in a manner reminiscent of the Christian charge, made over the centuries, that Jews were responsible for the death of Christ. But this perception, Sells argues, can be traced to the efforts of nineteenth-century Serb nationalists, and no earlier. The legend of Prince Lazar's defeat in 1389 was first 'marshalled' to define an uncrossable boundary, an 'unbridgeable gap between Slavic Muslim and Serb... only in the nationalistic literature of the nineteenth century'. It is in this literature that the figure of Prince Lazar becomes 'a Christ figure, with knight disciples, who is slain, and with him dies the Serb nation, to rise again only with the resurrection of Lazar. Turks are thus equated with Christ-killers and Vuk Brankovic, the "Turk within", becomes a symbol, and the ancestral curse, of all Slavic Muslims.'[94]

Drawing on *The Mountain Wreath*, a story of the destruction of Slavic Muslims in eighteenth-century Montenegro, written by Prince-Bishop Petar II under the pen name of Njegos, Sells illustrates how Slavic Muslims were referred to as 'Turks' in this literature, as though by converting to Islam they had changed their racial identity. This work placed Slavic Muslims outside the moral community. It contrasts the negotiation that was possible within the blood feud (violent as this was) between clans and the outsider status of Muslims. With the Muslims negotiation is not possible, regardless of their qualities as individuals and the play ends with their extermination: 'it's them or us'. Sells notes how the writer transposed the differences between Orthodox Serb and Slavic Muslim into a 'cosmic duality of good and evil', placing the Slavic Muslims 'in a

---

[91] Sells, 'Religion, History', p. 33.   [92] Ibid., p. 24
[93] Belgrade academic Miroljub Jevtic, professor of political science at University of Belgrade, cited in Sells, 'Religion, History', p. 24.
[94] Sells, 'Religion, History', p. 28.

permanent state of otherness',[95] or to return to Fein's phrase, pushing them outside the bounds of moral obligation. This 'Christological patterning' of the Kosovo myth was to be found in much art and literature of the nineteenth-century nationalist period. Interest in Kosovo, in Njegos's work and in Njegos himself as a national hero, was revived in the 1980s as preparations for the 600th anniversary of the fall of Kosovo got underway. By this time contemporary nationalist writers and artists were also choosing Kosovo as a theme for their work, citing Njegos to justify aggressive nationalist policies.[96] Thus the 'threat' to Serbs in Kosovo, who represented about 1 per cent of the population of Yugoslavia was translated into a threat to 'the integrity of a country with twenty-four million people'.[97] Conversely, the 'reclaiming' of Kosovo was a triumph for all Serbs: 'Throughout Serbia, Kosovo was in the air. Serbs gloated over their reconquest of the province. Serbian bookstores filled their shelves with books about Kosovo. Musical artists dedicated their work to Kosovo. There was even a new perfume called "Miss Kosovo 1389" – an allusion to the battle of Kosovo of that year.'[98]

The Orthodox Church took an active part in this reclaiming and re-memorialisation. Rehabilitated by Milosevic after being sidelined for decades by communism, the Church became an enthusiastic proponent of nationalism. This is not surprising given that '[t]he Serbian Church views itself as identical with the Serbian nation since it considers that religion is the foundation of nationality'.[99] The Church benefited in a number of ways under Milosevic with a construction programme, permission to publish religious material and the right to once again celebrate Orthodox Christmas. In 1990 classes on Marxism were removed from school curricula, to be replaced by religious instruction.[100] The Church and its escalating anti-Albanian rhetoric, which included the 'genocide' claim, played a central part in the increasing popular hostility towards ethnic Albanians. This climate of hostility provided the backdrop to the 1989 ceremonies to commemorate the fall of Kosovo in 1389. The anniversary brought pilgrims to Kosovo to view a commemorative passion play, though estimates of the numbers involved vary.[101] Sells notes that those foremost in the production and audience for this play were before too long at the forefront of ethnic cleansing.[102]

Another aspect of Serb history that was rememorialised in 1989 was the crimes committed by the World War II Ustasha regime. Revisionist

---

[95] Ibid., p. 29.   [96] Ibid., p. 33.   [97] Vermeer, 'Albanians and Serbs', p. 120.
[98] Ramet, *Balkan Babel*, p. 28.   [99] Ibid., p. 162.   [100] Ibid., p. 161.
[101] Noel Malcolm who was there at the time rejects the figure of 3 million given in the official media as vastly inflated and estimates 300,000–500,000 people. Noel Malcolm, *Bosnia: A Short History* (London: Macmillan, 1994), p. 292, n. 1.
[102] Sells, 'Religion, History', p. 31.

historians in Croatia had argued that the number of war dead at the hands of the Ustasha was lower than generally thought. Added to this was Tudjman's claim that the Serbs had not been a specific target of the Ustasha. Croat nationalists also resurrected the old red and white 'chess board' symbol of Croatia, which had been used by the Ustasha and thus represented the Ustasha state in the minds of many.[103] In this, claims about 'the return of the Ustasha' conflated all Croats with the policies of the Ustasha government.[104] The actions of both Serb and Croatian nationalists fed popular support for Serb nationalism and the memory of Jasenovac became a rallying cry for Serb nationalists.[105] Thus the ceremonial reinterment of the remains of World War II victims of the Ustasha played a central symbolic role in a ceremony which tied together the past history of defeat at the hands of the Ottoman Empire, victimisation by the Ustasha, and the claims that Serbs were suffering from genocidal policies in Kosovo.[106]

In addition to the use of mass demonstrations the nationalists used an increasingly compliant media. Thompson accurately identifies the media campaign over Kosovo as the keystone of Milosevic's rise to power. As illustrated above, the Serbian media took up Milosevic's cause of convincing Serbians that the matter was not 'just' about politics, but was:

a question of our fatherland . . . The new media language avoided moribund socialist terminology in favour of a language of demagogy and headlong irrationality, of rhetorical questions and exclamations, of destiny and mission: a 'celestial people' confronting its fate; a language of menacing ultimatums, of infinite self-pity, of immense accusations backed by no evidence or investigation; of conspiracy mongering, paranoia, and brazen incitement to violence. It was in fact, a language of war before war was even conceivable in Yugoslavia.[107]

Through such means the pro-government Serbian press was used to create a sense of a unitary Serbian national identity among Serbs, not only in Serbia, but also in Croatia and Bosnia-Herzegovina. The treatment

[103] What the nationalists did here also excluded those Croats who rejected this on account of its wartime association with fascism and genocide. Denich, 'Dismembering Yugoslavia', 378.

[104] See Banac, 'Fearful Asymmetry' for examples of virulent nationalist commentary and cartoons which depict all Croats as Ustasha, and all Albanians as intent on the destruction of Serbs. In this manner *any* resistance to Belgrade was portrayed as proof of sympathy to the Ustasha and genocide. It also implied that fascism was 'a continued Croat tendency', 155–6. Banac notes that the Croat reaction to this was 'slow and incredulous', 163.

[105] Roy Gutman, *A Witness to Genocide* (New York: Macmillan, 1993), p. xxi.

[106] Sells, 'Religion, History', p. 34.

[107] Thompson, *Forging War*, p. 53. On the language used see also Sabrina Petra Ramet, 'Introduction: The Roots of Discord and the Language of War', in Ramet and Adamovich (eds.), *Beyond Yugoslavia*, pp. 1–9.

of Serbs in Croatia by the post-1990 nationalist government in Croatia only aided this project of corporate identity building through denigrating a minority community. In large part the media in both Croatia and Serbia prepared the path to war with inflammatory reporting which aided the alienation of different communities and fed hostility.[108] In effect, the Serbian media helped to construct a 'national consensus'. This 'was the fruit of several years' labour by the government which used its power to marshal media workers'.[109] Some members of the media were happy to work in this capacity as they held nationalist convictions, others complied out of fear or economic necessity. For others, the habits of compliance learnt from the relationship between government and journalists throughout Yugoslavia's existence meant they remained obedient. Those who refused to follow the government line were quickly marginalised, with some resigning in the face of government pressure, some demoted or sacked, while others lost their lives.[110]

From symbolic manipulation to genocide

In the revitalised myth of Kosovo, nationalist discourse brought together a number of symbolic elements that were communicated to the population, including non-Serbs, through rallies and a compliant media. The past history of defeat at the hands of the Ottoman Empire, victimisation by the Ustasha and claims that Serbs were suffering from genocidal policies in Kosovo were combined into a powerful 'symbolic complex'. From the Serbian nationalist point of view, this legitimated the drawing of a sharp boundary between Serbs and non-Serbs and placed the latter firmly outside the bounds of moral obligation. The concrete consequence of this in Kosovo was the loss of autonomy in 1989. In 1990 the Kosovo parliament was dissolved and Kosovo annexed 'to all intents and purposes' by Serbia.[111] The symbolic complex that was developed around Kosovo legitimated ethnic cleansing in Bosnia-Herzegovina and, later, in Kosovo itself. In Bosnia-Herzegovina ethnic cleansing was driven initially by Serbian expansionism, rationalised by the ideology of 'Serbia for Serbs' and 'all Serbs in one state', and the same logic underpinned the campaign by Bosnian Serbs to carve out an ethnically homogeneous state if they could not be part of 'Greater Serbia'.

As we have seen, the 1990 elections brought nationalists to power across Yugoslavia. This did not bode well for minorities in the successor states.

---

[108] Thompson, *Forging War*, p. 52.   [109] Ibid., p. 52.

[110] Ibid., p. 52. Also see Milan Milosevic, 'The Media Wars', in Udovicki and Ridgeway (eds.), *Burn This House*.

[111] Vermeer, 'Albanians and Serbs', p. 119.

With the exception of Slovenia, which is relatively (though by no means completely) homogeneous, all had significant minorities. While nationalists did not gain a stranglehold on power in Macedonia (which is discussed further in chapter 7), elsewhere they implemented policies that removed the equal citizenship rights that had existed in Yugoslavia.[112] This further exacerbated the process of polarisation that was pulling Yugoslavia apart. In this breakdown, Bosnia-Herzegovina was most vulnerable to the predatory aspirations of Croatia and Serbia, both of which refused to recognise its independent existence, and claimed parts of it for themselves.

The breakup of Yugoslavia was precipitated by declarations of independence by Slovenia and Croatia. Slovenia had proposed a confederal model if Yugoslavia was to continue but this was rejected by Serbia which continued to push for recentralisation. Slovenia was highly sceptical about the likelihood of autonomy in a Yugoslavia led by Milosevic's Serbia. Consequently, the Slovenian constitution was amended in September 1989 – before multiparty elections – to allow secession from Yugoslavia. It was also late that year that the Slovenian police blocked a Serbian 'Truth About Kosovo' rally from being held in the Slovenian capital Ljubljana, which would have brought thousands of Serb nationalists flooding into Slovenia. This attempt, and the angry response of Serb nationalists when it was blocked, further heightened popular Slovenian distrust of Serbia, and made any agreement to a recentralised Yugoslavia under the leadership of Serbia even more remote.

In the 1990 referendum following the elections around 90 per cent of Slovenians opted for independence.[113] Slovenia, along with Croatia, declared its independence from Yugoslavia on 25 June 1991. To the Yugoslav National Army (JNA) this represented a threat to the territorial integrity of Yugoslavia, and the JNA moved on Slovenia within twenty-four hours, but this action lasted only ten days. The JNA withdrew in part due to the presence of European Community (EC) mediators. Another important element in reaching a ceasefire so quickly was that Slovenia was not a major issue for Serbia, as there was no major Serb population there and it was not that important to Greater Serb nationalists.[114] This brief conflict was also attended by desertion from the ranks by JNA soldiers, particularly those of non-Serb backgrounds, as the JNA began

---

[112] Hayden, 'Constitutional Nationalism'.

[113] John R. Lampe, *Yugoslavia as History: Twice There Was a Country* (Cambridge University Press, 1996), p. 351; Robert J. Donia and John V. A. Fine, *Bosnia and Hercegovina: A Tradition Betrayed* (London: Hurst & Co, 1994), p. 217.

[114] Donia and Fine, *Bosnia*, pp. 218–19.

its transformation from a federal Yugoslav army to an army fighting for Serbia.[115]

Conflicts were not to be so brief in either Croatia or Bosnia-Herzegovina. Though the JNA and Serbia were willing to let Slovenia go, this was not the case with Croatia, where neither the 12 per cent Serb minority nor the Serb government were prepared to let Croatia so easily secede from Yugoslavia. Serb nationalism in Croatia had already been heightened by both Milosevic's encouragement and the treatment of Serbs following the 1990 victory of nationalists under the leadership of Franjo Tudjman. Despite claims by Tudjman that there was no reason for Serbs in Croatia to be apprehensive,[116] after the elections the discriminatory treatment of Serbs in Croatia escalated: the Cyrillic script was removed from road signs, Serb workers were dismissed from their jobs, and the government encouraged the public display of the red and white 'chess board' emblem of Croatia, with its fascist associations. These policies, combined with Serbian encouragement, only fed the demands for autonomy on the part of the Serbs of Croatia, particularly in the Krajina region.[117]

A 1990 referendum among Croatian Serbs resoundingly supported autonomy and the 'Serbian Autonomous Region of Krajina' was declared in March 1991. The Croatian government opposed this and a weapons build-up on both sides ensued throughout 1990–91 and clashes escalated. In one clash in Borovo Selo in which twelve Croatian police and three Serbs were killed, some of the bodies of the Croatian police were mutilated in a 'symbolic re-enactment of Chetnik reprisals against Croats during WWII, calculated to inflame ethnic hatred by rekindling the passions of wartime genocide'.[118] Such acts were the harbinger of further violence. Although the conflict in Slovenia ended with relatively little loss of life and most of these casualties were from the military of both sides, the war in Croatia resulted in a high number of military and civilian casualties. Between July and December 1991 the JNA and Serbian paramilitaries took control of nearly one-third of Croatia, with more than 10,000 killed and around 30,000 wounded.[119] It was during this war between Serbia and Croatia that 'ethnic cleansing' was first put into practice, as Serbian

---

[115] After this transformation, that was finally completed with forced retirements in 1993, those left in authority in the JNA favoured Serbia's aims and supported Milosevic.

[116] Lenard J. Cohen, *Broken Bonds: Yugoslavia's Disintegration and Balkan Politics in Transition*, 2nd edn (Boulder: Westview Press, 1995), p. 211.

[117] Donia and Fine, *Bosnia*, p. 223. On the vocal critics of the government, including the stance of much of the Croatian Catholic clergy towards government policies, both in Croatia and in Bosnia, while the Catholic Church in Bosnia was more supportive of ethnic cleansing, see Cigar, *Genocide in Bosnia*, pp. 127–37.

[118] Donia and Fine, *Bosnia*, p. 223.   [119] Cohen, *Broken Bonds*, p. 229.

forces 'cleansed' non-Serbs from the parts of Croatia they claimed as their own. These operations included the wholesale destruction of cities such as Vukovar and Dubrovnik. For example, in addition to massacres like that of 260 patients dragged from their hospital beds in Vukovar in October 1991,[120] the assault on Dubrovnik, which was of no strategic importance, entailed the systematic destruction of buildings of religious and cultural significance.[121] Such practices supported the goal of ethnic cleansing, as they served to frighten people into leaving, and obliterated the physical signs of their communities, after which the military could resettle the areas that had been emptied of the 'wrong' group.

Thus Serb irregulars backed by the JNA set about expelling non-Serbs from areas with Serbian majorities. One of Slobodan Milosevic's first acts as President of Serbia had been to set up the Serbian Voluntary Guards under the auspices of the Interior Ministry. This allowed the formation of paramilitary organisations such as 'Arkan's Tigers', led by a known criminal, Arkan (Zeliko Razanotivic), or Vojislav Seselj's militia.[122] As Seselj acknowledged after Milosevic atttempted to distance himself from the militias in 1994, the militias were armed and trained by Serbia's police force and army.[123] The use of such ultra-nationalist irregulars in ethnic cleansing and the atrocities they committed was meant to destroy patterns of coexistence in a way that made it unlikely that people would ever want to live together again.[124]

The international community did nothing about the atrocities that occurred in Croatia at this time. It is a persuasive argument that decisive action at this time might have averted the ethnic cleansing that was to follow in Bosnia.[125] As it was, though, the inaction of the international community acted as a green light to both Milosevic and to Tudjman, signalling that they could continue their policies undisturbed. In September 1991, UN Security Council resolution 713 imposed an arms embargo on the former Yugoslavia in an effort to stop the violence. In effect, this merely served to strengthen the position of Serbia and its clients in Bosnia-Herzegovina as the JNA had maintained control of the military

---

[120] Jane M. O. Sharp, 'Dayton Report Card', *International Security* 22:3 (1997/98), 106.
[121] Donia and Fine, *Bosnia*, p. 226.
[122] Lampe, *Yugoslavia as History*, p. 353. Arkan was assassinated in Belgrade in January 2000.
[123] Cigar, *Genocide in Bosnia*, p. 54.
[124] Many JNA officers were willing to help Serbian irregulars in Croatia and it was with their assistance that irregulars often gained the advantage over Croatian Territorial Forces. 'By the fall of 1991 various YPA [JNA] field commanders were in effect prosecuting a civil war to unite the Serbs of Croatia with those living in the core republics of Serbia and Montenegro.' Donia and Fine, *Bosnia*, pp. 222–3; Malcolm, *Bosnia*, p. 226.
[125] See Sharp, 'Dayton Report Card', for this argument.

equipment in what was Yugoslavia.[126] The action of the international community in imposing this embargo paved the way for the further ethnic cleansing of populations either unarmed or seriously outclassed in terms of weaponry.

On 1 January 1992 the UN secretary general's personal envoy to Yugoslavia, Cyrus Vance, announced a ceasefire agreement between the JNA, Serbia and Croatia and that a UN Protection Force (UNPROFOR) would be deployed in Croatia.[127] On 2 January 1992 a formal peace agreement was signed in Sarajevo and UN personnel arrived in Croatia two weeks later to begin their peacekeeping role. This peace suited Milosevic, for as Jane Sharp points out, UN troops could protect the Serbs who remained in the UN designated protection areas which had been 'cleansed' of non-Serbs, 'thus freeing up the JNA for offensive operations elsewhere'.[128] In effect, the peace that had come to Croatia meant war for Bosnia-Herzegovina. During the latter half of 1991, for all intents and purposes, the JNA had been transformed from a federal Yugoslav army into a Serbian army. At the same time, the war in Croatia 'strengthened national extremists among Bosnian Serbs', and weakened the position of those who sought to defend the multiethnic character of the Bosnian state.[129] Areas of Bosnia-Herzegovina with significant Serb populations would be carved out as Serb enclaves along with a corridor to link them to the Serb Krajina. As Croatian policy changed, areas of Bosnia-Herzegovina would also be carved out as Croat enclaves.

War in Bosnia-Herzegovina

According to the 1991 census figures, of Bosnia-Herzegovina's population of 4.35 million people, 44 per cent identified themselves as Muslim, 31 per cent as Serb and 17 per cent as Croat. Following the 1990 elections, both Muslim and Croatian politicians in the coalition government supported an independent Bosnia rather than become part of a Serb dominated rump Yugoslavia. A proposal for an independent Bosnia submitted by the Muslim Party for Democratic Action (PDA) on 30 January 1991 was accepted by the Croatian Democratic Community (CDC), but was rejected by the Serb Democratic Party (SDP) under the leadership of Karadzic. It was unacceptable to the Serbs because it would mean the institutionalisation of Bosnian Serbs as a minority in an independent

---

[126] Ibid., 106.   [127] Donia and Fine, *Bosnia*, p. 227.

[128] Sharp, 'Dayton Report Card', p. 107.

[129] Donia and Fine, *Bosnia*, p. 220. On the opposition in Croatia see Cigar, *Genocide in Bosnia*, pp. 127–37; and Sven Balas, 'The Opposition in Croatia', in Udovicki and Ridgeway (eds.), *Burn This House*, pp. 265–78.

and sovereign Bosnia-Herzegovina,[130] something which the ideology of 'all Serbs in one Serbian' state would not allow. From this position it was impossible to reach a compromise. In October 1991 the Muslim and Croatian parties passed a resolution in favour of independence for Bosnia – members of the SDP having already left after the Serbian assembly president had adjourned the session. The Bosnian Serb party did not recognise this as valid, and on 21 December 1991 they declared their own republic within Bosnia-Herzegovina.[131]

In February 1992 a referendum on independence was held in Bosnia-Herzegovina.[132] This was boycotted by most of the Serb population at the behest of the Serbian Democratic Party (Srpska Demokratska Stranka, SDS). The result of the referendum supported independence and Bosnia-Herzegovina declared itself an independent state on 3 March 1992. This was not without misgivings on the part of Bosnian leaders, though. As Sharp explains:

Believing that Bosnia was not ready for either self-governance or self-defence and that the Bosnian Serbs were poised to attack once Bosnia was forced into independence, [Bosnian President] Izetbegovic in October 1991 began to ask the United Nations and the EC for some kind of transitional authority and/or preventive troop deployments. Neither UN nor EC officials whom Izetbegovic approached, nor any western government, however, would help Bosnia at this stage, forcing Izetbegovic to turn to Iran for assistance.[133]

At the same time, the Bosnian Serb leader Radovan Karadzic addressed himself to the shrinking rural Serb population of Bosnia-Herzegovina, and picked up on resentment of cosmopolitan Sarajevo and 'grievances from the Second World War against the local Muslims, whom these Serbs still called Turks'.[134] Karadzic played on these fears, with predictions that Serbs in Bosnia would be subjected to an Islamic fundamentalist regime.

As we have seen, the JNA had increased its activities in Bosnia in mid-1991, and while some of these activities were in support of the war in Croatia, many of their activities were clearly in preparation for a war in Bosnia itself. Throughout that year JNA units were moved out of cities into the countryside, and production facilities in Bosnia were either dismantled and shifted to Serbia or abandoned. By the beginning of 1992 the JNA was prepared for a full-scale assault on Bosnia.[135]

On 6 April 1992 the EC recognised Bosnia-Herzegovina as an independent state, with the United States following the next day. The Western

[130] Donia and Fine, *Bosnia*, p. 229.   [131] Ibid.
[132] Of the 64 per cent voter turnout, 99.5 per cent voted for a sovereign, independent and multinational Bosnia-Herzegovina. Thompson, *Forging War*, p. 205.
[133] Sharp, 'Dayton Report Card', 107.
[134] Lampe, *Yugoslavia as History*, p. 355.   [135] Donia and Fine, *Bosnia*, p. 229.

expectation that recognition of Bosnian sovereignty would calm things down was naive, if not wilfully blind. This recognition was not backed with any offers of protection for the vulnerable new state which was the object of the aspirations of Serb and Croatian nationalists both inside and outside Bosnia, and the newly fledged state was rendered even more vulnerable by the internationally sanctioned arms embargo. Thus, recognition without material support exacerbated the situation and 'unleashed a wave of systematic rape, murder, and evacuation of Croats and Muslims in those parts of Bosnia coveted by Milosevic'.[136] In this way Bosnia slid into a war that would last from mid-1992 until 1995, and in which Serbia and Croatia and their proxies within Bosnia-Herzegovina sought to divide its territory between them and used 'ethnic cleansing' as a means of doing so.[137]

The Muslim–Croat alliance

The position of Muslims in Bosnia-Herzegovina became even more precarious when the leadership of the Croatian party (HDZ) in Bosnia-Herzegovina changed. With Tudjman's protégé Mate Boban installed in January 1992 as leader of the Bosnian Croats, the HDZ policy changed to support the partition of Bosnia.[138] This reflected Tudjman's preference, highlighted by the 1991 agreement between him and Milosevic to 'carve up Bosnia between a Greater Serbia and a Greater Croatia'.[139]

In July 1992 the independent state of 'Croat Community of Herceg-Bosna' was declared by Boban in the Western Herzegovinan stronghold of Croat nationalism. This was despite the formal alliance between Croatia and Bosnia signed by Tudjman and Izetbegovic in June 1992[140] and it signalled that the 'shaky alliance' established between the Muslims and Croats in Bosnia-Herzegovina was falling apart. From the end of 1992 and into 1993, Croat–Muslim fighting spread as each side tried to control territory. Meanwhile, the international community sought to come up with some way of dealing with the conflict. The possibility of partitioning Bosnia-Herzegovina into up to ten cantons raised by the Vance–Owen plan caused some anxiety for the Bosnian Croats as Croats were in the minority. The January 1993 version of the Vance–Owen plan demonstrated that in struggling to deal with this conflict the international

---

[136] Sharp, 'Dayton Report Card', 107. In a similar vein Donia and Fine see the international community's actions as the ' "proximate cause" of the war in Bosnia' because their policies aggravated matters. Donia and Fine, *Bosnia*, p. 234.

[137] Sharp, 'Dayton Report Card', p. 103.

[138] Cohen, *Broken Bonds*, p. 248. On the split in the HDZ over policy towards Bosnia see Cigar, *Genocide in Bosnia*, pp. 128–9.

[139] Sharp, 'Dayton Report Card', 104.   [140] Ibid., 109.

community found itself drawn into legitimating the nationalists' ethnic exclusivist politics. As Noel Malcolm asserts:

> unlike the initial version proposed in October, the cantons were given 'ethnic' labels on the map, and at the same time the impression was given that the precise boundaries on the map were not yet final. This had the entirely predictable effect of inciting renewed competition for territory. And, worst of all, it incited competition between Croat and Muslim forces for parts of central Bosnia where there had been a mixed Muslim–Croat population. After the arms embargo this was the second most important contribution of the West to the destruction of Bosnia: it stimulated the development of a genuine Bosnian civil war, and in so doing it broke down the Croat–Muslim alliance which had been the only effective barrier to the Serbs.[141]

Whatever the intentions of the plan, non-Croats were expelled from areas allocated for Croatian self-rule.[142] In April 1993 Croat irregulars massacred Muslim residents of the mixed Muslim–Croat village of Ahmici. Early May saw the siege of the predominantly Muslim city of East Mostar and the coordinated expulsion of Muslims from Herzegovina.[143] By the time that the Bosnian Serbs had rejected the Vance–Owen plan in mid-May 1993, the Croat–Muslim alliance was broken and a three-way war was under way in Bosnia-Herzegovina. By June 1993 the leaders of Croatia and Serbia, along with their Bosnian clients, were again discussing partition of Bosnia-Herzegovina.

As fighting between Bosnian Croats and Bosnian Muslims continued through the middle of 1993, the 'spectre' of Islamic fundamentalism was raised by Croatian as well as Serbian nationalists. This rhetoric had little to do with the reality of the highly secularised community of 2 million Bosnian Muslims, many of whom were Muslim through culture and tradition, rather than by strong religious belief or practice.[144] Once again, though, stereotypical images were used to heighten fear and polarise communities, and also to deflect responsibility for the violence onto its victims. For example, President Tudjman blamed the fighting in 1993 on

---

[141] Malcolm, *Bosnia*, p. 248. Malcolm goes on to note, 'The UN human rights rapporteur Tadeusz Mazowiecki issued a report [in May 1993] clearly warning that the Vance–Owen plan was stimulating ethnic cleansing; but by then it was too late.' Malcolm, *Bosnia*, p. 249. Owen takes a different view of this. He points out that in January 1993 Bosnian Serbs held 70 per cent of Bosnia-Herzegovina. The 1993 Vance–Owen Peace Plan (VOPP) would have reduced this to 43 per cent As he points out, under the Dayton Agreement the Bosnian Serbs retained 49 per cent of Bosnia-Herzegovina and the state was partitioned into two entities. Still, at the time Izetbegovic regarded this solution as legitimating ethnic cleansing, and in any event the Bosnian Serbs eventually rejected it as they did not intend to give up territory voluntarily. See David Owen, *Balkan Odyssey* (New York: Harcourt Brace, 1995), pp. 91–3, for his views on this.

[142] Cohen, *Broken Bonds*, p. 277.   [143] Ibid., p. 277.   [144] Malcolm, *Bosnia*, p. 222.

the 'Mujahideen', arguing that as they had lost to the Serbs they were now trying to take Croatian territory, a view supported in the mainstream Croatian media, and in turn reflected in growing anti-Muslim feelings across Croatia.[145] As Muslim military successes against Croat forces increased in the autumn of 1993, thousands of Croatian civilians were killed and many more were forced out – themselves the victims of 'ethnic cleansing' and atrocities on the part of Muslim forces – and it appeared that the policy of Tudjman and his Bosnian client Boban had backfired.[146] Faced with domestic and international pressure against the Croatian role in Bosnia, combined with the military defeats there, Tudjman made a major turn around in policy. In early 1994 Boban was forced out of power and Tudjman shifted to join an anti-Serb coalition. The relevant factors here include economic inducements (the promise of aid), and the 3 February 1994 Security Council ultimatum, supported by the United States, that Croatia should withdraw troops from Bosnia or face sanctions,[147] combined with the opposition to Tudjman's policies within Croatia, which was better organised and more institutionally entrenched than the opposition in Serbia.[148]

So far, we have looked at the complex history of intercommunal relations in Yugoslavia, and the symbolic manipulation of the complicated legacy of an unresolved, violent (recent) past. Through this manipulation nationalist leaders emphasised the threat that minority groups posed to their own community and in turn labelled minorities as outside 'the universe of moral obligation'. This symbolic expulsion laid the groundwork for the physical expulsion and destruction that followed. It is to these acts that I now turn.

'Ethnic cleansing' in Bosnia-Herzegovina

As outlined above, 'ethnic cleansing' was first employed in Serb held areas of Croatia during 1992. In Bosnia-Herzegovina, Serb and Bosnian Serb forces engaged in a systematic programme directed at the construction of an ethnically homogeneous 'Greater Serbia', or failing that, an ethnically homogeneous Serb Republic within Bosnia-Herzegovina. The destruction of Muslim communities in Bosnia-Herzegovina displayed a systematic pattern that shows a 'general top-down policy guidance and a degree of coordination across the republic and, apparently, with unofficial and government circles in Belgrade'.[149]

[145] Cohen, *Broken Bonds*, pp. 278–9.   [146] Ibid., p. 279.   [147] Ibid., pp. 298–9.
[148] Cigar, *Genocide in Bosnia*, pp. 129–30.   [149] Ibid., pp. 47–61, quote at p. 47.

As in Croatia, the worst perpetrators of war crimes and crimes against humanity were paramilitaries, either 'special forces' (such as Arkan's 'Tigers', the 'White Eagles' led by Mirko Jovic or Sesejl's militia), or local police forces reinforced by local civilians. Army regulars were also involved, as were Territorial Defence Forces, who frequently acted under orders from, and in cooperation with, the regular army, although in some cases they acted independently. At times towns or villages formed their own paramilitary units. All this made it very difficult to trace the chain of command and therefore trace responsibility. The one common factor in the multiplicity of forces involved in the war in Bosnia-Herzegovina was that all forces received military hardware from their government backers.

Outline of a genocide

On 27 March 1992, the day the Bosnian Serbs declared their own constitution, the JNA attacked Bosnia. When the EC recognition of Bosnia came into effect on 6 April 1992, peace demonstrators in Sarajevo were attacked by snipers.[150] From then the violence quickly escalated, and within a couple of months Serb forces controlled about 70 per-cent of Bosnia-Herzegovina and engaged in wide-scale ethnic cleansing of both Muslims and Croats.[151]

Ethnic cleansing operations were preceded by Serb forces taking control of local media and communication facilities. Once the local media was controlled, it became the conduit for the claims that *Serbs* in the area were under threat of genocide at the hands of either 'Ustasha' or 'Mujahideen' or both. This propaganda was designed to heighten the fears of ordinary Serbs that *they* were in danger. This tactic played on the 'Kosovo symbolic complex' discussed above, which stressed the historic victimisation of Serbs, and was part of 'the social production of fear and vengefulness',[152] that served to legitimate violence against non-Serbs when the time came. At the same time, the local non-Serb populations were disarmed, though in some areas this was resisted more than in others. Serb civilians were often told to evacuate when operations against the non-Serb population were imminent.[153]

[150] Donia and Fine, *Bosnia*, p. 238.
[151] Aleksa Djilas, 'Fear Thy Neighbour: The Breakup of Yugoslavia', in Charles A. Kupchan (ed.), *Nationalism and Nationalities in the New Europe* (Ithaca: Cornell University Press, 1995), pp. 99–100.
[152] Paul Parin, 'Open Wounds; Ethnopsychoanalytic Reflections on the Wars in the Former Yugoslavia', in Alexandra Stiglmayer (ed.), *Mass Rape: The War Against Women in Bosnia-Herzegovina*, trans. Marion Faber (Lincoln: University of Nebraska Press, 1994), p. 42.
[153] Cigar, *Genocide in Bosnia*, p. 48.

In a pattern familiar from the Armenian genocide, the first victims in most communities were 'intellectuals and cultural leaders: teachers, lawyers, doctors, business people, religious leaders, artists, poets, and musicians', the object being to destroy the 'cultural memory' of a community.[154] Later, the killings were more random, aimed at terrorising people into leaving. In many areas life was made unliveable through the loss of employment, the cutting off of utilities and the imposition of petty rules that made it difficult for Bosnian Muslims to go about their daily lives, such as curtailing freedom of movement and association. Local authorities often played an active role in this, stripping Muslims of their property (usually claiming that it had been signed over voluntarily), or imposing exit taxes, as they left 'voluntarily'.[155]

An important part of the process was the systematic obliteration of mosques, churches and museums as if to wipe out the history of the co-existence nationalists were intent on destroying. Another, now infamous, part of this programme of destruction was the systematic use of violence against women.[156] Impregnation of the victims was often the goal of these rapes with women told by their attackers that they would have 'Serb babies'. 'Because this is ethnic rape, lacking racial markers, the children are regarded by the aggressors as somehow clean and purified, as "cleansed" ethnically. The babies made with Muslim and with Croatian women are regarded as Serbian babies.'[157] The international community was initially reluctant to acknowledge the reality of what was happening to women in Bosnia-Herzegovina. The first reports of systematic rape,

154 Sells, 'Religion, History', p. 26.   155 Ibid., p. 27; Cigar, *Genocide in Bosnia*, p. 57.
156 Ramet notes that a patriarchal backlash accompanied Milosevic's rise to power. 'The entire Milosevic phenomenon is, in fact, rooted in fear: fear of the Albanians, Croats, and even, eventually, Slovenes; fear of new political movements; fear of randomness, freedom, chaos; and fear of women.' Under the Milosevic regime jobs for women dried up and they were told to return to 'traditional duties'. Ramet, *Balkan Babel*, p. 110.
157 Catharine A. MacKinnon, 'Rape, Genocide, and Women's Human Rights', in Stiglmayer (ed.), *Mass Rape*, pp. 190–1. For a discussion of the patriarchal attitudes that make women's bodies a means of war and which also mean that forced impregnation *can* work as a means of cultural destruction because children of such rapes are understood by all parties to be 'Serbs', see Todd A. Salzman, 'Rape Camps as a Means of Ethnic Cleansing: Religious, Cultural, and Ethical Responses to Rape Victims in the Former Yugoslavia', *Human Rights Quarterly* 20:2 (1998); also see Tadeusz Mazowiecki, 'The Situation of Human Rights in the Territory of the Former Yugoslavia', UN Doc. A/48/92-S/25341 (United Nations: New York, February 1993); Theodor Meron, 'Rape as a Crime Under International Humanitarian Law', *American Journal of International Law* 87:3 (1993); United Nations, *Final Report of the Commission of Experts*, UN Doc. S/1994/674, 27 May 1994, part IV, <http://www.his.com:80/~cij/commxyu1.htm>, accessed 13 August 1997; F. Beverly Allen, *Rape Warfare: The Hidden Genocide in Bosnia-Herzegovina and Croatia* (Minneapolis: University of Minnesota Press, 1996); Kelly Dawn Askin, *Rape Crimes Against Women: Prosecution in International War Crimes Tribunals* (The Hague: Kluwer Law, 1997), pp. 261–375.

in November 1992, were not followed up. In early December the United Nations High Commissioner for Refugees (UNHCR) and the International Committee of the Red Cross (IRC) reported isolated cases of rape, and that they were being committed by all sides in the conflict.[158] However, by mid-December there was a turn around. Extensive publicity meant that the international community could not ignore the reality that, although all sides of the conflict did indeed perpetrate violence against women (as in all wars), it was Bosnian Muslim women who were being systematically targeted, often being 'incarcerated and repeatedly raped', and this was part of the programme of ethnic cleansing.[159] The rapes spread fear, demoralised the victims and their community, induced flight, and also made it unlikely that survivors would wish to return.[160] For the Muslim women who suffered these attacks, the social stigma attached to rape, let alone the fact that that most rapes were gang rapes, was part of a 'many layered trauma' and it is unlikely that the full extent of the rapes will ever be known as many women will never come forward to tell their stories.[161]

The wars in the former Yugoslavia saw the return of detention camps to Europe, the majority of which – though not all – were run by Serb forces.[162] The events in Opstina (district) Prijedor in north-western Bosnia, documented in the UN Commission of Experts Final Report, illustrates the pattern of events and the role of such camps.[163] In the wake of attacks on towns and villages in this district, 'hundreds, possibly thousands were killed . . . frequently after maltreatment'.[164] Survivors were divided into two groups, one of women, older men and children including younger boys up to around 16 years. The other was of younger men. The men were taken to concentration camps, such as those in Karaterm and at Ormarska. 'Massacres, tortures and appalling living conditions quickly depleted the number of detainees.'[165] Based on the numbers known to have gone into camps and those transferred elsewhere or later released, 'it may be assumed that the death toll was extremely high.

---

[158] Alexandra Stiglmayer, 'The War in the Former Yugoslavia', in Stiglmayer (ed.), *Mass Rape*, p. 24.

[159] Burg and Shoup, *The War in Bosnia-Herzegovina*, p. 170; Stiglmayer, 'War in the Former Yugoslavia', pp. 24–5. According to testimony given before the war crimes tribunal, rapes were ordered to boost Serbian 'morale'. MacKinnon, 'Rape, Genocide', p. 75.

[160] Alexandra Stiglmayer, 'The Rapes in Bosnia-Herzegovina', in Alexandra Stiglmayer (ed.), *Mass Rape*, p. 85.

[161] Vera Folnegovic-Smalc, 'Psychiatric Aspects of the Rapes in the War against the Republics of Croatia and Bosnia-Herzegovina', in Stiglmayer (ed.), *Mass Rape*, pp. 175–7, quote at p. 177.

[162] Burg and Shoup, *The War in Bosnia-Herzegovina*, pp. 175–81.

[163] United Nations, *Final Report*.

[164] *Final Report*, Part IV, Substantive Findings, Section A.5.   [165] Ibid.

The concentration camp premises were sometimes so packed with people that no more inmates could be crammed in. On at least one occasion this allegedly resulted in an entire busload of newly captured people being arbitrarily executed en masse.'[166]

Large-scale deportation was also part of the programme of ethnic cleansing. In the case of Opstina Prijedor, women were deported first, as soon as the first groups of non-Serbs were captured. Deportees were shoved into crowed buses and military trucks, to be 'dumped' within reach of non-Serb-held areas of Bosnia, though reaching these areas often necessitated long walks. Others were deported by rail, including many in cattle wagons. Some died due to being crowded into cattle wagons and closed military trucks in heat with no food or water.[167]

While news of the camps, and the ethnic cleansing of which they were but one aspect, was picked up in the international media, in the government controlled press reports of both the Croatian and Bosnian wars were distorted, portraying Serbs as only taking defensive actions whilst at the same time casting them as 'liberators'. The massive destruction of life and property was either ignored, or if this was not possible due to coverage in other sources, reports were met with 'parallel' reporting. For example, the release of the UN report on the systematic rape of non-Serb women was not mentioned, but a report which focused on Serbian rape victims was shown.[168]

In Bosnia-Herzegovina a systematic policy was implemented with the intention of changing the ethnic composition in a particular area claimed for either Greater Serbia, or once that goal became impossible, a Bosnian Serb Republic. The manner in which elites sought to build the state and buttress their own identity played on stereotypes and fears, and generated a whole new set of fears. As Hayden argues, this was about the 'unimagining' of Yugoslavia, and it was also about 'reimagining' the political communities which could 'legitimately' exist inside the boundaries of the redefined national and nationalist states that were being carved out.[169] In the context of the heterogeneity of Bosnia-Herzegovina, a 'forced unmixing of peoples' took place, and where heterogeneity once existed the memory of what was done in an attempt to create new boundaries will not easily be erased.

In chapter 6 I investigate how the international community struggled to deal with ethnic cleansing in Bosnia and what this means for

---

[166] Ibid.   [167] Ibid.

[168] Bosnian Serb rape victims were the subject of news bulletins when an EC report was released which 'estimated that 20,000 Muslim women had been raped by Serb soldiers'. This report was not mentioned. Thompson, *Forging War*, pp. 108–9.

[169] Hayden, 'Imagined Communities'.

the articulation of international norms of legitimate statehood. However, though peace came to Bosnia in 1995, Slobodan Milosovec was still entrenched in power in the Federal Republic of Yugoslavia and he continued to use the Kosovo issue as a means of legitimating his authority in the face of rising internal opposition. It is to this that I now turn.

Ethnic cleansing and legitimacy: Kosovo 1999 and Milosevic's fall from power

As we saw above, in 1989 Kosovo was stripped of its autonomous status, in response to which Kosovar legislators declared Kosovo's independence in July 1990. Subsequently, Belgrade dissolved the Kosovo parliament and ethnic Albanians were pushed out of all positions of public authority and responsibility in the province. A range of laws were passed that made life difficult for Kosovars, who suffered a range of human rights abuses during the 1990s, and were encouraged to leave the province.[170] Apart from Albania, no other member of the international community recognised Kosovo as an independent republic. In 1992 the ethnic Albanian community held elections in defiance of Serbian authorities, who declared the elections illegal. Despite this, a high voter turnout elected as president the leader of the Democratic League of Kosovo (LDK), Ibrahim Rugova. In 1998 elections were held again despite a Serb crackdown on Kosovo and Rugova was returned as President of the 'shadow' republic. However, between 1992 and 1998 the non-violent approach espoused by Rugova had been gradually losing the support of Kosovars, in no small part due to the way in which the West used Milosevic as a 'peacemaker' at Dayton and ignored the plight of the Albanian Kosovars in the Dayton Accord.[171] This led to a widespread perception that non-violence was not working.[172]

The years following Dayton saw the Milosevic regime engage in increasing repression of the ethnic Albanian population in Kosovo, the appearance of the Kosovo Liberation Army (KLA) in 1997, and the growing radicalisation of the ethnic Albanian population. Throughout the 1990s ethnic Albanians streamed out of Kosovo, with an estimated 350,000 leaving between 1989 and 1998 and another 100,000 leaving during the

---

[170] Sabrina Petra Ramet, *Balkan Babel: The Disintegration of Yugoslavia from the Death of Tito to the War for Kosovo*, 3rd edn (Boulder: Westview Press, 1999), p. 308; Malcolm, *Kosovo*, pp. 343–7, pp. 349–50 for an outline of human rights abuses.

[171] Ramet, *Balkan Babel*, 3rd edn, p. 309; Malcolm, *Kosovo*, pp. 353–5.

[172] Amanda Vickers, *Between Serb and Albanian: A History of Kosovo* (London: Hurst & Company, 1998), p. 287.

1998 crisis.[173] In February 1998, in the wake of the extrajudicial killings of civilians by Yugoslav security forces, the United States warned Milosevic that increasing isolation would be the price for further violence towards Kosovo Albanians.[174] Despite diplomatic efforts to bring about a change in policy, in July 1998 Yugoslav forces employed a renewed campaign of terror against the civilian population. The execution of unarmed civilians, including women and children, in an effort to crush support for the KLA, who controlled an estimated 40 per cent of Kosovo by that time, had the opposite effect of further radicalising the ethnic Albanian population and further alienating international public opinion.[175]

By early 1999 the international community was applying pressure to both Milosevic and the Kosovar Albanians to resolve their differences. However, the internationally brokered negotiations held in Rambouillet, France, in February 1999, proved unsuccessful and military intervention loomed. At the Rambouillet Conference it became increasingly clear that, unlike the Kosovar Albanians, the Yugoslav government was not taking negotiations seriously. Rather, the whole diplomatic process appeared to be a means of stalling the international community, from the Yugoslav point of view.[176] Despite some withdrawals of Serbian personnel and hardware, the agreements that were made during the course of negotiations were never fully complied with. During the break between the conference in late February and the March follow-up meeting in Paris, troops were building up on the border with Kosovo and in Kosovo itself, and attacks on civilians continued, leading to a sharp increase in the number of internally displaced people.[177] After a final attempt to negotiate a settlement with Belgrade failed, on 24 March 1999 NATO began air strikes against Belgrade that were to last eleven weeks.

Rather than backing down, Milosevic took the air strikes as an opportunity to embark on a massive expulsion of the ethnic Albanians of Kosovo, causing an estimated 900,000 refugees to flee the province.[178] Tactics similar to those used in Bosnia were employed with criminals released

---

[173] UNHCR, 'Kosovo's First Exodus', *Refugees* 116 (1999); Fernando del Mundo and Ray Wilkinson, 'A Race Against Time', *Refugees* 116 (1999).

[174] Ivo H. Daalder and Michael E. O'Hanlon, *Winning Ugly: NATO's War to Save Kosovo* (Washington, DC: Brookings Institution Press, 2000), p. 27.

[175] Human Rights Watch, *Federal Republic of Yugoslavia: Humanitarian Law Violations in Kosovo* (New York: Human Rights Watch, 1998), <http://www.hrw.org/reports/2000/fry/index.htm>, accessed 22 March 2000. This report also notes abuses by the KLA.

[176] Daalder and O'Hanlon, *Winning Ugly*, p. 88; Marc Weller, 'The Rambouillet Conference on Kosovo', *International Affairs* 75:2 (1999), 228–36.

[177] Weller, 'The Rambouillet Conference', p. 236.

[178] Nicholas Martin, 'UNHCR and Kosovo: A Personal View from the UNHCR', *Forced Migration Review* 5:August (1999), 14.

from prison combining with militia and regular army personnel in the onslaught against civilians, which, once again, included the systematic rape of women.[179] As Tim Judah notes, this ethnic cleansing backfired 'immediately' because it resulted in saturation coverage by the Western media of Kosovar refugees, which in turn helped maintain public support for the bombing campaign.[180] It also resulted in Milosevic and four others being indicted by the International Criminal Tribunal for the former Yugoslavia (ICTY) on charges of crimes against humanity and violations of the customs of war in Kosovo, the first time a serving head of state had been indicted as an international criminal. Milosevic has since appeared before the tribunal on these charges, and the tribunal has authorised two further indictments which charge him with responsibility, both individually and as part of a joint criminal enterprise, for crimes committed in Croatia and Bosnia-Herzegovina.[181]

It is not surprising that diplomatic efforts to resolve the conflict in Kosovo failed, as Slobodan Milosevic was not interested in a negotiated solution to the conflict which was, after all, of his own creation. For an authoritarian ruler like Milosevic the option of accepting the norms of legitimate statehood – democratic institutions, human and minority rights as well as a functioning market economy – was not acceptable, as it would have entailed remaking the bases of his domestic legitimacy in a way that would have made him vulnerable to domestic challengers, namely pro-democratic forces, when he was already under pressure from such forces. As public demonstrations throughout his time in power, and his final ousting from power in October 2000 have shown, there were many within Serbia who did not see the Milosevic regime as legitimate. However, the nationalist discourse of the regime, combined with the targeting of minorities, could mark such critics out as traitors to the Serb cause, at least for a time. This, combined with control of the police, army and

[179] Tim Judah, *Kosovo: War and Revenge* (New Haven: Yale University Press, 2000), p. 250. Also see Human Rights Watch, 'Federal Republic of Yugoslavia. Kosovo: Rape as a Weapon of "Ethnic Cleansing"', <http://www.hrw.org/hrw/reports/2000/fry/index.htm>.

[180] Judah, *Kosovo*, p. 251. On the Western response to Kosovar refugees, see Matthew J. Gibney, 'Kosovo and Beyond: Popular and Unpopular Refugees', *Forced Migration Review* 5:August (1999), 28–30.

[181] Milosevic was indicted on 8 October 2001 on charges of crimes against humanity, grave breaches of the Geneva Conventions and violations of the Customs or Laws of War in Croatia in 1991–92. On 22 November he was indicted on the same three charges with respect to events in Bosnia-Herzegovina between August 1991 and December 1995, but for the first time he was also indicted on the charge of genocide. See, respectively, ICTY, Case No. IT-01-50-I and ICTY Case No. IT-01-51-I, both available at: http://www.un.org/icty/ind-e.htm.

media and a weak and disorganised opposition allowed him to remain in power for more than a decade.[182]

In terms of the logic of state construction through pathological homogenisation Milosevic had 'nowhere else to go' by the second half of the 1990s. He came to power on the symbolics of Kosovo and he attempted to use the same tactics to hold on to power when there were few other options left to him. To back down would have undermined the basis of his legitimacy, which was increasingly shaky as the Serbian people tired of the hardships imposed on them by living in what had become, to all intents and purposes, a mafia state internally and a pariah state internationally. However, these 'symbolics' had very real consequences for Kosovar Albanians, as they also had for the many Serbs who – as in Bosnia and Croatia – have been the victims of reverse ethnic cleansing or revenge attacks.[183] Despite the short-term rise in Milosevic's domestic popularity as Serbia suffered the NATO bombing campaign in 1999, ultimately, the campaign contributed towards his loss of legitimacy and his hold on the state ended in October 2000, after a brief attempt to ignore the results of the September elections in which he lost power.

Conclusion

In this chapter I have demonstrated how, in the late twentieth century, pathological homogenisation still played a central role in state-building, especially in the absence of institutions that both constrain elites from engaging in such practices and that contribute towards constituting identities through non-pathological means. In fact, pathological strategies of identity construction have been used by elites to repress the development of such institutions. To illuminate how this policy could be chosen by state-builders as Yugoslavia collapsed, I have investigated the rise of assimilationist Serbian and exclusivist Croatian nationalism in the nineteenth century, and the influence of these ideologies on the path of development of the first Yugoslavia and during World War II. I then looked at how, under Tito's Yugoslav League of Communists, nationalism remained taboo, with any nationalist demands, such as those that arose in Croatia in the late 1960s and early 1970s, quickly quashed.

[182] Eric D. Gordy, 'Why Milosevic Still?', *Current History* 99: 635 (2000).
[183] When Kosovar Albanian refugees returned to Kosovo – with 600,000 returning within three weeks of the peace settlement, 200,000 Serbs and Roma fled to Serbia (and Montenegro). Those who went to Serbia joined 500,000 refugees already there as a result of the wars in Croatia and Bosnia. UNHCR, 'Europe's Latest Exodus', *Refugees* 116, 1999.

Yet, at the same time, nothing was done to challenge the way in which the constituent republics of the Yugoslav federal state were based on an ethnic conception of nationhood that saw each republic as the republic of, and for, the majority national group.

Efforts to devolve authority to the republics, as a way of countering complaints about Serb preponderance in the centralised system, resulted in communist elites in the republics jealous of their authority and resistant to change. The death of Tito, combined with economic downturn, demanded cooperative action between the federal and republican leaderships. Instead, a tired Party tried to reassert its authority, only to be met with increasing resistance from the republics. As the legitimacy of the Communist Party crumbled, elites in the republics followed different paths. In Slovenia a process of relative liberalisation occurred. In Serbia and Croatia nationalist leaders came to power. In the case of Croatia, this meant that the communists lost power to the long-standing nationalist, Franjo Tudjman, and his supporters. In Serbia, by contrast, Milosevic seized the moment, and with a fine sense of timing caught the rising current of nationalist fervour, and transformed himself from party man into a nationalist leader. Thus democratic reform was blocked in Serbia.

But Milosevic did not create nationalist sentiment in Serbia, though he undoubtedly pushed it to new heights (or depths). Milosevic tapped into strands of resentment that had their bases in recent historical experiences and a lack of knowledge about other cultures within Yugoslavia that the Titoist regime, despite its slogan of 'unity and brotherhood' had done little to rectify. Such resentment and lack of understanding was exacerbated by difficult social and economic conditions and a regime paralysed by its own inertia. As I have shown, the symbolic manipulation of the 'myth of Kosovo' combined with the reinterment of World War II victims of the Ustasha to create powerful images of the historic victimisation of Serbs at the hands of both Croats and Muslims. This served to push non-Serbs beyond the realm of moral obligation: it was 'they' who posed a threat to the very existence of all Serbs and Serbia. It was thus unacceptable that Serb communities could exist safely as minorities within the sovereign independent states of Croatia and Bosnia-Herzegovina. And as we have seen, the policies of Franjo Tudjman in Croatia certainly discriminated against Serbs, which in turn fed Serb fears and nationalism. If Yugoslavia could not be held together as a single state, then Serb enclaves would have to be carved out in both Croatia and Bosnia-Herzegovina, and non-Serbs would have to be removed from these areas. Thus, from the symbolic manipulation of the Kosovo myth, the regime moved to the political practice of 'ethnic cleansing'.

The 'pathological homogenisation' that occurred as Yugoslavia disintegrated and successor states struggled to emerge must be attributed to modern processes of state-building, rather than to any 'ancient hatreds'. Although nationalist leaders used cultural stereotypes and the unresolved past to buttress their own legitimacy and to reconstitute the state along ethnic-national lines, their object in doing so was to build and retain control over independent, territorially defined, sovereign states, which rest on an exclusive notion of sovereignty. This concept pre-dates nationalism as we have seen, but as this case shows, along with that of the Armenian genocide, nationalism as a populist ideology can legitimate pathological homogenisation as a means of state-building. In all the cases so far in this study, pathological homogenisation has occurred as a result of policy choices made by elites. However, such policies cannot be carried out without support, and thus require incitement, incitement that inevitably draws on the available cultural context. Through such policies elites have sought to construct the corporate identity of the state, but this has not occurred in isolation from the international social identity of the state. In chapter 6 I trace the development of international norms of legitimate state behaviour and how these have been articulated in response to practices of pathological homogenisation, and how the international community has sought – not always successfully – to institutionalise and enforce these. In the final chapter I turn to two threshold cases where elites have made different choices, the Czech Republic and The Former Yugoslav Republic of Macedonia.

6 Evolving international norms

This study has highlighted an important, and until recently, overlooked aspect of state formation and the creation of state boundaries – the practice of 'pathological homogenisation' – which may take the form of forced assimilation, mass expulsion or genocide, by which elites have sought to construct corporate identities that legitimate their authority. I now want to trace how such practices have come to be regarded as pathological and the concomitant development of international norms that proscribe them.

Despite the discourse of sovereignty, and claims by state elites that they possess the right to define corporate identities, there has long been a two-way relationship between such claims and the efforts of the society of states to articulate principles of coexistence which limit the actions a sovereign can legitimately take, inside the state as well as externally. Although at one level sovereignty and the principle of non-intervention in a state's domestic affairs have long been taken as the ground of international politics, in practice recognition of the legitimacy of governments, which rests on internal as well as external factors, has also played an important role in interaction between states. International standards which define legitimate state action towards citizens have gained increasing moral force this century, particularly since the end of World War II, and then again after the end of the Cold War.

However, as recent history demonstrates, these normative developments are by no means uncontested, in fact, they remain patchy and even where there is consensus that a state has gone too far, just how to deal effectively with massive abuses remains a pressing problem. Despite the now clearly articulated legal norms limiting state power over citizens, employing the most virulent exclusionary practices unfortunately remains an attractive option to some regimes. Understanding how such strategies can become a 'thinkable option', whether they take the form of forced assimilation, expulsion or mass murder, is thus of the utmost importance if the international community is to have any hope of preventing such practices in the future.

212

Throughout the book I have drawn on Alexander Wendt's distinction between the corporate and social aspects of state identity, characterising elites' use of pathological homogenisation as a form of 'corporate state identity construction' and the development of international norms that proscribe such practices as a form of 'societal state identity construction'.[1] However, unlike Wendt, I argue that corporate identity construction should not be neglected by international relations scholars, and that we need accounts of the relationship between corporate and social state identities that pay attention to how events within states influence the development of international social norms and, in turn, how social norms are diffused into states or, as in the case of Slobodan Milosevic's Yugoslavia, are rejected by particular regimes.

In this chapter I trace the impact that pathological strategies of corporate state construction have had on the development of international norms that define legitimate statehood. In the early modern period I trace a shift from the lack of any international normative response to the 1492 expulsion of the Jews from Spain to a more developed, albeit thin, normative environment that existed when Louis XIV revoked the Edict of Nantes in 1685. In the intervening years the Peace of Augsburg and the Peace of Westphalia, while codifying the rights of sovereigns within borders, had also articulated some basic minority rights. When Louis abrogated these rights his actions were rejected as illegitimate across much of Europe.

The nineteenth-century massacres of Armenians in the Ottoman Empire occurred in a context of growing humanitarian sentiment in Europe, including the anti-slavery movement, while throughout the Empire national consciousness was on the rise. The Great Powers tried to pressure the Sultan into treating his minority subjects as equal to his Muslim subjects. But although the Sultan appeared to acquiesce in this he ultimately rejected these standards and massacred subjects who he considered disloyal. Support for minorities by the Great Powers was taken as evidence of this treachery.

In the early twentieth century, when the Party of Union and Progress (CUP) embarked on its programme of creating a modern, national state using pathological means under cover of World War I, the allies called on them to stop what they were doing and asserted that they would punish those responsible for the systematic massacre of the Armenians when they had the opportunity to do so. There was one failed attempt to do this in 1919 but, in the end, those responsible for the genocide were not punished

---

[1] Alexander Wendt, 'Collective Identity Formation and the International State', *American Political Science Review* 88:2 (1994), 385.

for their actions. Yet at this time there was a clear awareness that what had been done to the Armenians constituted a crime against humanity, though this was ill-defined. There was an effort to translate this into legal principles under the conditions of the Treaty of Sèvres, yet this also failed as I explain below in greater detail.

It is in the late twentieth century, in the wake of the Holocaust, the Genocide Convention and the codification of international human rights norms, that we see the development of a more comprehensive normative and legal framework. It is under this framework that ethnic cleansing in the former Yugoslavia was recognised as constituting a crime under international law, for which a number of individuals are currently being tried. Of course, international norms and the creation of a war crimes tribunal to deal specifically with crimes committed in the former Yugoslavia did not stop the violence, and enforcing compliance has proved difficult and costly. Nonetheless, there have been significant normative developments over the course of the twentieth century, and I will characterise these trends across nine dimensions of normative change (see Table 2).

The sixteenth and seventeenth centuries

When Ferdinand and Isabella were engaged in laying the foundations for the modern Spanish state, there were no international norms governing the internal practices of monarchs, either within Europe or in any wider system. Thus the Ottoman Sultan Bajezet reportedly said on taking in Jews after 1492, 'Call ye this Ferdinand "wise" – he who depopulates his own dominions in order to enrich mine?'[2] The Jews were welcomed to the Empire as productive subjects, but there was no normative content to this remark and no sense of obligation on the part of the Sultan.

Although many acts of the Catholic Monarchs are best characterised as medieval, they were also innovators who were able to recast older social and cultural forms within the emerging state. This occurred in a context of normative flux as the bonds of universal Christendom frayed. Thus, although their actions can only be interpreted in terms of traditional Christian ethics, these no longer had universal purchase and came, along with dynastic claims, to form the basis of the legitimacy claims made by rulers *inside* the state. Two strands of thought regarding such expulsions existed simultaneously. One, inherited from Roman law, denied

---

[2] Cecil Roth, *History of the Jews* (New York: Schocken, 1961), p. 252, cited by Alan Dowty and Gil Loescher, 'Refugee Flows as Grounds for International Action', *International Security* 21:1 (1996), 58. Also see Michael Marrus, *The Unwanted: European Refugees in the Twentieth Century* (Oxford University Press, 1985), p. 6.

or devalued the independent identity of non-Christians.[3] Another more egalitarian strand, the legacy of early Christian (and earlier) universalism, asserted a wider human community in which differences should be tolerated.[4] As the universality of Christendom fragmented, and despite much debate within Christian society,[5] it was the exclusive strand which came to dominate in the early modern system of states.

The Respublica Christiana, though still providing the basis of a shared European identity in opposition to the Ottoman Empire, no longer provided a universal ethical system that could provide the basis for relations between emergent states. Indeed, although the Ottomans remained as a threat on the edge of Europe, even this could not rouse Europe to united action. 'Both the universal authorities in Christendom, the emperor in Sigismund's time and the popes continuously, made tremendous efforts to rouse Christian Europe to united activity in self-defence. Both failed totally. This is a touchstone of the emptiness of their universal authority.'[6]

As the universal Christian community broke down, the heterogeneity that characterised medieval political organisation was 'displaced' into the external realm of an emergent international system, and unity within the state became the order of the day. Though the idea of a 'European conscience' retained meaning, it was gradually rearticulated within the state by rulers such as Ferdinand and Isabella who changed Christianity while also drawing on it to consolidate their state-in-the-making. Thus we see the reassertion of traditional elements combined with innovation as states arose out of the breakdown of Western Christendom. In this process rulers such as Ferdinand and Isabella transformed the Church within their states into Churches *of* the state. This is highlighted by the example of the Spanish Inquisition which was the first institution to reach across both Aragon and Castile, and which answered directly to the monarchs. These rulers were able to make this transition without breaking with the Catholic Church, but they transformed Catholic identity into the criterion for membership in the moral community bounded by the state, making the presence of non-Christians problematic in a new way.

---

[3] Martin Wight, *Systems of States* (Leicester University Press, 1977), pp. 26–8.

[4] Ibid., pp. 20, 119. As a result of canon law few Popes supported expulsions of Jews and the Jews of Spain were offered refuge in the Papal states.

[5] Open dissent was recorded at the time of the expulsion. This was based on the argument that it was a mistake to throw out industrious subjects, and that their conversion was more likely to follow if they were allowed to stay rather than going off to live 'among the infidel' in the Ottoman Empire. The universalist strand did not completely disappear though, as according to late sixteenth-century opinion the edict of expulsion was not justified. Unbelievers should not be compelled to faith, as this was not justified by theology. See Henry Kamen, 'The Mediterranean and the Expulsion of Spanish Jews in 1492', *Past and Present* 119 (1988), 53–4.

[6] Maurice Keen, *The Penguin History of Medieval Europe* (London: Penguin, 1968), p. 312.

In the absence of any clearly articulated international norms other than the 'right to make war', however, the treatment of the Jews of Spain was of little relevance in relations between emergent states.

Augsburg and Westphalia

The Peace of Augsburg of 1555 marked peace between Lutherans and Catholics (though not between the latter and Calvinists) and codified the demand for religious unity within the state. The principle of *cujus regio ejus religio* established that the religion of the ruler defined the religion of the country, the implication of this being that 'religious dissent stood equal to political disaffection and even treason'.[7] Continuing the process already apparent in fifteenth-century Spain, while religious feeling as such did not diminish, regional differences pulled universal Christianity apart, as the sense of separate corporate identities within states and the principles of social interaction between these independent entities grew.[8]

Although the principle *cujus regio ejus religio* was formulated within the Empire, 'in practice it quickly extended throughout the Christian commonwealth of Europe'.[9] Though imperfect, this was a principle of regional coexistence, which recognised the rights of princes but also set some limits on their conduct, as it allowed emigration. This resulted in 'an extensive transfer of populations within Germany' as it allowed 'dissatisfied subjects to "vote with their feet"', in a wave of voluntary migration, if the ruler was not of their confession.[10] So while the Peace of Augsburg was an assertion of the sovereign rights of rulers in regard to the Empire, it also set some minimum requirement of religious toleration in that those subjects who wished to leave should be allowed to do so.

The Peace of Westphalia in 1648 reaffirmed the religious rights of sovereigns but once again these were limited by the requirement of tolerance, which was extended to Calvinists. The Treaty of Osnabrück of October 1648 allowed for liberty of conscience (Article 28), asserting the right of minorities (either Catholic or of the 'Confession of Augsburg') to practise their religions in both public and private, to teach their

---

[7] G. R. Elton (ed.), *The New Cambridge Modern History*, Vol. 2, *The Reformation 1520–1559* (Cambridge University Press, 1962), p. 5.

[8] Keen, *Penguin History*, p. 318.

[9] Adam Watson, 'European International Society and its Expansion', in Hedley Bull and Adam Watson (eds.), *The Expansion of International Society* (Oxford: Clarendon Press, 1985), p. 15. However it applied to Catholics and Lutherans, excluding Calvinists. H. G. Koenigsberger and George L. Mosse, *Europe in the Sixteenth Century* (London: Longmans, 1968), p. 187.

[10] Adam Watson, *The Evolution of International Society* (London: Routledge, 1992), p. 173.

children in schools of their religion, to be free of discrimination, to have equal rights to hospitals, alms houses and so on, 'so that in these and all other the like things they shall be treated in the same manner as Brethren and Sisters, with equal Justice and Protection' (Article 29). A member of a minority had the freedom to change abode and to 'keep or sell his Goods, and have them administer'd by his Relations, to visit them with all Freedom, and without any Letters of Passport, and to prosecute his Affairs, and make payment of his Debts, as often as shall be requisite' (Article 30). Those who wished to leave were allowed five years to do so, or three years for those who voluntarily changed religion, and those who left were to be granted all freedoms, 'nor shall they be oppress'd with unusual Reversals, or Decimation of the Goods they shall carry away with them, above what is just and equitable; and far less shall any Stop or Hindrance be made, upon pretext of Servitude, or any other whatsoever, to those who shall remove voluntarily'.[11]

Territorial rights were by no means completely settled at this stage, as the 'geographical extension of sovereign rule [was still] ill-defined'.[12] Westphalia thus resulted in a 'thin' mutual recognition of sovereignty, but the settlement (and that of Utrecht), was 'not animated by any deep normative commitment to establishing general rules of international conduct: "they looked to the past"'.[13] Yet, when compared to the context within which Ferdinand and Isabella expelled the Jews from Spain, the Westphalian system did have some content regarding what constituted legitimate behaviour of monarchs towards their subjects. This was a direct response to an important change that took place with the rise of absolute rulers – the way in which rulers sought to construct corporate identity within the territorial bounds of their states through the demand for religious conformity. Though absolutist society can hardly be said to have any notion of 'the people', nonetheless a homogeneous, unified population gradually became desirable, though this could never be fully achieved in practice. It could, however, be symbolised, and the expulsion or marking out of different groups served to symbolise the unity of the society as a whole. The principle of tolerance found in the Treaty of Osnabrück represents an attempt to limit the harmful effects of the desire for unity, and as such represents the beginning of an international social identity between states interested in finding some shared principles of coexistence. Thus Cardinal Richelieu who served under Louis XIII would refer in hindsight

[11] Clive Parry (ed.), *Consolidated Treaty Series*, vol. 1, *1648–1649* (New York: Dobbs Ferry, 1909), pp. 228–30.
[12] Christian Reus-Smit, *The Moral Purpose of the State: Culture, Social Identity, and Institutional Rationality in International Relations* (Princeton University Press, 1999), p. 171.
[13] Ibid., p. 159.

to the expulsion of the Moriscos from Spain (who, after all, were at least nominally Christian subjects of the Spanish King) as 'barbaric'.[14]

Louis XIV and the Revocation of the Edict of Nantes

Louis XIV's 1685 Revocation of the Edict of Nantes occurred in an international system that, although still normatively 'thin', was more developed than at the time of the expulsion of the Jews from Spain and which had seen the codification of emergent norms in the Peace of Westphalia. When Louis revoked the Edict of Nantes and forbade Huguenots to leave France ('except pastors who had two weeks in which to leave') he abrogated the, *jus emigrandi*, which had been granted to religious minorities in Germany under the Treaty of Osnabrück and had gained the status of a regional norm.[15]

Louis, like his father before him, pursued expansionist policies, motivated in large part by constant worry about Spanish ambitions, though Louis was also motivated by his own sense of glory. His expansionist pretensions brought a hostile response from other European powers, culminating in the Wars of Spanish Succession. Meanwhile, his attempts to create a homogeneous corporate identity for France only brought external condemnation. For instance, Frederick William, the Elector of Brandenburg, promulgated the Edict of Potsdam offering refuge to Protestants in response to Louis' policies. 'After the Treaty of Nymwegen and the subsequent pressure forcing him to give up his conquests on the Baltic, the great elector had been unwilling to do anything that might offend France, but he could not ignore the fate of his co-religionists. Much to the irritation of men at Versailles, other German princes followed suit.'[16]

Despite the hostility aroused by Louis' policies, at least in the short term, his treatment of the Huguenots was domestically popular and served his purpose of building a corporate identity that buttressed an absolutist authority that was in reality extremely fragile. Nonetheless, before too long the persecution of the Huguenots and the Revocation came to be seen as a political mistake as well as a religious crime.[17] In the international arena, the Revocation was regarded as illegitimate and it had a 'marked effect upon an international opinion growing increasingly hostile

[14] Henry Kamen, *Spain 1469–1714: A Society of Conflict* (New York: Longman, 1983), p. 221.
[15] Richard M. Golden, 'Introduction', in Richard M. Golden (ed.), *The Huguenot Connection: The Edict of Nantes, its Revocation and Early French Migration to South Carolina* (Dordrecht: Kluwer Academic Publishers, 1988), p. 17.
[16] John B. Wolf, *Louis XIV* (New York: W. W. Norton & Co., 1968), p. 395.
[17] Francois Bluche, *Louis XIV*, trans. Mark Greengrass (Oxford: Blackwell, 1990), p. 406.

to French pretensions and Bourbon methods',[18] bringing the condemnation of Protestant Europe upon France. 'Like other rulers who hoped to replace the pluralism in their lands by a formula like "one God, one law, one king", Louis encountered much difficulty, and in the end his efforts created disorder, suffering, and hatred, rather than the united kingdom of which he dreamed.'[19]

The responses that Louis XIV's policies, both internal and external, engendered within a Europe increasingly hostile to such absolutist and expansionary pretensions indicate that norms of acceptable state behaviour were changing. Though the Peace of Westphalia was a thin normative order, all the same it reflects the beginnings of a society of states resting on some shared norms. Though by no means uncontested, the effort to articulate minimum standards of coexistence extending to internal behaviour distinguish this period from the lack of such standards in the late fifteenth century when the system itself was taking shape. However, much as his contemporaries disapproved of Louis' actions, there was no attempt at direct intervention in France on behalf of the Huguenots, as within living memory of the religious wars there was a strong awareness that this would have undermined the purpose of the Westphalian settlement.

The nineteenth century

Over the next two centuries, as states consolidated internally, the concept of a European society of states developed and the idea of the law of nations replaced natural law. By the mid-eighteenth century positivist international law, based on the growing body of treaties and customary law, was on the rise. States came to be seen as the sole subjects of international law in a view that was predominant until the early twentieth century. As Hedley Bull notes, though individuals and non-state groups were considered to have moral rights, these were distinct from legal ones.[20] Concurrent with this developing perception of the European society of states, and of the law of nations as the public law of Europe, was the growth of the idea that a 'standard of civilisation' should be applied to non-European societies. According to this standard, which was based on the assumption of European superiority, entry into the European society of states required that non-European societies must be able to 'guarantee

[18] H. G. Judge, 'Louis XIV and the Church', in John C. Rule (ed.), *Louis XIV and the Craft of Kingship* (Columbus: Ohio State University Press, 1969), p. 243.

[19] Wolf, *Louis XIV*, p. 401.

[20] Hedley Bull, 'The Importance of Grotius in the Study of International Relations', in Hedley Bull, Benedict Kingsbury and Adam Roberts (eds.), *Hugo Grotius and International Relations* (Oxford: Clarendon Press, 1992), p. 86.

the life, liberty, and property of foreign nationals; to demonstrate a suitable governmental organisation; to adhere to the accepted diplomatic practices; and to abide by the principles of international law'.[21]

In the nineteenth century the Great Powers asserted their right to intervene in the Ottoman Empire on behalf of religious minorities, although in practice mistreatment continued and was often exacerbated by such pressure. The Great Powers intervened in the Ottoman Empire on four occasions.[22] Martha Finnemore argues that although the interventions in the Empire might be described as multilateral, at best this was 'quantitative' rather than 'qualitative' multilateralism, in the sense used by John Ruggie to mean the acceptance of norms and principles that apply equally to all parties. Though there may have been more than two states involved in intervention at any one time, interventions into the Ottoman Empire were not based on any generalised principles nor on any joint planning or implementation. Indeed, Finnemore argues, such interventions were driven by shared fear rather than 'by shared norms and principles',[23] as France and England feared Russia gaining influence in the crumbling Empire. Interventions generally tended to be made on behalf of a minority with which the intervening power had some affiliation, such as Russia's affiliation with the Orthodox subjects of the Empire.[24] This was not always the case, though, as the Great Powers did attempt to alleviate the ill-treatment of Jews in newly independent Romania and the treatment of minorities generally within the Ottoman Empire and newly independent states.

However, Great Power politics served to water down the protection offered to Armenians. Under Article 16 of the March 1878 Treaty of San Stefano, Russian withdrawal from the eastern provinces of Turkey was contingent upon the enactment of reforms in favour of the Armenians, and on guarantees of their protection from both Kurds and Circassians.

[21] Gerrit W. Gong, 'China's Entry into the International Society', in Hedley Bull and Adam Watson (eds.), *The Evolution of International Society* (Oxford: Clarendon Press, 1985), p. 179.
[22] During the Greek war for independence (1821–27); in Lebanon and Syria (1860–61); Bulgaria (1876–78); and Armenia (1894–97). See Martha Finnemore, 'Constructing Norms of Humanitarian Intervention', in Peter J. Katzenstein (ed.), *The Culture of National Security: Norms and Identity in World Politics* (New York: Columbia University Press, 1996), pp. 161–9.
[23] Finnemore, 'Constructing Norms', p. 182; John Gerard Ruggie, 'Multilateralism: The Anatomy of an Institution', in John Gerard Ruggie (ed.), *Multilateralism Matters: The Theory and Praxis of an Institutional Form* (New York: Columbia University Press, 1993), p. 14.
[24] The British helped national groups gain independence from the Empire, as in the case of Greece, but this also helped to counter the extension of Russian power into the West. Evan Luard, 'The Origins of International Concern Over Human Rights', in Evan Luard (ed.), *The International Protection of Human Rights* (New York: Praeger, 1967), p. 10.

British objections to Russian gains under this treaty led to the Congress of Berlin in mid-1878, where the protection afforded to Armenians underwent substantial reduction. Under Article 61 of the Treaty of Berlin, Russian troops were to withdraw immediately from the eastern provinces of Turkey, and the Great Powers accepted a pledge from the Sultan that reforms would be put into practice.[25]

This left the Armenians extremely vulnerable. Though at times it was politic for the Sultan to appear to give way to the wishes of the Great Powers, in reality from the beginning of his reign he was resistant to both what he saw as external interference in Ottoman affairs and to any claims made by his subjects that he saw as subversive. That the Armenians, once known as the 'loyal millet', would go outside the Empire and appeal to the Great Powers, particularly Russia, for protection made them traitorous in his eyes, as discussed in chapter 4. Hence the conditions of the treaty were quickly violated within the Empire. Over the next two years diplomatic pressure by the Great Powers had little effect and after 1881 the scramble for Empire among the powers meant that the Armenian question received less attention.

Although principle was not entirely absent from this international pressure, there were as yet no clearly generalised international principles, indeed the Treaty of Berlin marks the beginning of the decline in relations between Russia and Britain. Meanwhile, the Sultan saw the treaty as an attempt to impose standards that did not accord with his world view, and before long he acted in direct contravention of its requirements regarding the treatment of his Armenian subjects, with a series of massacres beginning in 1894.[26] The massacres aroused such international concern that the Great Powers insisted on sending representatives to take part in a commission of inquiry.[27] Following this the Sultan was presented with 'a reform programme, part of which he adopted, the British, French, and Russian Ambassadors expressing their satisfaction. Immediately afterwards, however, he inaugurated fresh massacres, while the Powers looked on in impotence.'[28]

At this time in the West there was a developing moral concern with the rights of individuals across states. Humanitarian concerns ranging from the anti-slavery movement to the rights of subjects in other states were on the rise, albeit in a mostly 'spasmodic and unorganized' manner and

---

[25] Vahakn N. Dadrian, *The History of the Armenian Genocide: Ethnic Conflict from the Balkans to Anatolia to the Caucasus*, 2nd edn, revised (Providence: Berghahn Books, 1997), pp. 61–3.

[26] C. A. Macartney, *National States and National Minorities*, 2nd edn (New York: Russell & Russell, 1968), p. 169.

[27] Luard, 'Origins of International Concern', p. 12.

[28] Macartney, *National States*, p. 170.

it was public outcry over abuses that pushed governments to act.[29] However, as Finnemore highlights, there were no fully articulated general legal
principles which could provide a framework for action, and the humanitarian standards that were developing did not accord with the prevailing
interpretation of international law as the law of nations. Thus, external
pressure to reform the treatment of minorities in the Empire placed those
minorities in a more vulnerable position, and when the Sultan turned on
subjects he perceived as disloyal they were offered no effective protection
and no legal recourse.

The twentieth century

The Armenian genocide 1915–1916

As I argued in chapter 4, the genocidal policies of the revolutionary Young
Turk regime can be distinguished from the massacres of Armenians
ordered by Sultan Abdul Hamid in the nineteenth century. The Sultan
had been concerned to keep the Armenians 'in their place' as a religious
community which was of lower status than Muslims, and he was prepared
to engage in massacres to do this, as he had done previously in Bulgaria
and elsewhere. By contrast, the Young Turks were influenced by a virulent
strand of Turkish nationalism which by the early twentieth century had
translated Islamic religious identity into a national identity based on the
assertion that Anatolia was the historical fatherland of the Turks. The
Young Turk regime set out to construct a rationalised modern state as
the state of the Turkish nation, centred on this heartland. In such a state
there was no place for the Armenians and they were to be 'deported'. This
'deportation' to the deserts, where most victims died, combined with
systematic massacres, was the first genocide of the twentieth century.

Despite the fact that it occurred during wartime, there was widespread
humanitarian concern for the plight of the Armenians, reflected in an
international relief effort, which was particularly active in the United
States, and a number of individual Germans (allies of Turkey) went to
great efforts to publicise the genocide. As we have seen, the Entente
powers called for Turkey to stop this assault on the Armenian population
'on the grounds of humanity and civilisation'. In response, Minister of
the Interior Talat declared that the Armenians posed a security threat, on
the grounds that they supported Russia in the war and that they were
on the verge of rebellion, and the deportations continued unabated.
Furthermore, the government asserted that what they did with their

[29] Luard, 'Origins of International Concern', pp. 11–14, quote at 11.

subjects was an 'internal' matter. While out of step with developing humanitarian norms this attitude was in accord with the traditional rule of international law, that the state had total discretion over the treatment of its citizens.[30]

Yet the international community – meaning concerned citizens of other states as well as the Great Powers – did recognise that what had happened in the Ottoman Empire was not merely a matter of state security and called for punishment of the architects of the 'massacres' and reparations to the Armenian community. The CUP was deposed at the end of 1918, and under pressure from the victorious powers and with the support of the Sultan, a trial of those accused of responsibility for the genocide was mounted in 1919.[31] However, this emergent social norm was at odds with Turkish domestic opinion and there was great internal resistance to these trials. Many of the accused fled the country, with the result that the architects of the genocide like Talat, Enver and Djemal were sentenced to death in absentia. These trials were soon sidelined by the struggle that brought the nationalist regime of Mustapha Kemal to power as the Empire finally collapsed. Those few individuals who were found guilty in 1919 were with few exceptions sent briefly into exile, only to return unabashed when the Kemalist regime came to power, and once it was established it denied that the genocide had ever occurred and repudiated the 1920 Treaty of Sèvres.

This treaty, imposed on the Empire by the Great Powers and signed by the Sultan's representative, made provisions for the return of Armenians to Anatolia, the recovery of Armenian owned property, the tracing of missing persons and the nullification of all religious conversions since the beginning of World War I.[32] It also recognised the independent Republic of Armenia that had been set up in Russian and Turkish Armenia at the end of the war, and ceded the eastern provinces of the Empire to the Republic.[33] Putting this into practice was a different thing, however, as 'the allies had made it clear that they would not furnish the troops to enforce the treaty', though they might give assistance with arms.[34]

[30] Finnemore, 'Constructing Norms'; Dadrian, 'Genocide as a Problem of National and International Law: The World War I Armenian Case and its Contemporary Legal Ramifications', *Yale Journal of International Law* 14:2 (1989), 278.
[31] Dadrian, 'The Turkish Military Tribunal's Prosecution of the Authors of the Armenian Genocide: Four Major Court-Martial Series', *Holocaust and Genocide Studies* 11:1 (1997); Dadrian, 'Genocide as a Problem', 278.
[32] Richard G. Hovannisian, 'The Armenian Question, 1878–1923', in Permanent Peoples' Tribunal, *A Crime of Silence*, pp. 26–7.
[33] For a detailed account of the short-lived republic that was absorbed into the Soviet Union in 1921, see Richard G. Hovannisian, *The Republic of Armenia*, Vols. 1–4 (Berkeley: University of California Press, 1971–96).
[34] Ibid., vol. 3, p. 325.

Without international support the Republic had little chance of survival, and the withdrawal of the United States from an active role in 1919 made this a certainty. The allies watched as Turkish troops took over most of the Republic and the terms of the Treaty of Sèvres were repudiated.[35]

In response, the Armenian government placed what remained of Armenia under Soviet rule, so that by 1921 the independent Armenian Republic was extinct. Once the nationalist regime of Mustafa Kemal made it clear that they had no intention of accepting the conditions of the Treaty of Sèvres, the allied powers sought to normalise relations with Turkey, accepting Kemal's demands that the treaty be rewritten, thus acquiescing in the rejection of any concessions to the Armenians. As Richard Hovannisian notes, the extent to which the will of the new Turkish regime prevailed is reflected 'in the fact that in the final versions of the Lausanne treaties neither the word "Armenia" nor "Armenian" was to be found. It was as if the Armenian Question or the Armenian people themselves had never existed.'[36]

The way the genocide was dealt with at the international legal level reflects the lag between emergent social norms and legal principle at the time. War crimes were the first item on the agenda of the Paris Peace Conference in 1919. The allies created a Commission on the Responsibility of the Authors of the War and the Enforcement of Penalties, and the findings of this commission reflect the clash between the prevailing interpretation of the principle of sovereignty and developing humanitarian norms.[37] The systematic destruction of the Armenian community was excluded from the category of war crimes, as it was regarded as an 'internal matter'. Yet there was by no means full consensus on this and one of the Committee members, Greek Foreign Minister Nicolas Politis, 'proposed the adoption of a new category of war crimes meant to cover the massacres against the Armenians'.[38] Politis argued that although the crimes did not *technically* come under international law, they nonetheless were offences against 'the laws of humanity' to be found in the Fourth Hague Convention. As Vahakn Dadrian observes, Politis was not alone in this:

Despite the objections of American representatives Lansing and Scott, who challenged the ex-post facto nature of such a law, the majority of the Commission 'hesitatingly' concurred with Politis. The Commission based its decision upon a Hague Convention principle which allowed for reliance upon the 'laws of humanity' and 'dictates of public conscience' whenever clearly defined standards and regulations to deal with grave offences were lacking.[39]

---

[35] Hovannisian, 'The Armenian Question', p. 27.   [36] Ibid., p. 28.

[37] Dadrian, *History of the Armenian Genocide*, n. 14, p. xxvii; Dadrian, 'Genocide as a Problem', 227, n. 12.

[38] Dadrian, *History of the Armenian Genocide*, p. 304.   [39] Ibid.

As a result, several articles in the Treaty of Sèvres clearly stipulated the Turkish government's responsibility for the genocide and the right of the allies to conduct trials of those accused of taking part.[40] However, as we have seen, the Treaty of Sèvres was repudiated by the Kemalist regime.

That the international community was struggling to articulate new principles of legitimate state behaviour at this time is reflected in the views of Politis and those who agreed with him, no matter how hesitant they were. According to the findings of the Permanent Peoples' Tribunal held in Paris in April 1984, which devoted a session to the Armenian genocide, the 'laws of humanity' not only express moral and ethical imperatives but also contain 'positive legal obligations which cannot be ignored by states on the pretext that they have not been expressed formally in treaties'.[41] In its findings the tribunal argued that although the Treaty of Sèvres was never ratified, its content, which clearly held Turkey responsible for the massacres on its territory, demonstrates that 'the states of that time were indeed conscious of the illegality of the crime which we now call genocide'.[42] However, this recognition did not translate into changed legal principles or political action. What consensus did exist was ultimately undermined by the lack of real cooperation among the Allies. Despite the 1915 allied declaration that they intended to punish those responsible for the genocide, there was no powerful state prepared to champion the Armenian cause after the war. Humanitarian ideals were dropped in order to deal with the Kemalist regime and in the end there were no sanctions against the Turkish state, whose representatives skilfully manipulated tensions between the allies to strengthen Turkey's position.[43]

The Kemalist regime and the 'exchange of populations'

Although the policies of the Young Turks were animated by chauvinist Turkish nationalism, it is the Kemalist regime that is generally recognised as the first to be overtly Turkist. David Kushner argues that it was only after World War I that 'Turkism could finally be adopted and transformed into a programme for action in the political, economic, social and cultural spheres.'[44] As I have demonstrated, though, the genocidal policy of the CUP laid the basis of Anatolian Turkey as a sovereign state, recognised as such by the Treaty of Lausanne in 1923.

[40] Ibid., p. 305.
[41] Permanent Peoples' Tribunal, *A Crime of Silence*, p. 223. The Permanent Peoples' Tribunal was founded by the Italian Senator and jurist Lelio Basso.
[42] Ibid., pp. 223–4.   [43] Dadrian, 'Genocide as a Problem', 226.
[44] David Kushner, *The Rise of Turkish Nationalism 1876–1908* (London: Frank Cass, 1977), p. 101.

The Kemalist regime continued to pursue a national state with the expulsion of over 1 million Greeks. Non-Turkish Muslims such as the Kurds, regarded as 'mountain Turks', were subjected to policies of forced assimilation, against which they rebelled in 1925, with their continued resistance leading to massacres during the 1930s and 1940s.[45] Picking up on the themes of nineteenth-century nationalists, from the 1930s onwards an 'official historical doctrine' developed in Turkey that located the early roots of the Turkish people in Anatolia.

Thus, the right to sovereignty continued to be interpreted in some quarters as granting governments complete authority over subjects and citizens and as giving state-builders the right to define the corporate identity of the state through pathological means, up to and including genocide.[46] Indeed, as we have seen in all the case studies above, such strategies of pathological homogenisation played a central role in constituting the state as a unitary, sovereign actor in the first place. The extirpation of Armenians from what was still the Ottoman Empire was part of the process by which the Empire was transformed into the territorial, sovereign and ostensibly homogeneous, national state of Turkey.

Although it was clear at the time that such acts were not considered morally acceptable, the translation of this widely held sentiment into international legal principles faltered. In the absence of a true multilateral basis for action, and in the face of the Kemalist regime's repudiation of the Treaty of Sèvres, its refusal to acknowledge the genocide, and its assertion of its sovereignty, international measures to punish the perpetrators of the genocide failed. Thus, when Interior Minister Talat asserted that what was done with the Armenians was an 'internal matter', he was out of step with rising humanitarian sentiment outside Turkey but he was not out of step with legally enforceable state practice. It was in this context, that the US Ambassador to the Empire, Henry Morgenthau, would remember his attempts to persuade the regime to act differently: 'Technically, of course, I had no right to interfere. According to the cold-blooded legalities of the situation, the treatment of Turkish subjects by the Turkish government was a purely domestic affair.'[47]

---

[45] Pierre Vidal-Naquet, 'By Way of a Preface and by the Power of One Word', in Permanent Peoples' Tribunal, *A Crime of Silence: The Armenian Genocide* (London: Zed Books, 1985), p. 4.

[46] Kuper, *Genocide: Its Political Use in the Twentieth Century* (New Haven: Yale University Press, 1981), pp. 161–85.

[47] Cited in ibid., p. 161. Dadrian notes that in a letter to President Woodrow Wilson, US Secretary of State Robert Lansing, a member of the Commission that excluded genocide from the category of war crimes, justified US interventions on behalf of the Armenians during the war, not on the grounds that the deportations were illegal, but because of the 'horrible brutality' with which the deportations were carried out. Dadrian, *History of the Armenian Genocide*, p. xxvii, n. 14.

By the time that the League of Nations was created after World War I, the processes that it sought to avert or limit through the minorities treaties were in fact well under way. Furthermore, in trying to deal with the treatment of minorities, the League became complicit with the dynamics of pathological homogenisation, at the very time that it sought to alleviate the effects of such processes. It is to these contradictions that I now turn.

Normative reevaluation and the League of Nations

Though ultimately unsuccessful, the League of Nations 'represented one of the first attempts to lay down explicit and institutionalized restraints on the rights of sovereign governments over their own subjects'[48] and for the first time the protection of minorities was regarded as an ongoing international responsibility.[49]

Despite this, the protection of minorities was certainly not understood in terms of general principles of conduct that applied equally to all states. On the contrary, the victors of World War I did not see the need to sign a general treaty which covered their own behaviour.[50] It was new states that were to come under the provisions of the treaty system, to which many strenuously objected, on the ground that the treaties were discriminatory. The country-specific nature of the treaties meant that many minorities, particularly those in 'civilised states' such as Germany were not covered, but, in any event, existing treaties proved to be ineffective.[51]

At one level the minorities treaties reflect an attempt to limit the worst methods of corporate state-building, which were by this time regarded as unacceptable at an international level. Unfortunately, this was under-pinned – and ultimately undermined – by the overriding concern with the stabilisation of state borders, and the preservation of international order, in the wake of war and the emergence of new states. However, as the preceding case studies have demonstrated, in the modern era such prac-tices have their roots in the construction of state boundaries as moral as well as territorial boundaries. The minorities treaties of the League, and their ineffectiveness, reflect the contradictions in the international system. While there was movement towards more clearly articulated social norms protecting the rights of minorities, at the same time new states continued

[48] Luard, 'Origins of International Concern', p. 15.
[49] Dorothy V. Jones, 'The League of Nations Experiment in International Protection', *Ethics and International Affairs* 8 (1994), 86; Jennifer Jackson Preece, *National Minorities and the European Nation-States System* (Oxford: Clarendon Press, 1998), pp. 67–94.
[50] C. A. Macartney, 'League of Nations' Protection of Minority Rights', in Luard (ed.), *International Protection of Human Rights*, pp. 23–6.
[51] Macartney, *National States*, pp. 390–1.

to construct corporate identities through exclusionary policies, and the concern with maintaining the stability of borders limited the effectiveness of the treaties and dragged the League into complicity over the sorts of practices it had hoped to prevent.

This is illustrated in the role the League played in the 1923 compulsory exchange of populations between Greece and Turkey. This exchange, provided for under Article 1 of the Convention of Lausanne Concerning the Exchange of Greek and Turkish Populations, required that from 1 May 1923 Turkish nationals should reside in Turkey and Greek nationals should reside in Greece.[52] The term that was used at the time was that the League was assisting with 'repatriation'. This was a euphemism which did not mask the fact that Turkey expelled over 1 million citizens of Greek origin who faced massacre if they stayed. In light of the genocide of the Armenians and the massacre of tens of thousands of Greeks in Smyrna in 1922, the Greek government had no choice but to accept these refugees and ask the League for assistance. In this exchange,

some 380,000 Turks were transferred from Greece to Turkey, reducing the size of the Turkish minority in Greece from 13.9 per cent (in 1920) to 1.6 per cent (in 1928). Unfair treatment, most notoriously on the Turkish side, exacerbated the already enormous social and economic problems: a favourite practice was to seize property from outgoing 'transferees' without compensation, to the cynical enrichment of the despatching state, leaving the now destitute evacuees to burden the resources of the receiving state.[53]

Thus the League became complicit in actions regarded as morally reprehensible by many of its personnel and by public opinion. But the alternative was to leave up to a million people to a fate similar to that of the Armenians, or, if no assistance had been given to the Greek government, to place an unmanageable burden on that receiving state. At the time, the 'exchange' did not have wide acceptance and as Jean-Marie Henckaerts notes, 'because of the highly unfavourable public response to the idea of a compulsory exchange',[54] both Greece and Turkey sought to deny responsibility for it. The British negotiator, Lord Curzon characterised the exchange as 'a thoroughly bad and vicious solution', but one made necessary by the actions Turkey had already taken against Greek nationals in its territory.[55]

For many policy-makers, the forced exchange of populations seemed like a simple solution to the problem of minorities, which would

---

[52] Jean-Marie Henckaerts, *Mass Expulsion in Modern International Law and Practice* (The Hague: Kluwer Law International, 1995), pp. 24–5.
[53] Raymond Pearson, *National Minorities in Eastern Europe 1848–1945* (London: Macmillan, 1983), p. 140. See also Stephen P. Ladas, *The Exchange of Minorities: Bulgaria, Greece and Turkey* (New York: The Macmillan Company, 1932).
[54] Henckaerts, *Mass Expulsion*, p. 125.   [55] Cited in ibid., p. 125.

ensure peace. Few saw the dangers of the precedent that was being set: 'Thus State interests were given priority over human rights and mass expulsions gained international respectability as a legitimate solution of demographic problems; in fact, the principle of compulsory population transfers was seen by many as a panacea, a final solution to the troublesome minority problem.'[56] This solution was particularly attractive to those new states with heterogeneous populations within their new borders and who resented the minorities treaties that had been imposed on them.

It is apparent that although new social norms regarding the treatment of minorities within states were developing, the claims of sovereignty still provided the overarching conceptual framework, which in the end undermined the new norms and, furthermore, set dangerous precedents in the way minority problems were handled. Though the minorities system did represent a normative shift towards challenging the right of states to do whatever they wanted with their citizens, at the same time it sought to stabilise the very system which underpinned such claims. As Dorothy Jones observes, despite emphasising the protection of minorities, states were most concerned with border protection and stablisation.[57]

While trying to deal with the worst excesses of state-builders, in the post-World War I period the international community also gave further legitimation to the exclusive principles on which such strategies of pathological homogenisation were based. Thus, although the League sought the protection of minorities, mass transfers occurred under its auspices, which set a further precedent for the mistreatment of minorities. As Alfred-Maurice De Zayas so aptly put it: 'Hitler himself became one of the leading advocates and practitioners of the principle of population transfers.'[58]

From minority to individual rights in the United Nations system

After World War II, mass deportation was labelled a war crime and a crime against humanity by the Nuremberg Tribunal.[59] In the wake of the Holocaust the term genocide was coined and the attempt to wipe out an entire people was for the first time recognised as a crime under international law under the Convention on the Prevention and Punishment of the Crime of Genocide of 1948.[60] The multilateral institutions that

[56] Alfred-Maurice De Zayas, 'A Historical Survey of Twentieth Century Expulsions', in Anna C. Bramwell (ed.), *Refugees in the Age of Total War* (London: Unwin Hyman, 1988), p. 20.
[57] Jones, 'The League'.   [58] De Zayas, 'A Historical Survey', p. 20.   [59] Ibid., p. 22.
[60] Convention on the Prevention and Punishment of the Crime of Genocide, in Burns H. Weston, Richard A. Falk and Anthony D'Amato, *Basic Documents in International*

were set up in the wake of the war meant that the rules were meant to apply equally to all states. However, while the mass deportations carried out by the Nazis were regarded as criminal, in the immediate post-war period the allies were party to massive deportations of ethnic Germans from Eastern Europe, in which an estimated 2 million people died and 14 million were made homeless.[61]

The years of war and Nazi war crimes 'led the Allies to retreat from their own moral commitments and to discard the Atlantic Charter with respect to the Germans. Just as the Nazis had disregarded the right to self-determination of the Czechoslovaks, the Poles, the Yugoslavs, the Russians – to name a few – so too would the victorious allies ignore the right of the German people to self-determination.'[62] Although the Allies had intended that the expulsions would be 'controlled' and 'humane', this was always unrealistic. As De Zayas notes, Churchill was wrong when he said in December 1944: 'Expulsion is the method which, so far as we have been able to see, will be the most satisfactory and lasting. There will be no mixture of populations to cause endless trouble . . . A clean sweep will be made.'[63]

While the Allies abhorred the genocide and mass expulsions carried out by the Nazis, they accepted the underlying premise that an ethnically homogeneous state is preferable to a heterogenous one, because they considered that it would be more stable. The post-war expulsions may have horrified some, but they were accepted by many. Once again, at the same time as the international community was trying to articulate norms of acceptable state behaviour it was also accepting the 'logic' of homogenising populations within state borders that had caused mayhem throughout the first half of the twentieth century.

Law and World Order, 2nd edn (St. Paul: West Publishing Co., 1990), p. 297; Leo Kuper, *International Action Against Genocide*, Report No. 53, revd edn (London: Minority Rights Group, 1984).

[61] De Zayas, 'A Historical Survey', p. 23.

[62] Ibid. As De Zayas notes, a number of factors led politicians who were at the time advocating commitment to human rights norms to endorse such policies. Among these were the problem of minorities in eastern European countries, a problem which had existed since World War I; the failure of a number of states to protect minorities; the role of some Germans as sympathisers for Hitler; and the pressures of territorial compensation after the war. The exchange of population was also meant to be limited to about 4 million, strictly controlled and 'humane' – which they were not. Finally, De Zayas notes that there was a sense that all Germans were collectively responsible for the war, which meant that the fact that any expulsion would affect guilty and innocent alike mattered little, pp. 23–4. Millions were also forcibly transferred within the Soviet Union in the post-war years. Also see Jackson Preece, *National Minorities*, pp. 103–4.

[63] Winston Churchill before the British House of Commons, 15 December 1944, cited in de Zayas, p. 25.

Universal human rights

In the years following the war, minority rights were discredited in reaction to both the failure of the League Treaties system, seen in the shadow of the Holocaust, and hostility towards Hitler's use of ethnic German minority rights in Europe. There were no minorities rights in the Charter of the United Nations and the international community turned to individual human rights as articulated in the 1948 Universal Declaration of Human Rights and the 1966 Covenants,[64] working on the assumption that individual rights applied to each individual member of any minority group. Until the end of the Cold War the only UN convention to explicitly deal with minority rights was Article 27 of the International Covenant on Civil and Political Rights (ICCPR), which states that in 'those States in which ethnic, religious or linguistic minorities exist, persons belonging to such minorities shall not be denied the right, in community with the other members of their group, to enjoy their own culture, to profess and practice their own religion, or to use their own language'.[65]

Whether or not Article 27 places any positive obligation on states to take affirmative action on behalf of minorities is the subject of debate.[66] It also allows states to define what groups constitute a minority, with the predictable result that minorities can be conveniently defined as belonging to some other category.[67] Post-Cold War, the 1992 Declaration on the Rights of Persons Belonging to National or Ethnic, Religious and Linguistic Minorities 'refers to such persons as having "the right to enjoy their own culture, to profess and practise their own religion, and to use

---

[64] Collectively referred to as the International Bill of Human Rights, in Weston, Falk and D'Amato, *Basic Documents*, pp. 298–301, 371–87. Also see Jack Donnelly, 'State Sovereignty and International Intervention: The Case of Human Rights', in Gene M. Lyons and Michael Mastanduno (eds.), *Beyond Westphalia? State Sovereignty and International Intervention* (Baltimore: The Johns Hopkins University Press, 1995), p. 117.

[65] In Ian Brownlie (ed.), *Basic Documents in International Law*, 3rd edn (Oxford: Clarendon Press, 1989), p. 280.

[66] Alain Fenet argues that this places no obligations on states. Alain Fenet, 'The Question of Minorities in the Order of Law', in Gerard Chaliand (ed.), *Minority Peoples in the Age of Nation-States*, trans. Tony Berrett (London: Pluto Press, 1989). For the argument that there is a positive obligation here see Nigel S. Rodley, 'Conceptual Problems in the Protection of Minorities: International Legal Developments', *Human Rights Quarterly* 17:1 (1995), 51. Also see N. Lerner, 'The Evolution of Minority Rights in International Law', in Catherine Brölman, Rene Lefeber and Marjoleine Zieck (eds.), *Peoples and Minorities in International Law* (Dordrecht: Martinus Nijhoff Publishers, 1993); M. Nowak, 'The Evolution of Minority Rights in International Law, Comments', in Brölman, Lefeber and Zieck (eds.), *Peoples and Minorities*; and Alfred-Maurice De Zayas, 'The International Judicial Protection of Peoples and Minorities', in Brölman, Lefeber and Zieck (eds.), *Peoples and Minorities*, pp. 259–61.

[67] Jackson Preece, *National Minorities*, p. 113.

their own language" '.[68] Although it requires more affirmative action on the part of states, this declaration is non-binding.

What other limits, if any, were placed on state-builders in the post-World War II era? Although the expulsion of nationals is not explicitly prohibited under international law, discriminatory or arbitrary treatment is prohibited. As Henkaerts notes, expulsions are inevitably accompanied by arbitrary or discriminatory treatment.[69] Furthermore, what is termed a mass expulsion may also amount to genocide, as we have seen in the cases of the Armenian genocide and ethnic cleansing in Bosnia-Herzegovina. The prohibition on the expulsion of nationals is also established as a norm under Article 9 of the Universal Declaration of Human Rights (UDHR), which states that, 'No one shall be subjected to arbitrary arrest, detention or *exile*.'[70]

In cases of extreme nationalism expulsion is often justified on the grounds that those expelled are not nationals. Although policies of denationalisation are not specifically prohibited under international law, according to the UDHR no one should be arbitrarily deprived of nationality. Hence, it is difficult for states to claim that there is no link between a policy of denationalisation and any expulsions that follow. Given that mass expulsions are proscribed, denationalisation must be considered arbitrary and may well lead to illegal and unacceptable policies.[71] Furthermore, under ICCPR Article 12 (4) individuals have the right to enter the state of which they are a national.[72] The forced removal of civilians during times of war is also prohibited under the Geneva Convention. 'Article 49 of the Fourth Geneva Convention Relative to the Protection of Civilian Persons in Times of War presents one of the clearest examples of positive international law forbidding removals during military occupations.'[73] Additional Protocols 1 and 2 also prohibit the forced removal of populations, as do the Nuremberg Principles, under which such practices constitute war crimes and crimes against humanity, as we have seen.[74]

[68] Rodley, 'Conceptual Problems', 51.   [69] Henkaerts, *Mass Expulsion*, p. 81.
[70] 'Universal Declaration of Human Rights,' in Weston, Falk and D'Amato, *Basic Documents*, p. 299.
[71] Henkaerts, *Mass Expulsion*, pp. 85–7.
[72] 'International Covenant on Civil and Political Rights', in Weston, Falk and D'Amato, *Basic Documents*, p. 378.
[73] Christopher M. Goebel, 'Population Transfer, Humanitarian Law, and the Use of Ground Force in UN Peacemaking: Bosnia and Herzegovina in the Wake of Iraq', *New York University Journal of International Law and Politics* 25:3 (1993), 632; 'Fourth Geneva Convention Relative to Civilian Persons in Times of War', 12 August 1949, in Weston, Falk and D'Amato, *Basic Documents*, pp. 170–80.
[74] Goebel, 'Population Transfer', 634–5.

While it is possible to trace the sort of provisions outlined above, minority groups within states were still highly vulnerable as the norm of non-intervention undermined such protection if state-builders saw fit to construct corporate identity through pathological means. Once again, it seems that the concern with limiting the damage that states could do to their own populations, and indeed the need for domestic transformation in many states if such practices were to be avoided, were undermined by the overwhelming concern with the stability of borders during the period of decolonisation and the Cold War.[75]

The right to national self-determination, first articulated after World War I according to ethnic and racial criteria, was reinterpreted in the light of World War II atrocities, the demands of colonised peoples for independence, and the desire to maintain the existing colonial boundaries between new states. Thus, from the 1950s a non-racial and non-ethnic concept of self-determination as a right of 'peoples' rather than 'nations' emerged, but despite this, the concept still often spelt trouble for minorities. Where self-determination has been interpreted in terms of the 'majoritarian principle' rather than racial or ethnic categories *per se*, in practice majorities and minorities have often been cast in ethnic or racial terms rather than in ways that build a shared civic identity. Once again, this has left minority groups vulnerable to those in control of the resources of the state.[76] Thus the right to self-determination provided yet another means by which rulers asserted their right to be free from external intervention as they were engaged in pathological methods of state-building. How the 'self' in self-determination was to be constructed was, once independence had been gained, asserted to be an 'internal' matter.

Despite the post-war articulation of human rights norms and the proscription of genocide, the UN Charter reaffirmed the prohibition on intervention in the domestic affairs of states on humanitarian grounds.[77] Those interventions that did occur during the Cold War period, such as the Tanzanian intervention into Uganda that ousted Idi Amin or the Vietnamese invasion of Cambodia that brought the Khmer Rouge's genocidal reign to an end, were neither justified in humanitarian terms (though they did have humanitarian outcomes) or accepted as legitimate by the international community. It was the end of the Cold War, and the massive atrocities that were witnessed soon after, that pushed further normative developments.

---

[75] Jackson Preece, *National Minorities*, pp. 106–14.
[76] Wight, *Systems of States*, pp. 168–72.
[77] Louis Henkin, 'Kosovo and the Law of "Humanitarian Intervention"', *American Journal of International Law* 93:4 (1999), 824.

Conditional sovereignty at the turn of the twenty-first century?

The international response to ethnic cleansing in Bosnia-Herzegovina and Kosovo

As Marc Weller observes, the international debate over how to deal with the Kosovo conflict, which culminated in the 1999 bombing campaign against the Federal Republic of Yugoslavia, represents a contest over 'core values' in the international system in which the principles of territorial unity, non-intervention and the non-use of force were all subject to debate.[78] This debate has been ongoing since the end of the Cold War but the Kosovo intervention took it to a new level of intensity. Advocates of intervention in the Kosovo case argued that such interventions may be legitimate if they are necessary to prevent or stop massive human rights abuses.[79] The pathological methods of corporate identity construction employed by Slobodan Milosevic's regime with its attendant human rights abuses, and, of course, the concerns for regional stability these policies provoked, led leaders of a number of states to argue in favour of intervention.

This was the latest episode in a decade of such methods employed by Milosevic and in the wake of Bosnia the international community knew who they were dealing with. In the first half of the 1990s the international community attempted to stop ethnic cleansing in Bosnia-Herzegovina, albeit in a halting, ill-considered and uncoordinated manner.[80] The conflict was initially seen as an opportunity for Europe to 'spread its wings' on a collective security issue, but its inability to deal effectively with this conflict highlighted the fact that although Europe has the highest level of institutional development of any region, reliance on European institutions to deal with Yugoslavia was overly optimistic.[81] Yet it was clear,

---

[78] Marc Weller, 'The Rambouillet Conference on Kosovo', *International Affairs* 75:2 (1999), 213–18.

[79] Nicholas J. Wheeler, *Saving Strangers: Humanitarian Intervention in International Society* (Oxford University Press, 2000). Henry Shue, 'Let Whatever is Smouldering Erupt? Conditional Sovereignty, Reviewable Intervention and Rwanda 1994', in Albert J. Paolini, Anthony P. Jarvis and Christian Reus-Smit (eds.), *Between Sovereignty and Global Governance: The United Nations, the State and Civil Society* (London: Macmillan, 1998).

[80] Tom J. Farer, 'A Paradigm of Legitimate Intervention', in Lori Fisler Damrosch (ed.), *Enforcing Restraint: Collective Intervention in Internal Conflicts* (New York: Council on Foreign Relations Press, 1993), p. 324; Ivo H. Daalder, *Getting to Dayton: The Making of America's Bosnia Policy*, (Washington, DC: Brookings Institution Press, 2000).

[81] Thomas G. Weiss, 'UN Responses in the Former Yugoslavia: Moral and Operational Choices', *Ethics and International Affairs* 8 (1994), 11; Philip H. Gordon, 'Europe's Uncommon Foreign Policy', *International Security* 22:3 (1997–98).

particularly once the 'ancient hatreds' explanation for the conflict had been challenged, that the methods of state-building being employed in the Balkans were widely regarded with abhorrence. While the failure to broker peace agreements quickly can be attributed to international reluctance to use the credible threat of force when diplomacy failed, the intransigence of Serb leaders in the rump Yugoslavia and Bosnia (as well as Franjo Tudjman in Croatia and his clients in Bosnia), and their indifference to the norms of legitimate statehood, must also be taken into account.

It was difficult for international negotiators to avoid being drawn into the logic of the ethnic cleansers and diplomatic activity resulted in a number of early proposals to divide Bosnia along ethnic lines, seen for example in the Vance–Owen plan.[82] These were, understandably, rejected by the Bosnian leadership. In a manner reminiscent of the dilemmas faced after both world wars, such proposals bought into the logic of ethnic nationalism by accepting cantonisation as a solution, and by seeking to negotiate a settlement with, and thus legitimate the position of, those who were perpetrating war crimes and crimes against humanity based on this very same logic.

The UN decision to send a peacekeeping force into Bosnia placed the peacekeepers in the invidious position of being helpless observers of various war crimes and crimes against humanity, and made military action more difficult as the peacekeepers themselves became targets. As Amir Pasic and Thomas Weiss point out, the attempt at humanitarian rescue was a poor substitute for 'robust diplomatic and military engagement' and in the end it 'prolonged the need for assistance', and damaged the UN.[83] Humanitarian assistance could not replace a coherent political and military policy for dealing with the former Yugoslavia, and addressing the causes of the humanitarian crisis there. And a policy of neutrality towards all parties was misguided when it was clear that, although there were casualties on all sides, a particular ethnic group was bearing the brunt of the atrocities being committed.[84]

The capture of UN peacekeepers and the fall of Srebrenica in July 1995, in which the world (and UN peacekeepers) watched as an estimated 8,000 Bosnian Muslim men and boys were herded off to be executed,

---

[82] Noel Malcolm, *Bosnia: A Short History* (London: Macmillan, 1994), p. 248.

[83] Amir Pasic and Thomas G. Weiss, 'The Politics of Rescue: Yugoslavia's Wars and the Humanitarian Impulse', *Ethics and International Affairs* 11 (1997), 108.

[84] The United Nations acknowledged this in its report on the fall of Srebrenica. United Nations, *The Fall of Srebrenica*, Report of the Secretary-General Pursuant to General Assembly Resolution 53/35, 15 November 1999, UN Doc. A/54/549, pp. 110–11; Ed Vulliamy, 'Bosnia: The Crime of Appeasement', *International Affairs* 74:1 (1998).

spurred decisive international action.[85] At the same time, Milosevic, acting on behalf of the Bosnian Serbs, was increasingly ready to negotiate an end to the conflict in the face of Bosnian Serb losses to resurgent Croat forces, which had resulted in a massive flow of Serb refugees into Serbia. Thus a combination of diplomacy and force led to negotiations that resulted in the implementation of the Dayton Peace Accord, signed in Paris in December 1995.

However, the Dayton Accord allowed the consolidation of ethnically defined political communities ('entities') within Bosnia-Herzegovina.[86] Dayton finally brought an end to the slaughter, but it reinforced contradictions between the social identity of the state – those international standards that are said to define legitimate statehood – and the basis on which the corporate identities within the two entities within Bosnia were to be constructed. From this it is apparent that although international action may be necessary to prevent or stop mass atrocities, if the preconditions that allow such atrocities to be thinkable are to be swept away domestic change is necessary. International standards have to be diffused into states, and in the longer term norms will only have constitutive, as well as constraining, effects when they are taken on by agents inside the state, who go about corporate identity construction accordingly. For example, despite the enormous resources that have been poured into Bosnia, since 1995 nationalists on all sides have displayed intense resistance to rebuilding Bosnia-Herzegovina as a multinational state,[87] though more moderate forces now seem to be on the rise. The politics of ethnic division will be left behind only if moderates, with international support, are able to draw on alternative strands in domestic cultures, strands that do not see ethnic differences as primary and instead stress coexistence, thus finding other means of building corporate identities.

Another important aspect of the Dayton settlement was that it did not deal with the problem of Kosovo, instead giving priority to bringing Belgrade on board in the peace process.[88] And even in the aftermath

[85] Jan Willem Honig and Norbert Both, *Srebrenica: Record of a War Crime* (New York: Penguin, 1996).

[86] Louis Sell, 'The Serb Flight from Sarajevo: Dayton's First Failure', *East European Politics and Societies* 14:1 (2000); Ronald C. Slye, 'The Dayton Peace Agreement: Constitutionalism and Ethnicity', *Yale Journal of International Law* 21 (1996).

[87] ICG, 'Preventing Minority Return in Bosnia-Herzegovina: The Anatomy of Hate and Fear', *ICG Balkans Report No. 73* (ICG, August 1999); ICG, 'Is Dayton Failing?: Bosnia Four Years After the Peace Agreement', *ICG Balkans Report No. 80* (Sarajevo: ICG, October 1999).

[88] Miranda Vickers, *Between Serb and Albanian: A History of Kosovo* (London: Hurst & Company, 1998), pp. 286–8. Milosevic negotiated on behalf of the Bosnian Serbs as indicted war criminals were banned from the negotiations, which excluded Radovan

of the 1999 NATO bombing campaign the international community remained loathe to fully reconsider the ambiguous status of Kosovo, as this may have implied the need to change territorial boundaries. As noted in chapter 5, after Dayton the Milosevic regime stepped up its repression of Kosovar Albanians. This, combined with the sense that they had been betrayed by the international community, led to an increasingly radicalised Kosovar community, less convinced of the merits of non-violence.[89] The Kosovo Liberation Army (KLA) meanwhile, began mounting attacks on Serb targets. In response, Serb forces began attacking not only the KLA but also ethnic Albanian civilians, destroying their homes and forcing hundreds of thousands to flee.

In February 1998 the United States warned Milosevic against continuing his repressive policies in Kosovo and in March the UN Security Council imposed an arms embargo on Yugoslavia, calling for a political settlement that granted autonomy to Kosovar Albanians.[90] A short-lived dialogue between the Yugoslav government and the Kosovar Albanians ensued, but in May a new offensive began, causing massive numbers of civilians to flee. In September 1998 the UN Security Council once again called on the Milosevic regime to desist from its repressive policies. Under Resolution 1199 the Council called for a ceasefire, an end to the repression of civilians, the withdrawal of the military and police personnel responsible for the violence, and insisted that a monitoring mission be allowed into Kosovo. In October the Yugoslav government agreed, along with NATO and the Organisation for Security and Cooperation in Europe (OSCE), to the creation of the Kosovo Verification Mission.[91] The Milosevic regime contravened the agreement, intensifying the conflict in Kosovo and impeding the Verification Mission.[92] On 5 October the UN Secretary General had issued a report condemning the killings in Kosovo. In response to this, Britain, the President of the Security Council at the time, proposed a draft resolution authorising the use of 'all necessary means' to stop the killings. This met with intense resistance from Russia and China, and led to NATO relying on the existing

---

Karadzic. At this time Milosevic had not been indicted by the Hague tribunal. No immunity was granted at Dayton which left the way open for his prosecution later.

[89] Vickers, *Between Serb and Albanian*, p. 287.

[90] UN Security Council Resolution 1160, 31 March 1998, under Chapter VII of the charter; Ivo H. Daalder and Michael E. O'Hanlon, *Winning Ugly: NATO's War to Save Kosovo* (Washington, DC: Brookings Institution Press, 2000), p. 27.

[91] This agreement was supported by the Security Council under Resolution 1203, 24 October 1998.

[92] For a refutation of the claim that the international community did not do enough to pursue a diplomatic solution to the crisis see Peter Christoff and Chris Reus-Smit, 'Kosova and the Left', *Arena Magazine* 43: (October–November 1999), 25–9.

UN resolutions as grounds for intervention in Yugoslavia in March 1999 rather than going back to the Security Council.[93]

Despite intense diplomatic efforts and numerous resolutions on the part of the Security Council there was clear evidence that agents of the state were employed in a systematic campaign of killing and expelling ethnic Albanian Kosovars.[94] This led the Contact Group for the former Yugoslav to set up talks at Rambouillet, backing the search for a diplomatic solution with the threat of force.[95] However, in the end, the Rambouillet talks made little headway, in great part because representatives of the Federal Republic of Yugoslavia evinced little genuine interest in reaching a diplomatic solution.[96] As noted above, accepting international norms of legitimate state behaviour and changing domestic policies was not an attractive option for a leader who had gained and maintained his authority through manipulation and violence.

This was another episode in a continuing normative clash between the Milosevic regime and those states that asserted that what he did within the borders of Serbia *was* of international concern. Milosevic never accepted the human rights standards that gained near universal assent after World War II, and to which Yugoslavia was a signatory. However, while there was a clear consensus that what was being done to ethnic Albanians in Kosovo was unacceptable, debates over the appropriate way to handle this put the 'core values' of territorial unity, non-intervention and the non-use of force on the table for debate, as noted above. As James Mayall observes, 'Throughout the early post-Cold War period, the Security Council exhibited a disturbing tendency to will the end but not the means. In Kosovo, NATO made it clear from the outset that it was prepared to commit whatever level of air power proved necessary to force President Milosevic to withdraw Yugoslav forces from the province.'[97]

Thus the Kosovo campaign was not only based on the assertion that affairs within a state were of international concern but that this was grounds for military action to stop the state-sponsored violence towards ethnic Albanians. But the legitimacy of the operation was hotly contested, as evinced by the draft resolution presented to the UN Security Council

---

[93] Wheeler, *Saving Strangers*, pp. 258–62; Adam Roberts, 'NATO's "Humanitarian War" Over Kosovo', *Survival* 41:3 (1999), 102–23.

[94] Human Rights Watch, *Federal Republic of Yugoslavia: Humanitarian Law Violations in Kosovo* (New York: Human Rights Watch, 1998).

[95] Christoff and Reus-Smit, 'Kosova and the Left', 28.

[96] See Weller, 'The Rambouillet Conference', for an account of the conduct of the parties at these talks.

[97] James Mayall, 'The Concept of Humanitarian Intervention Revisited', in Albrecht Schnabel and Ramesh Thakur (eds.), *Kosovo and the Challenge of Humanitarian Intervention: Selective Indignation, Collective Action, and International Citizenship* (Tokyo: United Nations University Press, 2000), pp. 328–9.

on 26 March, two days into the NATO operation, by Russia (supported by two states who were not sitting on the Security Council at that time, Belarus and India), which charged that NATO's operation was in breach of the UN Charter and was therefore illegal. Although it gained support from China and Namibia, twelve other members of the Security Council, including six non-Western states, rejected the draft resolution. While some members of the Security Council remained silent, others such as Canada and Slovenia were forthright in their arguments that the intervention was in fact legitimate, and Malaysia, Bahrain and Argentina all made statements in support of the intervention.[98]

There were miscalculations on both sides of this conflict as the NATO operation loomed. NATO miscalculated how quickly Milosevic would give way, based on a misreading of Dayton (that the threat of air strikes had brought Milosevic to the negotiating table on behalf of the Bosnian Serbs) and an assumption that Kosovo was the same as Bosnia. However, where Milosevic could let go of the idea of making Bosnia part of 'Greater Serbia' he could not easily let go of Kosovo. Not only was it within Serbia's borders, it was considered the heartland of Serb national identity and was the cornerstone of his use of Serb nationalism over the previous decade. As I argued in chapter 5, although Milosevic may have used this nationalism in the most instrumental manner, he was never a completely free agent, and by the late 1990s he had become enmeshed in the powerful symbolics that he used to gain power. If he walked away from the 'Kosovo myth', on what could he legitimate his authority? Though he had made the transition to nationalist demagogue in the late 1980s, he could hardly make a convincing transition to democratic leader in the late 1990s, with domestic opposition gaining momentum.

Milosevic miscalculated when he assumed that the NATO bombing would not last long. While at one level Milosevic was playing a game of bluff with the international community, his willingness to use mass violence as a weapon was not to be dismissed. On one occasion he is reported to have openly discussed killing all Albanians as a solution and on another he reportedly said to the German Foreign Minister, Joschka Fischer, 'I can stand death – lots of it – but you can't.'[99] Such statements explicitly signalled his rejection of certain norms of legitimate statehood and his understanding (*mis*understanding as it turned out) that because

---

[98] Wheeler, *Saving Strangers*, pp. 265–81. Also see 'Editorial Comments: NATO's Kosovo Intervention', *American Journal of International Law* 93:4 (1999), 824–62. As well as questions about the justice of the campaign, critics argued that the means employed were not just, pointing to the reliance on air strikes rather than ground troops, the targeting of civilian infrastructure and civilian deaths in Serbia, as well as the high numbers of Kosovars who were killed or displaced.

[99] Both cited in Daalder and O'Hanlon, *Winning Ugly*, pp. 58, 94.

others were working to a different set of norms he could manipulate this to his own advantage – playing to the theme of the historic victimisation of the Serb people by external powers once again – and NATO would back down. This normative clash had been going on since 1987 when Milosevic came to power. He never moved beyond a 'strategically motivated rhetorical position' towards other members of the international community.[100] Milosevic never entered into genuine dialogue but tried to play off, and to stave off, his interlocutors to his own advantage, while drawing on and manipulating domestic nationalist sentiment to construct a domestic normative environment in which non-Serbs posed a potential 'threat' and his critics were cast as enemies of the state. Meanwhile, his policies brought suffering and hardship to the very people in whose name he acted.

His actions ultimately pushed the international community, or at least significant sections of it, into taking military action to stop the systematic abuse of minority groups. What are the implications of this? Was it a 'watershed'?[101] Does it have 'the potential to be a defining moment in post-Cold War history'?[102] Lori Fisler Damrosch argues that 'The choice of NATO as the vehicle for intervention in Kosovo indicates that this was a European response to a European problem and would not necessarily prefigure comparable action anywhere outside Europe.'[103] While this is true up to a point, the fact that non-Western states were not prepared to support Russia's draft resolution against the NATO operation highlights that this has broader implications. Nonetheless, the debate over the legitimacy of the intervention emphasises that the conclusions we can draw from this operation are mixed and, importantly, that the political will and military means for such operations are unlikely to be found outside of Europe at the moment.

The conflict in Kosovo may represent a turning point because not only did states intervene to stop violence within another state but the head of the offending state was held personally responsible for the crimes committed against Kosovars and was indicted by the Hague tribunal, where he is currently on trial. Granted, the International Criminal Tribunal for the former Yugoslavia (ICTY) is an *ad hoc* tribunal, but the existence of this international court, along with the tribunal in Tanzania, set up to

[100] Thomas Risse, "Let's Argue!": Communicative Action in World Politics, *International Organization* 54:1 (2000).
[101] Wheeler, *Saving Strangers*, p. 297.
[102] Albrecht Schnabel and Ramesh Thakur (eds.), *Kosovo and the Challenge of Humanitarian Intervention: Selective Indignation, Collective Action, and International Citizenship* (Tokyo: United Nations University Press, 2000), p. 319.
[103] Lori Fisler Damrosch, 'The Inevitability of Selective Response? Principles to Guide Urgent International Action', in Schnabel and Thakur (eds.), *Kosovo*, p. 415.

try those responsible for the Rwandan genocide of 1994 (ICTR), boosted support for the development of general international judicial prosecution, in the form of a permanent international criminal court. These developments highlight the fact that we are witnessing normative change that has global implications.

Sovereignty and international accountability

In 1992 the Security Council first warned that individuals would be held responsible for breaches of the Geneva Conventions in the war in Bosnia-Herzegovina.[104] On 6 October 1992, in an effort to deter further abuses, it opened investigations of violations of these conventions through the establishment of a Commission of Experts.[105] Despite a serious lack of funding and lack of cooperation within the UN bureaucracy the Commission began collecting evidence for possible future prosecutions.[106] Following this, in early 1993 the Security Council advised the Commission to finish its work and announced the creation of the International Tribunal to Prosecute Violations of International Humanitarian Law in the Former Yugoslavia after 1 January 1991.[107] By Resolution 827 of 25 May 1993, the Security Council unanimously adopted the Tribunal's statute.

The Tribunal has the power to prosecute persons for serious violations of international humanitarian law, grave breaches of the Geneva Conventions, violations of the law or customs of war, genocide and crimes against humanity. Radovan Karadzic has been indicted for war crimes and crimes against humanity for his role in the siege of Sarajevo and the use of UN peacekeeping troops as hostages. On 16 November 1995 he was charged with genocide for his role in the murder of thousands in Srebrenica in July 1995. General Mladic, of the Yugoslav National Army and commander of Serbian troops in Bosnia-Herzegovina, was also indicted by the Tribunal on the same counts.[108] On 10 March 1998 the

---

[104] UN Security Council Resolution 764, July 1992.

[105] UN Security Council Resolution 780.

[106] James C. O'Brien, 'The International Tribunal for Violations of International Humanitarian Law in the Former Yugoslavia', *American Journal of International Law* 87:4 (1993), 641; M. Cherif Bassiouni, 'From Versailles to Rwanda in Seventy-Five Years: The Need to Establish a Permanent International Criminal Court', *Harvard Human Rights Journal* 10 (1997), 39–42.

[107] UN Security Council Resolution 808, 22 February 1993.

[108] As of August 2001 there are currently seventy-seven public indictments, forty-eight of which are currently in proceedings. Forty-six indictees are in detention with two (Biljana Plavsic and Momcilo Krajisnik) released pending trial. Twenty-six indictees remain at large and there are an unknown number of undisclosed indictments for crimes committed in the former Yugoslavia.

prosecutor's office of the Tribunal released a statement to the effect that the jurisdiction of the Tribunal covered the escalating violence, including violations of humanitarian law, in the province of Kosovo, in the Federal Republic of Yugoslavia. In May 1999, the Chief Prosecutor of the ICTY indicted Milosevic, along with four others, on charges of crimes against humanity, and violations of the laws or customs of war, in Kosovo, so that for the first time, a serving head of state was indicted as an international criminal.

While the establishment of this Tribunal was seen as a 'fig leaf' to cover international inaction by some, others have argued that it represents a normative shift. There are elements of truth in both these claims. While the conflict was raging in Bosnia, it did indeed seem that the establishment of the Tribunal would give small comfort to those who were the victims of ethnic cleansing. From the account given by one participant in both the Commission of Experts and the ICTY it seems that the motives of a number of states were certainly mixed. Yet this same account also demonstrates that the 'international community' is in practice much broader than a number of powerful states alone. A coalition of interested scholars, non-governmental organisations and committed states maintained the work of the Commission so that its final report could be published by the United Nations, and more recently they have worked to maintain support for the ICTY itself.[109] While it is still states that wield force, beyond this there is a broader coalition of concerned actors involved in the pursuit of international justice. At the same time a normative shift can be seen in that the ICTY cannot be attributed merely to victors' justice, as could the post-World War II war crimes tribunals, and the court has conducted itself with impartiality. Further, the statute for the ICTY establishes that crimes against humanity can occur in internal wars,[110] and rape was for the first time recognised as a crime against humanity.[111] More recently, three Bosnian Serbs were the first to be convicted and sentenced by the tribunal on charges of rape and enslavement as crimes against humanity.[112]

Establishing the ICTY was no substitute for effective action to stop atrocities, but this does not detract from the possible longer-term deterrent

---

[109] Bassiouni, 'From Versailles', 39–46.

[110] This was clearly articulated by the Appeals Chamber of the ICTY in 1995. See Prosecutor vs Tadic, Case No. IT-94-1-AR72, Appeal on Jurisdiction (2 October 1995).

[111] The tribunal for Rwanda goes even further in recognising that crimes against humanity can occur in peacetime. Theodore Meron, 'War Crimes Law Comes of Age', *American Journal of International Law* 92:3 (1998), 462–8.

[112] ICTY, *Judgement: Prosecutor vs Dragoljub Kunarac, Radomir Kovac and Zoran Vukovic*, 22 February 2001, Case No. IT-96-23-T & IT-96-23/1-T, available at <http://www.un.org/icty>.

effects of the Tribunal, along with the ICTR. As Payam Akhavan argues, the ICTY should also act as a deterrent and its effectiveness should not be judged only on whether or not particular individuals immediately desisted from perpetrating crimes but on how well it communicates the message that certain conduct is unacceptable:

> It is this expression of disapproval by the world community that is at the core of the ICTY's mandate. The punishment of particular individuals . . . becomes an instrument through which respect for the rule of law is instilled into the popular consciousness. Ultimately, the ICTY will be a success if it contributes to bringing about a culture of habitual lawfulness such that persecutions and atrocities do not present themselves as a real alternative to peaceful multiethnic coexistence.[113]

While the tribunal is still plagued by a shortage of funds and the failure to apprehend many high-ranking indictees, recent changes have seen greater cooperation with the tribunal by Croatia under a new government and the former President of the Serb Republic Biljana Plavsic (as well as Momcilo Krajisnik) voluntarily going to the Hague to face questioning in April 2001. Despite internal struggles over how to proceed, the Federal Republic of Yugoslavia did cooperate with the Hague and handed over Milosevic.[114] This contest between the nationalist Yugoslav President Vojislav Kostunica and Prime Minister Zoran Djindjic of Serbia reflects debate over the form that the corporate and social identities of Yugoslavia, particularly Serbia, should take in the future. Despite this debate, in the wake of the devastation that has befallen Serbia and amid revelations in the Serbian media of crimes committed against ethnic Albanians in Kosovo, rejecting existing norms of legitimate statehood is unlikely to be a realistic option.

Just as the rationale for the two *ad hoc* tribunals is of 'bringing about a culture of habitual lawfulness', this is also a goal of the International Criminal Court.[115] Under its 1998 Rome Statute, the Court will have jurisdiction over the crime of genocide, crimes against humanity, war crimes and the crime of aggression (Article 5). The definition of crimes against humanity is also wider, including 'forced pregnancy' (Article 7). However, the Court's jurisdiction is not retrospective and it may exercise its jurisdiction only over crimes committed after entry into force of the Statute for the state in which a crime was committed (Article 11).

---

[113] Payam Akhavan, 'Justice in the Hague, Peace in the Former Yugoslavia? A Commentary on the United Nations War Crimes Tribunal', *Human Rights Quarterly* 20:4 (1998), 749.

[114] Ian Traynor, 'Raids Exposed Rifts Between the Reformist Leaders', *The Guardian*, 2 April 2001.

[115] United Nations, *Rome Statute of the International Criminal Law Court*, UN Doc. A/CONF.183/9, adopted 17 July 1998.

The establishment of a permanent International Criminal Court clearly reasserts that genocide is a crime under international law and emphasises the obligation of all states to prevent, as well as punish, genocide. Under the Rome Statute the Court will be truly independent, as the Prosecutor has the authority to initiate investigations, 'on the basis of information on crimes within the jurisdiction of the court' (Article 15). The court is also capable of prosecuting nationals of non-signatory states for crimes committed on the territory of signatory states (Article 12). Importantly, as well as drawing on appropriate treaties and rules of international law and national laws that are consistent with international law and the Statute of the Court, the Court 'may also apply principles and rules of law as interpreted in its previous decisions' (Article 21). That is, it is within the Court's power to build on previous decisions and thus develop a body of legal precedent in international criminal law.

While some powerful states have been resistant to the court there is also significant support for it. There are 139 signatories to the 1998 Rome Statute for the Court, which, as of April 2002 had been ratified by 66 states, meaning that it will take effect as of 1 July 2002. A range of Western and non-Western states have ratified so far, including Argentina, South Africa, Botswana, Ghana, Gabon, Canada, France, Germany, the Netherlands, Croatia and also Yugoslavia, which signed on in December 2000 and ratified on 6 September 2001.[116]

The path of normative change

This chapter has traced the development of international standards which define legitimate state action with regard to the treatment of subjects and citizens. Humanitarian norms gained increasing moral and legal force in two bursts during the twentieth century, first following the violence of World War II and the Holocaust that accompanied it, and then in the decade following the end of the Cold War as the international community struggled to come to terms with continued violence within states. Standards of legitimate state behaviour have developed out of the social interaction of states as they respond to domestic policies, and attempts to argue that state leaders are not accountable for their actions at the international level are no longer readily accepted: legitimate sovereignty is, increasingly, conditional on how state leaders act towards their own citizens, that is, the way in which they go about constructing corporate state identity. As we have seen also, though, when state leaders choose

[116] The full list can be found at: <http://www.un.org/law/icc/statute/romefra.htm>.

Table 2 *Tracing international normative change*

	Spain	France	Turkey	Yugoslavia
1. No norms of internal constitution	*			
2. Treaty specific norms		*		
3. General social norms			*	*
4. General legal norms				*
5. Judicial prosecution (domestic)			*	
6. Judicial prosecution (*ad hoc* international)				*
7. Judicial prosecution (general international)				Emergent
8. Enforcement (*ad hoc*)				*
9. Enforcement (systemic)				

to turn their backs on international social norms, enforcing such norms remains a difficult task facing the international community.

The normative developments outlined in this chapter can be traced with reference to nine criteria (see Table 2). At one extreme is the complete lack of any international norms regarding the internal constitution of the state. Such an environment existed when the Catholic Monarchs, Ferdinand and Isabella, attempted to build a homogeneous state in early modern Spain through expelling the Spanish Jews. At this time there were no reciprocally recognised standards in the embryonic international system, beyond the right to make war.

By the time Louis XIV revoked the Edict of Nantes in 1685 there had been a normative shift in the system, reflected in the development of treaty specific norms, seen in the protection accorded to minorities under the Peace of Westphalia. Louis' actions contravened this fragile normative consensus, causing alarm across much of Europe. While there was no thought of intervention, Huguenots were able to find refuge outside of France.

By the late nineteenth century we see the development of general social norms proscribing mass slaughter reflected in the public outcry against the ill-treatment of minorities in the Ottoman Empire. While this was often limited to co-religionists, it was not always the case. However, while the late nineteenth-century interventions in the Ottoman Empire on behalf of minorities raised the hopes of Armenians that they would be treated as equal subjects, in fact the Sultan responded to their demands for equality with a series of massacres. Though these massacres were considered outrageous in moral terms at the time, ultimately no protection was accorded to the Armenians in the Ottoman Empire.

Likewise, although the Entente powers attempted to persuade the CUP to stop its 'deportation' of the Armenians during World War I, this merely resulted in the CUP issuing a formal order of deportation and their programme of extermination continued unabated. In the aftermath of the genocide, the international community struggled to articulate new international legal principles that would reflect the sense of moral outrage at what was clearly recognised at the time as a crime against humanity. This attempt to translate general social norms into legal principles can be found in the Treaty of Sèvres, but, as we have seen, this treaty was never ratified. In the face of the Kemalist regime's refusal to acknowledge the responsibility of the Turkish state for the genocide, their assertions of sovereignty as complete control over all internal matters, and the scramble for position as the Empire crumbled, the international consensus that systematic murder of a million people should be punished at an international level disintegrated. This reflected both the tentative nature of the legal finding that crimes against humanity had been committed by a state against its own people, and the lack of a truly multilateral basis from which to approach this issue. Prior to these findings, there was an attempt at domestic judicial prosecution in 1919, imposed on Turkey by the victorious allies. However, this failed in the face of high levels of domestic resistance and the nationalist revolution that swept through Turkey.

It was in the second half of the twentieth century that general legal norms regarding legitimate state behaviour were most clearly articulated. In the wake of World War II, horror at the Holocaust crystallised world opinion, the term genocide was coined, and the policies it represents were prohibited under the Genocide Convention. However, this was not straightforward, for, as noted earlier, the Allies supported the mass expulsion of ethnic Germans in which an estimated 2 million died. In their minds, this was obviously not in the same category as the genocide but, as I argued above, this massive displacement was underpinned by an acceptance of the 'logic' of homogeneity within states, which when put into practice is invariably a blunt instrument. A similar contradiction still plays out in the international system between human rights norms and the most conservative interpretation of the rights of sovereignty and non-intervention. Nonetheless, human rights norms gained increasing moral and legal force in the last decade of the twentieth century, and when states claim sovereignty over internal affairs while abusing significant sections of their populations, this is less and less convincing.

Ad hoc international prosecutions of crimes committed in the name of the state also contest the most conservative interpretation of sovereignty.

This is particularly the case with the contemporary tribunals dealing with Rwanda and the former Yugoslavia, which cannot so easily be dismissed as dispensing victors' justice, as was the case with the post-World War II tribunals in Nuremberg and Tokyo. Most recently we have seen a further development towards general international judicial prosecution, which is still in its early stages with the development of a permanent International Criminal Court which will have a Prosecutor authorised to independently instigate investigations. This is a new development, which despite the opposition of some states represents an emergent normative standard. This could not exist, even in its emergent form, if the norm of sovereignty was not undergoing revision.

However, ethnic cleansing in the former Yugoslavia occurred despite the development of clear norms proscribing such acts and the creation of the *ad hoc* tribunal for the former Yugoslavia. It is clear that under some circumstances only a clear and compelling threat of force may be enough to prevent or stop mass atrocities. The NATO campaign to stop ethnic cleansing in Kosovo is thus far the only case of collective intervention to stop ethnic cleansing, and it has not to date been taken as a precedent for further military intervention. Whether this remains a one-off intervention remains to be seen. Certainly, the legitimacy of such operations is still strongly contested as a conservative interpretation of sovereign rights remains compelling to many states, hence Russia's and China's response to the NATO intervention in Kosovo.

Does this debate mean that it is too early to say there is a new sovereignty norm at work today? The intervention in Kosovo, the ad hoc tribunals and the ICC do not represent a fully articulated and robust normative architecture. What they do represent, though, is a normative shift, so that it is very difficult for state leaders to argue, in the name of sovereignty, that they are not accountable for their actions. The social recognition that mass expulsions and slaughter are criminal acts grew throughout the course of the twentieth century. Since the middle of that century an international legal framework has developed which makes this a fact in law. But these social and legal changes, have not, in themselves, been enough to stop abuses. Although no systematic means of enforcement currently exist, recent events such as the creation of two ad hoc tribunals, the development of the ICC and the NATO intervention make it harder for would-be abusers, and their apologists, to assume that they will go unpunished or that 'sovereignty' will protect them. Over the course of the twentieth century and into the twenty-first, therefore, we have seen normative developments which may contribute towards constraining those who wish to use violence against their own citizens. As I have argued, this is certainly patchy, but sovereign immunity from prosecution is no longer inviolable.[117]

In chapters 2 to 5 I traced four cases of pathological homogenisation. In this chapter I have traced how these practices fuelled the development of international social norms proscribing such behaviour. In chapter 7 I investigate the circumstances that may inhibit strategies of pathological homogenisation, paying particular attention to the role of international norms, and the conditions under which these may influence the identities and interests, and thus the policies, of political elites. I investigate this through consideration of two 'threshold cases', the Czech Republic and the Former Yugoslav Republic of Macedonia.

[117] Also see Marc Weller, 'On the Hazards of Foreign Travel for Dictators and Other International Criminals', *International Affairs* 75:3 (1999).

7   On the threshold: the Czech Republic and Macedonia

In chapters 2 to 5 I traced the relationship between state-building and the strategies of pathological homogenisation used by elites in their efforts to construct political communities within the boundaries of states according to exclusive criteria of identity and difference. In chapter 6 I showed how these practices, although bound up with the development of the international system with its norm of non-intervention, have also pushed the development of international norms of legitimate state behaviour that clearly proscribe such acts. If such practices have been a recurrent feature of modern international politics, what are the chances that the now well-established norms of legitimate statehood will stop new state-builders from employing similar tactics? Under what conditions are state-builders less likely to take this path? These questions are particularly salient when practices such as ethnic cleansing and the forced displacement of peoples – let alone the genocide in Rwanda – seem so prevalent in the post-Cold War world.

In this chapter I investigate the relationship between corporate and social identity construction in the formative stages of two post-communist states. Both of these states, the Czech Republic and the Former Yugoslav Republic of Macedonia (FYROM),[1] are newly constituted following the dissolution of Czechoslovakia and the former Yugoslavia, respectively. Why choose these two states? First, their chances of a successful transition to democracy and the protection of human and minority rights seem very different. The Czech Republic is an example of a new state that was widely perceived as already part of the democratic club after the fall of communism. It is self-described as 'returning to Europe', it has signed on to numerous human rights conventions, and human and minority rights are enshrined in the constitution. Yet the path of corporate identity construction has not been as smooth as this might lead one to think. According to transitional studies, the Czech case should be an

---

[1] Formally known as the Former Yugoslav Republic of Macedonia, the provisional title under which it joined the United Nations in 1993, it will be referred to as Macedonia here.

'easier' case in that the state does not contain significant minority populations that have ties to surrounding states.[2] The Czech Republic does have a significant minority Roma population, though, which is the object of widespread hostility from the majority population, as is the case across Europe.[3] The Roma suffered disproportionately under the 1993 Czech citizenship law which rendered a large number of them stateless, and drew the condemnation of numerous international intergovernmental organisations, non-governmental organisations (NGOs) and domestic critics, many of whom argued that the law was specifically directed at the political exclusion and physical expulsion of members of this vulnerable group.[4] Below I investigate whether, distinct from the anti-Roma prejudice that is so widespread across Europe, the law represented a systematic attempt by agents of the state to deny citizenship rights to a significant proportion of this minority group. In light of the state's claims to democratic legitimacy, I then consider why the law was amended under pressure from both domestic and international critics.

Macedonia is certainly a harder case as it has a significant minority population with a strong sense of their own communal identity and strong ties to a neighbouring state, Albania. Ethnic Albanians represent at least one quarter of the population and they have been vocal in their demands for equal treatment and fair representation in government.[5] Macedonia gained its independence as the former Yugoslavia disintegrated violently. It is bounded by Albania, the Kosovo region of Yugoslavia, Greece, which was reluctant to recognise the state, and Bulgaria, which denied the existence of a distinct Macedonian nationality and language, arguing that these were 'really Bulgarian'. It has thus been subject to intense external pressure in a region beset by the ethnicisation of politics. In 1999 Macedonia dealt with a massive influx of ethnic Albanian refugees from Kosovo and most recently, in 2001, it teetered on the edge of civil war following attacks on police and army by ethnic Albanian guerrillas which

---

[2] Jon Elster, Claus Offe, Ulrich K. Preuss, *et al.*, *Institutional Design in Post-Communist Societies: Rebuilding the Ship at Sea* (Cambridge University Press, 1998).

[3] Referred to elsewhere as Gypsies, 'Romany', 'Romani' or the 'Roma' are the preferred designations of many of this group. The Roma are actually very diverse in ethnic, religious and cultural terms, so that defining one 'Roma' identity becomes difficult. Nonetheless, at a general level, 'all East European Roma share to some extent the same origins, language, culture and historical experiences in Europe'. Zoltan D. Barany, 'Living on the Edge: The East European Roma in Postcommunist Politics and Societies', *Slavic Review* 53:2 (1994), 324–5.

[4] Jirina Siklova and Marta Miklusakova, 'Law as an Instrument of Discrimination: Denying Citizenship to the Czech Roma', *East European Constitutional Review* 7:2 (1998), 338.

[5] There is also a significant Roma minority in Macedonia that is generally regarded as being subject to less discrimination and prejudice than elsewhere in Europe. For the argument that there is still pervasive and institutionalised discrimination against Roma in Macedonia, see European Roma Rights Center, *A Pleasant Fiction: The Human Rights Situation of Roma in Macedonia*, Country Reports Series 7 (July 1998).

escalated into open conflict. Since the breakdown of the former Yugoslavia many commentators have waited for Macedonia to descend into a nationalist driven conflagration. While the possibility of civil war certainly seemed more likely in 2001, the question remains, how did Macedonia defy such predictions for the best part of a decade? When many of the preconditions for ethnic cleansing existed in this state why did successive governments avoid targeting minorities and opt to build legitimacy within a broader European context?

An important difference between the Czech Republic and Macedonia is the state–society relations in each state. These have consequences for the ways in which international norms of legitimate state behaviour are diffused – or not diffused – into states, in particular the ways in which historically constructed cultural attitudes towards minorities, domestic debates about citizenship rights and national identity interact, and how these are articulated at the level of the state through society–state interaction. Do domestic cultures and the configuration of state–society relations in each of these states make acceptance of international norms more or less likely? Indeed, are international norms merely imposed from outside or have they played a constitutive role in the formation and development of these new states?

International norms of legitimate statehood

The international context of recent state formation in Europe is one in which the international norms of legitimate statehood have been defined in terms of democratic government and respect for human rights. These norms were most clearly articulated at the 1990 Conference on the Human Dimension held under the auspices of the Conference on Security and Cooperation (CSCE), now called the Organization on Security and Cooperation (OSCE). The Document of the Copenhagen Meeting (DCM) upholds the importance of human rights and fundamental freedoms as did the Helsinki Final Act of 1975. However, as Thomas Buergenthal argues, this was also a 'landmark international charter', as it was the first to explicitly focus on 'issues relating to the form and nature of government and the role of individuals and groups in society without, however, neglecting traditional human rights concerns. In this it is a document which, in its political scope and significance, is unmatched by other international human rights instruments.'[6] The signatories to the

---

[6] Thomas Buergenthal, 'The Copenhagen CSCE Meeting: A New Public Order for Europe', *Human Rights Law Journal* 11:1–2 (1990), 231. For an overview of the OSCE and minority rights see Jane Wright, 'The OSCE and the Protection of Minority Rights', *Human Rights Quarterly* 18:1 (1996).

DCM committed themselves to the principles of pluralistic democracy, the rule of law and respect for human and minority rights.[7]

In the post-World War II era the Council of Europe stressed human rights norms (European Convention on Human Rights, 1953) but since the end of the Cold War it has been active in the protection of minority rights, which are specifically addressed in the 1994 European Framework Convention on the Protection of National Minorities. This convention aims to specify 'the legal principles which States undertake to respect in order to ensure the protection of minorities', although how the principles are to be implemented is left to the discretion of each signatory state. Despite criticisms that the result was a vaguely worded and weak convention,[8] it represents an attempt to transform the CSCE/OSCE's political commitment to pluralistic democracy into legal obligations.[9] The convention can be said to carry some moral weight as to date it has been ratified by twenty states, including the Czech Republic and Macedonia, and entered into force in early 1998.[10] Finally, for those states wishing to accede to the EU, a working free market system is added to the Copenhagen criteria of legitimate statehood.[11] Therefore if states identify themselves as 'democratic' they can expect that they will be measured against a certain set of norms, including the election of governments through free and fair elections, a free market system and respect for human rights. These norms are by no means universally accepted but those governments, including the Czech Republic and Macedonia, that have recognised these norms as legitimate have taken on a social identity that makes voluntary compliance more likely and rejection more difficult.[12]

Despite this, signing on to international standards does not make compliance inevitable, passive or necessarily complete. As Thomas Risse, drawing on Jurgen Habermas' work on communicative action, demonstrates, even when there is general acceptance of a certain set of norms they are still subject to debate or 'argumentation'. Applying Habermas' framework to the international realm, Risse outlines how actors can move

---

[7] Document of the Copenhagen Meeting of the Conference on the Human Dimension Meeting of the CSCE, 29 June 1990, *Human Rights Law Journal* 11:1–2 (1990).

[8] Heinrich Klebes, 'The Council of Europe's Framework Convention for the Protection of National Minorities', *Human Rights Law Journal* 16:1–3 (1995), 97.

[9] Heinrich Klebes, 'The Council of Europe's Framework Convention', Appendix A: Explanatory Memorandum on the Framework Convention for the Protection of National Minorities, *Human Rights Law Journal* 16:1–3 (1995), 102–3.

[10] Ibid., 97–8; Jeffrey T. Checkel, 'Norms, Institutions, and National Identity in Contemporary Europe', *International Studies Quarterly* 43:1 (1999), 94.

[11] The criteria can be found at: <http://europa.eu.int/comm/enlargement//index/htm>.

[12] Thomas M. Franck, 'The Emerging Right to Democratic Governance', *American Journal of International Law* 86:1 (1992), 50.

from interaction that is based on strategic bargaining which has no interest in an other's point of view, to 'rhetorical action' in which actors try to convince or persuade others of the logic of an argument, albeit with no intention of changing their own position. However, this presupposes that at least one participant is prepared to be convinced by the better argument.[13] Risse argues that in some situations what begins as strategically motivated rhetorical argument can change towards a different form of reasoning in which debate is directed towards reaching some common understanding and in which all actors are prepared to be persuaded by the better argument. Such a shift is not merely a matter of deciding on an alternative strategy to achieve static interests, but reflects changes in how actors understand their interests and identities. Thus 'argumentative reasoning' has a constitutive effect on actors in which interests and identities are themselves the subjects of contestation and may undergo transformation.

As Risse explains, there are certain preconditions for such argumentative rationality including the capacity to empathise, that is to try and see the other's point of view, a 'common lifeworld' and recognition of all actors as equal. The common lifeworld that is reflected in a shared culture, language or norms provides a shared 'repertoire of collective understandings' to which actors 'can refer when making truth claims'.[14] Applying Habermas' insights about a common lifeworld to the anarchic international realm, Risse argues that we can see the development of lifeworlds in particular areas and on particular issues such as human rights and the environment.[15] In turn, international norms provide benchmarks against which critics may evaluate and contest the actions of a norm violating state, demanding that they give an account of themselves.

Another example of where an international common lifeworld might exist arises out of the shared values and norms of democratic states, creating the oft-cited zone of democratic peace. The leaders of the Czech Republic and Macedonia have voiced the desire to be included squarely in this zone or lifeworld with their avowed intentions of building democratic and inclusive states. This has resulted in an ongoing conversation – often debate – between these states and the international community. It has also given rise to debate, indeed struggle, within these states over

[13] Thomas Risse, ' "Let's Argue!": Communicative Action in World Politics', *International Organization* 54:1 (2000), 8–9.

[14] Risse, 'Let's Argue!', 11.

[15] Ibid. Also see Daniel C. Thomas, 'The Helsinki Accords and Political Change in Eastern Europe', in Stephen C. Ropp, Kathryn Sikkink and Thomas Risse (eds.), *The Power of Human Rights: International Norms and Domestic Change* (Cambridge University Press, 1999).

normative standards or the nature of the shared lifeworld inside the state. How should national identity and citizenship rights be defined? What are the rights of minorities within the new state? In both cases international pressure is towards more inclusive answers to these questions but they have been strongly contested at the domestic level, as I explain below.

Finally, Risse highlights the fact that it is clear whether or not we are in the realm of argumentative rationality when actors 'are accused of violating certain norms of appropriate behavior to which they have previously agreed. Do they dismiss such accusations as irrelevant or engage in some self-serving rhetoric? Or do they start justifying their behavior, give reasons for their action, or even apologize?'[16] If the latter cluster of reactions, then the norms are accepted as legitimate and the debate is over how the norms should be put into practice in a given situation.

The diffusion of international norms

An important factor in both the cases discussed below is the extent to which the new states genuinely see themselves as democratic states with all the changes that entails. However, states are not unitary actors and conflicting domestic norms including racial discrimination, ethnic or nationalist exclusiveness may be well entrenched and at odds with the democratic norm of the equality of all citizens. As George Schopflin notes, all post-communist societies have, to a greater or lesser extent, shared an investment 'in the supposed magical properties of nationalism and nationhood'.[17] While nationalist sentiment does not have to take a xenophobic turn, it does provide elites with the resources to build the corporate identity of the state through targeting out-groups if they so desire and there may also be counter-elites willing to use such means. These resources may become even more powerful when the imagined material rewards of the post-communist transition have not appeared for many people and a sense of betrayal may add to an already existing feeling of historic victimisation. As the domestic legitimacy of governments is vulnerable under such conditions, the ethnic or nationalist card can provide an attractive means of legitimation. Yet it is clear that a number of governments are cognisant of the longer-term costs of such strategies and are attempting to build stable corporate identities that are not dependent on the targeting of out-groups, and look to international norms for legitimation.[18]

---

[16] Risse, 'Let's Argue!', 19.
[17] George Schopflin, 'Culture and Identity in Post-Communist Europe', in Stephen White et al. (eds.), *Developments in East European Politics* (Durham: Duke University Press, 1993), p. 25.
[18] Franck, 'The Emerging Right', 50–1.

How do such norms diffuse into states when states are not unitary but contain complex societies with their own histories, cultures and internal debates? Indeed, is such diffusion possible? Jeffrey Checkel provides some answers to the question of how norm diffusion occurs with his typology of different state–society relationships. He uses this model to track how particular norms are likely to meet significant resistance or support within states. Focusing on citizenship and minority rights in Europe, he argues that the level of cultural 'match' between international and domestic norms will affect the likelihood of norm diffusion as an international norm that fits with 'historically constructed domestic norms' will be more readily accepted.[19] Recognising that states are not unitary actors, Checkel sets out to plot 'cross national variation among key actors' as they respond to new norms and, out of the debates that ensue, how the interests and preferences of domestic actors may change over time.[20]

According to Checkel, it is elites who are the 'gatekeepers who ultimately control the political agenda'.[21] He argues that change will occur through either a 'bottom-up' process when societal actors put so much pressure on elites they feel compelled to accept a norm, or 'top-down' when elites go through some process of social learning. Therefore, it is the structure of domestic institutions that will account, to a great extent, for whether international norms are diffused from the bottom up or top down.[22] As I argue throughout this book we cannot understand the social identities of states in isolation from their corporate identities. In both the cases studied below, while states have attempted to take on certain social identities, the 'push and shove' between these and corporate identities under pressure to change has to be considered as does the central role played by elites in constructing corporate state identities and mediating between these and the social identity of the state.

Ethnic and civic national identities in Eastern Europe

Even in a globalising world the contemporary state claims the primary, if not the exclusive, loyalty of its citizens. But what are the criteria of citizenship and national identity, the principles by which it is decided who

---

[19] Checkel, 'Norms, Institutions, and National Identity', 84–7. Also see Jeffrey T. Checkel, 'The Europeanization of Citizenship', in Maria Green Cowles, James Caporaso and Thomas Risse (eds.), *Transforming Europe: Europeanization and Domestic Change* (Ithaca: Cornell University Press, 2001); and Jeffrey T. Checkel, 'International Norms and Domestic Politics: Bridging the Rationalist–Constructivist Divide', *European Journal of International Relations* 3:4 (1997).
[20] Checkel, 'Norms, Institutions, and National Identity'.
[21] Ibid., 88.   [22] Ibid., 88–9.

is in and who is out? In the following cases we see two new states and the authority of their governments legitimated with reference to democratic values, commitment to a free market, and membership in European and other international institutions. Yet we also see tension between these norms and a tendency to define the political community in ethno-national terms. The ethnically based interpretation of national identity that is still prevalent in these states, despite civic principles to be found in their constitutions, poses problems for how minorities are treated within the nation-state and there are significant tensions between this conception of nationhood and building liberal-democratic institutions. 'The predominantly ethnic understanding of nationhood is very hard to reconcile with liberal-democratic politics, because it implicitly recognises full citizenship rights only for the majority ethnic group. Ethnic minorities tend to be treated as anomalous and problematic, even when they have inhabited the territory for centuries.'[23] This is the case even when minorities are formally guaranteed full citizenship rights.

Thus struggles over the way in which domestic or national identity is to be understood interact, and may clash with, these new norms even if international social membership rules for the new states have been defined through constitutional means. It is domestic cultural processes that have produced 'the master narratives that give shape to peoples' experience',[24] and while national sentiment may not necessarily be xenophobic, the new democratic norms with their implicit model of civic national identity pose a challenge to ethnically based conceptions of national identity. As a result, it is not difficult to find examples of resistance to attempts to change the 'master narrative'.[25] They can be seen at all levels of society, but are particularly apparent when state officials such as the police force or local governments resist changes that the central government has legislated. Thus there can be institutional blockage of change as well as institutions that reflect change.

As the previous case studies demonstrate, normative contest arises when established political arrangements lose legitimacy and are challenged by new ideas. This was certainly the case with the collapse of communism, a major crisis of legitimacy. Once the dust had settled it quickly became apparent that despite the turn to democracy in many

---

[23] Judy Batt, 'The International Dimension of Democratisation in Czechoslovakia and Hungary', in Geoffrey Pridham, Eric Herring and George Sanford (eds.), *Building Democracy? The International Dimension of Democratisation in Eastern Europe* (New York: St. Martin's Press, 1994), p. 182.

[24] Joel S. Migdal, 'Studying the State', in Mark Irving Lichbach and Alan S. Zuckerman (eds.), *Comparative Politics: Rationality, Culture, and Structure* (Cambridge University Press, 1997), p. 215.

[25] Ibid., p. 229.

states, there were also many competing interpretations of how the newly independent states should be constituted. This was particularly so when it came to the nature of national identities, where the ethnic and civic conceptions of national identity often clash. A necessary ingredient that may prevent people falling back on ethnic notions of national identity is a developed civil society, yet this is underdeveloped or non-existent in the wake of communism. For example, it has been very difficult to maintain voter interest, particularly when many voters view politicians with deepening cynicism.[26] While the behaviour of many politicians – one of the inheritances of the socialist era being self-serving and duplicitous elites – leaves much to be desired, there is also a lack of understanding of the demands of democratic systems. While citizens may want the perceived payoffs of liberal capitalism, understood as increased wealth, there is a less developed sense of civic duty. Claus Offe describes this as an instrumental attitude to liberalism and democracy – if we have *these* institutions we will get *these* (material) payoffs – rather than any deeply felt commitment to the liberal values of freedom and a civil society for their own sake.[27]

From this, it would be simple to give a materialist account of how international norms diffuse into new states. If there are material payoffs, why not comply? If the material payoffs are not good enough, forget it. But Offe's observation leads to a deeper understanding of the dynamics at work in this situation. For a start, while material interests are certainly important motivations in states wishing to accede to the European Union this is a story that cannot be told without taking account of wider European norms. Second, even if the incentives to comply with these norms that Europe provides are material, the norms reflect political values that are not reducible to material factors. Third, looking at the domestic factors which block the diffusion of wider social norms, we can ask why do some groups reject these norms when there may well be economic costs for doing so? The answer is that the material and normative dimensions of political life coexist and at times identity norms may trump material interests, resulting in widespread domestic resistance to less exclusionary norms, regardless of economic cost.

Elections were held very quickly after the downfall of communist regimes with parties funded by the state that did not, at least initially, have to rely on extensive networks of party membership and wider support within civil society. Many coalitions and parties themselves were unstable and this led to a focus on 'playing the electoral game' rather than thinking about the long-term practices needed to build stable parties and

[26] Charles Gati, 'The Mirage of Democracy', *Transitions* 2:6 (1996), 9.
[27] Claus Offe, 'Cultural Aspects of Consolidation: A Note on the Peculiarities of Postcommunist Transformations', *East European Constitutional Review* 6:4 (1997).

party systems.[28] Party politics in the new states tend towards shifting coalitions 'because no single political camp is strong enough to win and maintain clear-cut majorities',[29] and this is certainly the case in both the Czech Republic and Macedonia, which have had a succession of coalition governments.[30] It is to these two states that I now turn.

State formation in the Czech Republic

Cultural difference in Czechoslovakia

Czechoslovakia, created in the wake of World War I, brought together two dominant national groups, and a number of smaller ones. The Czechs and Slovaks had different histories under different rulers in the Austro-Hungarian Empire, but in the new state the 'Czechoslovak' national group, with a population of approximately 8.7 million, outnumbered the ethnic German population of 3 million, previously part of the dominant nationality under imperial rule.[31] During the inter-war period Czechoslovakia was a parliamentary democracy which, unlike many other new states, did not generally enact repressive policies towards minorities.[32] All the same, during the First Czechoslovak Republic, in both Slovakia and the Czech lands, Roma were prevented from moving around, which stopped them searching for work and resulted in their 'deepening pauperization'.[33]

In trying to control Roma in this way Czechoslovakia was no different from other European states. Indeed the story of the Roma in Czechoslovakia and now in the Czech Republic and Slovakia is only part of the story of the Roma, who are subject to widespread discrimination almost everywhere they are to be found. The Roma are very diverse due to their different historical experiences but they do share a history of exclusion and persecution.[34] First documented in Europe in the fourteenth and

[28] Elster, et al., *Institutional Design*, p. 134.   [29] Ibid., p. 16.

[30] Constitutional Watch, 'The Czech Republic', *East European Constitutional Review* 8:3 (1999).

[31] Carol Skalnik Leff, *The Czech and Slovak Republics: Nation Versus State* (Boulder: Westview Press, 1997), p. 29; Janusz Bugajski, *Ethnic Politics in Eastern Europe: A Guide to Nationality Policies, Organizations, and Parties* (Armonk: M. E. Sharp, 1994), p. 294.

[32] Leff, *The Czech and Slovak Republics*, p. 29; Bugajski, *Ethnic Politics*, p. 295.

[33] Kveta Kalibova, Thomas Haisman and Jitka Gjoricova, 'Gypsies in Czechoslovakia: Demographic Development and Policy Perspectives', in John O'Loughlin and Herman van der Wusten (eds.), *The New Political Geography of Eastern Europe* (London: Belhaven Press, 1993), p. 135; Otto Ulc, 'Integration of the Gypsies into Czechoslovakia', *Ethnic Groups* 9 (1991).

[34] On the ethnogenesis of a shared Roma identity in the face of discrimination in Eastern Europe see Nicolae Gheorghe, 'Roma-Gypsy Ethnicity in Eastern Europe', *Social Research* 58:4 (1991).

fifteenth centuries, the Roma arrived in waves of migration from India that may have started as early as the ninth century. From early on they were regarded with suspicion and by the seventeenth century they were the subject of numerous laws forbidding their residence or their nomadism. They were barred from a number of countries, including the Czech lands, on pain of death and were often hunted down in 'Gypsy hunts' during the seventeenth and early eighteenth centuries.[35] Across Europe they were accused of a range of crimes including theft, espionage, sorcery, spying, paganism, brigandage, spreading disease, abduction of children, evil-doing, being work-shy and being 'riff-raff'.[36] As Jean-Pierre Liegeois points out, the problem was their *existence* and for many state-builders their whole way of life and the fact of their visible difference meant they 'embodied subversion and perversion'. Therefore it was not a matter of what they had done but of what they *might* do. In the words of a nineteenth-century Strasbourg magistrate: 'I have no evidence of criminal acts committed by these people, but their situation is such that they must of necessity be tempted to commit them if the occasion presents itself . . . they cannot but be dangerous.'[37] According to Liegeois, the Roma have long been 'perceived as physically threatening and ideologically disruptive', regarded as setting a 'bad example of "asociality" and idleness'.[38] Their way of life and their refusal to assimilate was perceived as disruptive to the state and they were rarely left alone. By the nineteenth century and into the twentieth century policies of exclusion began to be replaced with policies of 'containment', that is forced assimilation, which often entailed the forcible removal of children from their families.[39] Forced assimilation policies were generally aimed at stopping Roma nomadism, as was the case in inter-war Czechoslovakia.

Czechoslovakia was the only industrialised state in southeastern Europe in the inter-war period, although most of the industrialisation was in the Czech lands. Greater economic development was reflected in higher education levels and greater life expectancy, and a more developed civil society.[40] However, there were significant tensions between the dominant national groups within Czechoslovakia. Where Czech national identity had tended to identify with the Czechoslovak state, Slovak nationalists were disgruntled with what they saw as the dominant role played by the larger partner in the state. After the Nazi invasion of Czechoslovakia in 1938, Slovakia gained independence under a Nazi puppet government, while the Czech lands became part of a German protectorate. The

[35] Jean-Pierre Liegeois, *Roma, Gypsies, Travellers* (Strasburg: Council of Europe Press, 1994), p. 128.
[36] Ibid., pp. 124–8.   [37] In ibid., p. 131.   [38] Ibid., p. 145.
[39] Ibid., pp. 136–45.   [40] Elster *et al.*, *Institutional Design*, p. 38.

war and its aftermath resulted in a homogenisation of the population, as an estimated 3 million ethnic Germans were deported from the Czech lands,[41] and out of approximately 350,000 Jews only 44,000 survived the Holocaust.[42] Most of the Roma in the Czech lands were exterminated once it was under German occupation. Here, as in Poland, Croatia and Serbia, 'extermination was pursued even more violently, and more systematically, than in Germany itself'.[43]

The events of World War II and its aftermath had a homogenising effect on Czechoslovakia, although this was not complete. The expulsion of the ethnic Germans was so 'successful' as it had international backing in the post-war era, when *all* Germans were considered morally responsible for Nazism, whereas both Budapest and Moscow opposed the expulsion of Hungarians from Slovakia and a sizeable minority remains there today. The Ukrainian minorities in both Czechoslovakia and Poland were absorbed by the post-war expansion of the Soviet Union.[44] There was significant migration of Roma from Slovakia to the Czech lands in the post-World War II period as they moved in search of work in mines and heavy industries or were forcibly resettled to fill the labour gap left by the expulsion of the ethnic Germans.[45] Thus the communists inherited a relatively more homogeneous population when they came to power in 1948, one in which the Roma were regarded as a 'problem' to be solved, as they were seen as an impediment to building a socialist society.[46] As a result, and despite some improvement in their socioeconomic position,

[t]he Gypsy, or Romani, population in Communist Czechoslovakia was subjected to forced resettlement, dispersal, the persecution of linguistic and cultural traditions, attempts at mass sterilization, and discrimination in housing, employment and education. The Communist authorities did not recognize Roma as members of a distinct nationality but, rather, as a backward ethnic minority that would be integrated into the emerging Socialist society.[47]

After a brief respite during the Prague Spring, efforts at forced integration continued until the end of communism. Yet the Roma had not been assimilated due to a combination of their resistance and majority prejudice towards them.[48] Furthermore, failed forced resettlement from Slovakia to Bohemia had resulted in government housing programmes in which

[41] Leff, *The Czech and Slovak Republics*, p. 8.   [42] Bugajski, *Ethnic Politics*, pp. 295–6.
[43] Liegeois, *Roma, Gypsies, Travellers*, p. 134. An estimated 400,000 to 500,000 Roma died in Europe during World War II.
[44] Bugajski, *Ethnic Politics*, p. 296.
[45] Kalibova, Haisman and Gjoricova, 'Gypsies in Czechoslovakia', p. 141; Liegeois, *Roma, Gypsies, Travellers*, pp. 148–9.
[46] Barany, 'Living on the Edge', 326–7; Ulc, 'Integration of the Gypsies', pp. 108–9.
[47] Bugajski, *Ethnic Politics*, p. 299.   [48] Barany, 'Living on the Edge', 326.

Roma from different areas were housed together. This resulted in conflict within housing estates and resentment from non-Roma when, in their view, Roma were given priority for state housing. 'The net effect was an exacerbation of antagonism and conflict between the communities, and a further strengthening of negative Gypsy stereotypes.'[49]

The velvet divorce

On 1 January 1993 Czechoslovakia was peacefully dissolved and the Czech Republic and Slovakia came into existence. The dissolution was in great part due to disagreement between elites who refused to compromise over the functioning of a bi-national state. Although Slovakia's Vladimir Meciar played a more overtly nationalist game in the lead up to the split, Czech nationalism which regarded the Czechs are superior to, and not needing, the Slovaks also played a role. Meciar's Slovak nationalism also produced a counter-nationalist response in the Czech lands. In short, even though the majority of voters wanted the federation to continue, they voted for parties that made very different choices, and it was a 'nationalist/ethnic divide' that dissolved Czechoslovakia, albeit in a non-violent manner.[50]

While Czechoslovakia was a small state, its successor states are even smaller, with populations of around 10 million in the Czech Republic and 5 million in Slovakia. Although the Czech Republic is now a relatively homogeneous state, there are a number of minorities there, the most visibly different, and the most discriminated against, being, as in the past, the Roma.[51] The open expression of hostility towards Roma increased after the fall of communism (as it did across Europe), as the liberalisation of societies gave racist groups the opportunity to air their views.[52] But discrimination is not limited to fringe groups, and Roma are often the target of resentment based on the view that they somehow gain greater assistance from the state.

Such discriminatory treatment is at odds with the proclaimed political status of Roma as equal citizens in the Czech Republic. Like other governments in Eastern and Central Europe that have sought both domestic and

[49] Liegeois, *Roma, Gypsies, Travellers*, p. 149.
[50] Elster et al., *Institutional Design*, p. 143.
[51] Significant minorities in a population of 10.3 million include Moravians, Slovaks, Poles and Germans, as well as Roma. Estimates of the Roma population vary widely, from 33,500 (0.3%) to 300,000 (2.9%). Minority Rights Group, *World Directory of Minorities* (London: Minority Rights Group International, 1997), p. 217. It is likely that the higher figure is more accurate as Roma often do not declare their background due to discrimination.
[52] Barany, 'Living on the Edge', 329.

international legitimacy through committing themselves to democratic institutions, the Czech government was faced with the problem of dealing with historically and culturally entrenched prejudice against the Roma. This in itself was a difficult enough task but the government seemed to contradict its avowed intention to address such issues when it promulgated the 1993 citizenship law that rendered tens of thousands of Roma aliens in their own country or led to their expulsion from the Czech Republic.[53] It is to the manifestly exclusionary effects of this law that I now turn.

Corporate identity of the state: national identity, human rights and the 'Roma Law'

There is a civic conception of national identity embedded in the 1992 constitution of the Czech Republic. The rights of ethnic minorities are upheld in the European Charter of Fundamental Rights and Freedoms, which was adopted by the Czechoslovak Federal Assembly in January 1991, and that was in turn adopted as Article 3 in the constitution of the Czech Republic in December 1992.[54] The Czech Republic has also ratified a raft of international human rights conventions and Article 10 of the constitution further declares that these 'are directly binding and take precedence over the law'.[55] While the legitimacy of government rests on the will of people, as expressed in majority voting, majority decisions must 'provide for the protection of minorities'.[56] The Roma are granted equal status as a recognised minority group.[57]

Despite these constitutional provisions, there is an extremely high level of antipathy towards Roma with most Czechs regarding them as 'outsiders' such that ill-treatment of this group is acceptable to many ordinary citizens.[58] That they are regarded by many Czech citizens as outside 'the sanctified universe of moral obligation', to use Helen Fein's phrase once again,[59] or 'outside the community of common concern',[60] is

---

[53] Human Rights Watch, *World Report 1999: Czech Republic*, <http://www.hrw.org/wr2k/ Eca-08.htm>.

[54] Constitution of the Czech Republic, in Albert P. Blaustein and Gisbert H. Flanz (eds.), *Constitutions of the Countries of the World* (New York: Oceana Publications, 1993), p. 159.

[55] Ibid., p. 119.   [56] Ibid., Article 6, p. 118.

[57] Barany, 'Living on the Edge', 333–6.

[58] Human Rights Watch, 'Roma in the Czech Republic: Foreigners in Their Own Land', *Human Rights Watch Country Report* 8:11 (1996).

[59] Helen Fein, *Accounting for Genocide* (New York: The Free Press, 1979), p. 4. Also see chapters 1 and 4, above.

[60] OSCE, *Report of the OSCE High Commissioner on National Minorities to Session 3 or the Human Dimension Section of the OSCE Review Conference*, RC.GAL/2/99, 22 September 1999, p. 1, <http://www.osce.org/inst/hcnm/recomm/roma/roma99.html>.

reflected in the widespread acceptance of attacks on Roma by skinhead or neo-Nazi groups and the level of support for the discriminatory treatment experienced by Roma at the hands of local administrators and police officers. Addressing this prejudice, President Vaclav Havel acknowledged in 1993 that legal standards are one thing, while bringing about 'a climate of tolerance, cooperation and coexistence' is another.[61]

Roma have a higher per capita crime rate than other groups in the Czech Republic, a state of affairs which reflects their low socioeconomic and educational status. They are widely regarded as a criminal class, with little recognition of the causes of criminalisation, such as their historic marginalisation and the resultant impoverishment and lack of educational opportunities, a situation that is exacerbated by the streaming of many Roma children into schools for the intellectually disabled.[62] Resistance to the equal treatment of Roma is often strongest, or at least most obvious, at the level of local government. At the time of the 'velvet divorce', in violation of the Charter of Fundamental Rights and Freedoms, a number of local government decrees were proclaimed under which Roma were evicted from their homes, or made to apply for visitors permits if they wanted to enter an area. These measures reflected panic that there would be an influx of Roma from Slovakia once the federation dissolved, but such discrimination is also an ongoing issue in the Czech Republic.[63] This reflects resistance to the norms of equality and the equal treatment of Roma amongst a significant proportion of the population.

The citizenship law

As noted above, most of the Roma on Czech lands were killed during World War II. After the war, many Roma were either forcibly moved to the Czech lands from Slovakia, or moved there voluntarily in search of work. When the state was recast as a federation in 1969 new citizenship legislation was introduced which made citizens of the Czechoslovak

---

[61] Cited in Barany, 'Living on the Edge', 337, n. 67. Such attitudes are prevalent amongst people who regard themselves as democrats, so that even a group of students who regard the slogan 'foreigners out!' as unacceptable regard the Roma as in another category and 'not liking them' does not mean being racist. Leff, *The Czech and Slovak Republics*, p. 170, cites one opinion poll in which 'an astonishing 91% of Czech and Slovak respondents express[ed] antipathy' towards Roma. Also see Chris Powell, 'Time for Another Immoral Panic? The Case of the Czechoslovak Gypsies', *International Journal of the Sociology of Law* 22:2 (1994), 110.

[62] Leff, *The Czech and Slovak Republics*, p. 170; European Roma Rights Center, *A Special Remedy: Roma and Schools for the Mentally Handicapped in the Czech Republic* (Bucharest: European Roma Rights Center, 1999), <http://www.errc.org/publications/reports/czech-republic.rtf>.

[63] Powell, 'Time for Another Immoral Panic?', 115–16.

Socialist Republic dual citizens of the federation and of their home republic. This legislation had no practical implications until the dissolution of Czechoslovakia in 1993. At this time, while Slovakian citizenship was made available to all former Czechoslovak citizens, the Czech Republic adopted a more restrictive approach. This automatically granted citizenship to anyone who had Czech citizenship under the 1969 law, while permanent residents who were now deemed to be Slovak citizens could apply to change their nationality, subject to certain conditions. It is these conditions that are central to the impact the law had, as many Roma could not meet them. Furthermore, the intricacies of the new laws were beyond the understanding of many citizens, including Roma, who in general have not had access to post-primary education,[64] and 'tens of thousands of Roma were made stateless, either de jure or de facto, by virtue of this law'.[65]

The conditions that applied to 'selecting' Czech citizenship under the citizenship law included a clean criminal record for the previous five years, the presentation of documentation proving Slovak citizenship, and at least two years' continuous residence in the Czech Republic.[66] The low socioeconomic status of the Roma population is reflected in higher crime rates, and the law had a disproportionate effect on this minority group, to the point where critics argued that the law had been aimed at the Roma. The law violated a number of principles of international law, for example, the principle of proportionality was violated as citizenship could be denied for shoplifting or murder, with no distinction made between these crimes.[67] Also, it imposed an *ex post facto* penalty for crimes committed before the law came into being:

The Czech citizenship law attache[d] to past criminal acts a heavier penalty (i.e. loss of the option of Czech citizenship) than existed at the time the crime was committed, in violation of article 11 (2) of the Universal Declaration of Human Rights, article 15 (1) of the International Covenant on Civil and Political Rights, and article 7 (1) of the European Convention on Human Rights. Principle X of the Helsinki Final Act requires OSCE participating States to fulfill in good faith their international legal obligations.[68]

---

[64] Law on Acquisition and Loss of Citizenship, Law No. 40/1993. Siklova and Miklusakova, 'Law as an Instrument'.

[65] OSCE High Commissioner on National Minorities, *Report on the Situation of Roma and Sinti in the OSCE Area* (The Hague: OSCE, March, 2000), p. 157.

[66] Siklova and Miklusakova, 'Law as an Instrument'; United States CSCE, 'Ex Facto Problems of the Czech Citizenship Law' (Washington: September, 1996), p. 4, <http://www.house.gov/csce/ czechlaw.htm>.

[67] Human Rights Watch, 'Roma in the Czech Republic', 17.

[68] United States CSCE, 'Ex Facto Problems', p. 3.

In practice, anyone without documents, including individuals born in the Czech Republic or who had spent most of their lives there, as well as Roma children in state care, were denied citizenship. A large number of Roma did not have documents to prove Slovak citizenship in the first place. A number that did have documents and gave up Slovak citizenship were then denied Czech citizenship, thus being rendered stateless.[69] For those who were not expelled from the Czech Republic, denial of citizenship often meant the withdrawal of social benefits.[70]

The previous case studies in this book all trace the shift from discrimination and sporadic violence against out-groups to systematically implemented state policies aimed at removing a given group from the territory of the state. In a comparative light we can ask whether the citizenship law in the Czech Republic represented a systematic attempt to remove the Roma from the Czech Republic. The answer to this question will depend on a reading of the intention behind the law, which will inevitably be controversial. Certainly, some critics claimed that this was a conscious policy by the government that was aimed at not only stemming the movement of Roma from Slovakia into the Czech Republic (which itself arose from prejudice against this group) but also at expelling the Roma from the Czech Republic.[71] Despite government denials that this was the intention of the law, Human Rights Watch argues that this claim is given some credence by the fact that it would have been simple to draft a very different law that did not have this effect on Roma resident in the Czech Republic.[72] They also pointed out that the state granted citizenship rights to ethnic Czechs resident elsewhere, thus highlighting the 'ethnic intentions' of the citizenship law,[73] which one critic described as 'a ridiculous and futile attempt to create as ethnically pure a state as possible'.[74] This 'intention' was at odds with the civic conception of national identity in the constitution of the Czech Republic and inherent in international instruments pertaining to the rights of minorities, to which the Czech Republic is party.

[69] Human Rights Watch, 'Roma in the Czech Republic', 21. This problem was reduced after the two governments began coordinating the administration of citizenship procedures in 1994.

[70] Powell, 'Time for Another Immoral Panic?', 117.

[71] Ibid., 115, notes that the debate over this supposed 'influx' was 'characterised by rumor and panic', rather than any objective analysis.

[72] Human Rights Watch, 'Roma in the Czech Republic', 15.

[73] Ibid., 20. Also see Beata Struharova, 'Disparate Impact: Removing Roma from the Czech Republic', *Roma Rights* 1 (1999); and Siklova and Miklusakova, 'Law as an Instrument'. As Powell noted in 1994, 'No-one seems keen to apply laws strictly to the large number of Americans who have overstayed their visas.' Powell, 'Time for Another Moral Panic?', 117.

[74] Tom Gross, 'Citizenship Law Codifies Racism', *Prague Post* 29 June 1994.

While there were vociferous domestic critics of the law from the beginning, the law was seen as legitimate in the eyes of many Czechs, as
it resonated with deeply entrenched attitudes towards the Roma. Many
politicians would have perceived great benefits in not challenging the
view that the Roma are an alien group that cannot be trusted, and that
rightfully belongs outside the state, regardless of what attachments they
may have. And many members of the elite may also hold these views.
As Chris Powell relates, 'When pressed a rather liberal official from the
Czech Republic's Office of the President said that the state was unlikely to
deal effectively with anti-Gypsy discrimination because the state benefits
from such discrimination.'[75]

A recent report noted that in spite of the increasing awareness of racism
as a problem in the Czech Republic, 'there appears to be still a very
widespread perception that most victims of racism and discrimination
are "outsiders" and do not really belong to Czech society. This perception contributes to rendering manifestations of racism and discrimination less unacceptable in the eyes of the majority population.'[76] However,
as noted above, domestic resistance to the law was by no means absent. A
number of domestic NGOs were active in challenging the law, as well as
the widespread discrimination against Roma, which made the law acceptable to so many people. These groups assisted Roma with information
about the law when the government failed to do so, and lobbied against
it both domestically and internationally.[77]

Search for legitimacy: social identity of the state
as a pluralistic democracy

The international norms that the Czech Republic had signed on to as
a democratic state gave domestic critics and international organisations
a standard by which to argue that the Czech state was accountable at
the international level. As we have seen, the Czech Republic (and before
that Czechoslovakia) sought to attain international legitimacy through
adherence to the political values articulated in the Document of the

---

[75] Powell, 'Time for Another Moral Panic?', 119.

[76] ECRI, *Second Report on the Czech Republic* (Strasburg: Council of Europe, 21 March
2001), p. 18. These findings were also echoed in the most recent European Union (EU)
accession report on the Czech Republic which notes, under the heading of political criteria for membership, that the Czech Republic needs to improve conditions for Roma and
put policies into practice. European Union, *Accession Partnership 1999: Czech Republic*.

[77] Tolerance Foundation, *A Need for Change in the Czech Citizenship Law: Analysis
of 99 Individual Cases* (Prague: Tolerance Foundation, 21 November 1994); Czech
Helsinki Committee, 'Rights of National and Ethnic Minorities', 1997, <http://
www.helcom.cz/en/r97_1.htm>.

Copenhagen Meeting, namely democratic institutions that reflect the rule of law, respect for human rights and respect for and protection of minority rights.[78] The desire to be seen as legitimate at the international level provided powerful incentives to amend the law and to put anti-discrimination provisions into practice.[79] Yet the pull of historically constructed prejudices against the Roma was also strong, resulting in a clash between international and domestic norms on this issue. However, this did not mean that the government could simply ignore international pressure as domestic actors were part of the pressure for normative change and they drew on and reported to international organisations in their campaign to have the law repealed. At the intergovernmental level pressure came from the Council of Europe, the CSCE/OSCE and the United Nations, particularly through the United Nations High Commission for Refugees (UNHCR), but also through the Committee on the Elimination of Racial Discrimination (CERD). The 1996 Council of Europe report on the Czech Republic and Slovakia asserted the principle that where individuals have 'genuine links' with a territory, having a criminal record is no justification for exclusion. The report also highlighted the non-proportional aspect of the law, noted above.[80]

The OSCE was vocal in its criticism of the citizenship law and questioned whether policy-makers should see the interests of the state in the way they did, arguing that the law undermined the creation of a stable, unified state. In the words of Max van der Stoel, then OSCE High Commissioner on National Minorities:

In no case should new citizenship laws be drafted and implemented in such a way as to discriminate against legitimate claimants for citizenship, or even to withhold citizenship from possibly tens of thousands of life-long and long-term inhabitants

---

[78] Document of the Copenhagen Meeting. This has also been a means of seeking support in both the economic and security realms; Batt, 'Czechoslovakia and Hungary', p. 176.

[79] Monitoring and discussion continues to be an ongoing problem, which reflects the high level of public antipathy towards Roma. The sorts of policies that are still attempted are exemplified by the wall built in the northern Bohemian town of Usti nad Lebem in order to separate Czechs from Roma. Condemned by the EU, the wall was dismantled on the orders of the national government but the Czech Constitutional Court ruled that the government did not have the right to order this. Despite this, an agreement was reached between the local council and the government. Lucian Kim, 'The Wall of Hostility on "Intolerance Street"', *US News and World Report* 127:18 (1999).

[80] Cited in Diane F. Orentlicher, 'Citizenship and National Identity', in David Wippman (ed.), *International Law and Ethnic Conflict* (Ithaca: Cornell University Press, 1998), pp. 304–7; Report of the Council of Experts of the Council of Europe on the Citizenship Laws of the Czech Republic and Slovakia, Doc. DIR/JUR (96), April 1996. The Council of Europe's European Commission Against Racism and Intolerance's 1997 and 2000 reports on the Czech Republic raise similar concerns. ECRI, *Report on the Czech Republic* (Strasburg: Council of Europe, September 1997); ECRI, *Second Report on the Czech Republic*.

of the state, most of whom are Roma. As a result, the status of these persons is essentially 'foreigner' in their own country. This would greatly undermine what I consider to be in the long-term interest of the state: the unequivocal establishment of a loyal bond between the state and its inhabitants and the prospect that they would be able to participate fully in the political, economic, and social life of the state.[81]

Similarly, the United Nations criticised the law through a number of its organs, in particular the office of the UNHCR and the CERD. The UNHCR's 1996 report 'unambiguously condemned the Czech law as incompatible with international law'.[82] In the view of the committee, the citizenship law was not acceptable as it excluded from the state individuals who 'had a genuine effective link and who had indicated their social attachment through exercise of civil and social functions'.[83] As the CERD noted, 'the act of rendering people stateless entails the deprivation of fundamental rights linked to citizenship, as well as exposing them to expulsion'.[84]

Critique and reform: amendments to the law

The Czech Republic's responses to criticisms of the law moved through a number of phases. At first, criticism was rejected as irrelevant, for example on the grounds that the law was not directed specifically at Roma. President Havel, while criticising discriminatory implementation of the law, argued that the law itself was not discriminatory.[85] The Czech Republic also argued that it was the sovereign right of the state to define its citizenship criteria. As the US Committee on Security and Cooperation argued in response to this claim, 'In fact, the right to determine one's nationals has been, historically, an expression of state sovereignty. Under modern legal standards, however, that right (like other sovereign rights) is circumscribed by the extent of any state's international human rights obligations.'[86] Such obligations played a constitutive role in the new state

---

[81] Statement by Max van der Stoel, OSCE High Commissioner on National Minorities, Human Dimension Seminar on Roma in the OSCE region, organised for the Office for Democratic Institutions and Human Rights and the High Commissioner for National Minorities, in Cooperation with the Council of Europe, Warsaw, 20–23 September 1994, cited in OSCE High Commissioner on National Minorities, *Report on the Situation of Roma and Sinti*, p. 158.

[82] Orentlicher, 'Citizenship', p. 308. Office of the UNHCR, *The Czech and Slovak Citizenship Laws and the Problem of Statelessness* (February 1996).

[83] Cited by Orentlicher, 'Citizenship', p. 309.

[84] CERD, Concluding Observations of the Committee on the Elimination of Racial Discrimination: Czech Republic, CERD/C/304.Add.47, 30 March 1998, section D, para 14.

[85] Tom Gross, 'On Czech Citizenship Law the President Has No Clothes', *Prague Post*, 7 December 1994.

[86] United States CSCE, 'Ex Facto Problems', p. 6.

as it sought to legitimate itself internationally. The state grudgingly acknowledged this but was uncooperative with domestic NGOs attempting to assist people vulnerable under the law and was initially uncooperative with international agencies, such as the UNHCR.[87] According to Human Rights Watch, the government only started a dialogue on the law when the Council of Europe handed down a highly critical report in 1996.[88]

However, the law was gradually amended. In 1994, while upholding the validity of the law, the Czech Constitutional Court recognised that permanent residency did not have to be fully documented to be a fact. But this recognition of the difficulty of producing documentation made little difference in practice as local officials still demanded that such documents be produced, which was an impossibility for many Roma.[89] The law was further amended in 1996, allowing the Ministry of the Interior discretionary powers to waive the requirement of a clean criminal record, and the law no longer applied to those who had served prison sentences of two years or less.[90] Critics argued that this did not go far enough, though, as it still allowed no scope to distinguish between minor and serious crimes and still required that applicants had to be permanent residents of the Czech lands at the end of 1992, something that many Roma could not prove.[91] Meanwhile, international pressure to further amend the law continued.[92] Finally, in 1999 under the new Social Democratic government the law was amended once again, this time to allow 'former citizens of the Czech and Slovak Federal Republic who were not citizens of the Czech Republic but were on the territory on December 31 1992, [to] acquire citizenship by declaration'.[93] The law still requires that applicants must have been on the territory of the Czech Republic for the whole time, which precludes those who were expelled or who left the country seeking asylum elsewhere from becoming citizens. There is no provision for compensation for those 'unjustly deprived of citizenship

---

[87] Human Rights Watch, 'Roma in the Czech Republic', p. 16.
[88] Ibid., p. 23; Siklova and Miklusakova, 'Law as an Instrument', p. 6. Report of the Council of Experts.
[89] Human Rights Watch, 'Roma in the Czech Republic', p. 18.
[90] Leff, *The Czech and Slovak Republics*, p. 172.
[91] Bella Edginton, 'The Czech Citizenship Law: Legally and Morally Wrong', *Prague Post*, 6 March 1996; Emma McClune, 'Proposed Changes to Citizenship Law Disappoints Helsinki Commission', *Prague Post*, 28 February 1996. While acknowledging some improvement in the situation due to the 1996 amendments, the 2000 ECRI report (finalised in June 1999 before the final amendment to the law) regards these as insufficient. The report took positive note of the debates current in the Czech Parliament at that time, that would lead to amendment. ECRI, *Second Report on the Czech Republic*, p. 6.
[92] For example, in 1998 the CERD noted that despite the 1996 amendments, some sections of the population still remained vulnerable as the question of citizenship had not been fully addressed. CERD, Concluding Observations.
[93] 'Czech Republic Amends Anti-Roma Law', *Roma Rights* 3 (1999).

and the benefits thereof for over six years'.[94] Nonetheless, this does show that over a period of six years successive governments did give way to international pressure and amended a discriminatory law that was in direct contravention of the principles which underpin the state's goal of international social legitimacy.[95]

While it is hard to conclusively prove that this law was designed with the intention of systematically removing Roma from the state, its acceptance by so many Czech citizens reflected entrenched discrimination against the Roma in the Czech Republic and there is strong circumstantial evidence that there may have been a systemic attempt to block citizenship rights for a significant number of this minority.[96] This is at odds with the norms of human and minority rights that the Czech Republic has signed on to, yet these international norms are not passively accepted by the Czech population, but are subject to a process of normative contestation and re-evaluation. This reflects what Checkel terms a lack of 'cultural match' between the domestic and international realms. Referring to Germany, Checkel notes that 'it is striking how ethnic and exclusive understandings of identity often appear as the default mode in public discourse'.[97] This is also the case in the Czech Republic where public figures often made statements that revealed an ethnic conception of identity that excluded the Roma, helping to turn them into the 'new foreigners' in their own land and often justifying discrimination and extreme violence as somehow deserved by this group. This ethnic conception of insiders and outsiders and the practical effects of the citizenship law highlighted a disjunction between the self-representation of Czech society as 'returning' to democracy and the withdrawal of citizenship rights from a significant number of a vulnerable minority.

The tensions highlighted here reflect a society in which, on this issue, dominant domestic norms do not 'match' the international social norms. The domestic norms of entrenched prejudice against the Roma may therefore have been an attractive or 'common sense' way of defining who belonged within the political community of the new state – by defining who most definitely did not! While anti-Roma sentiment was and is contested domestically by those individuals and NGOs who continue to

[94] Ibid.
[95] When the final amendment was passed in 1999 most members of the senior coalition partner in the 1992–96 governments (Vaclav Klaus's Civil Democratic Party) voted against the amendment, while most members of other parties, including the senior partner in the current coalition government, the Social Democratic CSSD, voted in favour.
[96] The OSCE High Commissioner for National Minorities notes the pervasive nature of the exclusion of Roma within OSCE countries, exclusion that is 'sometimes systematic and on occasion systemic', *Report on the Situation*, p. 3.
[97] Checkel, 'Norms, Institutions and National Identity', p. 98.

work at changing such attitudes, they could not have changed this law without reference to the *blatant* clash between the terms of the citizenship law and the avowed international social identity of the state and, most importantly, the strong international pressure for change. This provided a base from which to demand that the law, and the domestic norms that supported it, should be changed. On the other hand, in the absence of domestic activism it would have been harder, perhaps impossible, for international pressure to make a difference.

The effect of the law in rendering tens of thousands of long-term residents stateless brought the Czech Republic and the notions of citizenship at work there under harsh scrutiny. This led to strong pressure against what was clearly regarded as an unacceptable – perhaps even pathological – means of constructing national identity through exclusion of an easily targeted minority and over a period of six years the law was gradually amended. While this by no means ends the daily discrimination that Roma face in the Czech Republic, as they do elsewhere in Europe, it demonstrates a state that valued its international social identity enough to eventually change this law. However, there is still a significant gap between this identity and the reality of everyday experience for Roma in the Czech Republic, and monitoring and pressure to change this will continue. Legal changes are only a beginning. Deeper change, in which international social norms diffuse into the society is yet to occur. This is more likely if such norms resonate with the values of at least some of the domestic population, who are prepared to challenge dominant norms within their own community. Elites are also central to norm diffusion, as they are the gatekeeper able to block or facilitate such change. In the Czech Republic this story is still being played out. In the next section I turn to a very different story, that of relations between ethnic Macedonians and ethnic Albanians in the Former Yugoslav Republic of Macedonia.

On the edge of the storm: Macedonia and state-building at the turn of the twenty-first century

Macedonia, 'the epitome of a multiethnic state',[98] was the only republic to leave the former Yugoslavia peacefully. For a decade, this small state defied expectations of major ethnic conflict, despite internal ethnic tensions and a very unstable external environment. With at least a quarter of the population ethnic Albanians, who speak a different language and share different cultural and religious traditions to the Slavic Macedonian

---

[98] Duncan M. Perry, 'Destiny on Hold: Macedonia and the Dangers of Ethnic Discord', *Current History* 97:617 (1998), 120.

majority,[99] the construction of an inclusive corporate state identity – at both the constitutional level and in terms of daily practice – presents problems for the society as a whole, and for the policy-making elite. This is especially so in the context of a strong Slavic Macedonian nationalism that is on the defensive due to the relatively recent genesis of Macedonian national identity and the scepticism of many neighbours about the validity of Macedonia, both as an independent state and as a distinct nation. Thus, this new state has, for all of its short history, struggled with the construction of, and relationship between, the corporate and social identities of the state. Yet while ethnic minorities were subjected to ethnic cleansing in Croatia, Bosnia-Herzegovina and Kosovo, this did not happen in Macedonia. Rather than seeking legitimation by building the corporate identity in this manner, elites in Macedonia sought to legitimate the fragile new state through 'bringing the international community in'.

Despite this, in 2001 Macedonia came to the brink of civil war, with ethnic Albanian guerrillas, identifying themselves as members of the National Liberation Army (NLA), mounting attacks on Macedonian police and army posts in the first half of 2001. While ethnic Albanians have a number of legitimate grievances towards the Macedonian state, these acts and subsequent army retaliation have led to a polarisation of the situation, with the potential to set back, and possibly destroy, any chance of a genuine pluralist democracy in Macedonia. Not least is the potential for this situation to push nationalist elites to use the politics of fear to their own, short-term benefit, even though this would be at the cost of longer-term damage to this weak, economically struggling, state.[100]

Such strategies would deflect attention away from charges of high-level corruption against government officials who have been plagued by continuing scandals since the mid-1990s which have undermined trust in successive governments and raised doubts about the extent to which real progress has been made in the development of genuinely democratic institutions. As Duncan Perry notes, under conditions of economic hardship such revelations 'leave [the Macedonian people] feeling vulnerable and in

---

[99] According to the 1994 OSCE sponsored census, Macedonia's population of 2 million includes 66.5 per cent ethnic Macedonians, 22.9 per cent ethnic Albanians, 4 per cent Turks, 2.3 per cent Roma, 2 per cent Serbs and 0.004 per cent Vlachs. While most ethnic Macedonians are members of the Macedonian Orthodox Church, there are some Muslims and a few Protestants (including the current president). While most ethnic Albanians are Muslim, there are small numbers who are Orthodox or Roman Catholic.

[100] The idea of 'partition' was raised in 2001. This is a euphemism for 'mass deportation' of ethnic Albanians, which according to a recent International Crisis Group report is a 'fantasy' that has been part of Slavic Macedonian nationalist sub-culture for decades. ICG, 'Macedonia: The Last Chance for Peace', *ICG Balkans Report No. 113* (Skopje/Brussels: ICG, 20 June 2001), p. 12.

search of scapegoats, which in turn magnifies popular fears and promotes nationalism on all fronts'.[101] On the other hand, the desire to avoid major bloodshed and to take on the benefits of integration into Europe – to which all elites have adhered up to this point – may lead to rethinking the way the national identity has been constructed so far. It is in the *particular* interactions of the domestic and the international, or the corporate and the social, that Macedonia's future path will be decided.

To be sure, there is much for the aspiring nationalist demagogue to work with in a state in which two sizeable communities live in separate lifeworlds and have little understanding or empathy for each other. Many ethnic Macedonians distrust ethnic Albanians and are highly sceptical about their loyalty to the Macedonian state. Added to this is the 1999 NATO bombing campaign in Serbia, which saw rising anti-Western sentiment and sympathy for Serbia among ethnic Macedonians while ethnic Albanians were supportive of the bombing campaign and of the demands of Kosovar Albanians for independence. This in turn feeds ethnic Macedonian fears about the true object of the demands made by ethnic Albanians; that they wish to construct a Greater Albania, part of which would be carved out of Macedonian territory to be joined with Kosovo and Albania proper. However, over the last decade ethnic Albanian leaders have backed away from the idea of Greater Albania and insist that they are interested in securing equal rights for ethnic Albanians within the Macedonian state.[102]

What do developments in Macedonia mean for the questions posed in this book? This case helps us look at the pressures on elites, the relationship between elites and their society, and the sort of domestic institutions that exist or are being constructed and, in turn, how embedded these are in international institutions. Given the 'statist' structure of state–society relationships in Macedonia, ultimately the policy choices made by elites will be crucial for whether or not Macedonia follows the path of non-pathological forms of identity construction and further integration into Europe. This is all the more salient in terms of the policies that are pursued in dealing with the NLA insurgency which has revealed splits within the ethnic Macedonian leadership between nationalist hardliners

---

[101] Perry, 'Destiny on Hold', 123. In July 2001 the Skopje weekly *Start* ran a number of articles suggesting that the government leaders of both major ethnic groups have, since 1998, conspired to work against the interests of the state. One, headed 'Profiteers Need War Chaos', argued that the rhetoric of war served to deflect attention from corruption allegations. Such claims were rejected in the pro-government press. Radio Free Europe/Radio Liberty, *Balkans Report* 5:50 (20 July 2001).

[102] Throughout the crisis Albania has supported a political solution within Macedonia and has recently reiterated its commitment to joining the EU. Radio Free Europe/Radio Liberty, *Newsline* 5:160, part II (23 August 2001).

who wanted to pursue a military solution and moderates who argued in favour of a political solution.[103]

I begin this section with a brief history of Macedonia, looking at national identity construction within the republic that was part of the former Yugoslavia and the place and treatment of the ethnic Albanian minority up to the collapse of the second Yugoslavia. I then go on to trace developments in Macedonia as an independent state. In this I investigate the problems of constructing a coherent corporate identity in a multiethnic context and within the broader external environment, considering both security and normative issues. Here I look at both the pressures on Macedonia, the role of the international community and how successive governments have responded to these pressures, including the recent crisis. In doing this I highlight how successive governments in Macedonia have sought to solve the problem of corporate state identity construction by focusing on social identity construction. This was strongly supported by the international community and there were powerful external factors, not least the need for assistance in the economic and security realms that reinforced this strategy. However, recent events demonstrate that such a strategy will be fragile as an alternative to pathological methods of corporate identity construction if it is not matched by domestic normative change.

Development of a Macedonian national identity

During the nineteenth century the national idea spread across the Ottoman Empire and challenged the Ottoman organisation of diverse communities on the basis of religious identities. Like Turkish national identity, Macedonian national identity was a 'late developer', with many of those who lived in the three regions of historic Macedonia – Pirin, Vardar and Aegean Macedonia – identifying as respectively, Bulgarian, Greek or Serbian, though most peasants would have identified with Church, village and family in the first instance and took on national identities only when pushed by nationalist education, propaganda or terror campaigns. However, over time, religious identities were translated into national ones, although this did not make an impact on the vast bulk of the population until well into the twentieth century.[104]

---

[103] See Ana Petruseva, 'Macedonian Peace Deal in Jeopardy', *Institute for War and Peace Reporting's Balkan Crisis Report* 269 (9 August 2001); Ulrich Buechsenschuetz, 'New Rift in Macedonian Leadership?', Radio Free Europe/Radio Liberty, *Newsline* 5:151 (10 August 2001).

[104] Loring M. Danforth, *The Macedonian Conflict: Ethnic Nationalism in a Transnational World* (Princeton University Press, 1995).

The idea of a distinct Macedonian nationality developed first among intellectuals from the middle of the nineteenth century. By later that century, in the wake of the Treaties of San Stefano and Berlin (1878), Bulgarians, Serbs and Greeks were making conflicting claims on the territory, which led eventually to the Balkan wars of 1912–13.[105] The underground nationalist movement that emerged, the Macedonian Revolutionary Organisation (MRO),[106] later renamed the Internal Macedonian Revolutionary Organisation (IMRO), acknowledged their links with Bulgaria while advocating autonomy for Macedonia within the Ottoman Empire. The MRO, set up by an idealist band of teachers and other professionals, was envisaged as a populist organisation that would lead the peasants to revolt. Meanwhile, in Bulgaria the Supreme Macedonia Committee envisaged the Bulgarian army leading the struggle against the Ottoman Empire. The MRO was defeated by Ottoman forces in the failed Illinden uprising of August to November 1903. After this it never fully regained its former coherence, and, already committed to the use of terror tactics, it went further down this path.[107] Despite the complex national identifications of members of the MRO in the late nineteenth and early twentieth centuries, the organisation is now upheld as a 'national unifying symbol' in Macedonia, at least for ethnic Macedonians.[108]

In the aftermath of the Balkan wars and World War I, geographical Macedonia was split three ways between Greece, the Kingdom of Serbs, Croats and Slovenes and Bulgaria.[109] This engendered much suffering as massacres, and what we would now call ethnic cleansing were committed by all sides, including attacks on Bulgarian communities by Serbs and Greeks after the Bulgarians were defeated in the second Balkan

[105] Loring M. Danforth, 'Claims to Macedonian Identity: The Macedonian Question and the Breakup of Yugoslavia', *Anthropology Today* 9:4 (1993), 4. Danforth notes that for much of the twentieth century successive Greek and Bulgarian governments denied that there were Macedonian minorities in their states and have used policies of forced assimilation against these groups.

[106] Founded in Salonica in 1893, 'Internal' was later added to the name to make it the Internal Macedonian Revolutionary Organisation. The contemporary Internal Macedonian Revolutionary Organisation–Democratic Party of Macedonian National Unity (VMRO–DPMNE) was founded in 1990 and by its name sought to identify itself with the previous IMRO, while advocating a non-violent stance.

[107] Duncan M. Perry, *The Politics of Terror: The Macedonian Liberation Movements 1893–1903* (Durham: Duke University Press, 1988).

[108] Duncan M. Perry, 'The Republic of Macedonia: Finding its Way', in Karen Dawisha and Bruce Parrott (eds.), *Democratization and Authoritarianism in Postcommunist Societies: 2, Politics, Power and the Struggle for Democracy in South-East Europe* (Cambridge University Press, 1997), p. 251.

[109] Greece got more than 50 per cent, Bulgaria, punished for its role in the wars got 10 per cent of Pirin Macedonia and the nearly 40 per cent left (Vadar Macedonia) came under Serbian control. Jens Reuter, 'Policy and Economy in Macedonia', in James Pettifer (ed.), *The New Macedonian Question* (London: Macmillan, 1999), p. 29.

war (1913), and attacks by Serbs on Albanian Muslims in western Macedonia.[110] Along with the national-homogenising drive of attacks on civilians there was also a dimension that brought together class and religious affiliation as Christian peasants attacked Muslim landlords. The result of this was the movement of populations to safer territories, for example, ethnic Greeks to Greek territory. In 1915 Bulgaria, fighting on the side of the axis powers, returned to most of Vardar Macedonia. While this was popular with much of the Slavic population, for the Serb and Greek populations it meant persecution and forced displacement. Harsh treatment was also meted out in Serbia, including Kosovo, by the occupying Bulgarian forces.[111]

As in other areas of the Balkans in the first half of the twentieth century, in the process of imperial breakdown the various peoples in historical Macedonia were subjected to attempts at pathological homogenisation as elites sought to carve out national territories. Policies of murder and forced displacement of civilians were employed by many would-be state-builders. As Hugh Poulton notes, 'The three-way split [between Greece, Bulgaria and Serbia] that followed the second Balkan war has essentially continued until the present. This is because the new states would make the ethnic and national territories co-terminous by force, migration and state-sponsored homogenisation.'[112]

In a continuation of this logic both Albanians and Slavic Macedonians suffered attempts at Serbianisation in the early days of the first Yugoslavia. This led to disillusionment with the new state and the Serbian view of Macedonia as 'Southern Serbia' fed support for communists on the part of Vardar Macedonians. This gave a new burst of life to the IMRO, which used terrorist attacks and massacres, in turn resulting in violent counter-measures on the part of Serbian authorities.[113] The state clamp-down on the IMRO in Bulgaria, combined with its 'degeneration into gangsterism' and fratricidal disputes, meant that by the 1930s support for it was falling, especially among younger Vardar Macedonians.[114]

Despite the efforts of the IMRO, as late as World War II most Macedonians did not have a strong sense of Macedonian national identity and, if pressed, many would have identified themselves as Bulgarian. The Bulgarian invasion of Vadar Macedonia during World War II changed

---

[110] Hugh Poulton, *Who Are the Macedonians?* (Bloomington: Indiana University Press, 1995), pp. 74–5.

[111] Ibid., p. 76.   [112] Ibid., p. 77.

[113] Ivo Banac, *The National Question in Yugoslavia: Origins, History, Politics* (Ithaca: Cornell University Press, 1984), pp. 318–28.

[114] Stefan Troebst, 'IMRO + 100 = FYROM? The Politics of Macedonian Historiography', in James Pettifer (ed.), *The New Macedonian Question* (London: Macmillan, 1999), p. 69.

this, as the oppressive policies of the occupiers led many Vardar Macedonians to reject the idea of incorporation into the Bulgarian state.[115] For the first time, perhaps, there was a genuine mass response to the national mobilisation efforts of communist, non-communist, and in some cases, anti-communist Partisans during World War II. As the war came to an end the Communist Party was able to gain and maintain control of these different, often contradictory, currents.[116] Despite the shifting nature of identification outlined above, a process of ethnogenesis was occurring, to which the communists responded during and after the war. They had very good reasons for doing this, not the least of which was holding off the territorial ambitions of Bulgaria and controlling Greater Serbian ideas within the second Yugoslavia.[117]

Thus the People's Republic of Macedonia (later the Socialist Federal Republic of Macedonia) was proclaimed as a constituent part of the Federal Republic of Yugoslavia in February 1944 and a state-sponsored programme of nation-building within the republic ensued. Between 1944 and 1949 non-communists, and those with even slightly pro-Bulgarian sympathies, were 'ruthlessly eliminated'.[118] On the cultural front a national literary language was devised, based on Macedonian dialect,[119] and a 'reinterpreted' history, which claimed Bulgarian national heroes as Macedonian ones, was written. Texts were edited so that they accorded with the nationalist reading of history. In particular, references to the pro-Bulgarian sentiments of the IMRO were excised.[120] Harsh penalties were meted out to those who questioned this right up to end of the second Yugoslavia, with the repression of any evidence of pro-Bulgarian sympathies. It was a punishable offence to say there was no such thing as a Macedonian nation.[121]

The first Macedonian language primer appeared in 1946 and the Macedonian Department at Skopje University was set up in the same year with state education policy ensuring that the language came into

---

[115] Poulton, *Who Are the Macedonians?*, p. 115; Stefan Troebst, 'Yugoslav Macedonia, 1943–1953: Building the Party, the State, and the Nation', in Melissa K. Bokovoy, Jill A. Irvine and Carol S. Lilley (eds.), *State–Society Relations in Yugoslavia, 1945–1992* (New York: St. Martin's Press, 1997), p. 245.

[116] Troebst, 'Yugoslav Macedonia', pp. 245–50.

[117] Danforth, *The Macedonian Conflict*, p. 66; Perry, 'Republic of Macedonia', p. 230.

[118] Troebst, 'IMRO + 100 = FYROM?', p. 69; Troebst, 'Yugoslav Macedonia', pp. 250, 255–7.

[119] Danforth, *The Macedonian Conflict*, p. 67. Commentators differ on the exact source of the dialects that were the basis of the national language.

[120] Philologists were put to work devising the new language with instructions to differentiate it from Bulgarian while historians set to work on constructing a narrative of a nation with a long history in antiquity. Reuter, 'Policy and Economy', p. 30.

[121] Poulton, *Who Are the Macedonians?*, pp. 117–19; Troebst, 'IMRO + 100 = FYROM?', p. 66.

common use.[122] Because two thirds of the population was illiterate, folk music played an important role, as did radio, as well as print media.[123] The creation of a national Church was also central to building national identity, with the Macedonian Orthodox Church (MOC) established in 1967, much to the outrage of the Serbian Orthodox Church.

Despite the recent development of Macedonian identity, as Loring Danforth notes, it is no more or less artificial than any other identity.[124] It merely has a more recent ethnogenesis – one that can therefore more easily be traced through the recent historical record. As Stefan Troebst argues, though, there was no inevitable path to this development. Rather, 'the protagonists of Macedonian nationalism have been lucky twice'.[125] The first time was in the 1940s when Bulgarian nationalism pushed most Vardar Macedonians towards identification with a Macedonian Republic within Yugoslavia. The second time was in the early 1990s, when the hysterical Greek reaction to Macedonian independence and its choice of name and flag combined with Slobodan Milosevic's policies towards Slovenia and Croatia consolidated domestic support for a distinct national identity within an independent sovereign state.

However, this national identity is a Slavic Macedonian identity, in which 'one must be at least nominally Orthodox Christian and speak Macedonian'.[126] This conception of national identity does not include ethnic Albanians, and demands for Albanian to be accorded the status of a national language, and for Albanian secondary and higher education, pose a threat to the idea of national unity held by many ethnic Macedonians. Furthermore, as Yugoslavia was disintegrating, ethnic Albanians boycotted the 1991 referendum on independence (calling on the international community not to recognise Macedonia until ethnic Albanians were treated as equal citizens), as well as the 1991 census and the discussions on a new constitution. These acts, coming at a time when so many of Macedonia's neighbours were either sceptical or outright hostile towards an independent Macedonian state, seemed to be a betrayal of that state to many ethnic Macedonians.

Ethnic Albanians in Macedonia

While there is no doubt that there is widespread social discrimination against the ethnic Albanian minority and that tensions between them

---

[122] Poulton, *Who Are the Macedonians?*, p. 117.
[123] Troebst, 'Yugoslav Macedonia', pp. 253–4.
[124] Danforth, 'Claims', 8.   [125] Troebst, 'IMRO + 100 = FYROM?', p. 72.
[126] Perry, 'Republic of Macedonia', p. 251.

and ethnic Macedonians have deepened over the last decade, successive governments in Macedonia have not sought to legitimate themselves through the systematic expulsion or murder of ethnic Albanian Macedonians, even as such policies were being pursued as the Balkans erupted around them. In the period leading up to independence the nationalist Internal Macedonian Revolutionary Organisation – Democratic Party of Macedonian National Unity (VMRO–DPMNE) took an explicit anti-Albanian stance but they were not in a position to form a government and any such policies they might have implemented failed to come to fruition. However, as long as the ethnic Macedonian majority continued to regard the state as 'their' national state, the potential for inter-ethnic relations to destabilise the state remained.

The ethnic Albanian community is to be found mainly in western and northwestern Macedonia towards the borders with Albania and Kosovo, in areas such as Gostivar, Tetovo and in the capital Skopje. Generally, the Albanian and ethnic Macedonian communities have lived separately from one another and relations have been characterised by 'mutual ignorance about and mistrust of the other'.[127] Ethnic Albanians moved into Macedonia in the early nineteenth century. Under Ottoman rule, local elites were drawn from Albanian ranks ('along with Turks and some Greeks'), their privileged position causing resentment among other groups, hence the payback attacks during the Balkan wars.[128]

Following the collapse of the Empire, ethnic Albanians were treated harshly in the first Yugoslavia: 'State policy being either the assimilation or expulsion of Albanians, they became the most oppressed national group in Yugoslavia.'[129] Initially, Albanian language education was banned, but when ethnic Albanians used Serbian language education to pursue their own causes, 'Belgrade started discouraging public education for Albanians', allowing only religious instruction. However, Albanians turned the permitted religious schools into centres of 'national education and opposition activity'.[130] At the same time, under a Serb colonisation programme Albanian land was handed over to Serb settlers, the Albanians often getting little or no compensation. Many Albanians emigrated as a result, which was exactly what the authorities had in mind, while others took up arms against the Serbs.[131]

[127] Robert W. Mickey and Adam Smith Albion, 'Success in the Balkans? A Case Study of Ethnic Relations in the Republic of Macedonia', in Ian M. Cuthbertson and Jane Leibowitz (eds.), *Minorities: The New Europe's Old Issue* (Prague: Institute for EastWest Studies, 1993), p. 56.
[128] Perry, 'Republic of Macedonia', p. 251. While most ethnic Albanians are Muslim there are also some Catholic communities in Macedonia.
[129] Banac, *The National Question*, p. 298.   [130] Ibid., p. 299.
[131] Poulton, *Who Are the Macedonians?*, pp. 91–3; Banac, *The National Question*, pp. 300–3.

In post-World War II Yugoslavia, while Macedonians were recognised as one of the constituent nations, Albanians were accorded the status of 'nationality', as they had a 'home state'. Although their status was certainly better than in the first Yugoslavia, they were still subject to systematic discrimination and neglect. In particular, the state took an anti-Islamic stance that led them to persecute religious leaders and destroy mosques and other sites of religious significance. Fewer educational opportunities were available to ethnic Albanians and there was less economic development in Albanian majority areas as well as discrimination in employment practices.[132]

Following demonstrations in Kosovo in 1968 in support of Kosovo becoming a republic, demonstrations were held in Tetovo calling for 'Albanian areas of Macedonia to join with Kosovo in a seventh republic'.[133] From the Yugoslav perspective this represented aspirations for a Greater Albania and the state responded with repression in both Kosovo and Macedonia. Media portrayals of an 'Albanian threat' maintained fear among the ethnic Macedonian population and Albanians were kept out of positions of authority in state structures. Inferior education also made it difficult for them to move into positions of responsibility.[134]

In 1980–81 the predictable response to ethnic Albanian riots in Kosovo was the repression of all Albanian communities, including those in the Republic of Macedonia. As a consequence, any gains that may have been made since the 1960s were swept away. Albanian language education was limited or abolished and Albanian national names and symbols were banned,[135] as were folksongs, on pain of imprisonment. With the rise to power of Milosevic in the late 1980s, anti-Albanian rhetoric reached a new pitch in Yugoslavia, and it found a sympathetic ear among many ethnic Macedonians.

From this brief account we can see that while there is no long history of direct conflict between the two groups there are two very different stories within the Macedonian state and little mutual understanding. Where the ethnic Macedonian national identity had the backing of the Yugoslav state, ethnic Albanians suffered repression under communist rule, and were forced to accept the Titoist definition of a 'Macedonian' identity.[136] Up to the time of independence ethnic Albanians, with their own traditions and strong sense of communal identity, resisted a state that they

[132] Mickey and Albion, 'Success in the Balkans?', p. 57.
[133] Poulton, *Who Are the Macedonians?*, p. 126.
[134] Perry, 'Republic of Macedonia', p. 232.
[135] Mickey and Albion, 'Success in the Balkans?', p. 57.
[136] James Pettifer, 'The Albanians in Western Macedonia after FYROM Independence', in Pettifer (ed.), *The New Macedonian Question*, p. 137.

regarded as repressive. Because of the cycle of resistance and repression that this set up, at independence ethnic Albanians were not well integrated into the state structure on any dimension – social, cultural, political or economic.[137] Macedonia thus came to independence with at least a quarter – possibly a third – of its population having been mistreated by the state, a state in which national identity had been constructed in terms that excluded them.

Constitutional nationalism in a multiethnic state

As Yugoslavia was disintegrating nationalist fervour ran high in Macedonia, driven by fears for the survival of the new state as an independent entity. However, the 1991 constitution was drafted to suit international standards of legitimate government following a clear message from the international community that recognition was dependent on the construction of a multiparty system and respect for minority and human rights. According to the Badinter Commission, it was Macedonia, along with Bosnia-Herzegovina, that met the criteria for recognition, having held a referendum on independence and constitutionally upholding human and minority rights.[138] However, when drafting the constitution moderates had to compromise with nationalists, in particular the VMRO–DPMNE, which was adamant that concessions should not be made to minorities. As a result, despite efforts to integrate a civic conception of Macedonian citizenship into the constitution, including the constitutional right to the free expression of national identity,[139] the preamble was based on an ethnic conception of what it is to be Macedonian. This declares that: 'Macedonia is established as the national state of the Macedonian people in which full equality as citizens and permanent coexistence with the Macedonian people is provided for Albanians, Turks, Vlachs, Romanies and other nationalities living in the Republic of Macedonia.'[140] To ethnic Albanians this was taken to connote lower status within the new state and they consistently argued that the constitution should be amended.

Ethnic Albanians claim that current census figures do not give an accurate account of their numbers, which they put in the range of 40 per cent rather than 23 per cent of the population. Having boycotted the

[137] Poulton, *Who Are the Macedonians?*, p. 252.
[138] Duncan M. Perry, 'Macedonia: Balkan Miracle or Balkan Disaster?', *Current History* 95:599 (March 1996), 114; Reuter, 'Policy and Economy', p. 41.
[139] Mickey and Albion, 'Success in the Balkans?', p. 61.
[140] Constitution of the Republic of Macedonia, Preamble, in Blaustein and Flanz (eds.), *Constitutions of the Countries of the World*.

1991 census, they took part in the one held in 1994, arguing though that the numbers counted then are not accurate because of the effects of the 1992 citizenship law. This law required fifteen years continuous residence in Macedonia in order to gain citizenship. According to figures released by the Interior Ministry in 1994, this residency requirement resulted in an estimated 150,000 people not being counted in the census, 'despite having identity papers from the former Yugoslavia and even in some cases from the Socialist Republic of Macedonia, [having] failed to meet the requirements of citizenship . . . most of these are Albanians who had originally come from Kosovo'.[141] Ethnic Albanians found this hard to accept, when anyone of ethnic Macedonian background can claim citizenship under Article 11 of the constitution.

Under Article 7 of the constitution Macedonian is the official language but ethnic Albanians argued that Albanian should be recognised as a national language. Although Article 7 provides for the use of minority languages in 'the units of local self-government where the majority of the inhabitant belong to a nationality', ethnic Albanians argued that this had not been put into practice. Linked to language, education remained an explosive issue. Ethnic Albanians demanded the right to tertiary education in Albanian, which was resisted by successive governments. In late 1994 an Albanian language university was set up in Tetovo. At the opening celebrations in 1995 police attempted to close the university resulting in riots and the death of one ethnic Albanian, while a number of academics were arrested. After this the university went underground and the government more or less ignored it.[142] In July 2000, following the proposal of the OSCE High Commissioner on National Minorities, Max van der Stoel, parliament passed a new law on higher education that paved the way for the establishment of a private university to replace the underground university. Instruction is to be in Albanian as well as a couple of foreign languages, with study of Macedonian mandatory. The issue is still contentious, however, as many ethnic Albanians would prefer that Tetovo University simply be recognised. Critics also point out that the new university will be limited to training only teachers and public administrators.[143] Despite this, Prime Minister Ljupco Georgievski and the leader of the Albanian Democratic People's Party, Arben Xhaferi,

---

[141] Hugh Poulton, *Who Are the Macedonians?*, 2nd edn (Bloomington: Indiana University Press, 2000), p. 183. Poulton notes that the citizenship requirements have also affected many Turks and Roma, with the latter group particularly affected by the requirement to have a permanent income and a permanent place of residence.

[142] Ibid., p. 185.

[143] ICG, 'Macedonia's Ethnic Albanians: Bridging the Gulf', *ICG Balkans Report No. 98* (Skopje/Washington/Brussels: IGC, 2 August 2000), pp. 15–16.

attended a groundbreaking ceremony for the new university in February 2001.[144]

The tensions between civic and ethnic conceptions of national identity can be found again in Article 19 of the constitution. While freedom of religious expression is guaranteed, as is the separation of religion and state, the Macedonian Orthodox Church is the only religious organisation that is named in the constitution, implicitly giving it priority over all others in the view of critics. In sum, these constitutional issues link to a number of grievances regarding the status of ethnic Albanians and their sense of integration into the political community within the Macedonian state, reflected in low participation levels in the state bureaucracy, the police, the army and in higher education. Ethnic Albanians also claim that they are subject to daily discrimination, which reinforces their sense of unequal status within the state.

Search for legitimacy: social identity of the state
as a pluralistic democracy

Although Macedonia declared its independence in September 1991, entry into the United Nations and European regional organisations was blocked by Greece, which objected to the use of the name 'Macedonia', the choice of symbol on the new flag,[145] and the irredentist implications of references in the new constitution to the protection of Macedonians living outside Macedonia. Macedonia responded by amending its constitution, and eventually, changing the flag. When it was accepted into the United Nations in April 1993 it was under the temporary name of the Former Yugoslav Republic of Macedonia, which is still in official use. Despite this, Greece continued to lobby other states, particularly within the European Community, to withhold diplomatic recognition and imposed two economic blockades, one in 1992 and one from February to October 1995, which had a significant impact on Macedonia's struggling economy.

Despite the delays in gaining formal recognition, a number of international organisations were active in Macedonia. In the early 1990s, the first Macedonian 'government of experts' welcomed international support as President Kiro Gligorov negotiated Macedonia's peaceful exit from Yugoslavia and the withdrawal of Yugoslav National Army (JNA) troops

---

[144] Radio Free Europe/Radio Liberty, *Newsline* 5:29 (12 February 2001).

[145] K. S. Brown, 'In the Realm of the Double-Headed Eagle: Parapolitics in Macedonia 1994–9', in Jane K. Cowan (ed.), *Macedonia: The Politics of Identity and Difference* (London: Pluto Press, 2000).

in an agreement that also guaranteed Macedonia's borders.[146] As the
JNA took all military hardware and destroyed much of what could not be
moved when they withdrew in early 1992, vulnerable Macedonia looked
to the international community for protection and legitimation. Between
1991 and 1995 the violence in Croatia and then Bosnia-Herzegovina
loomed large, while Slobodan Milosevic continued to make remarks
such as the 1992 suggestion that Macedonia be split between Serbia
and Greece and Serbian troops made occasional border incursions.
Thus for the first half of the 1990s it was considered highly likely
that violence could spill over into Macedonia, with wider regional
implications.[147]

From the moment it became apparent that Macedonia would leave
the former Yugoslavia its leaders pursued membership in European and
international institutions in a quest for legitimacy, security and economic
development. This meant domestic restraint in dealings with the ethnic
Albanian minority and there is no doubt that moderation on the part
of Macedonia's leaders played an important role in avoiding the bloody
conflict seen elsewhere in the Balkans during the 1990s. Yet tensions
between the two largest ethnic groups persisted, even deepened, as ethnic
Albanians continued to demand resolution of the constitutional and social
issues outlined earlier. In the context of the 2001 crisis in Macedonia,
the International Crisis Group noted that the sort of changes demanded
by ethnic Albanian guerrillas and to which the government has agreed,
under immense pressure from the international community,

will be vastly unpopular with the [Slavic] Macedonians, who will blame the international community for destroying *their privileged position and (what amounts to
the same thing) the essential identity of the state*. The international community will
have to remain actively engaged to ensure that the changes are actually applied
throughout the country.[148]

Thus while Macedonia has pursued legitimation at the international level
through integration into international organisations, there is a disjuncture
between the corporate and social identities of the state. On the one hand,
Macedonia wants the benefits of a European social identity but on the
other hand significant sections of the population – including some elites –
are resistant to the notion of a genuinely pluralist, multiethnic society.

---

[146] Alice Ackermann, *Making Peace Prevail: Preventing Violent Conflict in Macedonia* (New
York: Syracuse University Press, 2000), p. 82.
[147] Ibid., p. 101.
[148] ICG, 'Macedonia: Still Sliding', *ICG Balkans Briefing* (Skopje/Brussels: ICG, 27 July
2001), p. 8.

International organisations in Macedonia

The first of the international organisations to begin work in Macedonia, and perhaps the least recognised, was the Working Group on Ethnic and National Communities and Minorities of the International Conference on the Former Yugoslavia. Aware of the dangers presented by ethnic tensions, this body was concerned with the facilitation of dialogue between contending ethnic groups.[149] Moderation on all sides was encouraged and ethnic Albanian leaders were persuaded not to seek territorial autonomy within Macedonia. The working group was dissolved in January 1996 following the Dayton Accord, but until then it had worked closely with the United Nations Preventive Deployment Force (UNPREDEP) and the CSCE/OSCE Spillover Mission to Skopje.[150]

The Spillover mission eventuated in late 1992 when the CSCE sent observers into Macedonia following the failure of the EU to do so, under pressure from Greece. This was one of the first international organisations 'on the ground' in Macedonia with the 'explicit task of preventive diplomacy'.[151] Small in number, the Mission was initially concerned with monitoring borders and with inter-ethnic mediation.[152] It also monitored the 1994 census and the elections of 1994 and 1998/99. The OSCE High Commissioner on National Minorities has also had an ongoing role in Macedonia through fact-finding missions and direct mediation efforts, as was the case with the issue of higher education for Albanians.

On 11 December 1992, following President Gligorov's request for assistance from the UN Secretary General, the UN Security Council unanimously resolved to send a peacekeeping force to Macedonia's borders with Albania and the Federal Republic of Yugoslavia. Part of the United Nations Protection Force (UNPROFOR) already operating in Croatia and Bosnia, this was the first preventive mission in the history of the United Nations. The small force of 1,000 personnel was intended to act as a deterrent, and despite its limited mandate of monitoring, reporting and good offices, it played an important role in maintaining Macedonia's territorial integrity in the early 1990s.[153] In March 1995 UNPROFOR was reorganised into three separate commands, with forces in Macedonia becoming the United Nations Preventive Deployment Force. This began

---

[149] Ackermann, *Making Peace Prevail*, p. 103.
[150] Ibid., pp. 103–5. This was despite the fact that Macedonia only had observer status at the CSCE at that time. It became a participating state in October 1995.
[151] Alice Ackermann, 'The Former Yugoslav Republic of Macedonia: A Relatively Successful Case of Conflict Prevention in Europe', *Security Dialogue* 27:4 (1996), 417.
[152] The number of observers was increased to sixteen in March 2001. For the Spillover Mission's mandate, see <http://www.osce.org/skopje/>.
[153] Ackermann, *Making Peace Prevail*, p. 84.

with a military mandate which was expanded to include political affairs in early 1994 and humanitartian-developmental affairs in 1995, in an attempt to address the 'economic and social roots' of conflicts within the state.[154] As the external threat posed by the FRY eased, greater emphasis was placed on political matters, that is, mediation of dialogue between the contending ethnic groups within Macedonia.[155] The UN mission was terminated in March 1999 following China's veto of a further mandate in February 1999,[156] just as the conflict in Kosovo was escalating and as refugees were already heading towards Macedonia.

Macedonia was admitted to the Council of Europe in September 1995 and NATO's 'Partnership for Peace' programme in November 1995. More recently, it has become party to the Balkans Stability Pact. Gaining membership of NATO and the EU are longer-term goals to which all political parties accede. In these goals Macedonia has 'signed on' to the shared norms of post-Cold War Europe: respect for human and minority rights, democratic institutions and a free market economy. In April 2001 Macedonia became the first Balkan state to sign a Stabilization and Association Agreement with the EU. At the signing ceremony in Luxembourg on 9 April, Prime Minister Georgievski said, 'The fact that we have become an associate member of the European Union today, believe me, is a great challenge for our country, and I assure you that we will do our best in the future to show serious results.' Thus, even as violence was escalating within the state the Prime Minister was reiterating the commitment of Macedonia to a European social identity. However, at the same ceremony the ethnic Albanian leader Arben Xhaferi highlighted that the standards which Europe demands were not being met as there had been no rethinking of the corporate identity of the state in Macedonia:

[I would like to see] only one simple thing – to correct the concept of the state which is incompatible with the multiethnic reality. We need a new concept, a new European concept of the state, which will be in harmony with reality. [We need] a new constitution, [and] to change some [elements] within the constitution, because we must put down our Balkan baggage and start changing all standards and values.[157]

Below I briefly trace the role of leaders in Macedonia in order to understand why they chose not to pursue nationalist politics before considering the implications of the recent conflict in terms of the extent to which any real change has taken place.

---

[154] Ibid., p. 119.   [155] Ibid., p. 119.
[156] Although denied by China, this was widely regarded as a response to Macedonia's diplomatic recognition of Taiwan in January 1999.
[157] Both Georgievski and Xhaferi cited in Radio Free Europe/Radio Liberty, *Balkan Report* 5:26 (10 April 2001).

Corporate identity of the state in the New Macedonia

According to Duncan Perry, there was 'little substantive cooperation among Albanian and Macedonian politicians' up to 1998 and tensions between the two groups have always remained high.[158] Following the failure to form a government after elections in 1990 a 'government of experts' was elected in 1991. The same year, Kiro Gligorov was elected President and he then steered Macedonia through a peaceful exit from Yugoslavia. Following a vote of no-confidence the government of experts collapsed in July 1992, blamed for the failure to gain recognition for Macedonia and to deal with economic problems. In the elections that followed Ljubco Georgievski's nationalist VMRO–DPMNE, with its explicitly anti-Albanian stance, gained the most votes, though not enough to govern in their own right. However, they refused to enter into coalition government with the ethnic Albanian and ex-communist parties. As a result, Brancko Crvenovski's Social Democratic Union formed a coalition that included the Reform-Liberal Party and the Albanian People's Democratic Party (PDP).[159]

In the 1994 elections the Social Democrat Coalition (SDSM) was returned. Once again, although Crvenovski's government included ethnic Albanians, there was no real progress on substantive changes such as their constitutional status and tensions rose when the government attempted to shut down the Albanian University that was opened in Tetovo in late 1994/early1995. Tensions continued to grow in the following years. In 1997 when parliament passed a law that reinstated Albanian language education at the Pedagogical Academy in Skopje, ethnic Macedonian students protested in the streets. Supported by the VMRO, these protests expressed explicit anti-Albanian sentiments such as 'Albanians to the gas chambers'.[160] Later that year the government responded in a heavy handed manner to activist mayors flying the Albanian flag in the town of Gostivar, leaving 3 dead and 400 wounded. The use of 'unwarranted violence' against unarmed civilians was followed by extremely harsh prison sentences for the main players.[161] These shifting policies showed a weak government that was unsure how to deal with inter-ethnic relations. The lack of any real reform led to a split within the PDP as ethnic Albanian moderates in the government coalition lost credibility.[162]

By 1996–97 the VMRO–DPMNE was toning down its nationalist rhetoric and even accused the SDSM government of using the flag incident

---

[158] Perry, 'Destiny on Hold', 124–6, quote at 124.
[159] Mickey and Albion, 'Success in the Balkans?', pp. 60–1.
[160] ICG, 'Macedonia: The Politics of Ethnicity and Conflict' (ICG, 21 October 1997), p. 11.
[161] Ibid., pp. 11–15.   [162] Ibid., p. 11.

to stir up nationalist sentiment. It ran on an economic platform in the 1998 parliamentary elections and won the most seats, although, once again, the leading party did not have an outright majority. When it came to looking for coalition partners, the VMRO–DPMNE joined forces with the centrist Democratic Alternative (DA) and the Democratic Party of Albanians (DPA), headed by Arben Xhaferi and regarded at the time as the most nationalist ethnic Albanian party.[163] These parties cooperated pragmatically, taking a 'centre-right' stance. However, the coalition was not particularly stable with the moderate DA leaving in 2000 and the more nationalist Liberal Party joining. In 1999 the VMRO–DPMNE candidate Boris Trajkovski won the presidential elections, assisted no doubt by his support for greater minority rights which garnered a high level of support from ethnic Albanians.[164]

One of the new government's first decisions was to allow NATO forces into Macedonia in late 1998 as the situation in Kosovo escalated. By mid-March there were over 10,000 NATO troops in the country. The crisis added another pressure as Macedonia was forced to deal with an estimated 350,000 refugees fleeing over the border from Kosovo in 1999. While international agencies were critical of the way the government handled the crisis, it argued that the international community, in the form of UNHCR and NATO, was very slow to provide assistance to a small and poor country beset by an influx of refugees who numbered more than three times the 100,000 predicted by international agencies. Support that had been promised 'did not materialize in a timely fashion, [but] Skopje feared that failure to cooperate would damage its chances of gaining its two most cherished foreign policy goals: entrance to the European Union and becoming an associate member of NATO'.[165] At the same time Macedonia's main market, Yugoslavia, collapsed compounding an already severe economic situation. The lack of understanding of the

---

[163] In 1997 a breakaway party from the PDP, the Party for Democratic Prosperity–Albania (PDP–A) emerged (after challengers were forced out) and in 1997 this group merged with the smaller Peoples Democratic Party to create the Albanian Democratic Party, now the Democratic Party of Albanians (DPA).

[164] The 1999 presidential election was marred by irregularities but the verdict of OSCE monitors was that overall the election of Boris Trajkovski as President is valid. However, all elections since 1994 have suffered from serious irregularities, leading to voter cynicism and loss of political legitimacy of the whole system. Duncan M. Perry, 'Macedonia's Quest for Security and Stability', *Current History* 99:635 (2000), 130; Constitutional Watch, 'Macedonia', *East European Constitutional Review* 9:1/2 (2000); OSCE, *Report of the OSCE*. The International Crisis Group argues that the international community bears some responsibility for voter passivity and cynicism – that is the erosion of what civil society exists – through allowing irregular results to stand. ICG, 'The Macedonian Question: Reform or Rebellion?', *ICG Balkans Report No. 109* (Skopje/Brussels: ICG, 5 April 2001), pp. 11–12.

[165] Perry, 'Macedonia's Quest', 133.

stresses – economic, cultural, social – that the crisis placed on Macedonia played a role in public opinion turning against NATO and the EU, though eventually Europe did recognise the strains placed on Macedonia.[166]

The continuing cleavage between the two ethnic communities was revealed by their different attitudes to the NATO bombing campaign in Yugoslavia. While most ethnic Macedonians were sympathetic to Serbia and increasingly hostile towards the bombing, ethnic Albanians were clearly in favour of the operation. The massive influx of refugees into Macedonia increased social tensions, and once again, revealed the cleavage between ethnic Albanians and ethnic Macedonians. Ethnic Albanians wanted all possible assistance given to the refugees and, as Arben Xhaferi urged, took refugees into their own homes. Ethnic Macedonians were less sympathetic due to the widespread fear that they were in danger of being swamped by the numbers of ethnic Albanians in Macedonia. The higher birthrate of ethnic Albanians has long been an issue for nationalists, and there was much anxiety that a significant number of Kosovars would remain in Macedonia. This fear was unfounded as most Kosovars had returned to Kovoso by September 1999. All the same, during the crisis, ethnic Albanian politicians, particularly the DPA, were very careful not to do anything to antagonise Macedonian nationalists and both sides refrained from nationalist incitements, although the DPA complained that they were not consulted on refugee related issues.[167]

More recently, domestic politics has been beset by corruption scandals and instability within the governing coalition. The government has been accused of engaging in phone tapping of members of the opposition and media. By 2000, parties were either leaving the coalition or splintering internally. Within the VRMO a splinter group, the VRMO–VRMO broke off, asserting the need to return to their 'nationalist roots'. The Democratic Alternative left the governing coalition in late 2000 and March 2001 saw the formation of a new ethnic Albanian political party, the National Democratic Party (NDP), which included two members of parliament.[168]

Corporate and social identity at odds?

By 2001 it was apparent that the inter-ethnic tensions that had been rising throughout the 1990s had not abated. In a region awash with weapons, the ambiguous status of Kosovo, run as a UN protectorate but with Kosovars

---

[166] Ibid.

[167] Ibid.; ICG, 'Kosovo's Impact on Macedonia' (ICG, 17 May 1999), p. 12.

[168] Corruption in the major parties was cited as the motivation for setting up this new party. ICG, 'The Macedonian Question', p. 14.

wanting independence, has been an important factor in the activities of ethnic Albanian guerrillas in Macedonia during 2001. Identifying themselves as the National Liberation Army (NLA), this group claimed to be fighting for greater rights for ethnic Albanians within the Macedonian state. There was some scepticism about this, and concerns that the true objective may have been to join Kosovo and northwestern Macedonia with Albania. Whatever the true motives of the NLA, it is clear that there was a situation of ethnic polarisation that provided a dangerous basis for ethnic cleansing on both sides. As a result, having survived the breakup of Yugoslavia without violence, Macedonia teetered on the verge of civil war during 2001, held back only by the interventions of the international community.

The NLA first made itself known on 23 January 2001 when it claimed responsibility for an attack on a police station the previous day, in a village halfway between Tetovo and the border with Kosovo. The border agreement that Macedonia struck with Serbia in late February, over which the United Nations Mission in Kosovo (UNMIK) and ethnic Albanian leaders in Kosovo, were not consulted may have further exacerbated tensions, creating another 'common cause' for ethnic Albanians on both sides of the border and an 'invitation to extremism' to groups that were already coalescing.[169] As the conflict developed, the mainstream ethnic Albanian parties became the spokesmen for the NLA, which was clearly setting the agenda.[170] The NLA's demands followed the list of grievances long held by the ethnic Albanians and they demanded changes to the constitution, in particular that ethnic Albanians be recognised as a constituent people of the state and that Albanian should be recognised as an official second language. They later demanded that an internationally monitored census should be conducted, which they argued would demonstrate that they make up 40 per cent of the population.[171]

By mid-March the fighting had spread to Tetovo. The 'rebels' or 'terrorists', depending on the point of view taken, claimed to be fighting to protect ethnic Albanians from abuses by security forces in the areas under their control. However, a significant number of ethnic Macedonians fled areas where they were in the minority. While some movements may be attributed to fear of conflict in general, it is clear that some fled due to 'direct threats' and that the NLA may have been engaging in ethnic cleansing of ethnic Macedonians from areas under their control. At the same time significant numbers of ethnic Albanians left their homes in the

---

[169] Ibid., pp. 5, 10.
[170] See ibid., for a detailed account of the first two months of the conflict.
[171] Constitutional Watch, 'Macedonia'; ICG, 'Macedonia: Last Chance for Peace', p. 5.

wake of anti-Albanian riots and the destruction of their homes by either the NLA or Macedonian forces. By late July, more than 150,000 people, over 7 per cent of the population, had been displaced.[172]

In early May, under pressure from the international community, a government of national unity was formed that brought together the major parties from both sides of the ethnic divide. Despite this, no political progress was made and by early June the NLA were threatening the capital, Skopje, and the likelihood of a political settlement seemed increasingly remote. Amidst the fighting, the international community played a central role in brokering a peace accord, which was finally signed on 13 August. NATO Secretary General Lord Robertson described this agreement as marking 'the entry of Macedonia into modern, mainstream Europe', before going on to note that a sustainable ceasefire was necessary before NATO would commit troops to weapons collection, the NLA having agreed to disarm.[173]

The peace deal includes the commitment to amend the contentious preamble to the constitution, removing references to an ethnic concept of Macedonian national identity which is to be replaced by a civic concept of the Macedonian people; the Albanian language is to be used in local government in areas where ethnic Albanians make up 20 per cent or more of the population; the number of ethnic Albanians in the police force is to be increased and there is to be proportional representation in public administration; legislation relevant to minorities will need a two-thirds majority in parliament, 'including at least half the affected minority's members of parliament'; while mention of the Macedonian Orthodox Church will not be removed from Article 19 of the constitution, other religious organisations are to be included as well. One lever that may assist is the possibility of international economic assistance.[174] While parliament voted in favour of accepting constitutional changes on 6 September, nationalists in the government argued that the proposed changes should be subject to a referendum and it was clear that at least some sections of the VMRO–DPMNE were playing the politics of ethnic fear. However, the referendum idea was eventually dropped and under pressure from the EU and Nato, the amendments were finally passed by parliament on November 16.[175]

---

[172] ICG, 'Macedonian: Still Sliding', p. 2.

[173] Nicholas Wood and Richard Norton-Taylor, 'Macedonians Sign Peace Deal', *The Guardian*, 14 August 2001.

[174] ICG, 'Macedonia: War on Hold', *Balkans Briefing* (Skopje/Brussels: ICG, 15 August 2001). Annex C of the agreement asks that an international donors' conference be held after ratification.

[175] ICG, 'Macedonia: Filling the Security Vacuum', *ICG Balkans Briefing* (Skopje/Brussels: ICG, 8 September 2001).

On 22 August NATO decided to go ahead with the mission to disarm the NLA. The British-led contingent of 3,500 went into this mission amid much skepticism as to how likely it was that the NLA would voluntarily disarm and how effective NATO could be in a mission planned to last for only thirty days.[176] Nonetheless, this operation saw the international community once again attempting to modify the internal politics of a sovereign state, and in this case, at least attempt to avert the descent into the sort of violence that would most likely result in at least some sort of partitioning, which would no doubt be attended by worst mass expulsions and killings as extremists on both sides set out to impose the logic of ethnic homogenisation, a story sadly familiar from these pages. Whether enough will be done to stop the worst happening remains to be seen.

International social identity and its limits

In the context of internal inter-ethnic tensions and external threats, nationalists on both sides of the ethnic divide pursued politics of moderation and have sought to legitimate the state, and their own authority, through the cultivation of Macedonia's international social identity. The international community fully supported this, displaying little enthusiasm for the VRMO–DPMNE in its early nationalist phase, and little patience with the recent, more nationalistic outbursts of some members of this party. Consequently, the desire for international legitimacy has been maintained and has so far prevented pathological homogenisation within Macedonia. While we see a cleavage between two very different communities, there has not been significant mass support for such policies and elites have backed away from them.

However, this strategy of attaining legitimacy through the social identity of the state has been pushed to its limits by, first, the receding of external threats and, second, the appearance of ethnic Albanian guerrillas who have been prepared to use force to attain their ends, no doubt spurred on by the intervention of the international community to protect the ethnic Albanians of Kosovo. These limits exist because the strategy of international societal identity construction has not been matched by any deep domestic diffusion of the international norms the state has signed on to. While domestic political culture has not, to date, supported violent

---

[176] 'Macedonia Rebels Agree to Disarm', BBC News Online, 14 August 2001, <http://news.bbc.co.uk>; 'Shadowy Rebel Assures Macedonia That He Seeks Peace', New York Times, 17 August 2001; Jonathan Marcus, 'Macedonia Mission "Too Short" ', BBC News Online, 17 August 2001, cites General Wesley Clarke, former commander of NATO troops in Yugoslavia in 1999, as of this opinion.

resolutions of the problematic relationship between ethnic Albanians and ethnic Macedonians, it is questionable to what extent these norms have been translated into real change at the level of daily practice and domestic institutions.

Thus a sharp disjunction remains between the social and corporate identities of this state and, as events in 2001 illustrate, without the support of the international community the most recent crisis would have escalated into civil war (if indeed the international community is, in the end, successful in guiding Macedonia away from this path). NATO unofficially brought the NLA into negotiations in a way that ethnic Macedonian leaders could not do due to public opinion. Most importantly, it was the envoys from the various international organisations (and the United States) who cajoled hardliners amongst the ethnic Macedonian members of cabinet into not pursuing a purely military solution. In so doing, they bolstered the moderates within government who, in the absence of international support, would not have been able to pursue a political solution.[177] How this international pressure affects the domestic legitimacy of all parties involved will be revealed in the elections due to be held some time in 2002, but the disjunction between the two forms of collective state identity is clear. As Loring Danforth notes, 'the price states must pay to avoid disintegration is to abandon their assimilationist policies and renounce the ultimate goal of an ethnically homogeneous nation-state. In order to save the state, in other words, it is often necessary to sacrifice the nation.'[178] So far, Macedonia has not been able to do this and the mismatch between the corporate and desired social identity of the state is currently painfully obvious.

Lessons learnt – or not? The Czech Republic and Macedonia

In this chapter I have addressed the question of why, in two threshold cases, 'pathological' methods of corporate identity construction have been avoided, if only barely. An important part of the answer lies in the social identity of states in Europe today. While this social identity is nested within international standards of human and minority rights, which have developed in response to the excesses of state-builders, it is in Europe that these norms are most institutionalised. In both the cases discussed above, the desire of elites in the new states to seek legitimacy by conforming to prevailing standards of legitimate statehood has been crucial. However, in both cases there remains a disjuncture between the social identity that

---

[177] Buechsenschuetz, 'New Rift'.   [178] Danforth, *The Macedonian Conflict*, p. 22.

has been taken on, and widely accepted domestic norms regarding the status of particular minorities. This highlights how fragile the strategy of legitimation through international social identity is when there is a strong clash between that identity and the domestic norms. On the other hand, it is the social identity of the state that gives minorities and reformers an external standard, combined with external support, with which to challenge their governments. What is crucial, though, is whether or not the potential for change exists at the domestic level. Where there is domestic debate over normative standards, there is more potential for change and advocates for more inclusive norms can point to the 'lack of fit' between domestic and international standards.

While the two case studies here are both threshold cases, there are, of course, many differences between the two states. The Czech Republic split from Slovakia peacefully and it did not suffer from external threats to its security. Furthermore, in the Czech Republic the Roma represent a minority of perhaps 2 per cent in a relatively homogeneous state, where party politics are not organised along the lines of ethnic cleavages. Domestic opponents to the citizenship law included human rights groups such as Czech Helsinki Watch as well as groups concerned specifically with the rights of Roma. While non-state actors are dependent on government support to push through the changes for which they lobby, there is some capacity to lobby in this way.

The citizenship law highlighted a clash between the domestic and international aspects of state identity, reflecting a lack of 'cultural match'.[179] But the international debate over the law quickly entered what Risse describes as the realm of 'argumentation'. The state responded to accusations of unacceptable behaviour by rejecting the criticisms as irrelevant in the first instance, then arguing, as Vaclav Havel did, that the law in itself was not unfair. These arguments were not accepted and in response to continuing pressure from domestic and international NGOs and intergovernmental organisations some amendments to the law were made. In turn, these amendments were criticised as insufficient and the pressure continued, resulting in another amendment in 1999. This does not mean that the ethnic conception of Czech national identity held by many Czechs or the deep, widespread antipathy towards Roma has changed and, indeed, it would take a concerted effort on the part of elites working with civil society to push the domestic diffusion of the norms of racial non-discrimination, something that has not happened to date. However, the law was amended and the state backed away from what appeared to be a systematically implemented policy aimed at denying

[179] Checkel, 'Norms, Institutions, and National Identity', 97–104.

citizenship rights to a significant section of a minority group. Thus, in the case of the Czech Republic the international social identity of the state worked to reinforce international and domestic criticisms of the citizenship law.

Why was pathological homogenisation avoided in Macedonia when for ten years this was so clearly the option of first choice for elites in other former Yugoslav states? The combination of external threats and the desire of leaders such as President Gligorov to avoid wholesale bloodshed led to the social identity of the fragile new state being cast as a pluralistic democracy. This was backed up by domestic policies of moderation in relations with the ethnic Albanian community, which in turn met with the approval of an international community that was extremely wary of the VMRO–DMPNE's overtly nationalistic and anti-Albanian rhetoric at the time.

However, international support on the one hand and restraint, if not reform, at home on the other, have not been enough to change the pre-conditions that exist should leaders opt to use pathological forms of identity construction in Macedonia in the future. After ten years the lack of 'cultural match' between the domestic and international aspects of state identity in Macedonia is striking. Despite attempts to write a civil conception of national identity into the constitution, the conception of national identity at work was, in the first instance, an ethnic Macedonian one that excluded ethnic Albanians and other minorities. While the constitution acknowledged the existence and rights of national minorities, the over-all effect was of a form of constitutional nationalism. Under sustained challenge over a period of ten years, the domestic resistance to changing the underlying way of thinking about the relation between nation and state has become apparent, highlighting that there has been little, if any, progress towards building a genuine pluralistic democracy within Macedonia.

The ethnic conception of the nation implicit in the constitution has been challenged by ethnic Albanians, who represent at least a quarter, and possibly more than one third of the Macedonian population. Their demands highlight the ethnic cleavage that has widened. On the one hand, ethnic Albanians have felt excluded by the state. On the other hand, many ethnic Macedonians have taken their complaints – and acts such as boy-cotting the first census in 1991 or calling on the international community not to recognise Macedonia at independence – as evidence of their lack of loyalty to the state. The reality that, until the recent open conflict, most ethnic Albanians would have conceded that they were relatively better off in Macedonia than in Kosovo (before 1999) or Albania made little difference to this perception. In short, no common lifeworld that transcends ethnic differences has been constructed in Macedonia, a fact reflected in the way party politics have been organised along ethnic lines, despite the existence of small non-ethnic parties.

Macedonia is still on the threshold of the 'common lifeworld' of Europe. Rather than a process of dialogue and norm diffusion the clash between ideas about the domestic corporate identity of the state and the international social identity of the state has become increasingly apparent over time. The lack of any real domestic change was masked to a great extent by the external pressures on this small state and the support of the international community, which accepted what now appears to be a status quo situation which did not deliver reform for ethnic Albanians and has engendered support amongst this community for the NLA. This is not to say that there are not moderate voices within Macedonia but the lack of real reform means that in a polarised situation they could easily be drowned out without international support.

The nature of society–state relations in Macedonia means that elites must play an active role in the diffusion of international norms into the domestic arena if there is to be any real change. This is difficult for those who are motivated to bring about domestic changes as they must struggle with other sections of the elite who have no interest in changing what they see as a legitimate, ethnic, conception of the state and, indeed, are prepared to use this to their own benefit at the 2002 elections. Reformers can easily be blocked in a state with so little institutional capacity, in which leaders often act as though the state is 'theirs', and amidst charges of corruption and electoral cynicism about politicians in general, in short in a state in which democratic institutions have not fully taken hold. This is a situation in which playing the exclusive nationalist politics may be hard to resist for some sections of the leadership, as illustrated by the Prime Minister's recent 'return' to an overt nationalist discourse.[180] This raises the question of just how genuine the VRMO–DPMNE's turn away from exclusivist nationalism in the mid-1990s really was, with all the indications being that it was little more than a rhetorical turn intended to win power and to placate the international community – while dividing the state into separate ethnic fiefdoms, with east and west corresponding, respectively, to ethnic Macedonian and ethnic Albanian control – with no real interest in promoting domestic change towards a pluralistic democracy.

[180] On the 'return' of Prime Minister Ljupco Georgeivski to hardline nationalism, see 'Macedonia's Born-Again Nationalist', BBC News Online, 27 August 2001. On the VMRO–DPMNE's portrayal of themselves as 'defenders of the nation' and how they are encouraging the perception of a security dilemma among ethnic Macedonians see ICG, 'Macedonia: Filling the Security Vacuum', pp. 5–7.

Thus Macedonia will remain reliant on international support for quite some time if it is to avoid civil war and the possibility that at least some sections of the elite could attempt to legitimate themselves through pathological strategies of corporate identity construction. The likelihood of this occurring once NATO forces leave is rising, if reports of the formation of paramilitary units under the command of the Ministry of the Interior and of arms acquisition by the government (or the hardline elements of it) are any indication. It is international pressure that may hold these developments back long enough for moderates to make a serious attempt to encourage a rethinking of the corporate identity of the state. Although such norm diffusion is a slow and difficult process, in the absence of any attempts to support this the future of a genuinely pluralist, democratic Macedonia looks bleak indeed. This highlights the fragility of a policy of relying on the international social identity of the state when it is so out of step with the dominant ideas of the corporate state identity.

Conclusion

This study has addressed several key questions regarding the recurrence of practices of pathological homogenisation in the international system of states: why have such practices been an enduring feature of international history? What role have such practices played in state formation? Why have state elites pursued policies that are, in the end, so often detrimental to their states and societies? Why has the international community failed to eradicate such practices, despite the development, particularly in the post-World War II era, of clear international norms proscribing them?

Until recently such practices gained little attention within international relations scholarship, but with the onset of episodes of 'ethnic cleansing' and genocide in Europe and Africa at the end of the twentieth century, they have attracted renewed interest. Understandably, the focus of most recent scholarship is on nationalism, particularly ethnonationalism. But practices of pathological homogenisation were employed by state-builders well before the age of nationalism. As I argued in chapter 1, national criteria of identity, which reflect the principle of political legitimacy that currently structures the international system, are profoundly powerful. However, there are other criteria according to which unified corporate identities have been constructed. Thus, it is state-building and the attendant process of corporate identity formation, and the relationship between these and the social identity of the state, which lie at the heart of this study.

Mainstream theories of international relations are ill-equipped to explain pathological homogenisation, as they explicitly bracket off state formation and the constitution of identities and interests. The state is taken as a 'given' and it is assumed that the primary interests and identities of states as actors are determined either by the rational calculations of self-interested individuals or by the nature of the international system (with the latter assumption drawing heavily on the former). These theories thus regard the formation of state identity and interest as irrelevant to the analysis of international politics, drawing a sharp distinction between the domestic and international realms, and taking the state as a unitary actor in international politics as their starting point. Likewise, theories of state formation also take the interests of state-builders as given either being interested in power for its own sake or, in material gain as in materialist accounts. Either way, these approaches do not inquire into how state-builders come to understand their interests in the way they do. Thus they cannot explain decisions made in spite of economic costs, or why elites may decide to use one strategy rather than another in building the state.

The argument restated

The central argument of this book is that understanding the construction of identities and interests is crucial to understanding political action, both domestic and international, and that culture and symbolism play important roles in this. There is an important cultural dimension to state formation that is ignored by both mainstream international relations scholarship and theories of state formation. If culture is mentioned at all in theories of state formation it is presented as an instrument of the pre-determined interests of state-builders. However, as I argued in chapter 1, 'culture' is more than an instrument through which material interests or raw power are pursued. State-builders are influenced by, and draw upon, the cultural resources of their time and place, although, as we have seen, as they do so they may simplify, manipulate and even distort these for their own purposes.

In chapters 2 to 5 I illustrated the relationship between state formation and cultural resources, and strategies of pathological homogenisation. The first two case studies, taken from before the age of nationalism, highlighted how state-builders sought to construct corporate state identities from the very inception of the modern state and system of states, in each case using the cultural resources available to them. In chapter 2 I showed how Ferdinand and Isabella drew on religious resources in their efforts to build a unified corporate identity as they laid the foundations of the modern Spanish state. In chapter 3 we saw how, despite the process of secularisation that was under way, Louis XIV also drew on religious criteria in his effort to represent the completeness of his rule through unity within the absolutist state.

Chapters 4 and 5 examined cases of pathological homogenisation in which national criteria of inclusion and exclusion prevailed. In chapter 4 I traced the breakdown of the traditional form of political organisation within the Ottoman Empire, and the transformation of religious communities (millets) into 'nations'. For many communities this transition led to national independence, but this was not the case for the Armenians. The

Armenian community sought not independence, but equality within the Empire. This claim, though supported by the European powers, clashed with the traditional Ottoman world view and resulted in widespread massacres at the end of the nineteenth century, as the conservative Sultan Abdul Hamid II sought to put them 'back in their place' as second-class subjects. In contrast, the genocide of the twentieth century was part of an attempt by the Party of Union and Progress (CUP) to build a homogeneous national state that had no place for the Armenians. This was the project of a modernising elite, yet in both conceiving and implementing this policy, the CUP drew on traditional attitudes towards Armenians which rejected the idea that they could be equal subjects of the Empire.

In chapter 5 I traced the roots of recent ethnic cleansing in the former Yugoslavia, identifying their source in the development of Croatian and Serbian nationalisms in the nineteenth century. It was these nationalist ideologies, rather than 'ancient hatreds', that had a significant impact on the history of Yugoslavia in the twentieth century. This was clearly apparent in how the first Yugoslavia was constructed under Serbian hegemony that was informed by an assimilationist ideology. In response to this, an exclusivist Croatian nationalist ideology developed, which animated the atrocities committed by the Ustasha during World War II. Under the post-World War II communist system, nationalism was repressed at one level, which meant that there was little public acknowledgement of the traumatic experiences of the war, while at the most fundamental level the constituent units of the second federal Yugoslavia remained national republics, understood as the republics of and for majority national groups. Furthermore, the concept that underpinned this – *narod* or 'the people' – retained an ethnic connotation.

As the communist regime lost legitimacy in the 1980s, the recent violent past, in which nationalist ideologies were so implicated, provided the cultural and historical resources on which nationalists – whether 'born again' from previous lives as communists, or those who had long challenged the communist system – could draw. This was exemplified in Serbia where Slobodan Milosevic's regime drew on the 'myth of Kosovo', and combined this with the threat posed by 'the return of the Ustasha', in a symbolic complex that served to incite virulent nationalism. This rationalised the ethnic cleansing of non-Serbs, first in the Krajina region of Croatia, then in Bosnia-Herzegovina, and finally in Kosovo itself. Such strategies provided a means of legitimating Milosevic's authoritiarian rule and supressing dissent for a decade. However, this was a short-term strategy that became increasingly hard to maintain. Milosevic fell from power in 2000 and was extradited to the Hague to stand trial for war crimes and crimes against humanity in mid-2001.

In chapter 1 I argued that the corporate and social aspects of state identity are mutually constitutive, and in chapter 6, in light of the four case studies outlined above, I traced the development of ideas of legitimate state action at the international social level. As we have seen, though, there are contradictory norms in the international system. This was apparent after the Armenian genocide and it is apparent still in the contemporary system.

At the time of the expulsion of the Jews of Spain in 1492, when the differentiation between the internal and external realms of the embryonic states system was first consolidating, the most basic reciprocal international norm was the right of sovereigns to make war. Beyond this, no other shared norms existed. Hence, the expulsion of the Jews raised no normative problems for other rulers in the system, although Christians debated the morality of the expulsion and the Ottoman Sultan was happy to exploit Spain's loss of an economically productive group.

By the time that Louis XIV revoked the Edict of Nantes in 1685, the international system had experienced some further normative development, though its normative structure remained quite thin. Louis' attempt at homogenisation through the forcible conversion of the Huguenots caused 200,000 people to flee. The Revocation and its consequences were widely condemned by European powers, reflecting that in the late seventeenth century such behaviour was regarded as illegitimate as it breached the minimal standards of coexistence that had been articulated at this time.

The massacres and genocide of the Armenians in the late nineteenth and early twentieth centuries, respectively, occurred in a very different normative context. By the late nineteenth century European states had developed a body of international law and a self-conscious identity as a society of states while the Ottoman Empire was still considered an 'outsider' knocking on the door of the European system, albeit through necessity rather than choice. European notions of a 'standard of civilisation', combined with Great Power interventions on behalf of minorities, put increasing pressure on the Empire to reform. This produced a clash of normative systems in which the European powers, taking for granted the superiority of their 'standard', failed to see that the implosion of the Empire was also an implosion of a whole world view. And they failed to see how the pressure they put on the Empire, combined with the lack of any practical support for the Armenians, placed that group in a perilous situation.

The leaders of the CUP determined to make the remains of the Empire 'fit the model' of the European state, and set about constructing a homogeneous national state, using genocide as a means to this end. The allies responded to these events with moral outrage and horror, yet under wartime conditions they could only threaten prosecution at a later date. In the wake of the genocide, international society struggled to reformulate norms of legitimate state action. Although the 'massacres' were not recognised as a crime under international law at the time, the conditions of the Treaty of Sèvres reflected a consensus that the Turkish state bore responsibility for what were clearly regarded as crimes against humanity. However, these findings were taken no further at this time. In the face of the rejection of the Treaty of Sèvres by the nationalist regime of Kemal Ataturk, its assertion of the sovereignty of the Turkish state, and the scramble for influence amongst the Allies as the Empire disintegrated, any thought of international justice for the Armenians dissolved, and Turkey was recognised as a sovereign state under the 1923 Treaty of Lausanne.

Although the League of Nations system represented the first institutionalised attempt to protect minorities, this system was not underpinned by general principles that applied to all states alike. While the League sought to provide protection to minorities in new states this was undermined by the preoccupation with stabilising borders, and the post-World War I grounding of the principle of self-determination in a racial conception of the nation, which in turn led to the role of the League in population exchanges. Ultimately, the League was caught in the contradictory position of trying to limit the worst excesses of a system that it also played a major role in supporting.

In the post-World War II era we have seen the development of clearly articulated norms that proscribe pathological homogenisation, from human and minority rights norms to the Genocide Convention. Yet this period has seen the systematic mistreatment of minorities, massive displacements of populations – including those sponsored by the Allies in the immediate post-war era, state orchestrated massacres and, more recently, genocides. It is within this context that the ethnic cleansing in Bosnia-Herzegovina and Kosovo and the attempts by the international community to induce and, finally, force an end to such activities must be understood. These attempts highlight the contradictions between competing norms in the international system. On the one hand, many states still assert that the right of non-intervention is one of the fundamental cornerstones of the system. On the other hand, there is a growing body of internationally recognised standards and laws that assert the rights of individuals and, increasingly, minorities, to be protected from abuse at the hands of those in control of the state. This implies that sovereignty today is conditional. For this to have any real meaning the principle of non-intervention must, on occasion, give way to higher values.

In chapter 7 I canvassed the possibilities of non-pathological forms of state-building, investigating the role that the international social identity of the state can play. In the Czech Republic an exclusionary citizenship law was gradually amended in response to both domestic and international pressure, based on the misfit between the law and the avowed identity of the Czech Republic. However, the entrenched prejudice against Roma, which made the law acceptable to many Czechs, is much harder to address, and highlights the limits of relying too much on the social identity of the state. This is even more so in the case of Macedonia which, in 2001, teetered on the brink of a conflict that threatened to escalate into ethnic cleansing of both the ethnic Macedonian and ethnic Albanian populations by opposing forces. The role played by elites is central to how this story will end and if elements of the Macedonian government use the politics of fear, recent Balkan history may be repeated in the one state that left Yugoslavia peacefully.

Theoretical implications

The argument developed in this study has several important theoretical implications. These concern what John Ruggie terms 'the paradox of absolute individuation', the relationship between culture and political action, the role of cultural resources and symbolic manipulation in the absence of institutional development, and the relationship between ideas and practices.

'The paradox of absolute individuation'

Ruggie argues that the claim to absolute sovereignty makes coexistence – and therefore existence within the system – difficult for states, as the more sovereignty approaches this ideal, the more it generates dysfunctional political, economic, environmental and humanitarian consequences. From early on in the history of the system, therefore, rulers have sought to 'unbundle' territoriality to compensate for these consequences. 'Thus, in the modern international polity an institutional *negation* of exclusive territoriality serves as the means of situating and dealing with those dimensions of collective existence that territorial rulers recognize to be irreducibly transterritorial in character. Nonterritorial functional space is the place wherein international society is anchored.'[1] Ruggie claims that it is the aspects that are 'irreducibly transterritorial' that have been

---

[1] John Gerard Ruggie, 'Territoriality and Beyond: Problematizing Modernity in International Relations', *International Organization* 47:1 (1993), 165.

of most concern to states. Yet because pathological homogenisation is a means by which state-builders attempt to constitute corporate identity within the state, which in turn can then be presented as the single, sovereign face of the state in the external realm, rulers have asserted that such acts are 'internal' matters and thus most definitely not of 'transterritorial' concern. As I have demonstrated, this claim to absolute sovereignty has long been challenged by the community of states and such acts are now regarded as illegitimate in terms of humanitarian norms and regional stability in a globalised states system: that is, they are now regarded as of 'transterritorial concern'. The problem is, though, as Ruggie highlights, that the system itself has been constituted on the differentiation of exclusive territorial jurisdictions and this logic still persists. As we have seen, some forms of exclusion are no longer considered acceptable at one level, yet if the claim to absolute sovereignty is no longer a moral or legal defence of pathological homogenisation, in practice it still presents a problem with which the international community struggles, as its members are individuated according to a version of the same principle.

Culture and political action

In chapter 1 I reviewed different approaches to the relationship between culture and human agents. As I argued, agents do not select from a range of options in their cultural repertoire as though they stand outside their own culture,[2] but neither are agents driven blindly by the cultural structures in which they are enmeshed. This is a mutually constitutive relationship in which cultural frameworks shape the self-understanding of actors, and determine the range of possibilities open to them, and which are in turn reconstituted through the interpretations and practical choices made by actors. It is how actors engage with cultural resources at any given time, therefore, that must be unravelled.

The policy choices made by elites that I have discussed in this book were not inevitable. Yet they were *thinkable* as policy options given the cultural context in which the actors operated. Not only were they thinkable, but elites have been able to put them into action, as they have been able to draw on the support of majority groups to do so. In each of the first four cases the choice to forcibly convert, expel or exterminate significant sections of the community in the name of homogeneity was conceived in terms of the available cultural criteria for moral inclusion

[2] The point was made with reference to Ann Swidler, 'Culture in Action: Symbols and Strategies', *American Sociological Review* 51:2 (1986).

and exclusion. As I demonstrated in chapters 2 to 5, the Spanish monarchs drew on growing popular hostility towards conversos and Jews, and though there were critics of their policy, it went ahead with the support of much of their population, and served to increase their legitimacy as the 'Catholic Monarchs'. Likewise, Louis XIV's policy towards the Huguenots drew on popular hostility towards the Huguenots exacerbated by the Church. In the two later cases state-builders drew on and manipulated nationalist ideologies in a manner that legitimated genocide and ethnic cleansing.

Cultural unification or institutional consolidation

In chapter 1 I noted Tilly's characterisation of the homogenisation of populations in early modern states as a function of administrative centralisation. As I argued there, the symbolic articulation of unity through pathological homogenisation actually provided an alternative means of building authority, in the absence or weakness of centralised institutions. Although it may seem that symbolic augmentation of authority plays a lesser role in contemporary states when compared to early modern states, it can still play a very important role. Under conditions of flux and political instability – which, by definition, periods of state formation must be as preceding forms of political organisation break down – the use of cultural and symbolic resources provide a potent means of corporate identity construction. In the early modern period, the reach of the state was shallow by contemporary standards, and the symbolic dimension of corporate identity construction served to unify the state in the absence or relative weakness of administrative integration, not merely as a function of it. Furthermore, it augmented the patchy coercive capacity of the state. In the pre-nationalist cases, therefore, we saw how symbolic resources did not merely serve to further the administrative centralisation of the state, but were an alternate means of building authority and legitimacy.

In both the Ottoman Empire and the successor states to the former Yugoslavia, however, administrative centralisation was relatively well developed. In these cases the use of symbolic resources provided an alternative means of building authority and legitimacy in the absence of representative institutions. Although the CUP came to power as a constitutional government, this quickly gave way to authoritarian rule, and they used populist means that relied heavily on the symbolic dimension to buttress their fragile legitimacy. In the former Yugoslavia the incitement and manipulation of virulent nationalism using populist methods was an attempt to foreclose the possibility of democratic reform, as Milosevic labelled his critics traitors to the 'Serbian cause'. Thus the way in which elites draw upon and manipulate cultural and symbolic resources as a means of resisting democratisation in the contemporary system is an important dimension of international politics that bears further investigation.

The Czech Republic and Macedonia both share the problems faced by all post-communist societies of how to build representative institutions that foster a sense of civil society and will not allow corrupt and mendacious politicians to use public office as a means of turning the state into personal fiefdoms. The Czech Republic displays relatively greater institutional development, reflected in its recent accession to NATO and, despite criticisms directed at the treatment of Roma, its accession status with the European Union. The non-governmental organisations (NGOs) that challenged the citizenship law could draw attention to the gap between the law and the international standards that the state has signed on to. They could criticise state policy without being pilloried as enemies of the state. Nonetheless the deeper cultural change they are pushing for, if it happens at all, will take some time and will not proceed without the active engagement of state elites.

Macedonia is in a weaker situation, with poorly developed institutions and having inherited a poor economy and then being buffeted by the economic blockade demanded by Greece and the sanctions against Serbia. One of the strengths that Macedonia did have in its early days was a leadership committed to moderation and easing the new state out of Yugoslavia non-violently. President Kiro Gligorov turned to the international community for security assistance when Macedonia was most threatened by Serbia in the early days of its independence and the vulnerable new state sought legitimacy through its avowed intention to turn towards Europe, with all this implied for democratic institutions and minority rights.

As I have demonstrated, though, the roots of ethnic nationalism have not been challenged at the domestic level and amidst allegations of high level corruption and with relatively weak institutional development the state is vulnerable to the politics of pathological homogenisation. If the moderates in government do win this battle they will need the ongoing support of the international community. But there are limits to the changes that can be brought about by taking on a particular social identity of the state if this clashes with domestic cultural mores. While international support is crucial in supporting contemporary state-builders who do not wish to pursue pathological methods, more work needs to be done on finding culturally appropriate ways of bringing about deeper domestic change. If we ignore this, the limits of social identity present us with a sobering picture.

Ideas and practices

According to Stephen Krasner, 'In the effort to construct sovereignty, ideas have been used to codify existing practices rather than to initiate new forms of order. Ideas have not made possible alternatives that did not previously exist; they legitimated political practices that were already facts on the ground.'[3] This view discounts the role of ideas in motivating and directing practices and draws a sharp distinction between ideas and practices. As explained in chapter 1, in this study culture is understood as the shared meanings and values that provide a framework for action as well as the practices through which social and cultural structures are remade. All actors act in reference to a framework that gives meaning to their practices, they do not merely 'act' and then think up explanations for such acts afterwards, as though they select from a repertoire of legitimating ideas that have no real impact on them. Agents are socially constituted, or to return to Margaret Archer's characterisation, 'we are all born into and can only live embedded in an ideational context which is not of our own making . . . However, there is the actual response of agency to this inherited cultural context and, in responding, actors can exploit their degrees of freedom to great (elaborative) effect.'[4]

Krasner's explanation is that actors were driven by 'usually mundane' interests – such as material gain or power. Once again, here the interests of actors are taken for granted rather than explained. However, as we have seen in the four cases of pathological homogenisation studied above, elites were influenced by and drew upon the cultural resources available to them in their attempts to construct corporate state identities. In turn, at the international level, over time states have collectively responded to such practices with evolving principles of appropriate state behaviour. These collective responses have not been simply codifications of already existing practices. As we have seen, the international community has struggled to articulate new ideas of legitimate state behaviour. Such norms are constitutive, as they represent changing concepts of what constitutes a legitimate international actor. That these are not merely *post hoc* legitimations of practices is reflected in how these ideas have developed ahead of the international capacity to gain compliance and, where necessary, enforce such norms. In short, there is a lag between changing norms and the capacity of states to put these into practice at the international level.

[3] Stephen D. Krasner, 'Westphalia and All That', in Judith Goldstein and Robert O. Keohane, *Ideas and Foreign Policy: Beliefs, Institutions, and Political Change* (Ithaca: Cornell University Press, 1993), p. 238.

[4] Margaret S. Archer, *Culture and Agency: The Place of Culture in Social Theory*, revised edn (Cambridge University Press, 1996), pp. xxv–xxvi.

Future research

States are no longer the only significant actors in contemporary global politics, yet they continue to claim a monopoly on the right to define legitimate political identity,[5] with the result that '[s]tatelessness is a condition of infinite danger' still.[6] Similarly, to be cast as an outsider within one's own state is perilous as this so often legitimates expulsion and extreme violence, up to and including genocide. In this study I have sought to trace the processes through which those who are in some way different to the majority population can be cast as political outsiders and subjected to processes of pathological homogenisation. I argued that such processes have been manipulated by elites engaged in the construction of corporate state identities that legitimate their rule. In turn, notions of legitimate state identity at the international social level have evolved in response to such practices, which have come to be regarded as unacceptable. I then went on to consider the factors that make such strategies less likely through considering two threshold cases, both of which demonstrate the important role played by elites in contemporary new states.

This argument suggests several avenues of future research: the application of the concept of pathological homogenisation in analysing state-building in contemporary non-Western states; the need for continuing work on the potential for norms of legitimate statehood to constrain pathological strategies or to reconstitute state identities and interests in ways that may preclude such strategies even being thinkable; and the role that such knowledge could play in the social recovery from the destructive policies used by leaders: what role can the international community play, if any, and how can society – both domestic and international – learn from the violent past in such a way that it does not provide resources for pathological homogenisation in the future?

The preceding chapters show that difference is not in itself the cause of pathological homogenisation, but rather it is the cultural construction of difference as inferior or threatening (or a combination of both) and the exploitation of such constructions under particular conditions – usually associated with a crisis of legitimacy – that is crucial. This has been the case in non-Western states as much as in Western ones, particularly post-colonial states where elites took on the sovereignty norm and the model of the sovereign state was imported as a means to political independence during the twentieth century. Although the focus of much of

---

[5] Andrew Linklater, 'The Problem of Community in International Relations', *Alternatives* 15:2 (1990), 149.

[6] Michael Walzer, *Spheres of Justice: A Defense of Pluralism and Equality* (New York: Basic Books, 1983), p. 32.

this book has been on European states, the framework developed here has relevance for further study of the processes of pathological homogenisation within non-Western states. As I briefly noted in chapter 1, although post-colonial states were legitimated on the basis of a non-racial concept of self-determination this did not necessarily translate into respect for the rights of minorities within the new states. The 'majoritarian principle', whether interpreted by those in control of the state in terms of political, ethnic, religious or any other criteria of identification, left numerous citizens at the mercy of those engaged in state-building. As Martin Wight put it, 'It follows from the majoritarian principle that minorities have no rights, or only such rights as majorities may care to concede... The elite who hold state power decide the political allegiance of all within the frontiers; the recusant individual may (if he is fortunate) be permitted to emigrate.'[7] Throughout the twentieth century the resort to such strategies of corporate identity construction was defended in terms of sovereign rights and the non-intervention principle was asserted with dire consequences for those deemed political misfits.[8]

In the contemporary international system there are clear prohibitory norms against pathological homogenisation, however there are also other norms that undermine these. The best chance of avoiding pathological practices is the prospect of international judicial punishment for perpetrators combined with the diffusion of prohibitory norms into new states, but as chapter 7 demonstrates such diffusion is a difficult and slow process. It is not enough for the international community to get new states to 'sign on' and then turn a blind eye to the mismatch between these standards and domestic norms and practices. An important area for further study is thus the ways in which international norms diffuse – or do not diffuse – into states. A number of scholars are now working on the diffusion of norms, particularly within Europe and with attention to the important role of social learning amongst elites.[9] Such approaches could be extended to complement the work of those scholars investigating the relationship between universal norms and cultural difference at a global level. In turn, this work could be brought to bear on the possibilities for the diffusion into non-Western states of norms of legitimate statehood that may render pathological practices less likely. This is particularly salient in

[7] Martin Wight, *Systems of States* (Leicester University Press, 1977), pp. 171–2.
[8] See Robert Jackson, *Quasi-States: Sovereignty, International Relations, and the Third World* (Cambridge University Press, 1990).
[9] The work of Jeffrey Checkel is exemplary in this regard. Jeffrey T. Checkel, 'Norms, Institutions, and National Identity in Contemporary Europe', *International Studies Quarterly* 43:1 (1999). Also see Maria Green Cowles, James Caporaso and Thomas Risse (eds.), *Transforming Europe: Europeanization and Domestic Change* (Ithaca: Cornell University Press, 2001).

cases where human rights and other standards are rejected as being based on culturally specific 'Western' values. How can respect for cultural difference be balanced with a clear message that sovereignty is conditional and that massive abuses committed in the name of the sovereign state can no longer be shielded behind the principle of non-intervention?[10]

Finally, how can societies recover from such violence perpetrated in the name of the state? A number of areas of research are relevant to answering this question. First, what role, if any, does the international community have in such recovery? Here, work on the role played by the United Nations, other international organisations and NGOs in rebuilding states could be combined with work on how domestic normative changes come about. International assistance may rebuild infrastructure but how can norms and values be reconstituted? Insights from this work could be combined with current research on the increasing number of domestic truth commissions as well as the role of international judicial prosecution: does giving people the opportunity to tell their story make a difference?[11] Related to both of the previous issues, we need to understand better the ways in which collective memories of events are constructed and how these may or may not provide the preconditions for ethnic cleansing and genocide. None of these are small tasks and there are scholars working in all of these areas. However, by bringing these areas of research together it may increase our understanding of the potential for recovery from, and the prevention of, such massive abuses. It is to the latter that I hope this book makes some contribution.

[10] Michael Barnett, 'The New United Nations Politics of Peace: From Juridical Sovereignty to Empirical Sovereignty', *Global Governance* 1:1 (1995).

[11] Robert I. Rotberg and Dennis Thompson (eds.), *Truth v. Justice: The Morality of Truth Commissions* (Princeton University Press, 2000); Elazar Barkan, *The Guilt of Nations: Restitution, and Negotiating Historical Injustices* (New York: W. W. Norton & Company, 2000); Martha Minow, *Between Vengeance and Forgiveness: Facing History After Genocide and Mass Violence* (Boston: Beacon Press, 1998).

Bibliography

Ackermann, Alice, 'The Former Yugoslav Republic of Macedonia: A Relatively Successful Case of Conflict Prevention in Europe', *Security Dialogue* 27:4 (1996), 409–24.

Making Peace Prevail: Preventing Violent Conflict in Macedonia, New York: Syracuse University Press, 2000.

Adams, Geoffrey, *The Huguenots and French Opinion 1685–1787: The Enlightenment Debate on Toleration*, Waterloo: Wilfrid Laurier University Press, 1991.

Ahmad, Feroz, *The Young Turks: The Committee of Union and Progress in Turkish Politics, 1908–1914*, London: Oxford University Press, 1969.

Akhavan, Payam, 'Justice in the Hague, Peace in the Former Yugoslavia? A Commentary on the United Nations War Crimes Tribunal', *Human Rights Quarterly* 20:4 (1998), 737–816.

Allen, F. Beverly, *Rape Warfare: The Hidden Genocide in Bosnia-Herzegovina and Croatia*, Minneapolis: University of Minnesota Press, 1996.

Allen, J. W., *A History of Political Thought in the Sixteenth Century*, London: Methuen, 1960.

Anderson, Benedict, *Imagined Communities: Reflections on the Origin and Spread of Nationalism*, Oxford: Blackwell, 1983.

Anderson, Perry, *Lineages of the Absolutist State*, London: Verso, 1974.

Archer, Margaret S., *Culture and Agency: The Place of Culture in Social Theory*, revised edn, Cambridge University Press, 1996.

Arendt, Hannah, *The Origins of Totalitarianism*, 2nd edn, New York: Harcourt Brace & Co., 1966.

Arfi, Badredine, 'Ethnic Fear: The Social Construction of Insecurity', *Security Studies* 8:1 (1998), 151–203.

Arnason, Johann, 'Figurational Sociology as a Counter-Paradigm', *Theory, Culture and Society* 4:2–3 (1987), 429–56.

Ashley, Richard K., 'Political Realism and Human Interests', *International Studies Quarterly* 25:2 (1981), 204–36.

'Untying the Sovereign State: A Double Reading of the Anarchy Problematique', *Millennium: Journal of International Studies* 17:2 (1988), 227–62.

Ashley, Richard and Walker, R. B. J., 'Reading Dissidence/Writing the Discipline: Crisis and the Question of Sovereignty in International Studies', *International Studies Quarterly* 34:3 (1990), 367–416.

Astourian, Stephan H., 'Genocidal Process: Reflection on the Armeno-Turkish Polarization', in Richard G. Hovannisian (ed.), *The Armenian Genocide: History, Politics, Ethics*, New York: St. Martin's Press, 1992, pp. 53–79.

Baer, Yitzhak, *A History of the Jews in Christian Spain*, vol. 2, Philadelphia: Jewish Publication Society of America, 1961.

Balas, Sven, 'The Opposition in Croatia', in Jasminka Udovicki and James Ridgeway (eds.), *Burn This House: The Making and Unmaking of Yugoslavia*, Durham: Duke University Press, 1997, pp. 265–78.

Banac, Ivo, *The National Question in Yugoslavia: Origins, History, Politics*, Ithaca: Cornell University Press, 1984.

'The Fearful Asymmetry of War: The Causes and Consequences of Yugoslavia's Demise', *Dædalus* 121:2 (1992), 141–74.

'Bosnian Muslims: From Religious Community to Socialist Nationhood and Postcommunist Statehood, 1918–1992', in Mark Pinson (ed.), *The Muslims of Bosnia-Herzegovina: Their Historic Development from the Middle Ages to the Dissolution of Yugoslavia*, Cambridge, MA: Center for Middle Eastern Studies, Harvard University, 1994, pp. 129–53.

'The Dissolution of Yugoslavia Historiography', in Sabrina Petra Ramet and Ljubisa S. Adamovich (eds.), *Beyond Yugoslavia: Politics, Economics, and Culture in a Shattered Community*, Boulder: Westview Press, 1995, pp. 39–65.

Barany, Zoltan D., 'Living on the Edge: The East European Roma in Postcommunist Politics and Societies', *Slavic Review* 53:2 (1994), 321–44.

Barkan, Elazar, *The Guilt of Nations: Restitution, and Negotiating Historical Injustices*, New York: W. W. Norton & Company, 2000.

Barkin, J. Samuel and Cronin, Bruce, 'The State and the Nation: Changing Norms and the Rules of Sovereignty in International Relations', *International Organization* 48:1 (1994), 107–30.

Barnett, Michael, 'The New United Nations Politics of Peace: From Juridical Sovereignty to Empirical Sovereignty', *Global Governance* 1:1 (1995), 79–97.

Baron, Salo, *A Social and Religious History of the Jews*, vol. 11, *Citizen or Alien Conjurer*, New York: Columbia University Press, 1967.

Bassiouni, M. Cherif, 'From Versailles to Rwanda in Seventy-Five Years: The Need to Establish a Permanent International Criminal Court', *Harvard Human Rights Journal* 10 (1997), 39–42.

Batt, Judy, 'The International Dimension of Democratisation in Czechoslovakia and Hungary', in Geoffrey Pridham, Eric Herring and George Sanford (eds.), *Building Democracy? The International Dimension of Democratisation in Eastern Europe*, New York: St. Martin's Press, 1994, pp. 168–87.

Bauman, Zygmunt, 'Intellectuals in East-Central Europe: Continuity and Change', *East European Politics and Societies* 1:Spring (1987), 162–86.

Modernity and the Holocaust, Cambridge: Polity Press, 1990.

Beloff, Max, *The Age of Absolutism 1660–1815*, London: Hutchinson, 1967.

Bendix, Reinhard, *Kings or People: Power and the Mandate to Rule*, Berkeley: University of California Press, 1978.

Biersteker, Thomas J. and Weber, Cynthia, 'The Social Construction of State Sovereignty', in Thomas J. Biersteker and Cynthia Weber (eds.), *State Sovereignty as Social Construct*, Cambridge University Press, 1996, pp. 1–21.

Bluche, François, *Louis XIV*, trans. Mark Greengrass, Oxford: Blackwell, 1990.

Boase, Roger, 'The Morisco Expulsion and Diaspora: An Example of Racial and Religious Intolerance', in David Hook and Barry Taylor (eds.), *Cultures in Contact in Medieval Spain: Historical and Literary Essays Presented to L. P. Harvey*, Exeter: Short Run Press, 1990, pp. 9–28.

Boban, Ljubo, 'Jasenovac and the Manipulation of History', *East European Politics and Societies* 4:3 (1990), 580–92.

'Still More Balance on Jasenovac and the Manipulation of History', *East European Politics and Societies* 6:2 (1992), 213–17.

Bonney, Richard, *Society and Government in France Under Richelieu and Mazarin, 1624–61*, London: Macmillan, 1988.

'Absolutism: What's in a Name?', in Richard Bonney, *The Limits of Absolutism in* ancien régime *France*, Aldershot: Variorum, 1995, pp. 93–117.

'Cardinal Mazarin and His Critics: The Remonstrances of 1652', in Richard Bonney, *The Limits of Absolutism in* ancien régime *France*, Aldershot: Variorum, 1995, pp. 15–31.

The Limits of Absolutism in ancien régime *France*, Aldershot: Variorum, 1995.

Bourdieu, Pierre, *In Other Words: Essays Towards a Reflective Sociology*, trans. M. Adamson, Cambridge: Polity, 1990.

Brass, Paul R., *Ethnicity and Nationalism: Theory and Comparison*, New Delhi: Sage, 1991.

Braudel, Fernand, *The Mediterranean*, vol. 2, London: Collins, 1973.

Breuilly, John, *Nationalism and the State*, 2nd edn, University of Chicago Press, 1993.

Brown, K. S., 'In the Realm of the Double-Headed Eagle: Parapolitics in Macedonia 1994–9', in Jane K. Cowan (ed.), *Macedonia: The Politics of Identity and Difference*, London: Pluto Press, 2000, pp. 122–39.

Brown, Michael E., 'Causes and Implications of Ethnic Conflict', in Michael E. Brown (ed.), *Ethnic Conflict and International Security*, Princeton University Press, 1993, pp. 3–26.

Brown, Michael E., (ed.), *The International Dimensions of Internal Conflict*, Cambridge, MA: The MIT Press, 1996.

Brownlie, Ian (ed.), *Basic Documents in International Law*, 3rd edn, Oxford: Clarendon Press, 1989.

Brubaker, Rogers, *The Limits of Rationality: An Essay on the Social and Moral Thought of Max Weber*, London: George Allen & Unwin, 1984.

'Rethinking Classical Theory: The Sociological Vision of Pierre Bourdieu', *Theory and Society* 14:6 (1985), 745–75.

Nationalism Reframed: Nationhood and the National Question in the New Europe, Cambridge University Press, 1996.

Buechsenschuetz, Ulrich, 'New Rift in Macedonian Leadership?', RFE/RL *Newsline* 5:151 (10 August 2001).

Buergenthal, Thomas, 'The Copenhagen CSCE Meeting: A New Public Order for Europe', *Human Rights Law Journal* 11:1–2 (1990), 217–32.

Bugajski, Janusz, *Ethnic Politics in Eastern Europe: A Guide to Nationality Policies, Organizations, and Parties*, Armonk: M.E. Sharp, 1994.

Bull, Hedley, 'The Importance of Grotius in the Study of International Relations', in Hedley Bull, Benedict Kingsbury and Adam Roberts (eds.), *Hugo Grotius and International Relations*, Oxford: Clarendon Press, 1992, pp. 65–93.

The Anarchical Society: A Study of Order in World Politics, 2nd edn, London: Macmillan, 1995.

Bull, Hedley and Watson, Adam (eds.), *The Expansion of International Society*, Oxford: Clarendon Press, 1985.

Burg, Steven L. and Shoup, Paul S., *The War in Bosnia-Herzegovina: Ethnic Conflict and International Intervention*, Armonk: M. E. Sharp, 1999.

Burke, Peter, *The Fabrication of Louis XIV*, New Haven: Yale University Press, 1992.

Calhoun, Craig, 'Nationalism and Ethnicity', *Annual Review of Sociology* 19 (1993), 211–39.

Critical Social Theory, Oxford: Blackwell, 1995.

Cederman, Lars-Erik, *Emergent Actors in World Politics: How States and Nations Develop and Dissolve*, Princeton University Press, 1997.

CERD (Committee on the Elimination of Racial Discrimination), Concluding Observations of the Committee on the Elimination of Racial Discrimination: Czech Republic, CERD/C/304.Add.47, 30 March 1998, section D, para 14.

Chaliand, Gerard and Ternon, Yves, *The Armenians: From Genocide to Resistance*, trans. Tony Berret, London: Zed Press, 1983.

Charny, Israel W. (ed.), *Genocide: A Critical Bibliographical Review*, vol. 2, New York: Facts on File, 1991.

Checkel, Jeffrey T., 'International Norms and Domestic Politics: Bridging the Rationalist–Constructivist Divide', *European Journal of International Relations* 3:4 (1997), 473–95.

'Norms, Institutions, and National Identity in Contemporary Europe', *International Studies Quarterly* 43:1 (1999), 84–114.

'The Europeanization of Citizenship', in Maria Green Cowles, James, Caporaso and Thomas Risse (eds.), *Transforming Europe: Europeanization and Domestic Change*, Ithaca: Cornell University Press, 2001, pp. 180–97.

Chejne, Anwar G., *Islam and the West: The Moriscos*, Albany: State University of New York Press, 1983.

Christoff, Peter and Reus-Smit, Chris, 'Kosova and the Left', *Arena Magazine* 43: October–November (1999), 25–9.

Church, William F. (ed.), *The Impact of Absolutism in France: National Experience Under Richelieu, Mazarin, and Louis XIV*, New York: John Wiley & Sons, 1969.

Cigar, Norman, *Genocide in Bosnia: The Policy of 'Ethnic Cleansing'*, College Station: Texas A & M University Press, 1995.

Cohen, Lenard J., *Broken Bonds: Yugoslavia's Disintegration and Balkan Politics in Transition*, 2nd edn, Boulder: Westview Press, 1995.

Cohn, Norman, *Europe's Inner Demons: The Demonization of Christians in Medieval Christendom*, revised edn, London: Pimlico, 1993.

Connolly, William E., *Political Theory and Modernity*, Oxford: Basil Blackwell, 1988.

Identity/Difference: Democratic Negotiations of Political Paradox, Ithaca: Cornell University Press, 1991.

Constitution of the Czech Republic, in Albert P. Blaustein and Gisbert H. Flanz (eds.), *Constitutions of the Countries of the World*, New York: Oceana Publications, 1993.

Constitution of the Republic of Macedonia, in Albert P. Blaustein and Gisbert H. Flanz (eds.), *Constitutions of the Countries of the World*, New York: Oceana Publishers, 1993.

Constitutional Watch, 'The Czech Republic', *East European Constitutional Review* 8:3 (1999).

'Macedonia', *East European Constitutional Review* 9:1/2 (2000).

'Macedonia', *East European Constitutional Review* 10:1 (2001).

Corrigan, Philip and Sayer, Derek, *The Great Arch: English State Formation as Cultural Revolution*, Oxford: Basil Blackwell, 1985.

Cox, Robert, 'Social Forces, States and World Orders: Beyond International Relations Theory', *Millennium: Journal of International Studies* 10:2 (1982), 126–55.

Crouzet, Denis, 'Henry IV, King of Reason?', in Keith Cameron (ed.), *From Valois to Bourbon: Dynasty, State and Society in Early Modern France*, University of Exeter, 1989.

Czech Helsinki Committee, 'Rights of National and Ethnic Minorities', 1997, <http://www.helcom.cz/en/r97_1.htm>.

Czech Republic, Law on Acquisition and Loss of Citizenship, Law No. 40/1993.

'Czech Republic Amends Anti-Roma Law', *Roma Rights* 3 (1999).

Daalder, Ivo H., 'Fear and Loathing in the Former Yugoslavia', in Michael E. Brown (ed.), *The International Dimensions of Internal Conflict*, Cambridge, MA: The MIT Press, 1996, pp. 35–67.

Getting to Dayton: The Making of America's Bosnia Policy, Washington, DC: Brookings Institution Press, 2000.

Daalder, Ivo H. and O'Hanlon, Michael E., *Winning Ugly: NATO's War to Save Kosovo*, Washington, DC: Brookings Institution Press, 2000.

Dadrian, Vahakn N., 'Genocide as a Problem of National and International Law: The World War I Armenian Case and its Contemporary Legal Ramifications', *Yale Journal of International Law* 14:2 (1989), 221–334.

'Documentation of the Armenian Genocide in Turkish Sources', in Israel W. Charny (ed.), *Genocide: A Critical Bibliographical Review*, vol. 2, New York: Facts on File, 1991, pp. 86–138.

'Ottoman Archives and Denial of the Armenian Genocide', in Richard G. Hovannisian (ed.), *The Armenian Genocide: History, Politics, Ethics*, New York: St. Martin's Press, 1992, pp. 280–310.

'The Secret Young-Turk Ittihadist Conference and the Decision for the World War I Genocide of the Armenians', *Holocaust and Genocide Studies* 7:2 (1993), 173–201.

The History of the Armenian Genocide: Ethnic Conflict from the Balkans to Anatolia to the Caucasus, 2nd revised edn, Providence: Berghahn Books, 1997.

'The Turkish Military Tribunal's Prosecution of the Authors of the Armenian Genocide: Four Major Court-Martial Series', *Holocaust and Genocide Studies* 11:1 (1997), 28–59.

Damrosch, Lori Fisler, 'The Collective Enforcement of International Norms Through Economic Sanctions', *Ethics and International Affairs* 8 (1994), 59–75.

'The Inevitability of Selective Response? Principles to Guide Urgent International Action', in Albrecht Schnabel and Ramesh Thakur (eds.), *Kosovo and the Challenge of Humanitarian Intervention: Selective Indignation, Collective Action, and International Citizenship*, Tokyo: United Nations University Press, 2000, pp. 405–19.

Damrosch, Lori Fisler (ed.), *Enforcing Restraint: Collective Intervention in Internal Conflicts*, New York: Council on Foreign Relations Press, 1993.

Danchev, Alex, and Halverson, Thomas (eds.), *International Perspectives on the Yugoslav Conflict*, London: Macmillan, 1996.

Danforth, Loring M., 'Claims to Macedonian Identity: The Macedonian Question and the Breakup of Yugoslavia', *Anthropology Today* 9:4 (1993), 3–10.

The Macedonian Conflict: Ethnic Nationalism in a Transnational World, Princeton University Press, 1995, pp. 56–65.

Davis, Natalie Zemon, 'The Rites of Violence', in Natalie Zemon Davis, *Society and Culture in Early Modern France*, Stanford University Press, 1975, pp. 152–87.

Davison, Roderic H., 'The Armenian Crisis 1912–1914', *American Historical Review* 53:3 (1948), 481–505.

'Turkish Attitudes Concerning Christian–Muslim Equality in the Nineteenth Century', *American Historical Review* 59:4 (1954), 844–64.

'Nationalism as an Ottoman Problem and the Ottoman Response', in William Haddad and William Ochsenwald (eds.), *Nationalism in a Non-National State: The Dissolution of the Ottoman Empire*, Columbus: Ohio State University Press, 1977, pp. 25–56.

Essays in Ottoman and Turkish History, 1774–1923: The Impact of the West, University of Texas Press, 1990.

De Zayas, Alfred-Maurice, 'A Historical Survey of Twentieth Century Expulsions', in Anna C. Bramwell (ed.), *Refugees in the Age of Total War*, London: Unwin Hyman, 1988.

'The International Judicial Protection of Peoples and Minorities', in Catherine Brölman, Rene Lefeber and Marjoleine Zieck (eds.), *Peoples and Minorities in International Law*, Dordrecht: Martinus Nijhoff Publishers, 1993, pp. 253–87.

del Mundo, Fernando and Wilkinson, Ray, 'A Race Against Time', *Refugees* 116 (1999).

Deng, Francis M., 'Dealing With the Displaced: A Challenge to the International Community', *Global Governance* 1:1 (1995), 45–57.

Denich, Bette, 'Dismembering Yugoslavia: Nationalist Ideologies and the Symbolic Revival of Genocide', *American Ethnologist* 21:2 (1994), 367–90.

Denitch, Bogdan, *Ethnic Nationalism: The Tragic Death of Yugoslavia*, Minneapolis: University of Minnesota Press, 1994.

Der Derian, James, and Shapiro, Michael (eds.), *International/Intertextual Relations, Postmodern Readings of World Politics*, Lexington Books, 1989.

Devetak, Richard, 'Incomplete States: Theories and Practices of Statecraft', in John MacMillan and Andrew Linklater (eds.), *Boundaries in Question: New Directions in International Relations*, London: Pinter Publishers, 1995, pp. 17–39.

Diefendorf, Barbara, *Beneath the Cross: Catholics and Huguenots in Sixteenth-Century Paris*, New York: Oxford University Press, 1991.

Diefendorf, Barbara and Hesse, Carla (eds.), *Culture and Identity in Early Modern Europe: Essays in Honor of Natalie Zemon Davis*, Ann Arbor: The University of Michigan Press, 1993.

Djilas, Aleksa, 'Fear Thy Neighbour: The Breakup of Yugoslavia', in Charles A. Kupchan (ed.), *Nationalism and Nationalities in the New Europe*, Ithaca: Cornell University Press, 1995, pp. 85–106.

Document of the Copenhagen Meeting of the Conference on the Human Dimension Meeting of the CSCE, 29 June 1990, *Human Rights Law Journal* 11:1–2 (1990), 232–46.

Donia, Robert J. and Fine, John V. A., *Bosnia and Hercegovina: A Tradition Betrayed*, London: Hurst & Co, 1994.

Donnelly, Jack, 'State Sovereignty and International Intervention: The Case of Human Rights', in Gene M. Lyons and Michael Mastanduno (eds.), *Beyond Westphalia? State Sovereignty and International Intervention*, Baltimore: The Johns Hopkins University Press, 1995, pp. 115–46.

Douglas, Mary, *Purity and Danger*, Harmondsworth: Penguin, 1970.

Dowty, Alan and Loescher, Gil, 'Refugee Flows as Grounds for International Action', *International Security* 21:1 (1996), 43–71.

ECRI (European Commission on Racism and Intolerance), *Report on the Czech Republic*, Strasburg: Council of Europe, September 1997.

ECRI (European Commission on Racism and Intolerance), *Second Report on the Czech Republic*, Strasburg: Council of Europe, 21 March 2000.

Edginton, Bella, 'The Czech Citizenship Law: Legally and Morally Wrong', *Prague Post*, 6 March 1996.

'Editorial Comments: NATO's Kosovo Intervention', *American Journal of International Law* 93:4 (1999), 824–62.

Edwards, John, *The Jews in Christian Europe, 1400–1700*, London: Routledge, 1988.

Elias, Norbert, *The Civilizing Process*, vol. 2, *State Formation and Civilization*, Oxford: Blackwell, 1982.

The Court Society, Oxford: Basil Blackwell, 1983.

Elliott, John H., *Imperial Spain 1469–1716*, Harmondsworth: Penguin, 1963.

Elster, Jon, Offe, Claus, Preuss, Ulrich K. with Boenker, Frank, Goetting, Ulrike, and Rueb, Friedbert, W., *Institutional Design in Post-Communist Societies: Rebuilding the Ship at Sea*, Cambridge University Press, 1998.

Elton, G. R., *Reformation Europe, 1517–1559*, London: Fontana/Collins, 1963.

Elton, G. R. (ed.), *The New Cambridge Modern History*, vol. 2, *The Reformation 1520–1559*, Cambridge University Press, 1962.

European Roma Rights Center, *A Pleasant Fiction: The Human Rights Situation of Roma in Macedonia*, Country Reports Series 7 (July 1998).

European Roma Rights Center, *A Special Remedy: Roma and Schools for the Mentally Handicapped in the Czech Republic*, Bucharest: European Roma Rights Center, 1999, <http://www.errc.org/publications/reports/czech-republic.rtf>.

European Union, *Accession Partnership 1999: Czech Republic*.

Farer, Tom J., 'A Paradigm of Legitimate Intervention', in Lori Fisler Damrosch (ed.), *Enforcing Restraint: Collective Intervention in Internal Conflicts*, New York: Council on Foreign Relations Press, 1993, pp. 316–47.
'How the International System Copes With Involuntary Migration: Norms, Institutions and State Practice', *Human Rights Quarterly* 17:1 (1995), 72–100.

Fearon, James D., 'Rationalist Explanations for War', *International Organization* 49:3 (1995), 379–414.

Fein, Helen, *Accounting for Genocide*, New York: The Free Press, 1979.

Fein, Helen (ed.), *Genocide Watch*, New Haven: Yale University Press, 1992.

Fenet, Alain, 'The Question of Minorities in the Order of Law', in Gerard Chaliand (ed.), *Minority Peoples in the Age of Nation-States*, trans. Tony Berrett, London: Pluto Press, 1989, pp. 12–51.

Findlay, Carter V., *Bureaucratic Reform in the Ottoman Empire: The Sublime Porte, 1789–1922*, Princeton University Press, 1980.

Finnemore, Martha, 'Constructing Norms of Humanitarian Intervention', in Peter J. Katzenstein (ed.), *The Culture of National Security: Norms and Identity in World Politics*, New York: Columbia University Press, 1996, pp. 153–85.
National Interests in International Society, Ithaca: Cornell University Press, 1996.
'Norms, Culture, and World Politics: Insights From Sociology's Institutionalism', *International Organization* 50:2 (1996), 325–47.

Folnegovic-Smalc, Vera, 'Psychiatric Aspects of the Rapes in the War Against the Republics of Croatia and Bosnia-Herzegovina', in Alexandra Stiglmayer (ed.), *Mass Rape: The War Against Women in Bosnia-Herzegovina*, trans. Marion Faber, Lincoln: University of Nebraska Press, 1993, pp. 174–9.

Foreign Policy Institute, Ankara, 'The Turkish Argument: The Armenian Issue in Nine Questions and Answers', in Permanent Peoples' Tribunal, *A Crime of Silence: The Armenian Genocide*, London: Zed Books, 1985, pp. 132–67.

Forsyth, Murray, 'The Tradition of International Law', in Terry Nardin and David Mapel (eds.), *Traditions of International Ethics*, Cambridge University Press, 1993, pp. 23–41.

Foucault, Michel, *Discipline and Punish: The Birth of the Prison*, London: Penguin, 1979.

Franck, Thomas M., 'The Emerging Right to Democratic Governance', *American Journal of International Law* 86:1 (1992), 41–91.

Fraser, Angus, *The Gypsies*, Oxford: Blackwell, 1992.

Frentzel-Zagorska, Janina (ed.), *From One-Party State to Democracy: Transition in Eastern Europe*, Amsterdam: Editions Rodopi B.V., 1993.

Gagnon, V. P., 'Ethnic Nationalism and International Conflict', *International Security* 19:3 (1994/95), 130–66.
'Ethnic Conflict as Demobilizer: The Case of Serbia', *Institute for European Studies Working Paper* 96:1, Ithaca: Cornell University, 1996, pp. 1–31.

Garrisson, Janine, *A History of Sixteenth-Century France, 1483–1598: Renaissance, Reformation and Rebellion*, New York: St. Martin's Press, 1995.

Gati, Charles, 'The Mirage of Democracy', *Transitions* 2:6 (1996), 6–12, 62.

Geertz, Clifford, *The Interpretation of Cultures*, New York: Basic Books, 1973.

Gellner, Ernest, *Nations and Nationalism*, Oxford: Basil Blackwell, 1983.

George, Jim, *Discourses of Global Politics: A Critical (Re) Introduction to International Relations*, Boulder: Lynne Rienner, 1994.

Gerber, Jane, *The Jews of Spain: A History of the Sephardic Experience*, New York: Free Press, 1992.

Gheorghe, Nicolae, 'Roma-Gypsy Ethnicity in Eastern Europe', *Social Research* 58:4 (1991), 829–44.

Gibney, Matthew J., 'Kosovo and Beyond: Popular and Unpopular Refugees', *Forced Migration Review* 5: August (1999), 28–30.

Giddens, Anthony, *The Nation-State and Violence: Volume Two of a Contemporary Critique of Historical Materialism*, Cambridge: Polity Press, 1985.

Glenny, Misha, *The Fall of Yugoslavia*, London: Penguin, 1992.

Godard, Charles, 'The Historical Role of the Intendants', in William F. Church (ed.), *The Impact of Absolutism in France: National Experience Under Richelieu, Mazarin, and Louis XIV*, New York: John Wiley & Sons, 1969, pp. 159–65.

Goebel, Christopher M., 'Population Transfer, Humanitarian Law, and the Use of Ground Force in UN Peacemaking: Bosnia and Herzegovina in the Wake of Iraq', *New York University Journal of International Law and Politics* 25:3 (1993), 627–98.

Golden, Richard M., 'Introduction', in Richard M. Golden (ed.), *The Huguenot Connection: The Edict of Nantes, its Revocation and Early French Migration to South Carolina*, Dordrecht: Kluwer Academic Publishers, 1988, pp. 1–27.

Golden, Richard M. (ed.), *The Huguenot Connection: The Edict of Nantes, its Revocation and Early French Migration to South Carolina*, Dordrecht: Kluwer Academic Publishers, 1988.

Gong, Gerrit W., *The Standard of 'Civilization' in International Society*, Oxford: Clarendon Press, 1984.

'China's Entry into the International Society', in Hedley Bull and Adam Watson (eds.), *The Evolution of International Society*, Oxford: Clarendon Press, 1985, pp. 172–83.

Gonzales de Caldas, Maria Victoria, 'New Images of the Holy Office in Seville: The Auto-de-Fe', in Angel Alcala (ed.), *The Spanish Inquisition and the Inquisitorial Mind*, New York: Columbia University Press, 1984, pp. 265–300.

Gordon, Philip H., 'Europe's Uncommon Foreign Policy', *International Security* 22:3 (1997/98), 74–100.

Gordy, Eric D., 'Why Milosevic Still?', *Current History* 99:635 (2000), 99–103.

Gow, James, 'Deconstructing Yugoslavia', *Survival* 33:4 (1991), 291–311.

Legitimacy and the Military: The Yugoslav Crisis, London: Pinter Publishers, 1992.

Green Cowles, Maria, Caporaso, James and Risse, Thomas (eds.), *Transforming Europe: Europeanization and Domestic Change*, Ithaca: Cornell University Press, 2001.

Greenfeld, Liah, *Nationalism: Five Roads to Modernity*, Cambridge, MA: Harvard University Press, 1992.

Greenfeld, Liah and Chirot, Daniel, 'Nationalism and Aggression', *Theory and Society* 23:1 (1994), 79–130.

Greengrass, Mark, *France in the Age of Henry IV*, Harlow: Longman, 1984.

The French Reformation, Oxford: Basil Blackwell, 1987.

Gross, Tom, 'Citizenship Law Codifies Racism', *Prague Post*, 29 June 1994.

Gurr, Ted Robert and Harff, Barbara, *Ethnic Conflict in World Politics*, Boulder: Westview Press, 1994.

Gutman, Roy, *A Witness to Genocide*, New York: Macmillan, 1993.

Habermas, Jurgen,*The Philosophical Discourse of Modernity*, Cambridge, MA: MIT Press, 1987.

Haliczer, Stephen, 'The First Holocaust: The Inquisition and the Converted Jews of Spain and Portugal', in Stephen Haliczer (ed.), *Inquisition and Society in Early Modern Europe*, London: Croom Helm, 1987, pp. 7–18.

Hannum, Hurst, 'Contemporary Developments in the International Protection of the Rights of Minorities', *Notre Dame Law Review* 66:5 (1991), 1431–48.

Hardin, Russell, *One for All: The Logic of Group Conflict*, Princeton University Press, 1995.

Harvey, L. P., *Islamic Spain 1250 to 1500*, University of Chicago Press, 1990.

Hastings, Adrian, *The Construction of Nationhood: Ethnicity, Religion, and Nationalism*, Cambridge University Press, 1997.

Hatton, Ragnhild, *Louis XIV and Europe*, London: Macmillan, 1976.

Hayden, Robert M., 'Balancing Discussion of Jasenovac and the Manipulation of History', *East European Politics and Societies* 6:2 (1992), 207–12.

'Constitutional Nationalism in the Formerly Yugoslav Republics', *Slavic Review* 51:4 (1992), 654–73.

'Imagined Communities and Real Victims: Self-Determination and Ethnic Cleansing in Yugoslavia', *American Ethnologist* 23:4 (1996), 783–801.

Hays, Sharon, 'Structure and Agency and the Sticky Problem of Culture', *Sociological Theory* 12:1 (1994), 57–72.

Held, David and Thompson, John B. (eds.), *Social Theory of Modern Societies: Anthony Giddens and His Critics*, Cambridge University Press, 1989.

Held, David, et al. (eds.), *States and Societies*, Oxford: Basil Blackwell, 1985.

Henckaerts, Jean-Marie, *Mass Expulsion in Modern International Law and Practice*, The Hague: Kluwer Law International, 1995.

Henkin, Louis, 'Kosovo and the Law of "Humanitarian Intervention"', *American Journal of International Law* 93:4 (1999), 824–8.

Henningson, Gustav, 'The Archives and the Historiography of the Spanish Inquisition', in Gustav Henningson and John Tedeschi (eds.), *The Inquisition in Early Modern Europe: Studies on Sources and Methods*, Illinois: Northern Illinois University Press, 1986, pp. 54–78.

Hess, Andrew C., 'The Moriscos: An Ottoman Fifth Column in Sixteenth-Century Spain', *American Historical Review* 74:1 (1968), 1–25.

Heyd, Uriel, *Foundations of Turkish Nationalism: The Life and Teaching of Ziya Gokalp*, London: The Harvill Press, 1950.

Hinsley, F. H., *Sovereignty*, 2nd edn, Cambridge University Press, 1986.

Hobsbawm, E. J., 'Introduction: Inventing Traditions', in Eric Hobsbawm and Terence Ranger (eds.), *The Invention of Tradition*, Cambridge University Press, 1992, pp. 1–14.

Nations and Nationalism Since 1780: Programme, Myth, Reality, 2nd edn, Cambridge University Press, 1992.

Hoffman, Mark, 'Critical Theory and the Inter-Paradigm Debate', *Millennium: Journal of International Studies* 16:2 (1987), 231–49.

Hoffmann, Stanley, *Duties Beyond Borders: On the Limits and Possibilities of Ethical International Politics*, Syracuse University Press, 1981.

The Ethics and Politics of Humanitarian Intervention, University of Notre Dame Press, 1996.

Hofmann, Tessa, 'German Eyewitness Reports of the Genocide of the Armenians, 1915–1916', in Permanent Peoples' Tribunal, *A Crime of Silence: The Armenian Genocide*, London: Zed Books, 1985, pp. 61–92.

Holt, Mack P., *The French Wars of Religion, 1562–1629*, Cambridge University Press, 1995.

Honig, Jan Willem and Both, Norbert, *Srebrenica: Record of a War Crime*, New York: Penguin, 1996.

Hopf, Ted, 'The Promise of Constructivism in International Relations Theory', *International Security* 23:1 (1998), 171–200.

Horkheimer, Max, 'Traditional and Critical Theory', in Max Horkheimer, *Critical Theory: Selected Essays*, New York: Free Press, 1972, pp. 188–243.

Hovannisian, Richard G., *The Republic of Armenia*, vols. 1–4, Berkeley: University of California Press, 1971–96.

'The Armenian Question, 1878–1923', in Permanent Peoples' Tribunal, *A Crime of Silence: The Armenian Genocide*, London: Zed Books, 1985, pp. 11–33.

Hovannisian, Richard G. (ed.), *The Armenian Genocide: History, Politics, Ethics*, New York: St. Martin's Press, 1992.

Human Rights Watch, 'Roma in the Czech Republic: Foreigners in Their Own Land', *Human Rights Watch Country Report* 8:11 (1996).

Federal Republic of Yugoslavia: Humanitarian Law Violations in Kosovo, New York: Human Rights Watch, 1998.

'Humanitarian Law Violations in Kosovo', *Human Rights Watch Report* 10:9 (1998).

World Report 1999: Czech Republic, <http://www.hrw.org/wr2k/Eca-08.htm>.

'Federal Republic of Yugoslavia. Kosovo: Rape as a Weapon of "Ethnic Cleansing" ', <http://www.hrw.org/hrw/reports/2000/fry/index.htm>.

ICTY (International Criminal Tribunal for the former Yugoslavia), *Judgement: Prosecutor vs Dragoljub Kunarac, Radomir Kovac and Zoran Vukovic*, 22 February 2001, Case No. IT-96-23-T & IT-96-23/1-T, available at <http://www.un.org/icty>.

ICG (International Crisis Group), 'Macedonia: The Politics of Ethnicity and Conflict', ICG, 21 October 1997.

'Kosovo's Impact on Macedonia', ICG, 17 May 1999.

'Preventing Minority Return in Bosnia-Herzegovina: The Anatomy of Hate and Fear', *ICG Balkans Report No. 73*, ICG, August 1999.

'Is Dayton Failing?: Bosnia Four Years After the Peace Agreement', *ICG Balkans Report No. 80*, Sarajevo: ICG, October 1999.

'Macedonia's Ethnic Albanians: Bridging the Gulf', *ICG Balkans Report No. 98*, Skopje/Washington/Brussels: ICG, 2 August 2000.

'The Macedonian Question: Reform or Rebellion?', *ICG Balkans Report No. 109*, Skopje/Brussels: ICG, 5 April 2001.

'Macedonia: The Last Chance for Peace', *ICG Balkans Report No. 113*, Skopje/Brussels: ICG, 20 June 2001.

'Macedonian: Still Sliding', *Balkans Briefing*, Skopje/Brussels: ICG, 27 July 2001.

'Macedonia: Still Sliding', *ICG Briefing Paper*, ICG, 27 July 2001, <http://www.intl-crisis-group.org/>.

'Macedonia: War on Hold', *Balkans Briefing*, Skopje/Brussels: ICG, 15 August 2001.

'Macedonia: Filling the Security Vacuum', *ICG Balkans Briefing*, Skopje/Brussels, ICG, 8 September 2001.

Israel, Jonathan I., *European Jewry in the Age of Mercantilism, 1550–1750*, Oxford: Clarendon, 1985.

Jackson, Robert, *Quasi-States: Sovereignty, International Relations, and the Third World*, Cambridge University Press, 1990.

Jackson Preece, Jennifer, 'Minority Rights in Europe: From Westphalia to Helsinki', *Review of International Studies* 23:1 (1997), 75–92.

National Minorities and the European Nation-States System, Oxford: Clarendon Press, 1998.

'Ethnic Cleansing as an Instrument of Nation-State Creation: Changing State Practices and Evolving Legal Norms', *Human Rights Quarterly* 20:4 (1998), 817–42.

Jones, Dorothy V., 'The League of Nations Experiment in International Protection', *Ethics and International Affairs* 8 (1994), 77–95.

Judah, Tim, *Kosovo: War and Revenge*, New Haven: Yale University Press, 2000.

Judge, H. G., 'Louis XIV and the Church', in John C. Rule (ed.), *Louis XIV and the Craft of Kingship*, Columbus: Ohio State University Press, 1969, pp. 240–64.

Kalibova, Kveta, Haisman, Thomas and Gjoricova, Jitka, 'Gypsies in Czechoslovakia: Demographic Development and Policy Perspectives', in John O'Loughlin and Herman van der Wusten (eds.), *The New Political Geography of Eastern Europe*, London: Belhaven Press, 1993, pp. 133–44.

Kamen, Henry, *Spain 1469–1714: A Society of Conflict*, New York: Longman, 1983.

Inquisition and Society in Spain: In the Sixteenth and Seventeenth Centuries, London: Weidenfeld and Nicolson, 1985.

'The Mediterranean and the Expulsion of Spanish Jews in 1492', *Past and Present* 119 (1988), 30–55.

The Spanish Inquisition: A Historical Revision, New Haven: Yale University Press, 1997.

Kantorowicz, Ernst H., *The King's Two Bodies: A Study in Medieval Political Theology*, Princeton University Press, 1957.

Katz, Jacob, *Exclusiveness and Tolerance*, Oxford University Press, 1961.

Katz, Steven T., *The Holocaust in Historical Context*, vol. 1, *The Holocaust and Mass Death Before the Modern Age*, New York: Oxford University Press, 1994.

Katzenstein, Peter J., *Culture, Norms and National Security: Police and Military in Postwar Japan*, Ithaca: Cornell University Press, 1996.

Katzenstein, Peter J. (ed.), *The Culture of National Security: Norms and Identity in World Politics*, New York: Columbia University Press, 1996.

Kaufmann, Chaim D., 'Possible and Impossible Solutions to Ethnic Civil Wars', *International Security* 20:4 (1996), 136–75.

'When All Else Fails: Ethnic Population Transfers and Partitions in the Twentieth Century', *International Security* 23:2 (1998), 120–56.

Kaufman, Stuart J., 'An "International Theory" of Inter-Ethnic War', *Review of International Studies* 22:2 (1996), 149–71.

Keen, Maurice, *The Penguin History of Medieval Europe*, London: Penguin, 1968.

Kelley, Donald R., *The Beginning of Ideology: Consciousness and Society in the French Reformation*, Cambridge University Press, 1981.

Kelsay, John, 'Bosnia and the Muslim Critique of Modernity', in G. Scott Davis (ed.), *Religion and Justice in the War Over Bosnia*, New York: Routledge, 1996, pp. 117–41.

Keohane, Nannerl O., *Philosophy and the State in France: The Renaissance to the Enlightenment*, Princeton University Press, 1980.

Keohane, Robert O. (ed.), *Neorealism and its Critics*, New York: Columbia University Press, 1986.

Kertzer, David I., *Ritual, Politics, Power*, New Haven: Yale University Press, 1988.

Kier, Elizabeth, 'Culture and Military Doctrine: France Between the Wars', *International Security* 19:4 (1995), 65–93.

Kim, Lucian, 'The Wall of Hostility on "Intolerance Street"', *US News and World Report* 127:18 (1999).

Kingdon, Robert M., *Myths About the St. Bartholomew's Day Massacres, 1572–1576*, Cambridge, MA: Harvard University Press, 1998.

Kirshner, Jonathan, 'Rationalist Explanations for War?', *Security Studies* 10:1 (2000), 143–50.

Klebes, Heinrich, 'The Council of Europe's Framework Convention', Appendix A: Explanatory Memorandum on the Framework Convention for the Protection of National Minorities, *Human Rights Law Journal* 16:1–3 (1995), 102; Appendix A: Explanatory Memorandum on the Framework Convention for the Protection of National Minorities, Commentary on Article 27, 103.

'The Council of Europe's Framework Convention for the Protection of National Minorities', *Human Rights Law Journal* 16:1–3 (1995), 92–115.

Knecht, R. J., *The French Wars of Religion 1559–1598*, 2nd edn, New York: Longman, 1996.

Koenigsberger, H. G. and Mosse, George L., *Europe in the Sixteenth Century*, London: Longmans, 1968.

Kowert, Paul and Legro, Jeffery, 'Norms, Identity, and Their Limits: A Theoretical Reprise', in Peter J. Katzenstein (ed.), *The Culture of National Security: Norms and Identity in World Politics*, New York: Columbia University Press, 1996, pp. 451–97.

Krasner, Stephen D., 'Approaches to the State: Alternative Conceptions and Historical Dynamics', *Comparative Politics* 16:2 (1984), 223–46.

'Sovereignty: An Institutional Perspective', *Comparative Political Studies* 21:1 (1988), 66–94.

'Westphalia and All That', in Judith Goldstein and Robert O. Keohane (eds.), *Ideas and Foreign Policy: Beliefs, Institutions, and Political Change*, Ithaca: Cornell University Press, 1993, pp. 235–64.

'Sovereignty and Intervention', in Gene M. Lyons and Michael Mastanduno (eds.), *Beyond Westphalia? State Sovereignty and International Intervention*, Baltimore: The Johns Hopkins University Press, 1995, pp. 228–49.

'Compromising Westphalia', *International Security* 20:3 (1995/96), 115–51.

Organized Hypocrisy, Princeton University Press, 1999.

Kratochwil, Friedrich, 'Of Systems, Boundaries, and Territoriality: An Inquiry into the Formation of the State System', *World Politics* 39:1 (1986), 27–52.

'Sovereignty as *Dominium:* Is There a Right of Humanitarian Intervention?', in Gene M. Lyons and Michael Mastanduno (eds.), *Beyond Westphalia? State Sovereignty and International Intervention*, Baltimore: The Johns Hopkins University Press, 1995, pp. 21–42.

Kuper, Leo, *Genocide: Its Political Use in the Twentieth Century*, New Haven: Yale University Press, 1981.

International Action Against Genocide, Report No. 53, revised edn, London: Minority Rights Group, 1984.

Kushner, David, *The Rise of Turkish Nationalism 1876–1908*, London: Frank Cass, 1977.

Labrousse, Elisabeth, 'The Political Ideas of the Huguenot Diaspora (Bayle and Jurieu)', in Richard M. Golden (ed.), *Church, State and Society under the Bourbon Kings of France*, Lawrence: Coronado Press, 1982.

'Understanding the Revocation of the Edict of Nantes from the Perspective of the French Court', in Richard M. Golden (ed.), *The Huguenot Connection: The Edict of Nantes, its Revocation, and Early French Migration to South Carolina*, Dordrecht: Kluwer Academic Publishers, 1988, pp. 49–62.

Ladas, Stephen P., *The Exchange of Minorities: Bulgaria, Greece and Turkey*, New York: The Macmillan Company, 1932.

Lake, David A. and Rothchild, Donald, 'Containing Fear: The Origins and Management of Ethnic Conflict', *International Security* 21:2 (1996), 41–75.

'Spreading Fear: The Genesis of Transnational Ethnic Conflict', in David A. Lake and Donald Rothchild (eds.), *The International Spread of Ethnic Conflict: Fear Diffusion and Escalation*, Princeton University Press, 1998, pp. 3–32.

Lampe, John R., *Yugoslavia as History: Twice There Was a Country*, Cambridge University Press, 1996.

Landau, Jacob M., *Pan-Turkism in Turkey: A Study in Irredentism*, London: C. Hurst & Co., 1981.

Lapid, Yosef, '*Quo Vadis* International Relations? Further Reflections on the "Next Stage" of International Theory', *Millennium: Journal of International Studies* 18:1 (1989), 77–88.

Lapid, Yosef and Kratochwil, Friedrich (eds.), *The Return of Culture and Identity in IR Theory*, Boulder: Lynne Rienner, 1996.

Le Roy Ladurie, Emmanuel, *The Royal French State 1460–1610*, trans. Juliet Vale, Oxford: Blackwell, 1994.

Leff, Carol Skalnik, *The Czech and Slovak Republics: Nation Versus State*, Boulder: Westview Press, 1997.

Lerner, N., 'The Evolution of Minority Rights in International Law', in Catherine Brölman, Rene Lefeber and Marjoleine Zieck (eds.), *Peoples and Minorities in International Law*, Dordrecht: Martinus Nijhoff Publishers, 1993, pp. 77–101.

Lewis, Bernard, *The Emergence of Modern Turkey*, London: Oxford University Press, 1962.

Libaridian, Gerard J., 'The Ideology of the Young Turk Movement', in Permanent Peoples' Tribunal, *A Crime of Silence: The Armenian Genocide*, London: Zed Books, 1985, pp. 37–52.

'The Ultimate Repression: The Genocide of the Armenians, 1915–1917', in Isidor Walliman and Michael N. Dobkowski (eds.), *Genocide and the Modern Age: Etiology and Case Studies of Mass Death*, New York: Greenwood Press, 1987, pp. 203–35.

Lichtenberg, Judith, 'National Boundaries and Moral Boundaries: A Cosmopolitan View', in Peter G. Brown and Henry Shue (eds.), *Boundaries: National Autonomy and its Limits*, Totowa, NJ: Rowman & Littlefield, 1981, pp. 79–100.

Liegeois, Jean-Pierre, *Roma, Gypsies, Travellers*, Strasburg: Council of Europe Press, 1994.

Lindo, E. H., *History of the Jews of Spain and Portugal*, New York: Burt Franklin, 1970 (1848).

Linklater, Andrew, *Men and Citizens in the Theory of International Relations*, 2nd edn, London: Macmillan, 1990.

'The Problem of Community in International Relations', *Alternatives* 15:2 (1990), 135–53.

'The Question of the Next Stage in International Relations Theory: A Critical-Theoretical Point of View', *Millennium: Journal of International Studies* 21:1 (1992), 77–98.

The Transformation of Political Community, Cambridge: Polity Press, 1998.

Little, Richard, 'Recent Literature on Intervention and Non-Intervention', in Ian Forbes and Mark Hoffman (eds.), *Political Theory, International Relations, and the Ethics of Intervention*, London: Macmillan, 1993, pp. 13–31.

Lloyd, Howell A., *The State, France, and the Sixteenth Century*, London: George Allen & Unwin, 1984.

Loescher, Gil, *Beyond Charity: International Cooperation and the Global Refugee Crisis*, Oxford University Press, 1993.

Loescher, Gil and Monahan, Laila, *Refugees and International Relations*, Oxford University Press, 1989.

Lossky, Andrew, *Louis XIV and the French Monarchy*, New Brunswick: Rutgers University Press, 1994.

Luard, Evan, 'The Origins of International Concern Over Human Rights', in Evan Luard (ed.), *The International Protection of Human Rights*, New York: Praeger, 1967, pp. 7–21.

Lynch, John, *Spain Under the Habsburgs*, vol. 1, New York University Press, 1981.

Macartney, C. A., 'League of Nations' Protection of Minority Rights', in Evan Luard (ed.), *The International Protection of Human Rights*, New York: Praeger, 1967.

National States and National Minorities, 2nd edn, New York: Russell & Russell, 1968.

'Macedonia Rebels Agree to Disarm', BBC News Online, 14 August 2001, <http://news.bbc.co.uk>.

'Macedonia's Born-Again Nationalist', BBC News Online, 27 August 2001.

MacKay, Angus, 'Popular Movements and Pogroms in Fifteenth-Century Castile', *Past and Present* 55 (1972), 33–67.

MacKinnon, Catharine A., 'Rape, Genocide, and Women's Human Rights', in Alexandra Stiglmayer (ed.), *Mass Rape: The War Against Women in Bosnia-Herzegovina*, trans. Marion Faber, Lincoln: University of Nebraska Press, 1993, pp. 183–96.

Magas, Branka,*The Destruction of Yugoslavia*, London: Verso, 1993.

Malcolm, Noel, *Bosnia: A Short History*, London: Macmillan, 1994.

Kosovo: A Short History, London: Macmillan, 1998.

Mann, Michael, *The Sources of Social Power*, vol. 1, *The History of Power from the Beginning to AD 1760*, Cambridge University Press, 1986.

The Sources of Social Power, vol. 2, *The Rise of Classes and Nation-States, 1760–1914*, Cambridge University Press, 1993.

Maravall, Jose Antonio, 'The Origins of the Modern State', *Journal of World History* 6:4 (1961), 789–808.

Marcus, Jonathan, 'Macedonia Mission "Too Short"', BBC News Online, 17 August 2001.

Marrus, Michael, *The Unwanted: European Refugees in the Twentieth Century*, Oxford University Press, 1985.

'The Uprooted: An Historical Perspective', in Goran Rystad (ed.), *The Uprooted: Forced Migration as an International Problem in the Post-War Era*, Lund University Press, 1990, pp. 47–57.

Martin, Nicholas, 'UNHCR and Kosovo: A Personal View from the UNHCR', *Forced Migration Review* 5: August (1999), 14–17.

Mattingly, Garrett, *Renaissance Diplomacy*, London: Jonathan Cape, 1955.

Mayall, James, *Nationalism and International Society*, Cambridge University Press, 1990.

'The Concept of Humanitarian Intervention Revisited', in Albrecht Schnabel and Ramesh Thakur (eds.), *Kosovo and the Challenge of Humanitarian Intervention: Selective Indignation, Collective Action, and International Citizenship*, Tokyo: United Nations University Press, 2000, pp. 319–33.

Mayall, James (ed.) *The New Interventionism 1991–1994: United Nations Experience in Cambodia, Former Yugoslavia and Somalia*, Cambridge University Press, 1996.

Mazian, Florence, *Why Genocide? The Armenian and Jewish Experiences In Perspective*, Iowa State University Press, 1990.

Mazowiecki, Tadeusz, 'The Situation of Human Rights in the Territory of the Former Yugoslavia', UN Doc. A/48/92-S/25341, United Nations: New York, February 1993.

McClune, Emma, 'Proposed Changes to Citizenship Law Disappoints Helsinki Commission', *Prague Post*, 28 February 1996.

McKim, Robert and McMahan, Jeff (eds.), *The Morality of Nationalism*, New York: Oxford University Press, 1997.

McNeill, William H., *Polyethnicity and National Unity in World History*, University of Toronto Press, 1986.

Mearsheimer, John J., 'Shrink Bosnia to Save It', *New York Times*, 31 March 1993.

Melson, Robert, 'A Theoretical Inquiry into the Armenian Massacres of 1894–1896', *Comparative Studies in Society and History* 24 (1982), 481–509.

'Provocation or Nationalism?: A Critical Inquiry into the Armenian Genocide of 1915', in Frank Chalk and Kurt Jonassohn (eds.), *The History and Sociology of Genocide: Analyses and Case Studies*, New Haven: Yale University Press, 1990, pp. 266–89.

Revolution and Genocide: On the Origins of the Armenian Genocide and the Holocaust, University of Chicago Press, 1992.

Meron, Theodor, 'Rape as a Crime Under International Humanitarian Law', *American Journal of International Law* 87:3 (1993), 424–8.

'War Crimes in Yugoslavia and the Development of International Law', *American Journal of International Law* 88:1 (1994), 78–87.

'War Crimes Law Comes of Age', *American Journal of International Law* 92:3 (1998), 462–8.

Mettam, Roger, *Power and Faction in Louis XIV's France*, Oxford: Basil Blackwell, 1988.

Meyer, John W., Boli, John and Thomas, George M.,'Ontology and Rationalization in the Western Cultural Account', in George M. Thomas, John W. Meyer, Francisco O. Ramirez, and John Boli, (eds.), *Institutional Structure: Constituting State, Society, and the Individual*, Newbury Park: Sage, 1987, pp. 12–37.

Mickey, Robert W., and Albion, Adam Smith, 'Success in the Balkans? A Case Study of Ethnic Relations in the Republic of Macedonia', in Ian M. Cuthbertson and Jane Leibowitz (eds.), *Minorities: The New Europe's Old Issue*, Prague: Institute for EastWest Studies, 1993, pp. 53–98.

Migdal, Joel S., 'Studying the State', in Mark Irving Lichbach and Alan S. Zuckerman (eds.), *Comparative Politics: Rationality, Culture, and Structure*, Cambridge University Press, 1997, pp. 208–35.

Miller, David, 'The Ethical Significance of Nationality', *Ethics* 98:4 (1988), 647–62.

Miller, Donald E. and Miller, Lorna Touryan, 'Women and Children of the Armenian Genocide', in Richard G. Hovannisian (ed.), *The Armenian Genocide: History, Politics, Ethics*, New York: St. Martin's Press, 1992, pp. 152–72.

'Milosevic to Face Charge of Genocide', *New York Times*, 30 August 2001.

Milosevic, Milan, 'The Media Wars', in Jasminka Udovicki and James Ridgeway (eds.), *Burn This House: The Making and Unmaking of Yugoslavia*, Durham: Duke University Press, 1997, pp. 108–29.

Minority Rights Group, *World Directory of Minorities*, London: Minority Rights Group International, 1997.

Minow, Martha, *Between Vengeance and Forgiveness: Facing History after Genocide and Mass Violence*, Boston: Beacon Press, 1998.

Montville, Joseph (ed.), *Conflict and Peacemaking in Multiethnic Societies*, Lexington Books, 1990.

Mosse, George L., *The Reformation*, Illinois: Dryden Press, 1963.

Naff, Thomas, 'The Ottoman Empire and the European States System', in Hedley Bull and Adam Watson (eds.), *The Expansion of International Society*, Oxford: Clarendon Press, 1985, pp. 143–69.

Nash, Margaret, 'The Politics and Norms of Self-Determination', unpublished paper, Melbourne: Monash University, 1996.

Nassibian, Akaby, *Britain and the Armenian Question, 1915–1923*, London: Croom Helm, 1984.

Nelson, Benjamin, 'Civilizational Complexes and Intercivilizational Encounters', *Sociological Analysis* 34 (1973), 79–105.

Netanyahu, Benzion, 'The Primary Cause of the Spanish Inquisition', in Angel Alcala (ed.), *The Spanish Inquisition and the Inquisitorial Mind*, New York: Columbia University Press, 1984, pp. 11–32.

The Origins of the Inquisition in Fifteenth Century Spain, New York: Random House, 1995.

Neumann, Iver B. and Welsh, Jennifer M., 'The Other in European Self-Definition: An Addendum to the Literature on International Society', *Review of International Studies* 17:4 (1991), 327–48.

The New Cambridge Modern History, vol. 2, *The Reformation, 1520–59*, Cambridge University Press, 1958.

North, Douglass C., *Structure and Change in Economic History*, New York: W. W. Norton, 1981.

North, Douglass C. and Thomas, Robert Paul, *The Rise of the Western World: A New Economic History*, Cambridge University Press, 1973.

Nowak, M., 'The Evolution of Minority Rights in International Law, Comments', in Catherine Brölman Rene Lefeber, and Marjoleine Zieck (eds.), *Peoples and Minorities in International Law*, Dordrecht: Martinus Nijhoff Publishers, 1993, pp. 103–18.

O'Brien, James C., 'The International Tribunal for Violations of International Humanitarian Law in the Former Yugoslavia', *American Journal of International Law* 87:4 (1993), 639–59.

Offe, Claus, 'Cultural Aspects of Consolidation: A Note on the Peculiarities of Postcommunist Transformations', *East European Constitutional Review* 6:4 (1997).

Office of the UNHCR (United Nations High Commissioner for Refugees), *The Czech and Slovak Citizenship Laws and the Problem of Statelessness*, February 1996.

Orentlicher, Diane F., 'Citizenship and National Identity', in David Wippman (ed.), *International Law and Ethnic Conflict*, Ithaca: Cornell University Press, 1998, pp. 296–325.

OSCE (Organization for Security and Co-operation in Europe) High Commissioner on National Minorities, *Report on the Situation of Roma and Sinti in the OSCE Area*, The Hague, March 2000, p. 157.

Report on the Situation of Roma and Sinti in the OSCE Area, The Hague, April 2000.

Report of the OSCE High Commissioner on National Minorities to Session 3 of the Human Dimension Section of the OSCE Review Conference, RC.GAL/2/99, 22 September 1999, <http://www.osce.org/inst/hcnm/recomm/roma/roma 99.html>.

Owen, David, *Balkan Odyssey*, New York: Harcourt Brace, 1995.

Parekh, Bhikhu, 'Ethnocentricity of the Nationalist Discourse', *Nations and Nationalism* 1:1 (1995), 25–52.

Parin, Paul, 'Open Wounds; Ethnopsychoanalytic Reflections on the Wars in the Former Yugoslavia', in Alexandra Stiglmayer (ed.), *Mass Rape: The War Against Women in Bosnia-Herzegovina*, trans. Marion Faber, Lincoln: University of Nebraska Press, 1994, pp. 35–53.

Parker, David, *The Making of French Absolutism*, London: Edward Arnold, 1983.

Parry, Clive (ed.), *Consolidated Treaty Series*, vol. 1, *1648–1649*, New York: Dobbs Ferry, 1909.

Pasic, Amir and Weiss, Thomas G., 'The Politics of Rescue: Yugoslavia's Wars and the Humanitarian Impulse', *Ethics and International Affairs* 11 (1997), 105–31.

Pavkovic, Aleksandar, *The Fragmentation of Yugoslavia: Nationalism in a Multinational State*, London: Macmillan, 1997.

Pearson, Raymond, *National Minorities in Eastern Europe 1848–1945*, London: Macmillan, 1983.

   'The Making of '89: Nationalism and the Dissolution of Communist Eastern Europe', *Nations and Nationalism* 1:1 (1995), 69–79.

Penrose, Jan, 'Essential Constructions? The "Cultural Bases" of Nationalist Movements', *Nations and Nationalism* 1:3 (1995), 391–417.

Permanent Peoples' Tribunal, *A Crime of Silence: The Armenian Genocide*, London: Zed Books, 1985.

Perry, Duncan M., 'Destiny on Hold: Macedonia and the Dangers of Ethnic Discord', *Current History* 97:617 (1998), 119–26.

   The Politics of Terror: The Macedonian Liberation Movements 1893–1903, Durham: Duke University Press, 1988.

   'Macedonia: Balkan Miracle or Balkan Disaster?', *Current History* 95:599 (1996), 113–17.

   'The Republic of Macedonia: Finding its Way', in Karen Dawisha and Bruce Parrott (eds.), *Democratization and Authoritarianism in Postcommunist Societies: 2, Politics, Power and the Struggle for Democracy in South-East Europe*, Cambridge University Press, 1997, pp. 226–81.

   'Macedonia's Quest for Security and Stability', *Current History* 99:635 (2000), 129–36.

Peters, Edward, *Inquisition*, New York: Free Press, 1988.

Petruseva, Ana, 'Macedonian Peace Deal in Jeopardy', *Institute for War and Peace Reporting's Balkan Crisis Report* 269, 9 August 2001.

Pettifer, James, 'The Albanians in Western Macedonia After FYROM Independence', in James Pettifer (ed.), *The New Macedonian Question*, London: Macmillan, 1999.

Poggi, Gianfranco, *The Development of the Modern State: A Sociological Introduction*, Stanford University Press, 1978.

Poolos, Alexandra, 'Czech Republic: A Wall Divides the Country', RFE/RL, 21 October 1999.

Poulton, Hugh, *Who Are the Macedonians?*, Bloomington: Indiana University Press, 1995; 2nd edn, 2000.

Powell, Chris, 'Time for Another Immoral Panic? The Case of the Czechoslovak Gypsies', *International Journal of the Sociology of Law* 22:2 (1994), 105–21.

Price, Richard and Reus-Smit, Christian, 'Dangerous Liaisons? Critical International Theory and Constructivism', *European Journal of International Relations* 4:3 (1998), 259–94.

Radio Free Europe/Radio Liberty, *Newsline* 5:29 (12 February 2001).

Balkans Report 5:26 (10 April 2001).

Balkans Report 5:50 (20 July 2001).

Newsline 5:160, part II (23 August 2001).

Ramet, Pedro, 'Religion and Nationalism in Yugoslavia', in Pedro Ramet (ed.), *Religion and Nationalism in Soviet and East European Politics*, 2nd edn, Durham: Duke University Press, 1989, pp. 149–69.

Ramet, Sabrina Petra, *Social Currents in Eastern Europe: The Sources and Meaning of the Great Transformation*, Durham: Duke University Press, 1991.

'Why Albanian Irredentism in Kosovo Will Not Go Away', in Sabrina Petra Ramet, *Social Currents in Eastern Europe: The Sources and Meaning of the Great Transformation*, Durham: Duke University Press, 1991, pp. 173–94.

Balkan Babel: Politics, Culture and Religion in Yugoslavia, Boulder: Westview Press, 1992.

'The Yugoslav Crisis and the West: Avoiding "Vietnam" and Blundering into "Abyssinia" ', *East European Politics and Societies* 8:1 (1994), 189–219.

'Introduction: The Roots of Discord and the Language of War', in Sabrina Petra Ramet and Ljubisa S. Adamovich (eds.), *Beyond Yugoslavia: Politics, Economics, and Culture in a Shattered Community*, Boulder: Westview Press, 1995, pp. 1–9.

Balkan Babel: The Disintegration of Yugoslavia from the Death of Tito to the War for Kosovo, 3rd edn, Boulder: Westview Press, 1999.

Ramet, Sabrina Petra and Adamovich, Ljubisa S. (eds.), *Beyond Yugoslavia: Politics, Economics, and Culture in a Shattered Community*, Boulder: Westview Press, 1995.

Ramsaur Jr, Ernest Edmondson, *The Young Turks: Prelude to the Revolution of 1908*, New York: Russell & Russell, 1957.

Report of the Council of Experts of the Council of Europe on the Citizenship Laws of the Czech Republic and Slovakia and their Implementation and Replies of the Governments of the Czech Republic and Slovakia, Doc. DIR/JUR (96), April 1996.

Reus-Smit, Christian, *The Moral Purpose of the State: Culture, Social Identity, and Institutional Rationality in International Relations*, Princeton University Press, 1999.

Reuter, Jens, 'Policy and Economy in Macedonia', in James Pettifer (ed.), *The New Macedonian Question*, London: Macmillan, 1999, pp. 28–46.

Risse, Thomas, '"Let's Argue!": Communicative Action in World Politics', *International Organization* 54:1 (2000), 1–39.

Roberts, Adam, 'NATO's "Humanitarian War" Over Kosovo', *Survival* 41:3 (1999), 102–23.

Rodley, Nigel S., 'Conceptual Problems in the Protection of Minorities: International Legal Developments', *Human Rights Quarterly* 17:1 (1995), 48–71.

Ropp, Stephen C., Sikkink, Kathryn and Risse, Thomas (eds.), *The Power of Human Rights: International Norms and Domestic Change*, Cambridge University Press, 1999.

Rosenau, Pauline Marie, *Post-Modernism and the Social Sciences: Insights, Inroads and Intrusions*, Princeton University Press, 1992.

Rotberg, Robert I. and Thompson, Dennis (eds.) *Truth v. Justice: The Morality of Truth Commissions*, Princeton University Press, 2000.

Roth, Cecil, 'Marranos and Racial Antisemitism', *Jewish Social Studies* 2:3 (1940), 239–48.

History of the Jews, New York: Schocken, 1961.

A History of the Jews in England, 3rd edn, Oxford University Press, 1964.

Ruggie, John Gerard, 'Continuity and Transformation in the World Polity: Toward a Neorealist Synthesis', *World Politics* 35:2 (1983), 261–85.

'Multilateralism: The Anatomy of an Institution', in John Gerard Ruggie (ed.), *Multilateralism Matters: The Theory and Praxis of an Institutional Form*, New York: Columbia University Press, 1993, pp. 3–47.

'Territoriality and Beyond: Problematizing Modernity in International Relations', *International Organization* 47:1 (1993), 139–74.

'What Makes the World Hang Together? Neo-Utilitarianism and the Social Constructivist Challenge', in John Gerard Ruggie, *Constructing the World Polity: Essays on International Institutionalization*, London: Routledge, 1998, pp. 1–39.

Rule, John C., 'Louis XIV, Roi Bureaucrate', in John C. Rule (ed.), *Louis XIV and the Craft of Kingship*, Columbus: Ohio State University Press, 1969, pp. 3–101.

Rusinow, Dennison, 'The Avoidable Catastrophe', in Sabrina Petra Ramet and Ljubisa S. Adamovich (eds.), *Beyond Yugoslavia: Politics, Economics, and Culture in a Shattered Community*, Boulder: Westview Press, 1995, pp. 13–37.

Rystad, Goran (ed.), *The Uprooted: Forced Migration as an International Problem in the Post-War Era*, Lund University Press, 1990.

Sack, Robert David, *Human Territoriality: Its Theory and History*, Cambridge University Press, 1986.

Salzman, Todd A., 'Rape Camps as a Means of Ethnic Cleansing: Religious, Cultural, and Ethical Responses to Rape Victims in the Former Yugoslavia', *Human Rights Quarterly* 20:2 (1998), 348–78.

Schnabel, Albrecht and Thakur, Ramesh (eds.), *Kosovo and the Challenge of Humanitarian Intervention: Selective Indignation, Collective Action, and International Citizenship*, Tokyo: United Nations University Press, 2000.

Schopflin, George, 'Culture and Identity in Post-Communist Europe', in Stephen White, Judy Batt, and Paul G. Lewis (eds.), *Developments in East European Politics*, Durham, NC: Duke University Press, 1993, pp. 16–34.

'Nationalism and Ethnicity in Europe, East and West', in Charles A. Kupchan (ed.), *Nationalism and Nationalities in the New Europe*, Ithaca: Cornell University Press, 1995, pp. 37–65.

Schroeder, Ralph, 'Nietzsche and Weber: Two "Prophets" of the Modern World', in Scott Lash and Sam Whimster (eds.), *Max Weber, Rationality and Modernity*, London: Allen & Unwin, 1987, pp. 207–21.

Scoville, Warren C., *The Persecution of the Huguenots and French Economic Development 1680–1720*, Berkeley: University of California Press, 1960.

Sedgwick, Alexander, *Jansenism in Seventeenth-Century France: Voices From the Wilderness*, Charlottesville: University Press of Virginia, 1977.

Seifert, Ruth, 'War and Rape: A Preliminary Analysis', in Alexandra Stiglmayer (ed.), *Mass Rape: The War Against Women in Bosnia-Herzegovina*, Lincoln: University of Nebraska Press, 1994, pp. 54–72.

Sell, Louis, 'The Serb Flight from Sarajevo: Dayton's First Failure', *East European Politics and Societies* 14:1 (2000), 179–202.

Sells, Michael, *The Bridge Betrayed: Religion and Genocide in Bosnia*, Berkeley: University of California Press, 1996.

    'Religion, History, and Genocide in Bosnia-Herzegovina', in G. Scott Davis (ed.), *Religion and Justice in the War Over Bosnia*, New York: Routledge, 1996, pp. 23–43.

Seroka, Jim, 'Yugoslavia and its Successor States', in Stephen White et al. (eds.), *Developments in East European Politics*, London: Macmillan, 1993, pp. 98–121.

'Shadowy Rebel Assures Macedonia that He Seeks Peace', *New York Times*, 17 August 2001.

Sharp, Jane M. O., 'Dayton Report Card', *International Security* 22:3 (1997/98), 101–37.

Shaw, Stanford J. and Shaw, Ezel Kural, *History of the Ottoman Empire and Modern Turkey*, vol. 2, Cambridge University Press, 1977.

Shoup, Paul, 'Titoism and the National Question in Yugoslavia: A Reassessment', in Martin van den Heuvel and Jan G. Siccama (eds.), *The Disintegration of Yugoslavia*, Yearbook of European Studies, vol. 5, Amsterdam: Rodopi, 1992, pp. 47–72.

Shue, Henry, 'Let Whatever is Smouldering Erupt? Conditional Sovereignty, Reviewable Intervention and Rwanda 1994', in Albert J. Paolini, Anthony P. Jarvis and Christian Reus-Smit (eds.), *Between Sovereignty and Global Governance: The United Nations, the State and Civil Society*, London: Macmillan, 1998, pp. 60–84.

Siklova, Jirina and Marta Miklusakova, 'Law as an Instrument of Discrimination: Denying Citizenship to the Czech Roma', *East European Constitutional Review* 7:2 (1998).

Simons, Marlise, 'War Crimes Tribunal Expands Milosevic Indictment', *New York Times*, 30 June 2001.

Skinner, Quentin, *The Foundations of Modern Political Thought*, vols. 1 & 2, Cambridge University Press, 1978.

Skran, Claudena M., *Refugees in Inter-War Europe: The Emergence of a Regime*, Oxford: Clarendon Press, 1995.

Slye, Ronald C., 'The Dayton Peace Agreement: Constitutionalism and Ethnicity', *Yale Journal of International Law* 21 (1996), 459–73.

Smith, Anthony D., *National Identity*, Reno: University of Nevada Press, 1991.
    Nations and Nationalism in a Global Era, Oxford: Polity Press, 1995.
    'Gastronomy or Geology? The Role of Nationalism in the Reconstruction of Nations', *Nations and Nationalism* 1:1 (1995), 3–23.

Smith, Roger W., 'Denial of the Armenian Genocide', in Israel W. Charny (ed.), *Genocide: A Critical Bibliographical Review*, vol. 2, New York: Facts on File, 1991, pp. 63–85.

Sonyel, Salahi Ramsadam, *The Ottoman Armenians: Victims of Great Power Diplomacy*, London: K. Rustem & Brothers, 1987.

Spierenburg, Peter, *The Spectacle of Suffering*, Cambridge University Press, 1984.

Spruyt, Hendrick, 'Institutional Selection in International Relations: State Anarchy as Order', *International Organization* 48:4 (1994), 527–57.

The Sovereign State and its Competitors, Princeton University Press, 1994.

Stiglmayer, Alexandra, 'The Rapes in Bosnia-Herzegovina', in Alexandra Stiglmayer (ed.), *Mass Rape: The War Against Women in Bosnia-Herzegovina*, trans. Marion Faber, Lincoln: University of Nebraska Press, 1994, pp. 82–169.

'The War in the Former Yugoslavia', in Alexandra Stiglmayer (ed.), *Mass Rape: The War Against Women in Bosnia-Herzegovina*, trans. Marion Faber, Lincoln: University of Nebraska Press, 1994, pp. 1–34.

Stiglmayer, Alexandra (ed.), *Mass Rape: The War Against Women in Bosnia-Herzegovina*, trans. Marion Faber, Lincoln: University of Nebraska Press, 1994.

Strayer, J. R., *On the Medieval Origins of the Modern State*, Princeton University Press, 1970.

Struharova, Beata, 'Disparate Impact: Removing Roma from the Czech Republic', *Roma Rights* 1 (1999).

Suny, Ronald Grigor, *Transcaucasia, Nationalism and Social Change: Essays in the History of Armenia, Azerbaijan and Georgia*, revised edn, Ann Arbor: The University of Michigan Press, 1996.

Sutherland, N. M., *The Massacre of St Bartholemew and the European Conflict 1559–1572*, London: Macmillan, 1973.

The Huguenot Struggle for Recognition, New Haven: Yale University Press, 1980.

Princes, Politics and Religion 1547–1589, London: The Humbledon Press, 1984.

'The Crown, the Huguenots, and the Edict of Nantes', in R. M. Golden (ed.), *The Huguenot Connection: The Edict of Nantes, its Revocation and Early French Migration to South Carolina*, Dordrecht: Kluwer Academic Publishers, 1988, pp. 28–62.

Swidler, Ann, 'Culture in Action: Symbols and Strategies', *American Sociological Review* 51:2 (1986), 273–86.

Taylor, Charles, *The Sources of the Self: The Making of Modern Identity*, Cambridge University Press, 1989.

Tenbruck, Friedrich H., 'The Problem of Thematic Unity in the Works of Max Weber', *British Journal of Sociology* 31:3 (1980), 316–51.

Ternon, Yves, 'Report on the Genocide of the Armenians of the Ottoman Empire, 1915–16', in Permanent Peoples' Tribunal, *A Crime of Silence: The Armenian Genocide*, London: Zed Books, 1985, pp. 94–125.

Tesón, F. R., *Humanitarian Intervention: An Inquiry into Law and Morality*, 2nd edn, New York: Transnational Publishers, 1997.

Thomas, Daniel C. 'The Helsinki Accords and Political Change in Eastern Europe', in Stephen C. Ropp, Kathryn Sikkink and Thomas Risse (eds.), *The Power of Human Rights: International Norms and Domestic Change*, Cambridge University Press, 1999, pp. 205–33.

Thompson, Mark, *Forging War: The Media in Serbia, Croatia and Bosnia-Hercegovina*, Article 19, London: International Centre Against Censorship, 1994.

Tilly, Charles, 'Reflections on the History of European-State-Making', in Charles Tilly (ed.), *The Formation of National States in Western Europe*, Princeton University Press, 1975, pp. 3–83.

Big Structures, Large Processes, Huge Comparisons, New York: Russell Sage Foundation, 1984.

'War Making and State-Making as Organised Crime', in Peter B. Evans, Dietrich Rueschemeyer and Theda Skocpol (eds.), *Bringing the State Back In*, Cambridge University Press, 1985, pp. 169–91.

Coercion, Capital and European States, AD 990–1990, Oxford: Basil Blackwell, 1990.

European Revolutions, 1492–1992, Oxford: Blackwell, 1993.

'States and Nationalism in Europe 1492–1992', *Theory and Society* 23:1 (1994), 131–46.

Todorov, Tzvetan, *The Conquest of America*, New York: Harper, 1992.

Tolerance Foundation, *A Need for Change in the Czech Citizenship Law: Analysis of 99 Individual Cases*, Prague: Tolerance Foundation, 21 November 1994.

Torov, Ivan, 'The Resistance in Serbia', in Jasminka Udovicki and James Ridgeway (eds.), *Burn This House: The Making and Unmaking of Yugoslavia*, Durham: Duke University Press, 1997, pp. 245–64.

Toulmin, Stephen, *Cosmopolis: The Hidden Agenda of Modernity*, University of Chicago Press, 1990.

Toynbee, Arnold (ed.), *The Treatment of Armenians in the Ottoman Empire: Documents Presented to Viscount Grey of Fallodon, Secretary of State for Foreign Affairs with a Preface by Viscount Bryce*, London: Hodder & Stoughton, 1916.

Traynor, Ian, 'Raids Exposed Rifts Between the Reformist Leaders', *The Guardian*, 2 April 2001.

Trevor-Roper, Hugh, 'The European Witch-Craze of the Sixteenth and Seventeenth Centuries', in Hugh Trevor-Roper, *Religion, the Reformation and Social Change, and Other Essays*, London: Macmillan, 1967, pp. 90–192.

Troebst, Stefan, 'IMRO + 100 = FYROM? The Politics of Macedonian Historiography', in James Pettifer (ed.), *The New Macedonian Question*, London: Macmillan, 1999, pp. 60–78.

'Yugoslav Macedonia, 1943–1953: Building the Party, the State, and the Nation', in Melissa K. Bokovoy, Jill A. Irvine and Carol S. Lilly (eds.), *State–Society Relations in Yugoslavia, 1945–1992*, New York: St. Martin's Press, 1997, 243–66.

Trumpener, Ulrich, *Germany and the Ottoman Empire 1914–1918*, Princeton University Press, 1968.

Tully, James (ed.), *Meaning and Context: Quentin Skinner and His Critics*, Cambridge: Polity Press, 1988.

Udovicki, Jasminka and Ridgeway, James (eds.), *Burn This House: The Making and Unmaking of Yugoslavia*, Durham: Duke University Press, 1997.

Ulc, Otto, 'Integration of the Gypsies into Czechoslovakia', *Ethnic Groups* 9 (1991), 107–17.

Ullmann, Walter, *A History of Political Thought in the Middle Ages*, Middlesex: Penguin, 1965.

UNHCR (United Nations High Commission for Refugees), *The State of the World's Refugees 1995*, London: Oxford University Press, 1995.

'Europe's Latest Exodus', *Refugees* 116 (1999).

'Kosovo's First Exodus', *Refugees* 116 (1999).

United Nations, *Final Report of the Commission of Experts*, UN Doc. S/1994/674, 27 May 1994, <http://www.his.com:80/~cij/commxyu1.htm>, accessed 13 August 1997.

Rome Statute of the International Criminal Law Court, UN Doc. A/CONF.183/9, Adopted 17 July 1998.

The Fall of Srebrenica, Report of the Secretary-General Pursuant to General Assembly Resolution 53/35, 15 November 1999, UN Doc. A/54/549.

United States CSCE (Commission on Security and Cooperation in Europe), 'Ex Facto Problems of the Czech Citizenship Law', Washington, September 1996, <http://www.house.gov/csce/ czechlaw.htm>.

van den Heuvel, Martin and Siccama, Jan G. (eds.), *The Disintegration of Yugoslavia*, Yearbook of European Studies, vol. 5, Amsterdam: Rodophi, 1992.

Van Evera, Stephen, 'Hypotheses on Nationalism and War', *International Security* 18:4 (1994), 5–39.

Verdery, Katherine, 'Whither "Nation" and "Nationalism"?', *Dædalus* 122:3 (1993), 37–46.

Vermeer, Willem, 'Albanians and Serbs in Yugoslavia', in Martin van den Heuvel and Jan G. Siccama (eds.), *The Disintegration of Yugoslavia*, Yearbook of European Studies, vol. 5, Amsterdam: Rodophi, 1992, pp. 101–24.

Vickers, Amanda, *Between Serb and Albanian: A History of Kosovo*, London: Hurst & Company, 1998.

Vidal-Naquet, Pierre, 'By Way of a Preface and by the Power of One Word', in Permanent Peoples' Tribunal, *A Crime of Silence: The Armenian Genocide*, London: Zed Books, 1985, pp. 1–7.

Vulliamy, Ed, 'Bosnia: The Crime of Appeasement', *International Affairs* 74:1 (1998), 73–92.

Walker, Christopher J., 'British Sources on the Armenian Massacres, 1915–1916', in Permanent Peoples' Tribunal, *A Crime of Silence: The Armenian Genocide*, London: Zed Books, 1985, pp. 53–8.

Walker, R. B. J., 'The Concept of Culture in the Theory of International Relations', in Jongsuk Chay (ed.), *Culture and International Relations*, New York: Praeger, 1990, pp. 3–17.

Inside/Outside : International Relations as Political Theory, Cambridge University Press, 1993.

Wallerstein, Immanuel, 'Culture as the Ideological Battleground of the Modern World System', in Mike Featherstone (ed.), *Global Culture: Nationalism, Globalization and Modernity: A Theory, Culture and Society Special Issue*, London: Sage, 1990, pp. 31–55.

Geopolitics and Geoculture: Essays on the Changing World-System, Cambridge University Press, 1991.

The Capitalist World-Economy, Cambridge University Press, 1979.

The Modern World-System, vol. 1, San Diego: Academic Press, 1974.

Waltz, Kenneth N., *Man, the State and War: A Theoretical Analysis*, New York: Columbia University Press, 1959.

Theory of International Politics, New York: Random House, 1979.

Walzer, Michael, *The Revolution of the Saints: A Study in the Origins of Radical Politics*, London: Weidenfeld & Nicolson, 1966.

'On the Role of Symbolism in Political Thought', *Political Science Quarterly* 82:2 (1967), 191–204.

Spheres of Justice: A Defense of Pluralism and Equality, New York: Basic Books, 1983.

Exodus and Revolution, New York: Basic Books, 1985.

Watson, Adam, 'European International Society and Its Expansion', in Hedley Bull and Adam Watson (eds.), *The Expansion of International Society*, Oxford: Clarendon Press, 1985, pp. 13–32.

The Evolution of International Society, London: Routledge, 1992.

Weber, Cynthia, *Simulating Sovereignty: Intervention, the State, and Symbolic Exchange*, Cambridge University Press, 1995.

Weber, Max, 'The Social Psychology of the World Religions', in H. H. Gerth and C. Wright Mills (eds.), *From Max Weber: Essays in Sociology*, London: Routledge & Kegan Paul, 1970, pp. 267–301.

Weiner, Myron, 'Bad Neighbors, Bad Neighborhoods: An Inquiry into the Causes of Refugee Flows', *International Security* 21:1 (1996), 5–42.

Weiss, Thomas G., 'UN Responses in the Former Yugoslavia: Moral and Operational Choices', *Ethics and International Affairs* 8 (1994), 1–22.

Weller, Marc, 'The International Response to the Dissolution of the Socialist Federal Republic of Yugoslavia', *American Journal of International Law* 86:3 (1992), 569–607.

'On the Hazards of Foreign Travel for Dictators and Other International Criminals', *International Affairs* 75:3 (1999), 599–617.

'The Rambouillet Conference on Kosovo', *International Affairs* 75:2 (1999), 211–51.

Wendt, Alexander, 'The Agent–Structure Problem in International Relations Theory', *International Organization* 41:3 (1987), 335–70.

'Anarchy is What States Make of It: The Social Construction of Power Politics', *International Organization* 46:2 (1992), 391–425.

'Collective Identity Formation and the International State', *American Political Science Review* 88:2 (1994), 384–96.

Social Theory of International Politics, Cambridge University Press, 1999.

Weston, Burns H., Falk, Richard and D'Amato, Anthony, *Basic Documents in International Law and World Order*, 2nd edn, St. Paul: West Publishing Co., 1990.

Wheeler, Nicholas J., *Saving Strangers: Humanitarian Intervention in International Society*, Oxford University Press, 2000.

White, Stephen, 'Poststructuralism and Political Reflection', *Political Theory* 16:2 (1988), 186–208.

Political Theory and Postmodernism, Cambridge University Press, 1991.

Wight, Martin, *Systems of States*, Leicester University Press, 1977.

Williams, Brackette F., 'A Class Act: Anthropology and the Race to Nation Across Ethnic Terrain', *Annual Review of Anthropology* 18 (1989), 401–44.

Wolf, John B., *Louis XIV*, New York: W. W. Norton & Co., 1968.

Wolin, Sheldon, *Politics and Vision*, Boston: Little Brown, 1960.

'Max Weber: Legitimation, Method, and the Politics of Theory', *Political Theory* 9:3 (1981), 401–24.

Wood, Nicholas and Norton-Taylor, Richard, 'Macedonians Sign Peace Deal', *The Guardian*, 14 August 2001.

Woodward, Susan L., *Balkan Tragedy: Chaos and Dissolution After the Cold War*, Washington, DC: The Brookings Institution, 1995.

Wright, Jane, 'The OSCE and the Protection of Minority Rights', *Human Rights Quarterly* 18:1 (1996), 190–205.

Yale, William, *The Near East: A Modern History*, 2nd edn, Ann Arbor: The University of Michigan Press, 1968.

Young, Iris Marion, 'Together in Difference: Transforming the Logic of Group Political Conflict', in Will Kymlicka (ed.), *The Rights of Minority Cultures*, Oxford University Press, 1995, pp. 155–76.

Zimmermann, Warren, *Origins of a Catastrophe*, New York: Random House, 1996.

Zolberg, Aristide, 'Strategic Interactions and the Formation of Modern States: France and England', *International Social Science Journal* 32:4 (1980), 687–716.

'Origins of the Modern World System: A Missing Link', *World Politics* 33:2 (1981), 253–81.

'Contemporary Transnational Migrations in Historical Perspective: Patterns and Dilemmas', in Mary M. Kritz (ed.), *US Immigration and Refugee Policy: Global and Domestic Issues*, Lexington Books, 1982, pp. 15–51.

'The Formation of New States as a Refugee Generating Process', in Elizabeth Ferris (ed.), *Refugees and World Politics*, New York: Praeger, 1985, 26–42.

Zürcher, Erik J., *Turkey: A Modern History*, London: I. B. Taurus & Co., 1993.

Index

Abdul Hamid II, Sultan, 124, 132–4,
    138–45, 148, 156, 162, 222, 300 *see
    also* Ottoman Empire
absolutism, 110, 116, 119, 120–3
    and Ferdinand and Isabella, 56
    and Louis XIV, 83, 85–8, 110–13
    see also Louis XIV; rulers; state/s
action/s, 18, 21, 22, 29, 31, 33, 252
    and culture, 11, 33, 44–9, 53, 303,
        304–5, 307
    political, 22, 25, 42, 44, 51, 299, 303,
        304–5
actors, 29, 34, 242, 252–5, 267, 304
    and change, 255, 294
    and culture, 45, 46, 304, 307
    and interests, 2, 16, 29–30, 38, 44, 46,
        298, 307
    identities of, 42, 298
    states as, 25, 31, 254, 255
    see also agents
agency, 29–30, 40, 41, 44, 46, 307
agent/s, 16, 29–30, 44, 50, 113
    and culture, 45–7, 49, 307
    and structures, 22, 23, 29–30
        cultural, 11, 34, 45, 304
        social, 22, 41, 44
    individual, 39, 41
    see also actors
Albania, 153, 174, 206, 250, 273, 280,
    290
Anatolia, 8, 52, 125, 126, 134, 151, 156,
    226
annihilation, 63, 130, 168
Aragon, 7, 56, 57, 59, 75, 76, 81,
    215
Archer, Margaret, 46, 307
Armenia, 131, 138, 140, 223, 224
Ashley, Richard, 19, 20
assimilation, 1, 5, 37, 63, 259, 279
    and Jews, 65–72
    and Moriscos, 78, 79
    in Turkey, 154, 226

assimilationism, 172, 293, 300
authority, 4, 31, 48, 59
    absolute, 47, 56, 111, 121, 218
    religious, 7, 37, 49, 71, 74
    sovereign, 31, 32, 48–9, 89, 226
    symbolic augmentation of, 4, 16, 71,
        185, 305
auto de fe, 70, 71–2

Balkan Wars, 150, 152–3, 275, 279
Balkans Stability Pact, 286
Banac, Ivo, 170, 173, 181, 182, 187
Bauman, Zygmunt, 32–3
behaviour, 29, 93, 125, 217
    legitimate state, 125, 161, 219, 225,
        238, 301, 307
    norms of, 1, 9, 15, 23, 230, 244, 246,
        302
    see also norms
Berlin Conference, 1878, 141
Bosnia-Herzegovina, 8, 138, 152, 166,
    168, 179, 281, 284
    civil war in, 189, 197–9, 200, 202, 205
    and Croatia, 173, 194, 199, 200, 201
    Croatians in, 188, 197, 199, 200, 202
    and Federal Republic of Yugoslavia, 174,
        175–6, 182, 194–7, 210
    in Kingdom of Yugoslavia, 172
    and Serbia, 194, 198, 199, 200, 201–5
    Serbs in, 166, 188, 197, 198, 202, 236,
        242
        and nationalism, 193, 197
        and Vance Owen plan, 200
    see also ethnic cleansing; international
        community; Muslims; nationalism
Bosnian Serb Republic, 53, 198, 205 *see
    also* Karadzic, Radovan
boundaries, 20, 49n113
    moral, 11, 14, 23, 54, 186, 227
    territorial, 122, 227
Bourdieu, Pierre, 45, 46–7, 111
Britain, 143, 221, 237 *see also* England

CAMBRIDGE STUDIES IN INTERNATIONAL RELATIONS